Praise for *People of the Pines*

"This is the book of record on the Oka crisis."
– *Montreal Gazette*

"*People of the Pines* offers a gripping, highly readable description of the confrontation between Mohawk Warriors and non-native authority." – *Globe and Mail*

"A visceral story with visceral impact, *People of the Pines* is a bitter slice of Canadiana." – *Calgary Herald*

"…a meticulous account of a 78-day standoff that could be called the first war zone in Canada since Riel's North-West Rebellion of 1885." – *Vancouver Province*

"The authors miss nothing…[they] have done an historic service in as much as they have written with great care and authority on a subject that will engage historians for as long as there are scholars to struggle with the full meaning of these events of the summer of 1990." – *Winnipeg Free Press*

"…an engrossing book."
– *Kitchener-Waterloo Record*

"…compulsory reading for anyone following native affairs in this country." – *Ottawa Citizen*

"Geoffrey York and Loreen Pindera have combined their journalistic talents in this insightful and informative look at the Oka crisis, its historical underpinnings, and its implications for the future." – *Edmonton Journal*

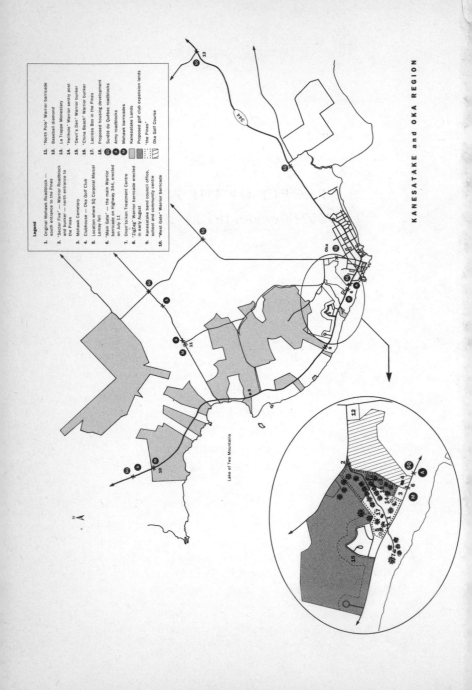

Legend

1. Original Mohawk Roadblock — south entrance to the Pines
2. "Sector Five" — Warrior Roadblock and bunker — north entrance to the Pines
3. Mohawk Cemetery
4. Clubhouse — Oka Golf Club
5. Location where SQ Corporal Marcel Lemay fell
6. "Main Gate" — the main Warrior barricade on Highway 344, erected on July 11
7. Onen'to:kon Treatment Centre
8. "ZigZag" Warrior barricade erected in early August
9. Kanesatake band council office, school and community centre
10. "West Gate" Warrior barricade
11. "North Pole" Warrior barricade
12. Baseball diamond
13. La Trappe Monastery
14. "Hellhole" Warrior sentry post
15. "Devil's Den" Warrior bunker
16. "China Beach" Warrior bunker
17. Lacrosse Box in the Pines
18. Proposed housing development

SQ Sûreté du Québec roadblocks
A Army roadblocks
M Mohawk barricades
Kanesatake Lands
Proposed golf club expansion lands
"the Pines"
Oka Golf Course

Lake of Two Mountains

Oka

KANESATAKE and OKA REGION

PEOPLE OF THE PINES
The Warriors and the Legacy of Oka

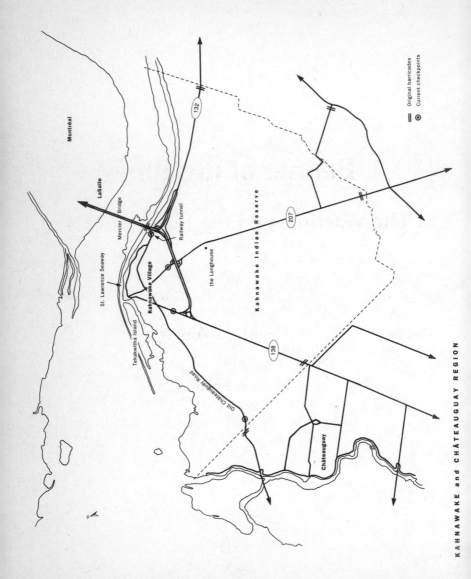

KAHNAWAKE and CHÂTEAUGUAY REGION

Montréal

LaSalle

Mercier Bridge

St. Lawrence Seaway

Tekakwitha Island

Kahnawake Village

Railway tunnel

the Longhouse

Old Châteauguay Road

Kahnawake Indian Reserve

Châteauguay

132

207

138

N

Original barricades
Current checkpoints

People of the Pines

The Warriors and the Legacy of Oka

by

Geoffrey York
and
Loreen Pindera

Little, Brown & Company (Canada) Limited
Boston • London • Toronto

Canadian Cataloguing in Publication Data

York, Geoffrey, 1960–
  People of the Pines

1st paperback ed.
Includes biographical references and index.
ISBN 0-316-90271-3

1. Quebec (Province) – History – Native Crisis, 1990.*
2. Warrior Society. 3. Mohawk Indians – Government
relations. 4. Mohawk Indians – Claims. 5. Mohawk
Indians – Land tenure. 6. Indians of North America –
Canada – Government relations – 1951–   .*
7. Indians of North America – Quebec (Province) –
Claims. 8. Indians of North America – Quebec
(Province) – Land tenure. I. Pindera, Loreen, 1959–
II. Title.

E99.M8Y67 1992   323.1'1975   C92-095026-4

Interior design and typesetting: Pixel Graphics
Printed and bound in Canada by Best Gagné Book Manufacturers

Little, Brown & Company (Canada) Ltd.
148 Yorkville Avenue, Toronto, Ontario, Canada

Contents

Acknowledgements

Not everyone will be happy with our documentation of the Mohawk saga. The reality of the story is not simple or easy; there are few heroes or villains, and the truth is sometimes unpleasant or painful. Ultimately, every person who lived through the crisis of 1990 has their own version of the story. But we would like to thank the hundreds of people who helped us to come as close to the truth as possible by sharing their stories of the summer's events, sometimes — as in the case of those men and women still facing charges — at great personal risk.

We could not have pieced together the history of Kanesatake without the help of the Kanesatake Mohawks who lent us their treasured letters, faded clippings, and family stories, especially Thelma David, Harvey Gabriel, and Richard Gabriel.

We are indebted to Brian Maracle and Dan David, whose advice and comments on the manuscript were invaluable. We would also like to thank our many fellow journalists who offered advice and shared anecdotes, tapes, photographs, and notes, especially Ann McLaughlin, John Kenney, Shaney Komulainen, Sylvain Julienne, Ian MacLeod, Kirsten Pendreigh, Suzanne Shugar, Leigh Ogsten, Paul Carvalho, Marcel Poulin, and Charles Bury. Thank you to Martin Therriault of the Canadian Center on Racism and Prejudices. Julian Sher and Charles Bury of the Canadian Association of Journalists and André

Noël of the Fédération Professionnelle des Journalistes du Québec deserve special mention for their work on behalf of journalists who covered the Oka crisis during the summer of 1990.

Thank you to Jeffrey Dvorkin and David Tweedie at CBC Radio News for their help and understanding.

This project could not have been completed without the enthusiasm and assistance of Kim McArthur and Sarah MacLachlan at Little, Brown and Co. and David Johnston of Peter Livingston Associates, and we are indebted to our editor, Kathryn Dean, for her patience and meticulous attention to detail.

Lastly, we are grateful to our families and friends for their support and encouragement, especially Sandro Contenta, Pauline Comeau, Dan Babineau, and Alison Burns.

Geoffrey York
Loreen Pindera
June 1991

Foreword

I wake up sometimes in the middle of the night, or in that quiet time just before dawn, feeling displaced and disoriented. I'm not quite sure where I am or where I've been. It takes me awhile before everything's okay; until the sweat on my forehead, the clammy feeling in my palms and the knot of fear in my gut subsides.

Some of my memories are stark and ugly and full of threat: of guns of all shapes and sizes, barricades and razor wire and the hatred in people's eyes. Strangely, confusingly, some of these same images are tinged with an almost surreal beauty: helicopter searchlights dancing across distant hills; people dancing to a Mexican drum between the barbed wire; and a Mohawk bunker under a full moon. These images repel me. But they fascinate me at the same time. I don't pretend to understand why.

Some people tell me to forget them. Leave the nightmares behind, they say. But I'm not sure I want them to fade away. Some are painful and I'd rather not remember them. But even these dreams force me to confront some things I know I must never forget.

It all seems so peaceful and serene. Everything, the trees lying across the road, the sand bunkers and the dew blanketing the grass, is infused with an almost eerie glow by some trick of a bright, full moon. But it doesn't fool anyone. Everyone is convinced that the police are planning to attack again, probably at dawn in a couple of hours. "Keep your head down," someone says gruffly. "The cops got snipers out there."

I move towards the Mohawk bunker on the eastern edge of the Pines. I'm nearly there when we all hear it; the loud, sharp snap of a twig somewhere in the woods to my left. Immediately, the whispered jokes and laughter stop. A rifle clip snaps into place. Someone draws back a rifle bolt and slams a bullet into the chamber. A rough voice commands everyone to "get your fucking asses down," as though we need the reminder. "Watch out for snipers, there. Keep down."

To my right, a pair of dark figures slip silently towards the noise. They pad quickly and easily through the night, like cats on a prowl. Their rifles ready, they hop over a log and disappear into the woods.

I look over my shoulder and I see four or five people in the bunker. They're hunched over their rifles. One person gazes through "night-vision" binoculars, scanning the forest for movement. "I can't see a damn thing out there," he whispers to no one in particular.

Time telescopes. Seconds feel like minutes and minutes drag on. The silence is broken only by the persistent crackle of a hand radio; someone, somewhere, wants to know what's going on. The alert is spreading to other bunkers along a mile-long stretch of dark forest overlooking the police lines.

Suddenly, there's another, louder, voice on the radio. "It's them," someone in the bunker says in a normal tone. "It's okay. They're coming back." Shoulders ease back from the rifles. The jokes and good-natured chatter begin again.

I'm surprised that everybody takes the alarm in stride. They're getting used to the routine after only a couple of days. No one, I notice, makes a fuss as five camouflaged figures file back from the woods with their AKs cradled in their arms. They're just kids, I think to myself.

As I edge over to a small hill overlooking the golf course, I'm interrupted by someone suddenly near me. He's looking off at the pine trees. Our great-grandfathers planted these trees by hand. They've always been there for us. "Y'know," he whispers, "I used to come here all the time when I was a kid." He stares at the first hint of northern lights above those trees. "But I can't remember it being this beautiful."

The chopper swooped low over the shoreline, looking for people trying to escape from or sneak into the barricades. Usually, it passed by the school. That's where most of the "civilians" — people who were too stubborn or too proud to leave their homes — had sought shelter when the army invaded. After nearly two months of daily brutality, fear, and steadily rising tension, words like "traumatized" can't do them justice.

The adults were in bad enough shape but everyone agonized over the children. Many of the kids were already permanently scarred by the constant threat of violence. Normally well-behaved and active children were prone to regular fits of temper or they woke screaming in the middle of the night. A lot of the kids asked their parents when, not if, the police were coming to kill them.

We had a promise from the army that it wouldn't fly its choppers directly over the school any more. The last time that happened, the children had run about screaming uncontrollably. They didn't understand what was happening.

"It's coming," yelled a woman standing near me, as the chopper burst over the treetops on the other side of the highway. A dozen or so people in front of the school began running in all directions. A couple of children ran wildly for the door to the gym. Some adults stood, shaking their fists at the chopper as it flew over. A few other people started running for the playground behind the school where they'd thought their children would be safe, shielded from the sight and sound of a steady stream of military vehicles passing by.

When I got to the corner of the building, I saw about two dozen children running, stumbling, and scrambling from the huge machine pounding the air above them. Their cries were drowned out by the chopper hovering there. One lone parent was torn between sweeping the children with her to safety or trying to chase the chopper off.

Everything seemed to move in slow motion. One little boy stopped running and turned to face the chopper. As he did, he stooped as if picking up something from the ground. He was pretending he had a rifle in his hands. He aimed his "rifle" in the air towards the chopper and a helmeted face framed in the doorway.

The chopper hung there for a long second before it tilted forward slightly and began to move off. As it did, other sounds filtered through the receding noise of the chopper's engines. "Bang, bang, bang …," the little boy cried as loudly as he could. "Bang, bang, bang …," he kept shouting as the tears streamed down his face and the chopper lifted over the treetops and out of sight.

My memories of that summer at Kanesatake are so different from the stories told by the media. Their attention was focused on the barricades. To most of them, this was just a cop story; the police and soldiers were there to "restore law and order," to put things back the way they were. But most of the people behind the barricades were my family, friends, and relatives. And they didn't want things to go back to the way they were. They knew that would mean a certain and steady ride down a one-way street to an oblivion called assimilation.

The summer began as the "Shoot-out at the Oka Corral," as one British newspaper called it, with the Mohawks portrayed as the righteous victims of a brutal raid by the police. Slowly, as the weeks dragged by, the story evolved into a cowboys and Indians "movie-of-the-night." Finally, the story turned into one of good guys and bad guys, "peace officers" and "terrorists." You just knew the Mohawks would end up wearing black hats in the end.

There were a few journalists who sought the truth from the many sides of this story. In doing so, most of them were condemned by their peers, some were attacked by officialdom, and a few have been beaten, threatened, and harassed. In the end, they remained true to their professions and to their own consciences. Among them I include the authors of this book.

Niawen-kowa.

Dan David
Winnipeg
June 1991

The Cast of Characters

People of the Pines: The Spring Occupation
Allen Gabriel
Curtis Nelson
Chief Samson Gabriel
David Gabriel
Marshall Nicholas
Dennis Nicholas
Walter David Sr.
Walter David Jr.
Joe "Stonecarver" David
Linda David-Cree
John Cree
Marie David
Valerie David
Susan Oke
Denise David-Tolley
Ellen Gabriel
Debra Etienne
Ronald Giroux
Linda Gabriel
Myrna Gabriel
Kelly Tolley
"Crazyhorse"
"Apache"
and many more Kanesatake Mohawks

Kanesatake Band Council: key players
Grand Chief George Martin
Chief Jerry Etienne
Jacques Lacaille, lawyer

Kanesatake Mohawk Coalition
Chrystal Nicholas — Group for Change
Harvey Gabriel — former chief
Ivan Nicholas — Group for Change
Bertha Bonspille-Peltier — Group for Change
Sheila Bonspille — Group for Change
Richard Gabriel — Group for Change
Clarence Simon — former grand chief
Ronald Bonspille — Clarence Simon supporter
Francis Jacobs — Clarence Simon supporter
Crawford Gabriel — Kanesatakeron League for Democracy
Jerry Peltier — advisor

Warriors at the Treatment Centre (September 1990)
Robert "Mad Jap" Skidders — Akwesasne
Dennis "Psycho" Nicholas — Kanesatake
Bill Sears — Akwesasne
Harold "Beekeeper" Oakes — Akwesasne
Ronald "Lasagna" Cross — Kahnawake/Kanesatake
Gordon "Noriega" Lazore — Akwesasne
Richard "Boltpin" Two Axe — Kahnawake
Joe "Stonecarver" David — Kanesatake
Mark "Blackjack" Montour — Kahnawake/Akwesasne
Hunter Montour — Kahnawake/Akwesasne
Jean Noël "Christmas" Cataford — Kanesatake
Roger "Twenty-Twenty" Lazore — Akwesasne
Larry "Wizard" Thompson — Akwesasne
Gerald "Slim" Marquis — Kahnawake
Mike "Wolverine" Mayo — Kahnawake
Herbert "Big Bear" Bush — Akwesasne
Donald "Babe" Hemlock — Kahnawake
Leroy "Splinter" Gabriel — Kanesatake
Randy "Spudwrench" Horne — Kahnawake
Dean "Sledgehammer" Horne — Kahnawake
"Blondie" (fifteen years old) — Oka
"Toad" (seventeen years old) — Kahnawake
"4-20" (seventeen years old) — Akwesasne
Tom "The General" Paul — Eskasoni, Nova Scotia
Kevin "Beaver" Gould — Whycocomagh, Nova Scotia

Brad "Freddy Krueger" Larocque — Regina, Saskatchewan
Paul "Sugar Bear" Smith — Oneida, Wisconsin
Kevin "Little Bear" Stanger — northwestern Quebec

Women at the Treatment Centre (September 1990)
Laura Norton — Kahnawake
Lorna Delormier — Kahnawake
Kahn-Tineta Horn — Ottawa/Kahnawake
Kahentiiosta — Kahnawake
Lorraine Montour — Kahnawake/Akwesasne
Shirley Scott — Kahnawake
Vicky Diabo — Kahnawake
Sandra Deer — Kahnawake
Cathy Sky — Kahnawake
Brenda Gabriel — Kanesatake
Arlette Van Den Hende — Kanesatake
Stephanie Horne — Kahnawake
Beverly Scow — Alert Bay, British Columbia
Jennie Jack — Taku River, British Columbia
Lucille Jack — Taku River, British Columbia
Georgina Michell — Pavilion, British Columbia
Cheryl Barney — Lillooet, British Columbia
Susan Oke – Kanesatake
Holly Pinsonneault – Kahnawake

Key Negotiators and Advisors at the Treatment Centre
Ellen Gabriel — Kanesatake
Denise David-Tolley — Kanesatake
Walter David Sr. — Kanesatake
Walter David Jr. — Kanesatake
Mavis Etienne — Kanesatake
Maurice Gabriel — Kanesatake
Joe Deom — Kahnawake
Laura Norton — Kahnawake
Eba Beauvais — Kahnawake
Nancy Deer — Kahnawake
Loran Thompson — Akwesasne
Francis Boots — Akwesasne
Diane Lazore — Akwesasne

Minnie Garrow — Akwesasne
Bob Antone — Oneida
Terry Doxtator — Oneida
Bruce Elijah — Oneida
Stanley Cohen — lawyer, New York City

Kahnawake Mohawk Council (elected council)
Grand Chief Joe Norton
Chief Billy Two Rivers
Chief Richard White
nine other chiefs

Kahnawake Longhouse (October 1990)
Frank Natawe, wellkeeper and chief, Turtle Clan
Ken Deer, chief, Turtle Clan
Mike Nolan, chief, Turtle Clan
Bryan A. Deer, chief, Bear Clan
Sewatis Diabo, chief, Bear Clan
Donald Hemlock, chief, Bear Clan
Wendell Beauvais, chief, Wolf Clan
Pat Nolan, chief, Wolf Clan
Joe Deer, chief, Wolf Clan
Norma Delaronde, clan mother
Eba Beauvais, clan mother
Francis Dione, clan mother
Laura Norton, clan mother
five other clan mothers

Kahnawake Warrior Society
Allan Delaronde, war chief
Donnie Martin, assistant to the war chief, Wolf Clan
Mark "Cookie" McComber, assistant to the war chief, Turtle Clan
Michael Thomas, assistant to the war chief, Bear Clan

Town of Oka: key players
Jean Ouellette, mayor
Gilles Landreville, deputy-mayor
Luc Carbonneau, lawyer
Lambert Toupin, lawyer

Lise Bourgault, MP for Argenteuil-Papineau

Châteauguay: key players
Jean-Bosco Bourcier, mayor
Yvon Poitras, leader of Solidarité Châteauguay
Ricardo Lopez, MP for Châteauguay

The Quebec Government
Robert Bourassa, premier
Gil Remillard, justice minister
John Ciaccia, native affairs minister
Sam Elkas, public security minister
Claude Ryan, chairman of cabinet crisis committee
Robert Lavigne, director of the Sûreté du Québec
Pierre Coulombe, negotiator
Alexander Paterson, negotiator

The Federal Government
Brian Mulroney, prime minister
Tom Siddon, minister of Indian Affairs
Kim Campbell, justice minister
Bill McKnight, defence minister
Harry Swain, deputy minister, Indian Affairs
Roger Gagnon, assistant deputy minister, Indian Affairs
Frank Vieni, regional director, Indian Affairs
Yves Désilets, negotiator
Bernard Roy, negotiator

The Canadian Armed Forces
General John de Chastelain, chief of defence staff
Lieutenant-General Kent Foster, commander of Mobile Command
Brigadier-General Armand Roy, commander of 5th
    Mechanized Brigade
Lieutenant-Colonel Pierre Daigle, commanding officer at Oka
Lieutenant-Colonel Robin Gagnon, commanding officer at
    Kahnawake
Major Rémi Landry, deputy commanding officer at Oka
Major Alain Tremblay, C company, 2nd Battalion

CHAPTER 1
Get Ready to Rock and Roll

July 11, 1990

It was still dark when Eba Beauvais awoke and made her way to the sacred fire in the clearing in the Pines. Almost everyone was still sleeping. A few men who had been on guard all night were standing around the fire. Eba savoured the stillness. There was scarcely a sound, except for the rustle of the great pine trees and the chirp of restless birds, stirring in anticipation of the dawn of another day.

As the first hint of light coloured the eastern sky, John Cree, the faithkeeper, made his way to the tents where the women and children were asleep. He began to wake them for the sunrise tobacco-burning ceremony that was held every morning to greet the new day.

The Mohawks had been up most of the night, on patrol or talking around the fire, and some of the women could not be roused from their sleep. Sixteen-year-old Myrna Gabriel got out of the car where she had spent the night, next to her mother. She lay down near the fire and promptly fell back to sleep. Her mother, Linda Gabriel, joined Eba Beauvais and John Cree and the others.

They stood in a circle under the majestic white pines, sleepy-eyed, still in the rumpled clothes they had slept in, and looked east towards the Mohawk graveyard that they were protecting. As they faced the sunrise, John Cree burned tobacco and said the traditional prayers. He thanked the Creator for everything on Mother Earth — the insects that purify the ground, the birds that sing, the eagle that protects the people, the food that nourishes life — and everything in the Sky World, including the sun, the moon, and the stars.

Denise David-Tolley was feeling uneasy. Just before she woke up, she had had a troubling dream about an attack and someone's death. She kept gazing around the woods and staring up towards the tops of the giant trees, trying to rid herself of the feeling that someone was watching the tiny group of Mohawks clustered around the fire. The feeling was all the more troubling because David-Tolley had always felt safe in the Pines, protected by the spirit of her grandmother who was buried in the tiny graveyard in the southeast corner of the Pines. Just east of the graveyard was the Oka Golf Club, and beyond that, at the bottom of a hill, was the town of Oka, nestled on the shore of the Lake of Two Mountains.

David-Tolley looked up again, then checked her watch. It was 5:15 a.m. Suddenly she heard the faint noise of cars driving west up Highway 344 from the town of Oka. The vehicles crested the hill and came into view.

"Holy fuck, they're here!" she yelled. Two bulky blue rental trucks sped up the highway, with a long line of police cars and vans behind them. Cruiser after cruiser pulled up along the side of the highway. One of the trucks drove right up to the Mohawk barricade that blocked the south entrance to the Pines and parked there. Police officers spilled out of the vehicles. They wore dark uniforms and bullet-proof vests and carried semi-automatic guns. Most of them took positions along the shoulder of the highway; others climbed up trees on the far side of the road, ducked down into the ditches, or crouched behind their vehicles with their guns ready. A third group, the main corps, planted themselves side by side in front of the makeshift barrier at the entrance to the Pines. They were the tactical intervention squad of the Sûreté du Québec — the Quebec provincial police.

Denise David-Tolley grabbed her two-way radio to alert the warriors deep in the woods. "They're here," she shouted. "The SQ are here."

The men did not need to be alerted. Six hundred metres away, at a second barricade set up at the north end of the dirt road that cuts through the Pines, a Mohawk woman from Oka had just sped up from the town in her car, careening past the baseball field on the northeast edge of the golf course. She slammed to a halt at the roadblock, where several warriors stood around, drinking coffee and stretching the sleep from their limbs. "The cops are right behind me!" she yelled.

As she spoke, a van and four police cars turned the corner near the baseball field and stopped about 150 metres away. The doors burst open and four officers jumped out of each car. More policemen poured out of the van. Some took up position near the cars, while the others spread out along the edge of the golf course or scattered into the woods.

One of the Mohawks had a two-way radio and it crackled to life. "They're here, boys! They're here! This is not a drill. Get ready to rock and roll!" The warriors burrowed into their bunkers dug out on the edge of the dirt road or ducked out of sight in the woods.

Like the other police officers, those at the back barricade wore dark jumpsuits and bullet-proof vests and carried assault rifles and semi-automatic weapons.

Altogether, the SQ had sent in about one hundred officers to flush the Mohawks from the patch of forest they had been guarding for four months. On Highway 344, the members of the tactical intervention squad were reinforced by riot police — several dozen men wearing shielded helmets and carrying sticks and service revolvers. They milled about the highway, behind the tactical squad, waiting for their turn to act.

Denise David-Tolley's mind was racing over the plans the Mohawks had prepared in case of a police raid. She was a tough, stocky, no-nonsense woman from the Mohawk community of Kanesatake, just west of the Pines. Much of her inspiration came from Anna Mae Aquash, a Micmac activist who was gunned down in mysterious circumstances in 1976, three years after she participated in the armed standoff between Indians and U.S. authorities at Wounded Knee in South Dakota. David-Tolley regarded Anna Mae Aquash as her mentor, but until 1990 she had had no deep involvement in the struggle for native rights. The closest she had come was a 1977 confrontation, in which she had helped to reclaim the Mohawk baseball diamond on the edge of the Oka golf course northeast of the Pines.

David-Tolley had helped patrol the Pines since the early spring of 1990, when the Mohawks began occupying the area to prevent the expansion of the golf course onto their ancestral territory. For more than two centuries, they had been demanding legal title to four hundred square kilometres of land that made up the original seigneury of the Lake of Two Mountains. Now, after watching their land whittled away by decades of urban encroachment and private development, the Mohawks were fighting to protect a small tract of eighteen hectares of forest just west of the Pines, which was in danger of being razed to make room for the golf course.

The private land developers who owned that land planned to sell it to the town of Oka to lease to the golf club, then build sixty luxury homes along the borders of the new eighteen-hole course. If their plans went ahead, all that would be left of the magnificent forest, considered by the Mohawks to be the heart of their territory, was the twenty-two hectares of the Pines themselves. Even that, like the Mohawk graveyard, legally belonged to the town of Oka.

David-Tolley had been uncompromising in her efforts to have the Pines and surrounding forest recognized as Mohawk territory. Realizing that her resistance might land her in jail, she nevertheless refused to obey a court injunction ordering the people of the Pines to dismantle their roadblocks on the dirt road that ran through the site.

Denise David-Tolley and the other Mohawk women had already decided that they would be the ones to confront the authorities, since, according to Mohawk tradition, the care of the land is always entrusted to the women. But no one had been expecting a hundred police officers. Just a few days earlier, an SQ officer had assured the Mohawks that the police would not intervene in a civil injunction unless a criminal act were committed. The Mohawks did not believe they had been responsible for any crimes. Ever since the town of Oka had obtained the injunction on June 29, the protesters had been prepared for municipal workers to come up from the town with heavy equipment to take down the barricades, and they expected the SQ to follow with warrants for their arrest if they resisted. But there was no sign of a front-end loader or other heavy equipment and no sign of officials from the town — just the SQ, rifles ready, standing grim-faced on the highway.

John Cree's sister, Debbie Etienne, had slept through the beginning of the tobacco-burning ceremony, but she woke up when the police arrived. She climbed out of her tent, still wrapped in a blanket, her bare feet wet from the early morning dew. She saw people running around in a panic and her brother standing near the fire, looking frightened. A child was crying. A few of the women stood in a little cluster, pointing out the police, trying to spot them in the trees.

An SQ officer bellowed into a megaphone: "We want to talk to your leader. Have your leader approach the lines immediately."

About a dozen of the Mohawk women, who had been gathered by the fire in the clearing, walked nervously towards the barricade at the south entrance of the Pines. The police officers stood shoulder to shoulder along the edge of the highway, their guns trained on the women as they came forward.

"Show them you're not armed," one of the women yelled to the others. Linda Gabriel looked straight at the officers and stretched out her hands. "We're not armed, we're not armed," she kept repeating as the women walked toward the police.

When they reached the barricade, the women stood side by side in a long row, facing the police. Eba Beauvais stood at one end of the row. At forty-eight, she was a grandmother, a clan mother of the Turtle clan, and a veteran of a decade of confrontations between Indian militants and police. Beauvais had first come to the Pines a few weeks earlier from Kahnawake, the Mohawk reserve on the south shore of Montreal, about forty-five kilometres southeast of Kanesatake. As a trained mediator — she had taken courses in alternative dispute resolution in Montreal — and as a respected elder in the Longhouse, the traditional spiritual and political institution of the Mohawks, she had been asked to help resolve the internal tensions among the Longhouse people of Kanesatake. Like most people in Kahnawake, she had friends and relatives among the Mohawks of Kanesatake. Her son-in-law, Dennis Nicholas, and her grandson were putting in long hours on patrol in the Pines. So when the women had asked her to return to the Pines to stay, a few days before July 11, she had not refused. She felt obligated to her family, to her people and to the land.

Eba Beauvais' lined, motherly face and her serene temperament belied her steely nature. Eye-to-eye with the police, their weapons aimed at her, she was calm and unafraid. There were police officers in front of her and off to the side, almost behind her. But she and the other women locked eyes with the officers in front and stared them down until they looked away.

Denise David-Tolley spoke first. "What the hell do you want?" she demanded.

"Where's your leader?" the officer with the megaphone said. "We want to speak to your leader." He was standing behind his vehicle, several metres away from the Mohawks.

"What's the matter with you?" David-Tolley yelled back. "You want to talk to us, come out here and talk."

"You come here," he replied.

When the officer didn't move, she shouted again. "There is no leader here," she said. "You are looking at the leaders. Everyone's the leader. The people are the leaders."

The policeman shook his head. "No, no, I want your leader now."

He was getting agitated. The women could hear it in his voice. They heard the click, click of the guns as the policemen readied their rifles. David-Tolley's daughter, Kelly, started to cry as she stood at the end of the line with her teenaged friends. David-Tolley turned on her: "Knock it off! Don't you dare cry. We are a proud people. Don't you dare show them tears."

Then she faced the police again. She fixed her eyes on one officer and uttered a threat. If her daughter or any of the children were killed, his own children would be cursed.

He slowly shifted his gun, pointing it skyward. The officer behind him pushed him out of the way and stepped forward. He aimed his gun at David-Tolley.

"Come on, fucker, shoot," she told him. "If that's what you want to do, do it now."

The officer in charge was still asking for a Mohawk leader to come forward. Finally, one of the women returned to the fire and asked John Cree to talk to him. The women turned to the faithkeeper, since he had been acting as one of their spokespersons whenever government officials came to the Pines. Cree approached the police officer at the barricade. He was accompanied by Ellen Gabriel, a softspoken thirty-one-year-old artist from Kanesatake and a member of the Turtle clan, whose own nickname was Turtle.

The SQ officer made it clear that negotiations were out of the question. Negotiations were for politicians, not for the police, he said. Then he gave John Cree five minutes to talk to the women and decide what they were going to do. But Cree pleaded for more time. Finally, the police agreed to give them forty-five minutes to finish the tobacco-burning ceremony.

The Mohawks returned to the fire and prayed for a long time. They asked the Creator for protection, especially for the children. They prayed that the children would hear or see nothing that would harm them that morning.

A warrior named Mad Jap stayed close to the front of the barricade, hurling insults at the police and ordering them to leave. Mad Jap, whose real name is Robert Skidders, had arrived in Kanesatake a few days earlier from the Mohawk reserve of Akwesasne, the Mohawk reserve that straddles the borders of Quebec, Ontario and New York State, sixty kilometres southwest of Oka. He had been an elected councillor in Akwesasne for three years in the mid-1980s, but he had moved away from the Indian Act system and had become an ally of Mohawk traditionalists such as Francis Boots, the Akwesasne war chief. Mad Jap, a short, wizened man and a reformed cocaine addict, had accompanied Boots on several trips to Kanesatake in the late spring, after the people in the Pines had called for help from warriors in other Mohawk communities. The warriors saw themselves as the defenders of Mohawk territory, and they believed that all their communities belonged to a single Mohawk nation. Many had come from Kahnawake and Akwesasne, bringing food, tents, and other supplies — including weapons — to bolster the defence of the Pines.

Mad Jap never carried a gun, but now he was brandishing his fists at the police like a weapon. "This is Mohawk land," he yelled at them. Some of the women, worried that he might provoke the police into an attack, urged him to cool down.

By now, more people were awake. Kahentiiosta, a thirty-three-year-old Mohawk woman from Kahnawake, took her two young sons, Rorhare and Aniatariio, to the middle of the Pines, and left her teen-aged niece there to watch them. Kahentiiosta was another veteran of armed confrontations with the police. She had spent three years at Ganienkeh, the militant Mohawk community in upstate New York, and had come to the Pines reluctantly at first, exhausted after a tense standoff with New York state police at Ganienkeh in the spring. Her family had set up camp in the Pines just two days earlier.

A cheerful and unflappable woman, Kahentiiosta showed no fear as the police surrounded the Pines. She had complete confidence in the warriors, armed and hidden deep in the woods, who had the job of defending the Pines and the women and children at the front. "The men know what's going on," she reassured some of the frightened young girls. "They're watching. They're not going to leave us."

As soon as the tobacco-burning ceremony was finished, she got the gas barbecue going for coffee and told the girls to make peanut butter sandwiches for the warriors. Eba Beauvais and three other women gathered up hot ashes from the sacred fire in styrofoam cups. They approached the line of police officers, burning sweetgrass and sprinkling the ashes at their feet. For Beauvais and the others, the ashes were more than just a symbolic line of defence. They believed in the power of those ashes to protect the Mohawks from harm. "Don't one of you dare to cross this line," Beauvais told the police.

A couple of policemen were crouched down in the trees, near another dirt road that cut across the Pines onto the highway, a few dozen metres west of the Mohawk barricade. When Beauvais approached one of them, he screamed at her to get back. She saw fear in his eyes. Mad Jap came up behind the clan mother and yelled back at the police officer: "You shut up! Get back where you belong! She has a job to do, and you have a job to do. You let her do her job."

Eba Beauvais had felt a flicker of fear when the officer shouted at her, but she quickly regained her confidence and threw some ashes in the policeman's face. He recoiled, his face pale.

Beauvais continued sprinkling the ashes around the entire perimeter of the Pines. As she worked, Mohawks from all over Kanesatake were congregating at the back entrance. They were curious to find out what was going on, and they were anxious to help.

One of the women in Kanesatake had received a frantic call at her home from a Mohawk in Oka, warning her that dozens of police cars were heading for the Pines. She and her husband jumped into their car and raced up Highway 344 toward the Pines. When she saw all the police vehicles blocking the highway, she screeched to a halt and backed up at full speed, then drove around the Pines on back roads through Kanesatake to get to the barricade at the rear entrance. There she dropped off her husband, who had a hunting rifle in his hand. He disappeared into the Pines, discarding his dress shoes when he found himself slipping all over the thick bed of pine needles on the forest floor. When he re-emerged from the Pines several hours later, he was still in his stocking feet.

Dennis Nicholas had also arrived in the Pines by then, limping on a swollen leg. Codenamed "Psycho," Nicholas was the recognized "head of security" at the Mohawk camp in the Pines. He had been helping to patrol the woods since the beginning of the protest in March. Two days earlier, he had injured his leg and broken his right wrist when an all-terrain vehicle he was driving had flipped over in the Pines. He had just returned from the hospital early that morning and had been sitting in his kitchen having a coffee when he got word of the raid. He sped down to the Pines and joined the warriors in the woods.

By the time Eba Beauvais had finished spreading the ashes, forty-five minutes had passed and the police were calling again for the Mohawks to approach the barricades. The women walked forward once more, a long line of them, hand in hand. The police ordered them to cross over the barricade and come out onto the highway.

"Are you crazy?" yelled Denise David-Tolley. If they went out onto the highway, she was sure they would be arrested and the police would rush in to ambush the men.

The tension mounted as the Mohawks and the SQ stared at each other across the barricade. The women were resolute: they were not going to leave the Pines. But the Sûreté du Québec were under orders from Oka Mayor Jean Ouellette to enforce the civil injunction to dismantle the roadblocks, and they were determined to clear the Mohawks from the area.

The SQ were heavily armed, obviously prepared to use force. They had a long history of using truncheons and tear gas to quell disturbances by native people — in Restigouche in 1981, in Lac Barrière in 1989, and in several other violent confrontations with native protesters at Indian reserves across the province. Primarily a rural police force, the SQ were accustomed to patrolling highways and ticketing traffic offenders, and they had virtually no training to help them understand cultural minorities. A senior provincial official later admitted that the SQ had little interest in finding a peaceful solution to the Mohawk dispute on July 11. "They wanted to show the natives who was in control," the official said.

Later, the SQ complained that they should have been supplied with high-powered military technology to overcome the Mohawks in the Pines. But the greater problem was their failure to understand the deep conviction and stubborn toughness of the Mohawks. Many of the warriors had gone through armed confrontations in the past, and they were willing to risk a shoot-out with the police, even at the cost of their lives, in defence of their land.

A number of senior SQ officers had recognized the dangers of the operation in the Pines and had recommended sending in a specialized team of criminal negotiators. But they lost the internal debate on tactics. One officer later said the police commanders had expected a relatively easy operation, counting on the psychological effect of the surprise early-morning raid to flush out the Mohawks. When that failed to work, they resorted to other tactics — tear gas and concussion grenades — in an attempt to frighten the Mohawks into giving up the occupied territory.

On that morning of July 11, as the women stood arm in arm in front of the roadblock, the police lost patience. Without warning, they lobbed a canister of tear gas over the barrier. Then they hurled another one. The first two canisters fell short of the women, and a gust of wind came up from nowhere, blowing the smoke back in the direction of the police. To the Mohawks, it seemed that the wall of smoke was walking back slowly toward the police and they felt that the wind was a gift from the Creator, protecting them from harm.

The police lobbed two more canisters. One hit Denise David-Tolley in the leg. Another grazed Eba Beauvais' leg as it whizzed by, smoke already whooshing out of the canister. It landed and exploded a foot from where she stood.

For several long moments, Beauvais could not see anything. As the smoke cleared, she could just make out the police officers' faces, now covered by gas masks. Her heart jumped at the frightening sight. The women retreated, coughing and choking. But as soon as the smoke settled, they ran forward again, where they were met with another barrage of tear gas. This time the projectiles hit Mad Jap's truck, which was parked at the front of the barricade near a makeshift bunker of dirt and logs, shattering a window and denting the side of the vehicle.

In the midst of the smoke, explosions, and confusion, Francis Boots stood by the fire, clutching a bag of tobacco that one of the women had handed him a short time before. He sprinkled the tobacco on the fire and resumed the prayers, asking for guidance and strength for the

Mohawks in the Pines. He felt a strange sense of calm, even while cans of tear gas and concussion grenades exploded around him.

Boots was wiry and baby-faced and wore his black, curly hair tied back in a single braid. He looked younger than his forty-one years — too young to be an experienced war chief. He had been a traditionalist since he had attended his first Longhouse ceremony as a twenty-year-old youth, and he was with other Mohawk militants when they took over the Seaway International Bridge in Akwesasne in 1968. He was a quick study, and his knowledge and interest in traditional ways had caught the attention of the elderly war chief, John Tebo, who chose Boots as his understudy. Tebo died in 1974, and Boots had replaced him as the war chief in the Akwesasne Longhouse. His sacred tobacco was his only weapon; like his friend Mad Jap, Francis Boots never carried a gun.

At the other end of the Pines, Joe David, codenamed Stonecarver, could hear the tear gas canisters popping. At first he thought the sound was gunshots, and a chill went down his spine. All spring, the thirty-three-year-old artist from Kanesatake had campaigned against using weapons to block the expansion of the Oka golf course. But now, with tear gas exploding a few hundred metres away, his misgivings about the weapons disappeared. He could not see an alternative anymore.

One of the Mohawk warriors, who called himself Rambo, had fled in fear within minutes of the arrival of the police, leaving behind his AK-47, a semi-automatic rifle, propped up against a log at the back of the Pines. Stonecarver had never held an AK-47 before; he had deliberately avoided even looking at the guns closely. But now, with the police all around the Pines, he picked up Rambo's gun. He felt totally calm.

Another warrior — a man with combat experience — showed Stonecarver how to lock and load the rifle. Despite his background, the warrior's hands were shaking as he locked in the ammunition clip. For the first time, Stonecarver felt a flicker of fear.

The moment the police had arrived at the Pines, one of the Mohawks had grabbed a cellular phone and made an emergency call to Allan Delaronde, the war chief of the Kahnawake Longhouse. Because there was no formal Warrior Society at Kanesatake, the people in the Pines relied on the warrior societies of Kahnawake and Akwesasne for technical support and expertise. Delaronde was a senior leader of the Kahnawake Warrior Society and supervisor of the society's territorial patrol. The warriors had a sophisticated network of communications at Kahnawake, including a system of two-way radios and police scanners, and Delaronde was the man at the centre of the network.

The war chief was astonished by the news of the police raid at Kanesatake. He had planned to drive out to the Pines the following day to take tents, kitchen equipment, food, and another gas cookstove to the people at the barricade. Now it was too late for that.

Delaronde immediately swung into action. Over the cellular phone, as he talked to Psycho and other Mohawks in the Pines, Delaronde could hear the blasts of the tear gas canisters. He started making calls to key people, relying on a "telephone tree" to spread the word around his community.

Delaronde's son, Johnny, made some of the first calls to warriors around Kahnawake. At about 6:20 a.m., he called Mark "Blackjack" Montour and told him that the warriors were planning to seize the Mercier Bridge and the highways leading to it. He instructed Montour to meet a group of warriors at the traffic circle on Highway 138, just south of the bridge that crossed Kahnawake territory and linked Montreal to Châteauguay and other south shore suburbs.

Blackjack was a thirty-year-old former ironworker and a veteran of the armed standoffs between Mohawk warriors and state troopers at the Mohawk communities of Moss Lake and Ganienkeh in upper New York State. His earliest experience with the warriors was in 1974, at the age of thirteen, when he picked up a gun in defence of the Mohawk militants who had taken over an abandoned camp at Moss Lake. Despite his long history of involvement in armed confrontations, Blackjack was boyish and cheerful. He had a childlike sense of mischief, which sometimes landed him in trouble, but he always had an innocent smile on his face.

Often he jumped into his red sports car and drove to the home of his mother and stepfather in upstate New York, near the Mohawk reserve at Akwesasne. To an outsider, the Montours would look like an affluent, all-American family. Their sprawling ranch-style house, located on a forty-five hectare estate on the outskirts of Westville, New York, was full of sports trophies and hunting rifles. Blackjack and his younger brother, Hunter, had hockey pennants and rock star posters on their bedroom walls. Their stepfather, Dr. David Gorman, was a physician and former speedboat racer and skeet-shooting champion. Their mother, Lorraine Montour, was a clan mother and a longtime Mohawk activist who had invested $200,000 in a bingo palace at Akwesasne. They kept a stable of expensive horses and purebred English setters

Just three days before the July 11 police raid, Blackjack had bought a new gun. It was a Ruger Mini-14 with a laser sight, purchased for more than $1,200 U.S. at a gun store in Massena, New York. He also bought another Mini-14 for his brother. They had intended to use the guns for deer hunting. But those plans were all changed now.

After he received Johnny Delaronde's telephone call, Blackjack put on his boots and jeans and drove to the traffic circle on Highway 138, where he met a dozen other warriors. They stood around nervously, perhaps a little frightened and uncertain how to proceed. "What are we doing standing here?" Blackjack asked the warriors. "Let's get going."

Blackjack swung his car onto Highway 138 and blocked one lane of northbound traffic. Rush hour had just begun, and the traffic was heavy. Thousands of commuters from Châteauguay were speeding northward through Kahnawake to their jobs in Montreal. "All these cars were doing everything they could to get to work," Blackjack recalled later. "They were going into the ditch to get around us. There were thousands of cars."

Another warrior drove his car into the second lane of traffic, forming a V-shape with Blackjack's car. But the motorists kept coming, still frantically trying to get to work, somehow avoiding the roadblock by driving through the ditch or along the median. Finally, Blackjack and another warrior pulled out their semi-automatic rifles and waved them in the air. The motorists screamed to a halt. "All these drivers — their eyes got as big as golf balls," Blackjack recalls. "They started to back up. We went down the road, pushing the traffic back."

It took only fifteen minutes to stop the traffic, but it took two hours for the warriors to push the cars back to the outskirts of Châteauguay. Then they realized they were too close to the town, so they created a no-man's-land of several hundred metres between two barricades to help protect their position from police attack. Blackjack found a cement block and put it in the middle of the highway and stuck a Mohawk Warrior flag into it. Somebody else found a flag of the Iroquois

Confederacy — the alliance of six Iroquois nations of which the Mohawks are a part — and stuck it beside the warrior flag.

Groups of warriors were blocking every other highway that intersected Kahnawake: Highway 132, Highway 207, and the paved road known as Old Châteauguay Road. Then they completed their operation by seizing the Mercier Bridge. "We took the strategic point — the highest point on the bridge, in the middle, where we could see both sides," Allan Delaronde recalls.

Debbie Etienne was sitting by the fire, her feet still bare, a blanket wrapped around her. She was trying to make sense of the chaos around her. She felt trapped. The police were everywhere. A helicopter hovered overhead. There was nowhere to run.

Mohawk songs and chants were blaring from a stereo in Mad Jap's truck parked near the dirt bunker at the front of the barricade, and some of the young girls were dancing to the haunting music. Others hung back, frightened and uncertain what to do next. One of the teenaged boys had been badly affected by the tear gas. He was coughing and choking, and a woman was holding wet cloths to his burning eyes. The residue of the tear gas stuck to everyone's clothes. It itched and stung on the skin, and rubbing it made it worse. When people walked on the dirt where the smoke had settled, the gas vapours would rise up again, and they would cough and choke. One of the women handed out wet hankies so people could cover their faces.

At about 7:00 a.m., when the news came over the cellular phone that the Kahnawake warriors had seized the Mercier Bridge, Debbie Etienne felt some of her courage return. People started to cheer around her; the sense of isolation was broken. Etienne felt her fear turning to anger. "Now we're going to kick your asses!" someone yelled at the police.

At about 7:30 a.m., a front-end loader arrived from Oka. It parked on the highway, behind the police line, and made no move towards the roadblock. The police were still volleying tear gas at regular intervals. Then they began shooting off concussion grenades. The grenades made a huge, explosive sound, and every time they went off, one of the women yelped in terror.

Kahentiiosta remained calm. By now her two boys, aged five and seven, were running around the fire, playing. She warned the boys to stay away from the police. "They might take you," she said. "Okay, okay, okay," the youngest boy answered impatiently, showing no sign of fear.

Ellen Gabriel was pacing nervously up and down the western edge of the Pines, a few metres from a small group of SQ tactical squad members, who were crouched behind a tree. Kahentiiosta tried to calm her down, telling her war stories about Ganienkeh. "This is all scare tactics," she told Ellen Gabriel. "They just want us to go home."

The police helicopter was flying low overhead. Each time it swung past, everyone in the Pines would look up, and the police who were positioned close to Gabriel and Kahentiiosta would inch closer towards them. Kahentiiosta called for help from the warriors to prevent the police from advancing any farther. Someone found a chainsaw and started to saw down one of the majestic trees to block their path.

The police hesitated as they looked up at the tree looming over them. Then one of them fired a canister of tear gas, forcing the Mohawk with the chainsaw to back off. The tree, its trunk half-severed, swayed in the wind. Then a concussion grenade exploded, followed by a second blast. Kahentiiosta grabbed her children and sent them off with her niece to a camp in the middle of the pine forest, where she thought they would be safer.

The boys were more curious than frightened by the series of explosions. They thought it was fireworks going off. All their lives, they had seen their parents involved in armed confrontations, and they had grown up around guns.

More squad cars raced up the highway from the town, with another van behind them. Police officers jumped out and began putting on their gas masks and tactical gear in the middle of the highway. By now, Mohawk men were milling about among the women and children, some of them carrying baseball bats. There were still no guns in sight — the men with weapons remained hidden in the forest — but more and more people from the community were spilling into the Pines, walking in from the back entrance where they had left their cars along the road. Other Mohawks stood on the highway just west of the Pines, piling up tires and setting them ablaze. They were hoping the thick, black smoke would force the police to retreat.

At about 8:30 a.m., the front-end loader roared up and started moving toward the Mohawk barricade. It had been parked on the highway for over an hour, but now the police had decided to make their move. "Where's the men?" one of the Mohawk women began screaming to Kahentiiosta. "Where are our men now?"

"The men are in their positions," she answered. "They're not going to be standing in the front there. They know what they're doing."

Kahentiiosta spoke with confidence, but she didn't really know where the men were. She told the women to get behind the lacrosse box that stood in the middle of the clearing, a couple of hundred metres north of the roadblock. She did not realize that some of the warriors were hiding behind the lacrosse box with their guns ready.

The police blasted several more volleys of tear gas and concussion grenades, sending some of the women scurrying towards the lacrosse box and the tents in the northeast corner of the clearing. Hervey Nicholas, a big, burly Mohawk, bellowed at the rest of the women to move away from the front of the Pines. His sister, Janet, had been sitting in her car, parked just a few metres from the barricade. When she heard her brother's orders, she drove the car up the dirt road and stopped near the lacrosse box. The concussion grenades were exploding all around her. "You know what my first thought was?" she recalls, shaking her head. "Somebody call the police."

The Mohawks heard the roar of the front-end loader as it moved forward and made one swipe at the roadblock. Ellen Gabriel stood off to one side of the dirt road, cursing. "This is their justice system," she said angrily to another Mohawk woman. "What the fuck kind of people are they? Over a goddamn golf course and their fucking greedy lust for money."

Eba Beauvais told her to get back. "We're in the line of fire," she said. "They're moving in."

Denise David-Tolley's voice crackled over the two-way radio from a spot in the Pines where she was watching the front-end loader lumber forward. "Let them do it," she told the warriors. "We can always replace it."

The gas and smoke had created a huge screen between the police and the Mohawks in the Pines. From where the Mohawks stood, a couple of hundred metres back, they could not even see the remains of the roadblock. If the police had simply intended to dismantle the barricade, they were now free to do so: the Mohawks were retreating and could no longer protect it. One after another, four heavily-equipped police officers leaped over the barricade and raced into the Pines, brandishing their weapons. The police spotted one Mohawk man dashing from a hiding place near the front of the barricade, heading northwest towards the west side of the lacrosse box. Three officers took off after him. One of them was Corporal Marcel Lemay.

"They're coming in!" a Mohawk woman yelled. "They're in. The cops are in."

A warrior called Crazyhorse was standing with a group of Mohawk men who were concealed in the dense bush behind the lacrosse box, their weapons loaded and ready to fire. They watched as the police ran forward into the clearing. They were in plain view, an easy target if the warriors chose to shoot at them.

Crazyhorse heard a rapid succession of gunshots, but he did not recognize the sound as gunfire until he saw dirt flying up into the air as the bullets struck the ground. "They're shooting!" he yelled. The firefight had begun, with bullets flying from both sides. At the peak of the brief battle, several warriors were firing their assault rifles from their hiding places behind the lacrosse box.

Children and women were running in all directions. Within seconds, most of them had hit the ground, looking for cover. One woman clung to the trunk of a tree. Her husband, a warrior, appeared out of nowhere and threw himself against the woman to shield her from the barrage.

Kahentiiosta was standing beside Eba Beauvais when the gunfire began. She pulled the older woman down to the ground beside her. "They're shooting at us!" she said. "And you're standing there like a damned idiot!"

"I can't breathe!" Eba Beauvais yelled, her voice muffled in the grass. "I'm going to die!" She turned her head and pulled off the wet hankie covering her face, waiting for the rapid fire to stop. Finally the barrage of shots ended, trailing off into a series of single blasts.

The gunfire had lasted for exactly twenty-three seconds.

Eba Beauvais looked back at the highway as the smoke was clearing and saw an ambulance hurtling toward the western fringe of the Pines.

"I think we got one!" a warrior was yelling excitedly.

The couple who had been pressed against the tree near the front still stood there, clinging to the trunk, sobbing. In the other direction, near the lacrosse box, a woman stood on the dirt road with a baby in her arms. She was crying. A warrior burst out of the forest, grabbed the baby, and took the infant into the woods for safety.

"Get in the bush!" one of the warriors screamed at the women. "All you girls, in the bush! Now!"

Some of the Mohawk women were standing dazed in the clearing. One of the warriors drove up in a blue pick-up truck and ordered the women to get into the back. Everyone assumed that the police were preparing for another assault.

Dozens of Mohawks were milling about the road at the back entrance to the Pines. Stonecarver tried to clear them away. "There are police snipers in the woods," he shouted at them.

From a ravine in the woods north of the Pines, he could hear Ronald Cross — a tough-talking warrior codenamed Lasagna — yelling at the police. "Get out of here!" he was shouting. "You've got five minutes to clear out."

Stonecarver ran across the road in the direction of the warrior's voice. He was wearing black trousers and had an ammunition clip stuffed in each pocket. They kept falling out onto the ground, and several times he had to stop to pick them up.

Lasagna had spotted three police snipers crouched down in the gully. When he confronted them, two took off right away, but the other stood his ground. The warrior and the police officer aimed their assault rifles at each other. Lasagna was trembling with fear. He did not want to shoot or be shot at, and he was certain the police sniper felt the same way, but for several long seconds neither of the men would back down. They just stared into each other's eyes.

"Look at that, your buddies left you behind," Lasagna shouted. "Drop your weapon or you're dead meat!" The police officer looked around and realized that the other officers had left. He retreated.

Back on the highway, eight hundred metres south of where Lasagna stood staring down the police sharpshooter, the Mohawks watched in awe as the ambulance sped down towards Oka. The police officers followed, jumping into the back of the vans and trucks as they pulled away, leaving behind a half-dozen vans and cruisers in their hasty retreat.

A Mohawk climbed into the cab of the deserted front-end loader, which had been abandoned by the police at the front barricade. The keys were still in it. He fumbled around for a moment, trying to figure out how to unlock the ignition. An armed warrior jumped onto the machine and shoved the muzzle of his weapon into the cab, not realizing it was a Mohawk in the driver's seat. "Put that gun down!" another Mohawk screamed. "That's my cousin in there."

The front-end loader roared to life. Other Mohawks were breaking into the abandoned squad cars. A warrior jump-started one of the vehicles, then drove it into the Pines, siren blaring.

The women were already busy in the middle of the pine forest. A few of them were tearing strips off sheets for bandages and gathering blankets to set up a makeshift first-aid centre in case anyone had been hurt.

When the warrior sped up the dirt road in the cruiser with his siren wailing, the Mohawks thought the police had come back. Some of the women hid in the bushes until they realized it was a warrior behind the wheel. "It's one of our guys!" one of the women yelled in jubilation.

Several women jumped onto the hood of the police car, cheering as they drove through the Pines. But the driver could not see a thing, and he smashed into a van parked along the edge of the dirt road. Two of the women were badly hurt when they fell to the ground, but they were too giddy to pay attention to their injuries.

On the highway, the front-end loader lowered its shovel onto one of the deserted police vans, crushing its roof. It backed up, then roared forward, pushing two police vans onto the crest of the hill overlooking the town of Oka. Someone felled a tree across the crushed vehicles, forming a barricade across the highway. It became the main Mohawk barricade for the rest of the summer.

Other warriors pumped bullets into three of the deserted police cars, forcing open the trunks and doors in search of police weapons. The cars, with their windshields smashed and pockmarked with bullet holes, were pushed several hundred metres west on the highway and left on their sides, creating an obstacle course to slow down any police vehicles that might try to enter the area. Young Mohawks, wrenches in hand, stripped the police cars of every workable part.

Francis Boots looked on in horror as the vehicles were demolished. "No, no, don't destroy those damned things," he pleaded. "We can use them. We can use the radios."

But it was too late. The Mohawks — including many people who had never set foot in the Pines to help the protesters during the early days of the roadblock — were united in an orgy of destruction, a collective venting of anger.

One of the warriors — a Kanesatake warrior codenamed Apache — climbed into the shovel of the front-end loader and was lifted to the top of the newly formed barricade across the highway. He held up his rifle in a gesture of defiance, smirking down at the police who were clustered on the road at the bottom of the hill.

Mohawks from the town of Oka had gathered behind the police line at the bottom of the hill and were now cheering as they watched the front-end loader push the damaged vans into place at the top of the hill. Many of them had been standing there since early morning, watching the police cars speed up the hill, one after another. Some had tried to block a police van after it hit a car parked on the side of the road in Oka, until the van's driver had told them they would be under arrest if they did not get out of the way.

At 8:40 a.m., when the people of Oka had heard the rapid exchange of gunfire in the Pines, one woman cried, "Oh my God, they'll all be killed!" But some of the white townspeople started to laugh when they heard the shots.

Several fights nearly broke out between supporters and opponents of the Mohawks. One young blond kid shook his head angrily. "All over a stupid golf course," he muttered.

Later, when the front-end loader overturned the police vans, the blond teenager joined in the cheers of the Oka Mohawks. Three days later, the fifteen-year-old French Canadian went behind the barricades, looking for excitement and eager to do whatever he could to help save the Pines. He became a warrior, and his codename was "Blondie."

Over in Kahnawake, it had taken the warriors about three hours to seal off the highways that passed through their reserve. They set up barricades at the borders of their territory and chased out any stray vehicles. The police were busy on the other side of the barricades, diverting traffic away from the Mohawk reserve.

By 9:30 a.m., the barricades were established, and dozens of Mohawks were manning them. The Mercier Bridge was now under their control. The warriors had gone through a dress rehearsal in 1988, when they seized the bridge in retaliation for an RCMP raid on the discount cigarette stores in Kahnawake. This time, the whole operation went smoothly. And the seizure of the bridge seemed to have achieved its objective: the police did not attempt a second assault on the Mohawks in the Pines.

It was nearly mid-morning before the people in the Pines knew for sure that a police officer had been killed in the gunfight. Corporal Marcel Lemay, a thirty-one-year-old member of the SQ tactical intervention squad, had been shot while trying to intercept the warrior who had fled the front barricade as the police moved into the Pines. Lemay was married and the father of a two-year-old daughter. His wife was expecting a second child.

According to one of Lemay's colleagues, Lemay ran towards three large trees to take refuge from the gunfire. He was about thirty metres west of the barricade when he suddenly fell face first, uttering a feeble cry. His colleague rushed towards Lemay and tore off his gas mask. It was filled with blood. A single bullet had entered through Lemay's left armpit, at a spot unprotected by his bulletproof vest, and ripped through his lungs, his oesophagus, the base of his heart, and his aorta, fragments of the bullet lodging in his right shoulder. A Quebec coroner later concluded the shot had come from the direction of the escaping warrior.

The SQ later told investigators that they did not fire any shots until they were retreating, after they had rescued Lemay. But journalists did not record any further gunshots after the short, twenty-three-second fusillade, and the SQ did not explain how they could have rescued Lemay and fired the shots to cover their retreat within the same short burst of gunfire.

At first, some of the Mohawks did not believe the news of Lemay's death. With all the smoke and confusion during the exchange of gunfire, most of them did not see the ambulance pull into the Pines, and no one seemed to have seen the officer go down. Some people were convinced he had fallen out of a tree and shot himself. Others said he had been shot from behind, by one of his own men.

The Mohawks later admitted that half a dozen warriors had fired their weapons. They had been standing behind the lacrosse box, a few hundred metres from the spot where Lemay fell. They insisted that the police had fired first, and that the warriors had aimed high, above the heads of the officers. Their orders, crackling over the two-way radios in Mohawk and in English, had been to hold their fire unless they were shot at — and once they responded, not to shoot to kill.

At the end of the crisis, Montreal Urban Community police determined the shots had come from three directions in the Pines: from behind the lacrosse box, from the eastern edge of the Pines, and from the direction of the retreating warrior, northwest of the roadblock at Highway 344. Lemay was killed by a steel-tipped "full metal jacket" .223 calibre bullet. While the SQ tactical intervention squad uses .223 calibre bullets, they do not normally use the "full metal jacket" type — a fact which led the Quebec coroner to conclude the shot that killed Lemay could not have come from one of his colleagues. The gun that fired the fatal bullet was never found.

There had been about thirty warriors in the Pines when the police arrived at 5:15 a.m. Within an hour, nearly everyone in Kanesatake knew about the raid, and dozens of Mohawks joined the people in the Pines. Many were boys and men who brought guns with them to help defend the land. By the time of the shooting at 8:40 a.m., there were an estimated fifty to seventy-five armed men in the forest.

A few hours later, one of the Mohawks did an inventory of the weapons that the Mohawks had at their disposal that day. At least twenty people in the Pines had .22-calibre rifles or shotguns. There were about ten bolt-action .303s; several pistols, including at least one high-powered nine-millimetre pistol; a .45-calibre semi-automatic Colt pistol; a police-style Taurus .357 magnum revolver; and a .22-calibre Ruger pistol. There were plenty of assault rifles: a sniper version of an M-14, five SKS rifles (including one that took a thirty-round clip), three M-1 Carbines (a World War II era semi-automatic American service rifle), five heavy-barrelled AR-15s (a semi-automatic civilian version of an armed services rifle), a fully automatic CAR-15, and an RPK (a Russian-designed light machine gun). The warriors had several thousand rounds of ammunition.

Clearly, the Mohawks had enough firepower to mount a lethal counterattack when the police rushed into the Pines. The vast majority of the warriors — most of whom were caught completely off guard when the gunfire began — chose not to open fire. A few of the warriors had been in position along the eastern edge of the Pines, their guns trained on police officers who were clustered in and around the tiny Mohawk graveyard between the Pines and the golf course. Contrary to the conclusions of the police investigation, they denied firing any shots. "We had them in our sights," one warrior said later. "If we'd wanted to kill them, we would have."

Publicly, all the warriors insisted that Lemay's killer had not been a Mohawk. But no one could prove it — and privately, among a few Mohawks, a nagging doubt persisted. There was that ominous shout — "I think we got one" — that some warrior had yelled out soon after the shooting. In all the hysteria and confusion, it is possible that even the man who killed Lemay does not know he did it.

The Mohawks expressed sorrow at the death of Corporal Lemay, but no one expressed shame. They blamed the mayor of Oka. "He sent the sQ in here," one Mohawk said.

The news of Lemay's death dampened the jubilation that had swept through the Pines after the police retreated. It sent a cold chill through the veins of all who had confronted the police that morning. Regardless of how Lemay had died, they knew the police would blame the warriors.

For the rest of the day, the warriors conducted sweeps through the Pines and the golf course, looking for hidden snipers. They took up positions where they could look down at the town of Oka and braced themselves for a second attack.

CHAPTER 2

Golfballs among the Headstones

Fighting the Mayor's Dream

The bones of the Mohawk dead are piled on top of one another in the tiny graveyard just off the highway west of the town of Oka. Wedged between the driveway to the Oka Golf Club and the club's parking lot, the cemetery has been left with no room to expand. The graves are tightly packed together, and stray golfballs are sometimes found strewn among the decaying headstones. The ninth hole is just a few metres away. The names on the headstones read like a genealogy of the Kanesatake Mohawks: Gabriel, Nicholas, Nelson — the parents, grandparents, and great-grandparents of the people who stood together in the Pines during the spring and summer of 1990.

Thirty years ago, when the Oka Golf Club was built and the little Pine Hill Cemetery was boxed in, no one paid attention to the Mohawks' outcry. The encroachment of the golf course on the Mohawk graves became for them a symbol of the relentless appetite of developers and municipal politicians for the shrinking forest. West of the cemetery are the Pines — a forest of majestic white pine trees, some of them over a hundred years old. A dirt track that leads north off the highway runs into a clearing where a lacrosse box stands, its weathered boards in need of a fresh coat of paint. Mohawk kids play lacrosse here in the summer, and as far back as anyone can remember, the Kanesatake Mohawks have held a community picnic here every July 1. The municipality of Oka legally owns the clearing in the Pines and calls it a municipal park, but the Mohawks refuse to recognize Oka's title. They say they never gave up the land or sold it. To demonstrate their attachment to the Pines, the Mohawks take care of the area. Every spring, they organize a clean-up of the grounds.

The Pines are the heart of the territory the people of Kanesatake have called their own for more than 270 years. Their ancestors named their settlement after this place on the crest of the hill above Lake of Two Mountains: Kanesatake, "where the sandy crust dunes are." The soil is fine and sandy here, and after it rains, the sand drifts and hardens into a tough crust. A century ago, when the deforested hillside was in danger of collapsing into the town of Oka and the lake below, the Mohawks planted tens of thousands of trees in the shifting sand, under the direction of the Sulpician priests who then held title to the territory — though the Mohawks never recognized the priests' ownership. The Pines and a belt of forest running along the northern fringe of Oka are all that is left of that hand-planted forest, known by the Mohawks as the Commons. Now the Mohawks are fighting to keep what is left of the forest from being chopped down.

The Mohawk settlement of Kanesatake is spread out over eight hundred hectares just west of the Pines. It is not a reserve, but a patchwork of lots scattered among French Canadian farms — the meagre remnants of a once-vast seigneury, sold by the Sulpician priests to the federal government in 1945. About 625 Mohawks live on federal lands in the municipal parish of Oka. The rest — about 250 people living on sixty Crown-owned lots — reside in the town of Oka itself. That checkerboard configuration has created a jurisdictional nightmare which has strained relations between the Mohawks and municipal governments in the town and parish of Oka for many years. The Mohawks refuse to recognize municipal by-laws within their territory. One Mohawk, for example, began building a three-storey apartment block on Crown-owned land in Oka without seeking a municipal permit. The conflict led to a messy court fight that is still wending its way to the Supreme Court. The shell of that half-finished apartment building stands as a constant reminder of the Mohawks' defiance. Twice during the summer's long standoff, attempts were made to burn it down.

The Mohawks believe that all the land of the original Lake of Two Mountains seigneury — including the entire parish and town of Oka

— is their property. But they have legal title to none of that land, not even their burial ground. In the wake of the police raid on the Pines, the federal government purchased the graveyard from the town of Oka for one dollar. That transaction, done without the knowledge or consent of the Mohawks, heaped insult upon injury.

For years, the Mohawks have watched new housing and recreational developments take over the last remaining undeveloped land around Kanesatake. Across the highway, south of the cramped graveyard and the Pines, affluent French Canadians have built beautiful, high-priced houses on expansive, treed lots that look south out over the Lake of Two Mountains. The Mohawks contend that the luxury homes, with their neatly manicured lawns and in-ground pools, were built on land stolen from them. But unlike the Mohawks, deprived of any recognition of their claims even though their ancestors hunted and farmed on this land for generations, the newcomers have legal documents to show they own their lots.

The undercurrent of hostility between the Mohawks and their white neighbours surfaced in 1986 when the owners of some of those homes tried to block a Mohawk initiative to open a drug and alcohol treatment centre for aboriginal people in a vacant residence next to their property. The homeowners feared the native-run centre would devalue their property and threaten the peace and tranquility of the neighbourhood. They skirted allegations of bigotry by demanding the closing of a non-native treatment centre nearby at the same time, but most Mohawks perceived thinly veiled racism at the heart of the campaign. The group's lobbying efforts failed, and the Onen'to:kon Treatment Centre opened in 1987. But soon that same group of citizens, bitterly hated by many Mohawks, adopted a new cause that would once again pit them against the people of Kanesatake. They led the campaign to support the golf course expansion.

Oka's Mayor, Jean Ouellette, did not consult the Mohawks before he proudly unveiled plans for the expanded golf course at a municipal council meeting in March 1989. The town had acquired an option to buy a strip of eighteen hectares of forest and swampland just west of the clearing in the Pines for $70,000. It planned to lease that land to the Oka Golf Club so nine holes could be added to the existing course. The golf club was to put up the money for the land purchase, in lieu of several years' rent to the municipality. The French owners of the land, Maxime Maurice and Jean Michel Rousseau, planned to retain enough of their property to build a row of sixty luxury townhouses that would back onto the golf course. Mayor Jean Ouellette, himself a member of the golf club, described the deal as a win-win situation for the town — it did not have to front the money for the golf course expansion, and it could look forward to one million dollars in rent over the thirty-five-year period of the golf club lease as well as property taxes from the proposed $10 million housing development for years to come.

Jean Ouellette knew there was bound to be a jurisdictional fight with the Mohawks over the project, because the Mohawks had tried to keep town employees out of the forest before. In 1988, the Oka town council had taken out an injunction against the Kanesatake band council and the Mohawk Warrior Society, after some unidentified Mohawk men tried to stop three of its employees from pruning trees in the forest. Following the incident, the municipality had received a letter purportedly from the Kanesatake war chief, warning Oka that its "continued invasion of (Mohawk) territories would not be tolerated." (One of the employees who had been sent to prune the trees — a Mohawk named Jean Noël Cataford — quit his job and joined the warriors' defence of the Pines in 1990. He was codenamed Christmas.)

Ouellette was not too concerned about the Mohawks because he knew he had the strict rule of law on his side: the government and the courts had consistently denied the Mohawk land claim for 150 years. So he simply dismissed the inevitable Mohawk protests as a potential annoyance. When an angry townsperson at the March 1989 municipal council meeting demanded to know if the mayor had consulted the Mohawks before making his plans, Ouellette merely shrugged. "You know you can't talk to the Indians," the mayor replied.

The atmosphere at that municipal council meeting was explosive. Helga Maeder, a potter who had settled in Oka two years earlier, was stunned by the council's attitude. Many townspeople in the audience resented Ouellette and his council for presenting the project to them as a *fait accompli*, without asking either the Mohawks or the Oka voters if they wanted the development and without making any plans to study its environmental effects. Helga Maeder had never been politically active, but when the mayor refused to hold a referendum on the golf course expansion issue, she organized a petition to have the project stopped.

The response was extraordinary. Nearly nine hundred people from Oka and the surrounding parish signed the petition. Many white townspeople opposed the project because the golf course was, after all, a private club, and few of them stood to enjoy its benefits. Others were opposed for environmental reasons: the more trees that were cut in the sandy soil of the Pines, the greater they believed was the danger of repeating the erosion problems that had plagued Oka in the nineteenth century, when the shifting sands of the hillside had threatened to bury the town.

The project's opponents solicited the support of the provincial environment minister of the day, Lise Bacon. Her ministry also had grave concerns about the soundness of the golf course expansion. But because the law did not require the municipality to conduct an environmental impact study for a recreational project, the department was powerless to stop the town of Oka from chopping down trees to make way for nine more holes.

Immediately after Ouellette announced plans for the expanded golf course, there were isolated acts of vandalism in Oka. Mohawks were blamed for smashed windows at the town's offices and in stores. But most Mohawks staged polite demonstrations to show their opposition to the proposed expansion. Allen Gabriel, a Mohawk conservation officer for the band council who was head of a committee to research the Kanesatake land claim, organized a protest march through the town of Oka on April 1, 1989. Big, wet snowflakes were falling as about three hundred Mohawks walked down the hill from the Pines towards the town. Children from the Mohawk elementary school carried placards, mothers pushed strollers, and drummers sat perched in the back of a pick-up truck that led the procession through Oka.

The march was sanctioned by the provincial police, the Sûreté du Québec, but the demonstration had little impact. "They let us play in the town for the day," Debbie Etienne recalls wryly.

By summer, the golf club's board of directors was planning a symbolic tree cutting in the Pines to kick off the planned expansion of the golf course. The ceremony was scheduled for August 1, 1989. The media were all present. So were the Mohawks.

"About seventy-five or a hundred of us showed up there early in the morning," Allen Gabriel recalls. "We warned the president of the expansion committee, Pierre Phaneuf, you're not going to cut down any trees — symbolic or otherwise. We told him that if he did, he'd be responsible for the consequences."

Pierre Phaneuf really couldn't understand what all the fuss was about. "We only want to cut down twenty-two acres out of seventy," he told reporters.

With the media watching and threats from Kanesatake's grand chief, Clarence Simon, and the Quebec Ministry of the Environment to go to court to stop the tree cutting, the project's launch was called off.

Two days later, representatives of the Quebec Native Affairs Secretariat and the federal Department of Indian Affairs and Northern Development, as well as both the municipality and the parish of Oka, met the band council's lawyer and the Mohawks who were leading the Kanesatake land claim committee, Allen Gabriel and his father Raymond, at a hotel in the Montreal suburb of Dorval. The Mohawks called for a moratorium on all development in the area — not just the golf course expansion, but other projects slated to be built on disputed Mohawk territory as well.

The regional director of Indian Affairs, Frank Vieni, also wanted to resolve more than the immediate problem of the golf course project. As the top Indian Affairs bureaucrat in Quebec, Vieni held the purse-strings for all aspects of social and economic development in Kanesatake. He realized most community development efforts were thwarted by the way the Kanesatake Mohawks were dispersed throughout the parish and the town of Oka, without a unified geographic base. But Vieni balked at the Mohawk demand to freeze all municipal development in the area until the land issue was resolved. "It's unthinkable to even consider imposing a moratorium on all development under municipal jurisdiction," he told the Mohawks at the meeting. "Life must go on for these people."

Vieni proposed instead to work out an arrangement whereby the town of Oka, the parish, and the Mohawks would have to consult each other on future projects. He suggested they negotiate some kind of binding mechanism to make sure each community's development plans were compatible with those of its neighbours — though Vieni later acknowledged that a consultation process would not guarantee the Kanesatake Mohawks a means to stop any municipal project that encroached on land they claimed. But Kanesatake's white neighbours had never before sought the Mohawks' opinion on their development plans, and Vieni thought an agreement to start Oka and Kanesatake talking to each other was at least a first step towards avoiding potential conflicts.

Mayor Ouellette agreed to a fifteen-day moratorium on some of Oka's planned developments, including the golf course expansion, with a commitment to extend the freeze as long as discussions with the Mohawks proceeded "in a positive direction."

"The obvious question was, positive for whom?" Allen Gabriel remarks. "That was his big stick: You guys sit down and behave or else I'll lift this moratorium." Although the Mohawks knew Oka could lift the development freeze at any time, they believed the town's desire to resolve the land dispute was sincere, so they agreed to Ouellette's terms.

In September 1989, the federal government tabled its first proposal. The government termed it a "framework agreement" for negotiations. Frank Vieni now admits that calling it an "agreement" was misleading because the Mohawks never undertook to do anything more than consult their community about the contents of the proposal. Despite the fact that the government's proposal was rejected by almost every person in Kanesatake who took the time to study it, federal officials continued to insist that they had a "framework agreement" with the Mohawks. By the summer of 1990, Indian Affairs Minister Tom Siddon's constant references to this "agreement" had thoroughly muddied the situation. It left Canadians with the impression that the Mohawks had backed out of a deal — even though the federal proposal had never been ratified by the people of Kanesatake.

The federal proposal had a dual purpose: first, to unify Kanesatake's land base and create a reserve; second, to resolve the jurisdictional problems between Kanesatake and the parish and town of Oka. The government planned to create a "land unification package," by purchasing for the Mohawks parcels of land that were contiguous to the patchwork quilt of lots already owned by the Crown, spread out over the parish of Oka.

But when it came to the golf course expansion land, there was a catch: the government would only buy that land, including the Pines and the cemetery, if the Mohawks first settled their jurisdictional squabble with Oka over the Crown-owned lots in the town. That condition doomed the proposal from the start. The reason the Mohawks had embarked on the negotiations in the first place was to stop Oka from razing much of the Pines for its golf course. But under the federal proposal, they could only attain that goal if the Mohawks living in the town of Oka agreed to comply with the municipality's by-laws. The Mohawks had always refused to recognize Oka's authority over the Crown-owned lands in the town because they considered those lands to be exclusive Mohawk territory. They were not prepared to begin now to trade off their rights over those lands in exchange for the lands slated for the golf course expansion. So they rejected the government proposal. "We tore the thing apart," says Linda Cree, one of the first Mohawks to look at the document.

Linda Cree was an education counsellor in Kanesatake and the wife of the Longhouse faithkeeper, John Cree, who performed the tobacco-burning ceremony the morning the police raided the Pines. She was the eldest of the eight children of Thelma and Walter David Sr., a proud and fiercely traditional family whose members were respected by some in the community and despised by others for their outspoken and uncompromising belief that the Longhouse is the only valid form of government in the Mohawk settlement. Most of Thelma and Walter's children — including Walter David Jr., Denise David-Tolley, and Joe David — were to be deeply embroiled in the summer's events. Over the years, Cree had immersed herself in Mohawk history, poring through archives in Ottawa and in New York State, trying to prove that Mohawks had settled in the Lake of Two Mountains long before the French staked claim to the territory. Her mind was like a computer, filled with dates and details of historic treaties. In her view, Oka's plans to clear-cut part of the Commons for an eighteen-hole golf course represented an illegal intrusion on Mohawk territory.

Allen Gabriel, who had been given the mandate by the band council to consult the Kanesatake Mohawks on the land issue, sought the help of Cree and other members of the Kanesatake Joint Services Council — a committee of band employees who worked in education, health, and social services. After reading and rejecting the federal proposal, they set to work to draft their own principles for negotiations. They wanted clear jurisdiction over their territory, including the Crown-owned lots in the town.

Throughout November of 1989, they held public meetings for the Mohawks to discuss both the government's proposal and their own options. "They were very lively meetings," Allen Gabriel recalls. "What we had known all along was starting to happen: People saw that framework agreement as blackmail, as something that undermined the historical position we've always maintained — that this is our territory."

That attitude of distrust towards the federal government and towards Oka poisoned the atmosphere of the meetings. Most people were unwilling to trade off their rights over land in the town of Oka for territory elsewhere which they believed was already theirs. They did not believe Oka's assurances that it did not want to appropriate the Crown-owned lots in the town or evict the Mohawks living there; it just wanted everyone in the town to live by the same regulations and by-laws. They were suspicious of the federal negotiator's insistence that he sit in on the workshops, and, after the first few meetings, Yves Désilets was barred from attending the rest. By late fall, 201 out of the 203 people who had shown up for the workshops had rejected the government's proposal. The other two had abstained.

Allen Gabriel says the Mohawks never formally ended talks with the various levels of government, but the consultation process was put on hold when the people of Kanesatake became embroiled in a political dispute over who had the right to run the band's affairs. In January 1990, the clan mothers who appoint chiefs to the band council dismissed Grand Chief Clarence Simon over allegations of conflict of interest. He refused to accept the decision of the clan mothers, and for a time the golf course issue was all but forgotten by the community while the faction supporting Clarence Simon feuded openly with Simon's replacement, Grand Chief George Martin.

The Mohawks in the Simon and Martin camps were not the only rival groups feuding. The political in-fighting re-ignited a twenty-year-old controversy over Kanesatake's system of government. Since 1969, the Department of Indian Affairs had used a provision in the Indian Act for traditional or "custom" councils to recognize a form of band council which was unique to Kanesatake — a hybrid of Mohawk customs and Indian Act regulations. The Kanesatake council still complied with the Indian Act, passing band council resolutions that required a stamp of approval from Indian Affairs and administering the funds that came from Ottawa. But instead of being elected, the nine chiefs on this "custom" council were appointed by clan mothers, in consultation with each of the three Mohawk clans, the Turtle, the Bear, and the Wolf.

Not everyone supported the "custom" council. Two rival groups — one called the Kanesatakeron League for Democracy, the other known as the Group for Change — wanted a return to band elections. Some of the Mohawks in these two factions said the existing system simply did not work, and they pointed to the recent history of political upheaval in Kanesatake. Between 1987 and 1990, the clan mothers of the "custom" council had appointed new chiefs six times. Many of the Mohawks who sought a return to elections had lost their clans, traditionally passed down by their mothers, because of intermarriage with non-Mohawks. Without a clan, they had no voice in decision making. Other Mohawks who opposed the "custom" council complained that they were seldom consulted by the clan mothers, which went against the principles of grassroots democracy on which the system was supposed to be based.

The other faction in Kanesatake was the Longhouse — the traditional political and spiritual institution of the Mohawks. The Longhouse followers had their own set of clan mothers, whose role was to listen to the people of their clans and counsel the Longhouse chiefs. The Longhouse community in Kanesatake was tiny. Its members met at a modest, wooden building next to the property of their aging chief, Samson Gabriel. But they were the most outspoken and defiant people in Kanesatake. They considered themselves a sovereign nation, and they regarded the Kanesatake band council as a distorted imitation of their traditional system of government. They refused to recognize the jurisdiction of the Indian Act over their lives.

Throughout his consultations, Allen Gabriel walked a tightrope, trying to maintain support from each of these groups without alienating any of the others. Gabriel himself could not be slotted into any single faction — he drew a salary from the band office, while describing himself as a Longhouse follower. He sided with neither the new grand chief George Martin nor his predecessor, Clarence Simon.

Until the in-fighting flared up in January 1990, it had been relatively easy to keep everyone in the settlement focused on the land issue, because it was one of the few issues everyone in Kanesatake agreed on. Virtually every Mohawk in the community believed they had been unjustly deprived of their territory. But with the political upheaval, that focus was lost, and the Oka municipal council took advantage of the opportunity to resurrect its plan for the golf course expansion.

In early March, after the band council announced it was breaking off plans for negotiations until it had more time to study the land issue, Mayor Jean Ouellette declared he had run out of patience. "No one can agree, no one gives us firm propositions on what they want to do — what does Ottawa want? What do the Mohawks want?" he asked. In fact, the Mohawks had made their objective perfectly clear — the cancellation of the golf course project. But the mayor and his council were resolute.

"When the municipal council voted to proceed with the golf course, we almost fell out of our chairs," says Helga Maeder, who attended the Oka council meeting in early March 1990. Maeder had been confident that there was enough opposition to the project from the Mohawks and the Oka townspeople to force the council to set it aside. Instead, the mayor called off the tree-cutting moratorium.

The Mohawks accused Oka of taking advantage of the political turmoil in Kanesatake to move ahead on the project while the new band council was too disunified to mount any opposition to it. Oka's lawyer, Luc Carbonneau, says the golf club simply could not afford to keep waiting. "Some of the golf club members had a lot of money already invested in the project," Carbonneau said later. There was also the question of the ten-million-dollar housing development that would border the golf course, he added. It, too, was being delayed by the stalled negotiations.

On March 9, 1990, the day the moratorium was to end, the Department of Indian Affairs and the Kanesatake band council convinced Oka's mayor to hold off on the golf course expansion for two more weeks. That night, the Mohawks held a demonstration at the golf club.

About one hundred Mohawks, backed by environmental groups that opposed the expansion, marched up the golf club driveway and past the cemetery to gather in the parking lot of the golf club, where the directors were meeting. A couple of the club's directors came outside and stood on the porch impatiently. They listened coolly as Allen Gabriel read out a letter of protest.

"We are here to express to you our great concern over your plans to expand this golf course to eighteen holes," he read. "It is common knowledge that these lands are part of the Mohawk territory of Kanesatake and that our title to these lands has never been ceded or extinguished." The letter went on to ask the club's members to postpone their expansion plans until the land issue was resolved.

Walter David Jr., the band's economic development officer, stood near the back of the crowd and started to chant, "No Golf! No Golf!" But no one joined in. Instead the Mohawks stood around in little groups, shivering, griping about how ineffective the demonstration was and arguing amongst themselves.

The demonstration at the golf club ended without any indication from the club's directors that they would take heed of the Mohawks' concerns. Walter David Jr., Marshall Nicholas, and a couple of other Longhouse men went back to Walter's two-storey log house, sat around the kitchen table, and talked about what to do next. There was not much time to come up with a new strategy: rumours were already circulating around Oka that work on the golf course would begin any day. In a last-ditch plan to stop the expansion, David and the others decided to establish an "early warning system" to alert the community if anyone tried to start construction in the forest. They set up a round-the-clock watch over the Pines.

Early the next morning, March 10, one of the men borrowed John Cree's tractor and dragged a fishing shack down from his backyard to a clearing in the Pines. Word soon spread around Kanesatake that a camp had been set up in the forest. Throughout the day, people wandered down to the area to find out what was going on there. Some scoffed and said it would never achieve anything. Others stayed. The occupation had begun.

CHAPTER 3
Camouflage and Ugly Sticks

The Occupation of the Pines

Denise David-Tolley stood shivering beside the campfire that was burning just outside the fishing shack set up in the Pines, clutching her jacket around her tightly and stamping her feet to keep warm. It was the first night of the occupation of the Pines — March 10, 1990. David-Tolley had arrived to take a turn on duty as soon as her shift at CKHQ, the Kanesatake radio station, ended at midnight.

"It was so cold," she remembers. "The men stayed inside the shack, and the women were outside by the fire, trying to keep it going and trying to keep warm."

At first there was just a handful of people keeping watch over the Pines. One of the men brought a small woodstove to heat the shack, and others carted in tables and chairs to make it more comfortable. They took turns parked in their cars, staking out either end of the dirt road that ran through the Pines to see if municipal contractors would try to come in. Someone erected a banner between two trees, near the edge of the golf course. "Are you aware that this is Mohawk land?" it asked, in French and English.

One of the men put up the blue and white flag depicting the Hiawatha belt that symbolized the link between the Mohawks and the other nations of the Iroquois Confederacy. He also put up a Warrior Society flag — the silhouette of a warrior on a backdrop of red, with the yellow sun blazing behind him. But that flag came down after a couple of days. The people in the Pines wanted to keep the camp non-political, a welcome place for any Mohawk who opposed Oka's plans for the golf course, and the flag represented a political faction that many Kanesatake Mohawks did not support. It was identified with the militant Mohawk nationalists in Kahnawake who had captured the Mercier Bridge two years earlier to protest against an RCMP raid on the south-shore reserve's illegal cigarette businesses, and with the gun-toting security patrols in Akwesasne who backed gambling and high-stakes bingo as a means of building a national Mohawk economy.

In Kahnawake and Akwesasne, the warrior societies had grown out of a long tradition of Mohawk militancy. With the growth of Mohawk nationalism in those communities had come the rebirth of the men's societies of the Longhouse, whose role it was to defend Mohawk rights and territory.

In contrast to its sister Mohawk reserves, there were fewer traditionalists in Kanesatake, and the Longhouse people there, who had for many years been unwelcome by the Christian majority, had a reputation in the other Mohawk communities for being timid and not rocking the boat. Kanesatake also had a tiny population, without a defined territory, making it difficult to defend. Only about eight hundred Mohawks lived on the patchwork of lots scattered throughout the town and parish of Oka.

But most Kanesatake Mohawks had relatives and friends on the other Mohawk reserves, and Longhouse followers often went to socials and spiritual gatherings at each others' Longhouses. So while there was no long-established Warrior Society in Kanesatake, there were people with links to the warrior societies in Kahnawake and Akwesasne. A few of the older teenagers in Kanesatake who attended the Kahnawake Survival School — the high school established by militant Mohawk nationalists in the late 1970s — had worked for the warriors on their territorial patrol in Kahnawake. A similar system of patrols had been set up in Kanesatake around 1988. It called itself the Kanesatake Warrior Society, drafted its own letterhead and operated out of the home of Dennis Nicholas. The patrols had been set up in response to a series of police raids on underground slot machine operations in Kanesatake, but once that crisis passed, the patrols petered out and the loosely organized Warrior Society faded from existence.

Nicholas, later codenamed "Psycho" by the warriors, was regarded by some of the enthusiastic young men in Kanesatake as the war chief, and although he was never officially given that title by the local Longhouse, he considered himself the leader of the Kanesatake warriors. His phone number was given as the contact number for the Kanesatake war chief in a letter to the municipality of Oka in 1988, in which a man using the name "Aroniahes Otonion" and the title "war chief" warned a town employee that further incursions onto land claimed by the Kanesatake Mohawks could lead to confrontation. The thirty-eight-year-old Mohawk owned one of the illegal slot-machine operations that was raided that year. While they were functioning, proceeds from Nicholas's slot machines had paid the salary for the Mohawk language kindergarten teacher at the local elementary school.

Dennis's brother, Marshall, ran a cut-rate cigarette business in Kanesatake, part of a healthy illegal cigarette trade in the community. Some of the Mohawks in the Kanesatake cigarette trade had business connections to warriors in Akwesasne and Kahnawake, but few were actively involved in the warrior movement and its fight for Mohawk sovereignty.

Despite his codename, Nicholas was a placid, softspoken man whose air of quiet authority gained him the respect and trust of most people in Kanesatake. He had left behind him a troubled marriage and a history of alcohol abuse, after going through the program at the Onen'to:kon Treatment Centre across from the Pines soon after it opened.

Nicholas was also something of an electronics wizard. After the first protesters in the Pines passed around a hat to collect money for two-way radios and a police scanner, he was the one who erected an antenna in the Pines and showed the men how to wire the scanner to pick up the Sûreté du Québec's frequencies. They set up a generator at the fishing shack to keep the radios charged.

It did not take long for rumours to start circulating around the town of Oka that the camp in the Pines was a Warrior Society outpost. Although most of the people putting in shifts in the Pines had never had anything to do with the warriors, one or two of the Mohawk men had brought arms into the camp right from the start. One man wore a pistol strapped underneath his coat. Hunting rifles were kept hidden in vehicles or propped out of sight in a corner of the fishing shack.

"It was a macho thing — to show the men, 'Come on, join us, look what we've got,'" one of the women says about the men who were carrying the first guns. But the men told the women that they wanted the weapons there for protection, in case they were harassed. Some of that harassment came from other Mohawks who didn't support their stand in the Pines, and some of it came from white townspeople who lived near the Pines. The Mohawks were, after all, barring all non-natives from entering what was legally a municipal park.

A couple of weeks after the camp was set up, some white men from Oka crept onto the golf course in the dead of night and tried to sneak up to the camp in the Pines to tear down the banner hanging there.

"There was only a couple of guys on duty," one of the Mohawks recalls. "These guys were all dressed in black — I don't know who they were trying to impress. We caught them. We could have done some major damage to them if we'd wanted to. We laughed as we chased them out."

In April, someone set fire to a shed on the golf course. The people sitting in the Pines heard two loud explosions, and they called the fire department. But the Mohawks themselves were suspected of starting the fire, as a gesture of ill will towards the golf club. A police cruiser, its high beams on, stayed parked on the golf course that entire night, watching the people on duty in the Pines. The Mohawks, in turn, suspected that golf course supporters had set the fire to undermine the public support the Mohawks were getting from environmentalists and other groups. The Sûreté du Québec investigated the incident, but no one was ever charged.

During the first weeks of the occupation, the snow was still deep in the Pines, and the nights were long and cold. Joe David, a son of Walter David Sr., was one of the men who took turns staking out the dirt road at the north entrance to the forest, parked in his 1966 black Chevy truck and watching for intruders.

"I didn't have a lot of money, so I didn't have a lot of gas. I couldn't start the truck to warm myself up. I spent a lot of freezing nights. But it was nice, going down there, walking through the slush. There'd be three or four people sitting inside the cabin. We'd be pretending to be working hard, but for the most part, we were just trying to stay warm. People would drop by now and then, John Cree would be telling his cornball jokes, everybody would be having a good time. There was one guy who used to spend every second day or so inebriated. He felt so good, because after three weeks of being there almost constantly, he hadn't touched a drop. He couldn't believe himself that he could have done that."

Joe David was an artist, a stonecarver and painter who had made his first major art sale a few months earlier. It was a haunting painting of an unsettled spirit that had been purchased by the federal Public Service Commission for its 1990 calendar, and forty thousand prints of his work now hung in federal bureaucrats' offices across the country. He was a loner who spent his time painting and reading, someone who usually shunned causes. But his grandmother was buried in the Mohawk cemetery next to the Pines, and most of his family was involved with the camp, so he felt a commitment to take part in the protest. He was also a pacifist, who believed non-violent civil disobedience was the best way to force political change. He saw a chance to adopt the tactics of radical American and European environmental groups and put them into effect in the Pines. Throughout the spring of 1990, those kinds of tactics were used. The Mohawks combed the forest, looking for the surveyors' stakes that marked the layout of the expanded golf course and the proposed housing development. They pulled up every stake they could find.

The people in the Pines had vowed that they would not budge from their camp until the Oka Golf Club had abandoned its plans for expansion. But after three weeks of keeping watch round the clock, even some of the protesters were amazed by their own perseverance.

"I'll bet they didn't think we'd last this long!" Debbie Etienne remembers telling someone. "We were surprised at the commitments coming from the community, keeping it going."

Debbie Etienne and her husband Ronald Giroux, a non-Mohawk, were spending long hours in the camp whenever they could get away from their jobs. Often she would stand at the front entrance to the Pines, telling curious passersby to go and speak to Oka's mayor, Jean Ouellette.

Every day, some of the older women would come around with coffee and homecooked meals — macaroni casseroles and sandwiches, and sometimes, when the protesters were lucky, traditional Mohawk food like corn soup and fried bread. One of the women in the town had a son-in-law who worked in a twenty-four-hour doughnut shop. Often she would come up to the Pines in the morning with trays of day-old doughnuts and thermoses of coffee.

"We didn't have to leave," Joe David says. "We could stay there all night long, all day long. We had our sacred fire going, an eternal flame. It rained so heavy one night, it drowned the fire out. But it didn't matter — just sitting around the fire, freezing, our boots almost right in the flames, trying to stay warm — the feeling was so good. It was just people, sticking together."

Teenagers would drop by the Pines on their way home from school. Sixteen-year-old Myrna Gabriel and her two girlfriends became regulars, showing up at the fishing shack by five o'clock in the afternoon, and staying until after it got dark. The girls were dubbed "the three Amigos." Myrna keeps a calendar marking all the important events in her day-to-day life, and March 31 is blocked off in bold red ink: the first time she slept overnight in the Pines. "It hit me, there were no other girls my age involved. We were there defending our land, while all these other teenagers were out partying it up. It made me proud."

Another young woman, Susan Oke, started out covering the story of the camp in the Pines for the Kanesatake radio station. She'd been raised in Montreal, in a middle-class neighbourhood. For her, the days and nights spent sitting around the sacred fire, talking about Mohawk traditions and participating in spiritual ceremonies were part of the journey of discovering her Mohawk roots. Susan went on night patrols with the other women, carrying their "ugly sticks" — broken-off branches or axe handles — for protection, in case they ran into intruders in the dark.

Some nights no one was around to take a shift, so John Cree would park his truck at the entrance, leaving a giant stuffed Snoopy doll with a cap on its head on the driver's seat.

Every morning, John Cree came into the Pines at sunrise before heading off to his job as a fueller at the Montreal International Airport in Dorval. He would burn tobacco at the fire, which was part of the Mohawk tradition of giving thanks to the Creator for the dawn of a new day.

Curtis Nelson was another Mohawk who often spent long hours in the Pines, sharing a night shift with Marshall Nicholas, sitting at the entrance to the forest in his big Chevy Blazer or Marshall's jeep.

"It brought together people who hadn't spoken to each other in years," Nelson says. "Even people who never actually put time in, they'd come by just to wave, or they'd come along and say, 'Don't say anything, but here's twenty dollars for gas.' I thought this was the thing that was going to bring this community together once and for all. And it did — for a little while."

One night about sixty people were gathered around the fire, talking over strategy and how far everyone was prepared to go. Curtis Nelson made a rousing speech, telling people he was ready to die for the land if it came to that. He was a compelling orator, an avowed traditionalist despite a brief foray into band office politics and a devoted family man who spoke only Mohawk to his two pre-school children.

Not everyone in Kanesatake supported the stand of the people in the Pines, however. On April 22, some Mohawks opposed to the occupation tried to burn down the fishing shack. It was Earth Day, and the people in the Pines had organized a giant clean-up of the area, in which bagloads of garbage and debris were carted off. Just after nightfall, a couple of drunk Mohawks came into the camp and smashed windows and poured gasoline around the shack. They said later they had done it just to cause trouble, because they did not like the self-righteous attitude of the Longhouse people. (Despite that act of hostility, those men joined the warriors on July 11 when the police raided the barricade in the Pines, taking up posts in the bunkers for about two weeks after the raid.)

The vandalism and threats from within the community led to new arguments from some of the men about whether they should arm and protect themselves. The debate had begun in late March, as soon as protesters spotted the first unmarked police cars patrolling past the Pines, but it grew more heated as harassment from both Mohawks and non-Mohawks increased. The argument consumed hours around the campfire and at people's kitchen tables. Then one Sunday in late April, a number of Mohawks from the Pines met in a United Church hall in Oka. The main topic of discussion was whether or not they should invite warriors from other communities to help protect the camp.

A warrior flag was draped over the table when Joe David arrived at that meeting, and it made him furious. "He kept saying, 'No way — no guns here,'" recalls one of the men who attended the meeting.

Other people reminded Joe David of what had happened in the "Salmon War" at the Micmac reserve at Restigouche in 1981, where Sûreté du Québec officers had waded into a crowd of women and children to break up the protest. One officer had kicked a three-year-old boy, and another, swinging his truncheon, had launched into the crowd shouting "*maudit sauvage!*" (damned savage). And when the Algonquins of Lac Barrière had set up barricades to prevent pulp and paper companies from logging in the La Vérendrye Wildlife Reserve, once again the SQ had used force to quell the demonstrations.

"We're going to get clubbed and beaten at the barricade and you're saying all we should be armed with is our resolve?" Joe David's brother, Walter David Jr., demanded.

Walter David's argument was convincing, but Joe David was worried that the support they were getting from environmentalists and other groups would be lost if people discovered there were arms in the camp. He also feared that an invitation to the warriors would give some Mohawks a reason to boycott the camp in the Pines. But he felt increasingly isolated and distrusted. The other Mohawks had dubbed him Gandhi.

In mid-April, a week or two before the meeting in the United Church hall, Joe David had gone on his own initiative to Akwesasne. The reserve was consumed by a power struggle between pro-gambling and anti-gambling factions. The pro-gambling side was backed by the Akwesasne Warrior Society. By the time Joe David arrived, the community was on the brink of war. People on both sides were living in armed fortresses, trained dogs chained to their houses, guns at arms' reach.

Joe David had relatives on both sides of the dispute, but his instinct was to oppose the warriors. He went to the home of one of the men in the anti-warrior camp to talk about the situation in Kanesatake.

"He had these lights set up outside the house, so that the minute a car door would slam, or there was some other sound, these big flood lights would go "BSH!" and light up the whole yard ... I asked if they would consider coming up to Kanesatake to help us if it looked like there was going to be a raid, to show strength in numbers."

But within a few days of that meeting, war had broken out in Akwesasne. Over a period of several days, the two sides engaged in gun battles, in which two men died. Joe David never heard back from the anti-warriors. Pleas for help were going out to every faction of the

Iroquois Confederacy in several communities, but it was only the warriors who answered the call.

After their fishing shack was vandalized on April 22, the protesters decided to erect barricades across the dirt road that ran through the Pines, to discourage further intruders. They dragged cement blocks across the south entrance to the Pines, just a few metres back from Highway 344. A large log was pushed across the north entrance, where the dirt track through the Pines met a back road that ran through Kanesatake.

Once the roadblock was in place, the town of Oka lost no time in seeking an injunction ordering the Mohawks to take down the barricade. Oka's lawyer, Luc Carbonneau, argued that the dirt road going through the Pines, which the town of Oka called Chemin du Mil, was a municipal thoroughfare that had to be kept open for emergency vehicles. In fact, the road was rarely used by anyone and it was impassable all winter, because it was rarely cleared of snow. Carbonneau nevertheless produced affidavits showing that Oka's fire department had used the dirt track on at least two occasions. The injunction was granted on April 26. The people in the Pines decided to ignore it.

"I don't recognize the authority of the province over this land," said Curtis Nelson, who later travelled with Allen Gabriel at the peak of the summer's crisis to bring other Iroquois Confederacy chiefs into negotiations with the government. "You can have ten or twelve injunctions — it doesn't matter to me."

Rumours flew through the camp that the town had hired a contractor to clear the barricade on May 1. Word was sent to Kahnawake, and when the day dawned, a group of Kahnawake warriors had joined the protesters in the Pines. The licence plates of the warriors' vehicles were covered by rags and they wore masks over their faces as they zipped in and out of the Pines, putting on an impromptu performance for the police and the journalists who were watching the barricades. Like most other non-native members of the public, the media were barred from entering the Pines. The strategy of the Mohawk protesters was to intimidate the police and to maintain an aura of mystery about what was actually going on behind the barricades. They were also trying to sustain the media's curiosity and engender publicity about their occupation.

At about 1:00 p.m., a Sûreté du Québec helicopter came into view and hovered over the camp. Several police cars drove by, and one tried to force its way past a protester who was blocking its path. When the protesters did not move, the car rammed him. A TV cameraman emerged from the bushes, where he had been capturing the scene on tape, and as soon as the officer spotted him, the cruiser backed up.

Scores of Kanesatake Mohawks flocked into the Pines to show their support for the protesters and to watch what would happen when the contractor that Oka had hired to remove the main roadblock arrived with his heavy equipment. But with the threat of a confrontation in front of the TV cameras, municipal councillors decided to postpone the dismantling of the barricade and to try to resume negotiations.

Late in the afternoon, a provincial negotiator and representatives of the municipality of Oka arrived in the Pines to meet the protesters. Despite the continuing tensions among the various Kanesatake factions, the Mohawks formed a united front at the meeting. The elected grand chief, George Martin, and his rival, the ousted grand chief, Clarence Simon, came to the Pines to support Allen Gabriel and the Longhouse followers who led the occupation of the Pines. The factions temporarily set aside their lingering resentments. "We'll back up whatever you say," George Martin told Allen Gabriel's ally, Curtis Nelson. Everyone sat together under the pine trees and the Mohawks put forward their new demands: a fifteen-day moratorium on the golf course expansion and a resumption of negotiations with the federal government.

The next day, the same alliance of Mohawks met officials from Oka and the provincial and federal governments at the Kanesatake Longhouse, about a kilometre northwest of the Pines. The atmosphere was still tense. Warriors in camouflage gear raced in and out of the Pines in their trucks, their faces masked by bandanas, some brandishing weapons. A Sûreté du Québec helicopter kept buzzing over the Pines.

Inside the Longhouse, an angry debate was going on. Oka's acting mayor, Gilles Landreville, demanded to know if the Mohawks could deliver a consensus from their community.

"Do you have the consensus of *your* community?" one of the Mohawks threw back at Landreville, knowing that many people in Oka were opposed to the golf course project.

The Mohawks reiterated their argument that they had never ceded their territory to anyone. "When did the women of the Mohawk Nation sell this land to you?" the sister of one of the band council's clan mothers, Madeleine Montour, asked the Oka negotiators. "Did you ever ask the women?" she demanded. Her question was ignored.

The municipality wanted the barricades and the Mohawk signs dismantled before agreeing to the fifteen-day moratorium and proceeding with negotiations. But by then, there was such deep distrust towards Oka that the Mohawks refused to consider the town's proposals. Nobody was hiding the possibility that the blockade could result in violence. "If blood is shed, it will be on your hands," Dennis Nicholas warned the representatives from the town.

The talks had been proceeding for a couple of hours when two Mohawks rode up to the Longhouse in an all-terrain vehicle. They reported seeing suspicious activities across the golf course. Trucks escorted by the police were dropping off long wooden boxes in a shed behind the clubhouse. The men were convinced that the boxes contained guns — proof that the police were gearing up for a raid. The talks broke off and the negotiating team, with reporters trailing behind them, went to investigate. There was no sign of the police or their arsenal, although the Mohawks later complained that the search had not been done thoroughly.

None of the non-Mohawks saw any boxes, and no one ever confirmed what was in them, but by then, paranoia filled the air. More and more people began to talk about the need to establish a strong defence. For many of the people in the Pines, there was no longer any question about the need for the warriors. A distress call was sent to the other two Mohawk reserves, and the response was immediate.

The Akwesasne war chief, Francis Boots, had made his first trip to the Pines in early May. He was first made aware of the seriousness of the situation when David Gabriel, the son of Longhouse chief Samson Gabriel, travelled to Akwesasne in April to ask for financial support. On a second trip, later in May, David Gabriel asked for a patrol vehicle, a supply of two-way radios, and $200 for gas and groceries. The warriors gave him the money, along with a 1983 Chevy Blazer truck and four radios.

Francis Boots himself never carried a gun. But when he went back to the Pines for a second time in May, he was accompanied by three or four other warriors from Akwesasne, and they brought their weapons with them. Indeed, they never travelled to a trouble spot without their guns. "The guys just knew," Boots explains. "The consensus was to keep the guns out of view. They weren't there for public consumption."

The warriors also brought truckloads of food, tents, sleeping bags, and other equipment for the protesters. Most of the Mohawks who opposed the presence of weapons, including Joe David, had already drifted away from the camp. But the hardline Longhouse followers — including Ellen Gabriel, Denise David-Tolley, Linda Cree and Walter David Jr. — remained in the Pines, and they were grateful for the advice and support the experienced warriors were offering. They realized they could not rely on the men of Kanesatake to guard the Pines. Despite their rhetoric about defending the Pines to the death, most of the local Mohawks had never experienced a confrontation with the police, and they were unprepared to pick up a weapon.

A few of the young Mohawk men from Kanesatake, however, were inspired by the arrival of the warriors from Kahnawake and Akwesasne. One of the young men, later codenamed Crazyhorse, was enthusiastic about the idea of becoming a warrior. He spent his welfare cheque to purchase an assault rifle on the black market in nearby St. Eustache.

All weapons remained hidden, but the camp was beginning to resemble a practice field for war games. The Mohawks obtained an expensive night-vision scope which allowed them to see into the forest at night. Masked men in camouflage gear raced around in all-terrain vehicles, patrolling the woods. Everyone knew the police were keeping a close watch on their activities.

Some of the Mohawks who had sneered at the occupation of the Pines in the early spring were now showing up at the barricades to help. Others, however, were worried about the guns and the danger of a conflict with the police. Marshall Nicholas — who had been named in the April 26 injunction as a key player in the Pines — washed his hands of the whole affair. He sold his weapons, and his appearances at the barricade became more and more infrequent.

The armed men in the Pines asked the women to decide if the weapons should stay. As the traditional caretakers of the land, the women had the responsibility of dealing with this issue, but the decision was not one they wanted to make. There were strong arguments both for and against being armed.

Linda Cree had been an avowed anti-warrior, but her opinion began to shift after the events of May 1. "It was hard to justify not having arms after that," she said. She was nervous about the hazards of guns, but she was equally afraid of the consequences of a police attack if the Mohawks were unarmed.

"What choice did we have by then?" asks Linda's sister, Denise David-Tolley. "We said, 'Bury them, hide them, keep them away. Only if they come in to harm us do you bring them out — only then.'"

She pauses for effect.

"They came in to harm us."

With tensions running high between the people in the Pines and Oka, the town did not make another attempt to send in a front-end loader to dismantle the roadblock before its injunction expired on May 4. The white homeowners who lived across the highway from the Pines had been watching the comings and goings of Mohawks there nervously since the occupation began in March. By early May, they were growing increasingly distressed by the failure of the police to intervene. By then they had organized a citizens' group to pressure the municipality to move ahead with the golf course project.

Privately, the town council was considering abandoning the whole undertaking, in exchange for a commitment from the Mohawks to resolve the jurisdiction problem and other contentious issues after the barricades were lifted. On May 2, Yves Désilets informed Mayor Ouellette that the federal government was prepared to purchase the golf course expansion land. Figures for compensation were bandied about. However, convinced that the golf course expansion was a worthwhile project and under pressure from the *Regroupement des citoyens d'Oka* to proceed with it, the municipal councillors wavered. And the Regroupement would hear nothing of giving into Mohawk demands.

"We ask that the federal government intervene so that the problem is settled once and for all," said Dr. Jacques Imbeau, a dentist who lived across the highway from the Pines. Imbeau knew the Mohawk land claim had been consistently rejected, even by the highest court of appeal of its day, the Privy Council in London, in 1912. "There is no reason for this debate to continue," Imbeau said. He accused the Mohawks of holding Oka hostage.

Although many people in the town still opposed the expansion, the pro-golf citizens managed to attract about two hundred golf club members and locals to a town meeting on May 7. A small group of Mohawks showed up uninvited. The councillors allowed Allen Gabriel to address the meeting but refused to let any other Mohawk in his contingent speak.

"I come here armed with words, not a machine gun," Gabriel told the crowd as the Mohawks stood by the door and listened. He went on to say that the citizens of Oka could move out of the town if they could not co-exist peacefully with the Mohawks. He was openly jeered.

"You may succeed in convincing the SQ to come in to forcibly remove us, but we will still be there," Gabriel continued. "Do you really think that expanding this private golf course is worth jeopardizing the social peace?"

Afterwards, the mayor was defiant. "There is no question of yielding one inch of the land," he told reporters. "It belongs to the town of Oka."

That same day, the mayor of Oka wrote to Quebec Public Security Minister Sam Elkas and Premier Robert Bourassa, demanding that the police be sent in to dismantle the roadblock and clear the Pines. Elkas refused to comply. "I don't want to send in anyone to play cowboys over the question of a golf course," he declared publicly.

On May 8, the mayor met Quebec Native Affairs Minister John Ciaccia in the Cabinet minister's office. Ciaccia had a long history of dealing with aboriginal people. Before entering politics, he had served as an associate deputy minister of Indian Affairs under Jean Chrétien in Ottawa. In the early 1970s, he had helped to negotiate the historic James Bay and Northern Quebec Agreement with the Cree and Inuit of northern Quebec. Unlike his federal counterpart, who was reluctant to deal with any Indian leaders who were not elected under the Indian Act, Ciaccia was willing to recognize the traditional Longhouse leaders. He had taken the time to learn about Iroquois treaties and Mohawk grievances and had already met the leaders of the Kahnawake Longhouse on several occasions.

Ciaccia was convinced that negotiations with the warriors was the only way to resolve disputes. "The Mohawk tradition, even that of the so-called 'warriors', leads me to believe that discussions conducted in a calm and serene climate can succeed," Ciaccia had said in a letter to Sam Elkas the previous November, when he intervened to prevent a police raid on a new super-bingo scheduled to open in Kahnawake. "The risk that any such police intervention would degenerate into a violent confrontation is great, if not inevitable," Ciaccia warned in his letter. "The consequences of a confrontation would be dramatic." Ciaccia knew the Mohawks well enough to understand that they would never back down on their territorial claims. He could see that the Mohawks and the town of Oka were on a collision course.

Ciaccia persuaded Jean Ouellette to suspend the golf course project while he tried to convince the federal government to buy the land slated for development and to compensate the town for foregone taxes and rent. Ouellette told Ciaccia he was open to any proposal, as long as the terms of Oka's original injunction were respected and the barricades were removed.

The next day, Ciaccia drove to Ottawa to meet Tom Siddon, the federal Indian Affairs minister. He left the meeting optimistic that he could work out a deal with Siddon and called Ouellette on his car phone on the drive back to Montreal to tell him the good news. But by then Ouellette was already starting to back away from the commitment he had made the previous day. He told Ciaccia he had not given him a mandate to sell the municipality's property.

"There's only one way we're going to be able to build the golf course," the mayor told John Ciaccia. "That's with the army." Little did Ouellette realize how prophetic those words would prove to be.

Two days later, Ciaccia met members of the band council in his office. The Longhouse people had decided not to attend the meeting, preferring to deal "nation-to-nation" with the federal government. Ciaccia told the band council about his efforts to get Ottawa to buy the land in the Pines to put a stop to the golf course project, and the band council was ready to consider the offer.

The Longhouse people learned of Ciaccia's gesture from band council lawyer Jacques Lacaille after the meeting, but they were unenthusiastic about it. They felt that they already had title to the land. So if the government wanted to compensate those landowners who, in the Mohawks' view, had misappropriated the property, that was fine, but they wanted no part of any discussions with the government about buying the land on their behalf. In any event, nothing more came of Ciaccia's intervention in Ottawa. It would be nearly three months — well into the crisis — before the federal government made a firm offer to the town of Oka to purchase any of the disputed land.

The protest camp, which had begun as a non-political effort, was now clearly under the control of the Longhouse. Until early May, the band council had actively supported the blockade in the Pines, purchasing two-way radios for the protesters and lending them a four-by-four truck. But the alliance grew more tenuous as some of the Longhouse followers became convinced that the band council might compromise their claim to sovereignty. They believed the only way to settle the land question was by forcing the government to recognize the historic treaties that successive colonial powers had signed with the Iroquois Confederacy. This, they felt, could only be done through the Longhouse, as the only legitimate Mohawk government and the only direct link to the original treaty-makers, and they wanted the band council to take a back seat in the negotiations.

Twice more, in May and early June, the town of Oka tried to renew the temporary injunction it had been granted in late April. Superior Court Judge Vital Cliche, who presided over the hearing in May, could see no urgent reason to clear the roadblock, and he told the parties to negotiate. But by then the municipality and the Mohawks were no longer meeting face to face. The federal negotiator, Yves Désilets, was acting as a go-between. The Mohawks did not trust him, however. He had been seen having dinner with members of the Oka council, and the Mohawks felt he was too cozy with the municipality. Désilets still continued to shuttle back and forth between the two sides, though, and told the Mohawks that the Oka council was willing to extend the moratorium on the golf course expansion — but only if the Mohawks left the Pines.

In late May, Walter David Jr. erected a small log cabin in the Pines, reasserting the Mohawk claim to the territory. Oka insisted that the cabin be dismantled. The atmosphere of distrust worsened, and every Oka council meeting was packed by a crowd of angry citizens who demanded the intervention of the Sûreté du Québec.

Because of the civil war going on in Akwesasne all this time, the Akwesasne warriors were too busy to offer much assistance to the people of Kanesatake. A few warriors from Kahnawake remained in the Pines through most of May.

One day in May, some of the men were digging foxholes in the Pines. They believed there was still a threat of police intervention and were preparing the foxholes as hiding places to be used in the event of a raid. As they were digging, another Mohawk roared up to the foxholes in his truck and reported that a police car was coming into the forest by the back entrance. The men threw down their shovels and ran to the back of the Pines to confront the officers.

A single cruiser was parked on the road at the north entrance to the Pines. A couple of the men went forward to talk to the police, while the rest hid out of sight in the forest. The police said they had received a report that a Mohawk had threatened a golfer with a shotgun. The men denied it. One of them — a "hothead," according to another warrior — got into an argument with the police officer and spat at him. The policeman reached for his gun and took a step towards the Mohawk.

"Suddenly, you could hear all the guns cocking in the woods," a warrior recalls. "The policeman just looked around, got in the car and took off." Because of incidents like that one, the police continued to keep a close watch on the Pines. Several times, the Mohawks caught a glimpse through their night-vision scope of intruders in the woods whom they took to be police, and sometimes they heard men signalling each other late at night with poor imitations of bird calls.

The Mohawks knew the police were having a hard time figuring out just how many people were in the Pines. One officer struck up a conversation with a Mohawk whom he met at the courthouse in St. Jérôme, digging for information on the Mohawk protesters. But the Mohawk kept his silence. The only advantage the people in the Pines had over the police and the municipality was the fear of the unknown, so they did everything they could to keep the police wondering how heavily guarded the area was. For a while they left a dummy — clothes propped up by logs and stuffed with pine needles — to guard the camp. One night, when they knew they were being watched, a couple of men ran back and forth in front of the police, changing their jackets each time they made another pass, hoping to make them believe the Pines were full of warriors. People in Oka began to whisper that there was a warrior behind every tree. In reality, very few people were in the Pines most of the time. Many had jobs to go to in the daytime, and by late May, a lot of people were too exhausted to spend their nights on patrol. Sometimes there were only a handful of women by the fire or at the roadblock.

Most of the warriors had drifted home to Akwesasne and Kahnawake, and even the Kanesatake Mohawks found their commitment waning. Often there was no one in the Pines at all. It looked as if the protest might die out on its own.

Few people outside the three Mohawk territories knew about the protest camp in tiny Kanesatake, so one of the influential warrior leaders in Kahnawake, Paul Delaronde, promised the people in the Pines that he would spread word about the occupation. In late May and early June, he and a few other Kahnawake warriors travelled to Iroquois reserves in Ontario and upstate New York, including Six Nations, Oneida, and Onondaga, asking for physical and spiritual support for the Kanesatake Mohawks. In Kahnawake itself, some people collected money to buy more two-way radios; others raffled off tickets to raise money for food and other supplies.

The federal negotiator, Yves Désilets, was still trying to persuade the Mohawks to consider the unification of Kanesatake lands, as proposed by the federal government in the so-called "framework agreement" of 1989. At a meeting in early June, representatives of the band council and the people in the Pines angrily reminded Désilets that the Kanesatake Mohawks had already rejected the 1989 proposal. They told him that if he had no authority to discuss other options, they wanted a face-to-face meeting with the Indian Affairs minister himself. Désilets arranged the meeting for June 21.

In the two weeks that preceded that meeting, the relationship between the band council and the people in the Pines grew increasingly strained. The Longhouse people felt the band council was relying too heavily on the advice of their young white lawyer, Jacques Lacaille. Grand Chief George Martin was not an assertive or articulate man, and Lacaille was doing so much talking on Martin's behalf that the people in the Pines dubbed him "Chief Lacaille." Lacaille maintained that the band council had the only legal authority to negotiate with the federal government. The Longhouse people accused him of trying to usurp their role.

There were also growing tensions among the Longhouse people in the Pines. Allen Gabriel, Curtis Nelson, and Marshall Nicholas had been asked by the Longhouse chief, Samson Gabriel, to represent the Longhouse on the land issue. Three of the women involved in the occupation — Linda Cree, Ellen Gabriel, and Debbie Etienne — had also played an important role. But on June 14, the women officially severed their ties with the other Longhouse negotiators, as they felt intentionally excluded from key decisions and planning sessions. In her June 14 letter to Lacaille, Linda Cree insisted that the land negotiations had to involve the women. The Longhouse women cited the Great Law of Peace, the founding constitution of the Iroquois Confederacy, which states: "Women shall be considered the progenitors of the Nation. They shall own the land and the soil."

Throughout the occupation, the people in the Pines had worked hard to reach a consensus on every decision, and even after the serious split on June 14, they tried again to resolve their differences. With the help of Eba Beauvais and others from Kahnawake, an uneasy peace was restored in the Pines.

The meeting with Tom Siddon on June 21 did not go well, however. The Longhouse people had spent all night drafting their terms for dismantling the barricades, but they were virtually ignored when the meeting began. Siddon focused his attention on Jacques Lacaille and the band councillors, and he was unwilling to discuss anything except the federal proposal to unify the land — the same proposal that the Mohawks had rejected in 1989.

The Longhouse people listened patiently. Finally, at the end of the meeting, they delivered their own position paper. Describing themselves as members of the sovereign Mohawk Nation of the Iroquois Confederacy, the Longhouse people laid out their demands: a suspension of all development on Mohawk traditional land until an agreement on land rights was reached and a review of all existing developments (including the golf course), which would be placed under the jurisdiction of the Mohawk Nation.

The Longhouse people had privately discussed the possibility of taking down the barricades if Siddon seemed willing to consider their proposal. But they had heard nothing from the minister to indicate that the federal government's position had changed. "We're going to leave now and go back to our barricades," Allen Gabriel informed Siddon. "They're up and they're going to stay up."

For most of the meeting, Siddon seemed to have no idea who the Longhouse people were. Later, he dismissed them. "Don't worry about them," Siddon told a band councillor. "We don't recognize the Longhouse, and we're not going to deal with them."

The Longhouse followers returned from the meeting with Siddon more firmly resolved to stand their ground. They took Siddon's remark that he was not prepared to recognize the Longhouse as the final insult.

Despite their renewed resolve, there was still a shortage of people willing to spend long hours in the Pines. Francis Boots found the roadblock deserted when he answered a call for assistance in late June and returned to Kanesatake with three other warriors from Akwesasne. He drove on to the settlement and found many of the Mohawks at the elementary school, attending a graduation ceremony for the grade six students.

The director of education assumed that Boots and his contingent were the Mohawk singers she had been expecting to show up for the ceremony. Of the four men, Boots was the only one with a repertoire of Mohawk songs, so the Akwesasne war chief went up to the front of the audience and sang four songs for the graduating students. He was roundly applauded.

On June 29, Oka lawyer Luc Carbonneau returned to the Quebec Superior Court in St. Jerome to seek another injunction to remove the roadblocks in the Pines. Lacaille went to court to fight the injunction on behalf of the band council, but the Longhouse people refused to attend the hearing. "We don't recognize the authority of that court," Allen Gabriel told Lacaille. "Why should we go?" Judge Anthime Bergeron granted the injunction, criticizing the Mohawks for their "nearly anarchistic" attitude and for using illegal means to force their territorial claims on Oka. But he also warned the municipality not to use his judgment as a pretext for proceeding with the golf course project. "Even if I am a golfer," Bergeron said in his ruling, "I believe that a golf project that will not be open to the public should not be undertaken at the expense of the public. No golf project is valuable enough to necessitate the wiping out of an important forest, especially in the context of the evidence I've heard."

The injunction, which was granted against Chief George Martin and all members of the Kanesatake band, was served on the band office. But the chief admitted he was powerless to order the people in the Pines to take the barricades down, even if he had wanted to do so. He said he refused to do the "dirty work" of the municipality.

By early July, Longhouse people from Kahnawake were driving back and forth to the Pines every day. Randy Horne, a Mohawk ironworker later codenamed "Spudwrench," made three or four trips to the Pines with vanloads of groceries for the people at the barricade.

It was during the first week in July that Ronald Cross became a warrior. The thirty-three-year-old ironworker had grown up in Kahnawake, but he had been living and working in New York City for several years. His mother and younger brothers lived in Kanesatake, and in late spring he quit his job and came home. He had been doing a lot of cocaine in New York, and he wanted to kick the habit.

"I saw what it was doing to me," he said, "and I knew if I stayed in New York I'd just get back into it." He planned to enter the native treatment centre in Kanesatake, across from the Pines. He was a heavy drinker, but he had never been in serious trouble until May, when he and his brother were arrested after an altercation with police at a bar in LaSalle, a Montreal suburb just across the St. Lawrence River from Kahnawake.

Ronald Cross was known as Lasagna because his mother was Italian. To the consternation of his Italian uncles, he considered himself a Mohawk and a warrior by birthright, if not by experience. The shooting death of his unarmed cousin, David Cross, in a confrontation with a police officer in Kahnawake in 1979 had left him with a deep sense of distrust and anger toward all white authority. But he was raised a Catholic, knew little about the Longhouse movement, and had never been a political activist. In the late spring, after his arrival in Kanesatake, he sometimes wheeled his motorcycle through the Pines and sat at the roadblocks with the men on guard there. He told them they were wasting their time.

On July 1, Lasagna dropped by the Pines to watch the annual lacrosse match between Mohawks from Kahnawake and Kanesatake. For the first time, he talked to some of the more experienced warriors who had just arrived — including Gordon Lazore, a warrior from Akwesasne codenamed "Noriega," who later became his close buddy. For a long time, Lasagna had been fascinated by guns and military tactics, but it was more than the military image of the warriors that attracted Lasagna to the Pines. For the first time, he was beginning to understand and respect the commitment of the protesters. On July 1, he decided to join the fight.

Ellen Gabriel, Denise David-Tolley, Debbie Etienne, and the other Kanesatake Longhouse women in the Pines were holding daily women's meetings to discuss strategy and keep their spirits up. They decided they would be the front line of defence if the municipality tried to tear down the barricade, and the warriors would stay in the background unless weapons were needed.

Allen Gabriel and Curtis Nelson believed that the women were being unrealistic. They were worried about the danger of an assault on the Pines by the police. "They're not going to come in here and have tea with you," Allen Gabriel told the women.

But the women dismissed Gabriel's concerns. They were no longer prepared to be conciliatory. In early July, they issued an invitation to women from Kahnawake and Akwesasne to join the protest camp.

At first, the Kahnawake women were reluctant to travel to the Pines. Unlike the battle-hardened traditionalists of their own community, the people of Kanesatake were untested and inexperienced, and some Mohawks doubted that they had enough commitment and determination to resist a possible police raid. Stephanie Horne, Kahentiiosta, and a couple of other Kahnawake women sat up most of the night on July 1 around Kahentiiosta's kitchen table in Kahnawake, discussing whether they should accept the invitation.

Kahentiiosta had spent the spring in Ganienkeh, the militant Mohawk territory in upstate New York that had just gone through a lengthy standoff against the state police. She was tired and she wanted to spend some time at home with her children. But she agreed to go to Kanesatake with the other women to check out the situation.

When she arrived at Kanesatake on about July 5, one of the Kanesatake women gave her a tour of the Pines, telling her the story of all the land they had lost over the years. When they came to the tiny graveyard, hemmed in by the golf course and the highway, Kahentiiosta was amazed. "Why didn't you take a stand before?" she asked. "Why did you let them go so far in the first place?"

She decided to stay, and after a few days she returned to Kahnawake and brought her two young sons to the Pines.

Joe David, who had stayed away from the Pines throughout most of May and June, spent two days fasting at the top of the mountain overlooking Kanesatake at the start of July, trying to decide what stand he should take. He was still opposed to the weapons, but when he thought about his grandmother buried in the Mohawk cemetery, next to the golf course, he could see no way of staying out of the conflict without abandoning her memory and her spirit.

As he stood on a rocky outcrop, praying for guidance, three eagles swooped down from the sky and hovered over him silently. A few moments later, a hawk landed on the branch of a dead oak nearby. It perched there, staring at him, unafraid. This was the sign he had been waiting for. The hawk and the eagle are strong symbols of power for the Mohawks and the other nations of the Iroquois Confederacy. Joe David believed he had been given a confirmation that the people in the Pines would be protected, and that they were justified in their actions to defend the land. He climbed back down the mountain and returned to the Pines.

On July 3, a group of protesters from the Pines went to the Sûreté du Québec detachment in St. Eustache. They were nervous about the possibility of a police raid, and they wanted to know their rights. A police officer assured them that the injunction was a civil matter and the police would not intervene unless they suspected a criminal act had been committed.

Almost every day during that first week of July, the Oka municipal council issued new ultimatums, ordering the Mohawks to clear out of the Pines. Tensions were moving close to the breaking point. On Thursday, July 5, Sam Elkas announced that the Mohawks must clear the barricades within four days or else the government of Quebec would take action. He did not specify what kind of action the Mohawks should expect, but the threat of police intervention was implicit.

Chrystal Nicholas, a thirty-two-year-old university student from Kanesatake who had just joined the protest in the Pines, listened in shock to the news reports of the Elkas announcement. Most of her cousins and brothers and sisters were participating in the occupation, and she knew there was potential for violence. It was clear that nobody was in a mood to strike a compromise — the Mohawks were preparing to put up an armed defence. She called the office of Sam Elkas and spoke to one of his assistants, emphasizing that the situation could turn violent, but her warning was ignored.

The Elkas announcement was a turning point. Allen Gabriel and Curtis Nelson believed that a police raid was imminent, and they urged the other Mohawks to find a way to dismantle the barricades. "What the hell is it going to take to bring the barricades down?" Gabriel asked angrily during a heated debate in the Pines on July 5. "We're not going to stay here for the rest of our lives. We have to resolve this thing one way or another."

"We'll leave when we get all our land back," a young Kanesatake warrior answered.

There was no room left for compromise. Allen Gabriel and his closest allies in the Longhouse, Curtis Nelson and Marshall Nicholas, left the Pines and did not return. Ellen Gabriel and the Longhouse faithkeeper John Cree, who both spoke passable French, became the main spokespersons for the Kanesatake Mohawks who stayed behind.

On July 6, the Quebec Human Rights Commission sent an urgent telegram to both Quebec Native Affairs Minister John Ciaccia and his federal counterpart Tom Siddon, warning them of the escalating risk of conflict at Oka and urging them to set up an independent committee to study the historical land claim of the Kanesatake Mohawks. The Commission believed the protesters in the Pines could be convinced to dismantle the barricades if they were given a say in the makeup and the mandate of the committee. It would be nearly four months before the Commission received a reply to its telegram to Tom Siddon, but John Ciaccia replied the same day he received it. Ciaccia welcomed the proposal, but even as he considered it, the risk of a clash between the police and the warriors was increasing.

Within a day or two, the Sûreté du Québec had stepped up their patrols. Police were placed on standby in Oka, and some of the officers told a reporter they were waiting for the green light to raid the barricade. One boasted that it would be "a big party" if they were sent in to make arrests.

Mohawk warriors were arriving daily from Kahnawake and Akwesasne, setting up tents in the Pines or sleeping in vans and cars around the clearing. By the second weekend in July, the log blocking the north entrance to the Pines had been reinforced by a row of concrete blocks.

The men had piled sand and sandbags on top of the blocks to protect the military-style bunkers they had already dug out on the edge of the golf course, which they had camouflaged and surrounded with home-made traps. They had also dug a trench from those bunkers to another one, farther back in the woods, so they could retreat without being seen if the police moved in.

John Ciaccia was desperate to avoid a violent confrontation. On Sunday, July 8, and again the next day, he phoned Mayor Jean Ouellette and pleaded with him not to call in the Sûreté du Québec. Ouellette refused to make the Cabinet minister any such promise. When Ciaccia asked him directly if he was going to ask for police intervention, his only reply was, "Not today."

On July 9, Ciaccia sent a letter to Ouellette, again asking the municipality to suspend indefinitely its plans for the golf course expansion. Ciaccia warned the mayor that the situation could degenerate into a confrontation that would have serious consequences for the Mohawks and for Quebec society.

"We are often accused by aboriginal people of not paying attention to their claims and of reneging on our commitments," he wrote. "The situation at Oka lends credibility to those accusations."

Ciaccia went on to remind Ouellette of his promise to suspend the golf course project indefinitely when they had met in May, and he underlined the fact that Ouellette had originally consented to Ciaccia's proposal to negotiate an agreement in which the federal government would buy the disputed land.

"On the one hand, you sat at the negotiating table, and on the other hand, you are now maintaining that the Mohawks, who have been there for 250 years, already have enough land and you want to limit the extent of their territory," Ciaccia wrote Ouellette. "These people have seen their lands disappear without having been consulted or compensated, and that, in my opinion, is unfair and unjust, especially over a golf course."

Although Oka had the right to apply the court injunction according to the strict rule of law, Ciaccia threw the law itself into question: "I believe the situation goes beyond strict legality," he wrote, and then quoted the late Quebec premier, René Lévesque, citing the famous Charles Dickens line — "sometimes the law is an ass" — in a debate in the Quebec National Assembly. "And if that is the case," wrote Ciaccia, "elected officials must not hide behind laws, but act in a generous and responsible manner." By suspending the golf course project indefinitely, Ouellette would be permitting the Quebec government to "ask the Indians to lift their barricades," Ciaccia concluded. "That sign of goodwill would re-establish a climate in which to negotiate a solution that is acceptable and fair to all."

On the same day, July 9, Ciaccia offered to meet the people in the Pines — but the offer was rejected outright by Ellen Gabriel, who said that only the direct intervention of the federal government could resolve the situation. She called for "nation-to-nation" talks with the prime minister. That same day, the federal negotiator, Yves Désilets, showed up to meet the Longhouse representatives, but they refused to see him.

Some of the Mohawks in the Pines could still see room for a negotiated settlement, but they were unable to shake the resolve of the Longhouse leaders. Some of them felt desperate. Tears pouring down her face, Chrystal Nicholas pleaded with one of the Longhouse men to reconsider Ciaccia's offer. But he was already preparing for a police raid. "We're ready for them," he said grimly.

On Tuesday, July 10, Jean Ouellette replied to the appeal Ciaccia had made the previous day by accusing Ciaccia of not understanding native issues. The same day, Ouellette made a formal request to the Sûreté du Québec to clear the barricades and stop the "criminal acts" in the Pines. "We are counting on you to settle this problem without any further delays or requests on our part," Ouellette told the police in a letter.

Jacques Lacaille, acting on behalf of the Kanesatake band council, announced that he would appeal the injunction in court on July 11 — the next day. Meanwhile, Lacaille and members of the band council met Ciaccia at three o'clock on July 10. The Cabinet minister was scheduled to travel to the Soviet Union on a business trip on July 13, but he assured Lacaille that nothing would happen before then. "Don't worry," he said. "When I come back I'm going to settle this matter." (Ciaccia was not the only key player who was leaving the scene. Sam Elkas was already on holiday in the Eastern Townships.) Lacaille left Ciaccia's office at five o'clock, confident that he had enough time to take legal action to prevent a police raid. But later that evening, he got a call from the SQ at St. Eustache, who wanted an urgent meeting with Lacaille and the band council that very night.

When the police officers arrived at Lacaille's office in downtown Montreal, they described an act of vandalism near the Pines that had taken place the previous night. Someone had slashed tires and smashed eggs against the windshield of a car parked in the driveway of Jacques Imbeau, the dentist and Oka citizens' group leader who lived across the highway from the Pines. Witnesses had reported seeing three Mohawks running away from Imbeau's driveway. (The Mohawks later alleged that the vandalism was a setup, carried out by supporters of the Oka citizens' group.)

Since a crime had allegedly been committed, the police said, they had to intervene. "They told me it was out of their hands," Lacaille recalled later. "I told them we would appeal to various ministers the next morning. We didn't think they had the authority to act without the permission of the minister of public security, and we knew Sam Elkas was away."

Lacaille's partner, John Pepper, returned to the office late that night and worked until two o'clock in the morning to prepare legal arguments against a police intervention in the Pines. The lawyers planned to present their case in the St. Jérôme courthouse later that morning.

Four hours before, at about ten o'clock that night, Crazyhorse had received a call from an old friend who worked as a dispatcher for the Sûreté du Québec. Something was up, he said. He was pretty sure there was going to be a raid the next morning.

It was not the first time the Mohawks had received a tip that the police were planning to raid, and nobody was sure how seriously to take the new information. But Crazyhorse and the rest of the warriors at the north entrance to the Pines worked through the night to improve their defences. They shifted the locations of their bunkers to surprise the police. They set up booby traps — sharpened sticks buried in a pit and covered with loose dirt and pine needles. They hid homemade pipebombs on the west side of the golf course. These were tricks that one of the warriors had learned from a book on Vietnam-style tactics. Some of the warriors put fish hooks on tree branches at knee and ankle level to injure anyone who tried to sneak through. Fishing line, attached to tin cans filled with pebbles, was strung through the brush along the edge of the forest. If anyone tripped over the fishing line, the rattling pebbles would act as an alarm.

Crazyhorse worked until about four o'clock in the morning. Then he went to sleep, hunched down in the bunker where he had been working. At around the same time, Stonecarver was waking up after two hours of fitful dozing in the front seat of his truck at the north entrance to the Pines. He got out of the car to stretch his legs and stood around with a couple of the other men, shivering and feeling like a zombie.

In the clearing at the front of the Pines, a few men were gathered around the fire. They had spent the night watching for intruders. Aside from the sound of their quiet conversation, the woods were dead quiet in the stillness of pre-dawn.

In the town of Oka, Joyce Nicholas was already awake. She was frying pancakes and brewing coffee to take up to the Pines for breakfast for the men who had been awake all night. Just before five o'clock, she strolled out to her porch. Her eyes widened. Dozens of police cars and rental trucks were rumbling down Oka's main street and up the hill, heading toward the Pines. She raced inside to her phone and dialed her sister Janet in Kanesatake.

As the cruisers sped through the town, Denise David-Tolley was dozing in a tent in the Pines. She tossed restlessly, troubled by a frightening dream. She was dreaming about an attack on the Pines. In her dream, somebody was dying.

CHAPTER 4

The Two Dog Wampum

Oka's First Mohawk Wars

It was three o'clock in the morning when the Quebec provincial police arrived in Oka, armed with warrants for the arrest of forty-eight Indians. They burst into homes and dragged the sleeping men from their beds, firing off pistols in their ears. Eight suspects were rounded up altogether and hauled off to jail.

The episode reads like an excerpt from the summer of 1990, but it happened on June 13, 1877. Just as it would be 113 years later, the issue was land rights. At the heart of the dispute was a pasture the Mohawks had fenced in for their cattle, on common lands they had been using for over a century. The Mohawks had chopped down nearby trees to rebuild the fence. But they had encountered opposition from the missionaries at the Seminary of St. Sulpice, who claimed that the Mohawks could use the land and the trees only at the pleasure of the priests. They called on the Quebec provincial police to arrest the Mohawks who had cut down the trees.

It was not the first time the Sulpicians had called on the provincial police to assert control over the rebellious Mohawks. There would be countless other such incidents in the years to follow. But this time, the arrests sparked an open revolt by the embittered Mohawks.

The day after the raid, the Mohawks met in council and resolved to fight the heavy-handed methods of the police. They armed themselves and met at a Protestant school house in Oka, where they spent the night on watch. Their chief, Sose Onasakenrat, urged them to resist further arrests. "If the police come to take you without warrant, fire at them," he said. "Fear not, I am your Grand Chief and you must listen to me."

In the town of Oka itself, wild rumours began circulating that the Mohawks planned to burn down the entire community. Witnesses later testified that they had heard the Indians uttering mysterious threats.

At four o'clock the next morning, the worst fears of the townspeople were confirmed when they were awakened by the sound of a cannon and the sight of flames leaping from the Catholic church. By dawn, the 150-year-old stone structure was a smoking ruin.

Since the Mohawks had a motive for starting the fire — their long-standing dispute over the land with the Sulpician priests — they were presumed to be responsible for it. They admitted to setting off the cannon, which they claimed they did to alert villagers to the fire, but they disclaimed any connection with the church burning. Fifteen Mohawks were nevertheless charged with arson and court proceedings began in nearby Ste. Scholastique. When the first two trials resulted in hung juries, the judge concluded it was impossible to arrive at a fair verdict in the district, and the case was moved to Aylmer, Quebec, near Ottawa.

In all there were five trials, but only the last, before an all-English jury, resulted in a unanimous verdict to acquit the Mohawks. The only concrete result of the church-burning trials was publicity that inflamed French Catholic versus English Protestant sentiments as debate over "The Oka Question" filled the editorial pages of rival Montreal newspapers. Some people openly accused the Sulpician priests of buying witnesses' testimony and even of coercing Catholic Mohawks to set fire to the church's stable in order to frame the dissident Mohawks.

No one ever proved decisively who was responsible for the fire. "It was simply the culminating event in a long, ugly squabble between the French Canadian priests and the Iroquois Indians, who happened to be Protestants," one historian concluded.

But it was not by mere happenstance that the Mohawks had converted *en masse* to Protestantism in 1869, eight years before the fire. The gesture was intended to prove that the Sulpicians were no longer needed or wanted in Oka. One hundred and fifty years before, in

1717, the Governor of New France had granted the priests of the Seminary of St. Sulpice the seigneury on the Lake of Two Mountains as a Catholic mission for the Indians. Believing the land had been set aside for them, the Indians had settled there in 1721, only to have their pleas for recognition of their property rights flatly rejected. By turning their backs on Catholicism, the Mohawks hoped they could finally expel the priests and gain undisputed control of the forests and fields of the region.

By the time of the Oka Mohawks' mass conversion to Protestantism in 1869, the fight for recognition of their land claim had already been underway for several generations. Over the next 270 years, the Indians delivered a steady stream of petitions — in 1781, 1788, 1794, 1802, 1818, 1828, 1839, 1848, 1869, and on into modern times — to successive colonial administrators and Canadian politicians, demanding recognition of their claim to the seigneurial lands.

Although the written history of the Indian settlement at the Lake of Two Mountains begins in 1717, the traditionalist Mohawks of Kanesatake said, and still say today, that the north shore of the lake was their territory long before the Christianized Indians settled there under the tutelage of the Sulpicians. Their claim is important because in order to have their land rights recognized under the federal land claims process, the Mohawks must prove that they are not merely early immigrants to the region, but that they have lived there since "time immemorial." They offer as proof of the early presence of their ancestors the pottery shards and clay pipes and other remnants of an ancient settlement that can still be found in the forest beside the lake. Archaeologists have dated the pottery shards back thousands of years.

Anthropologists are uncertain how closely related the Mohawks were to the Indians who populated the shores of the Lake of Two Mountains, but they were most likely St. Lawrence Iroquoians — the name given to the Indians that Jacques Cartier found living in and around Montreal and Quebec City when he first visited the St. Lawrence Valley in 1535. Little is known about the St. Lawrence Iroquoians, because their settlements had disappeared by the time Samuel de Champlain retraced Cartier's voyage up the St. Lawrence some seventy years later. But it is known that their language and culture were similar to those of the Mohawks and others in the alliance of nations known collectively by the French as the Iroquois. Like the other Iroquois, they were corn farmers who supplemented their food by hunting and fishing.

Scholars have surmised that the St. Lawrence Iroquoians were driven out of the St. Lawrence Valley by the Mohawks in the late 1500s as the Mohawks moved north to gain control of the fur trade. Some of the defeated St. Lawrence Iroquoians are believed to have been absorbed by the Mohawks through adoption and intermarriage. As a result, it is likely that the Kanesatake Mohawks of today do have blood-links to the earliest known inhabitants of the region.

By the early seventeenth century, the Mohawks controlled the entire St. Lawrence Valley. For decades, they warred with the French and their native allies, the Algonquin and Montagnais. It was not until the late seventeenth century, after a French expedition succeeded in burning down Mohawk towns south of the Mohawk River (in present-day New York State) and destroying their corn supplies, that the Mohawks made a tenuous peace with the French. At this point, many of the Mohawks left their homeland in the Mohawk Valley to settle on the St. Lawrence River, around the town of Montreal.

One of those settlements was at the foot of Mount Royal. It was a mission settlement, established by the Roman Catholic Sulpician order, which was by then the seigneurial administrator of the Island of Montreal. Despite their affiliation with the Catholic church, the Mount Royal Mohawks maintained their warrior tradition, and by 1687 about eighty Mohawk warriors were living in the settlement. Indians from all over the fur-trading territory came to live there, but the Mohawks were the dominant group, and Mohawk became the common language of the community.

The Mohawks and other Christianized Indians weren't destined to stay at the foot of the mountain for long. In 1694, the settlement burned down as a result of a fire started by a "drunken Indian." The Sulpicians constructed a stone fort to replace the burned-out town, but the priests blamed the proximity to white settlers and the corrupting influence of liquor for the drunk and disorderly conduct of many Indians at the mission, and by the turn of the eighteenth century, they had moved the settlement to Sault-au-Récollet, fourteen kilometres north of Mount Royal on the Rivière des Prairies.

That forced move did not put an end to the friction between white colonists on the Island of Montreal and the Indians. By 1714, the

Sulpicians were petitioning the French king, Louis XV, to grant them land off the island for a permanent mission, where they might have more success in their evangelization efforts. They wanted a site far from the evils of civilization — a place where the Indians could fish, hunt, and farm.

The Christianized Indians at Sault-au-Récollet were reluctant to move away from the centre of trade at Montreal, but the missionaries and colonial officials persuaded the chiefs to travel north of the Rivière des Prairies to the mainland to choose a site for a permanent settlement. They chose the north shore of the Lake of Two Mountains, where other Mohawks had settled around the turn of the century.

Seventy years later, in a speech to the Superintendent of Indian Affairs in 1788, the Mohawk chief Aughneeta recalled the move: "Again our priests ... told us we should remove once more with our families for that it was no longer proper that any Indians should live on this island, and that if we should consent to go and settle at the Lake of Two Mountains we should have a large tract of land for which we should have a Deed from the King of France as our property to be vested in us and our heirs for ever, and that we should not be molested again in our habitations."

The Governor of New France, Philippe de Rigaud de Vaudreuil, granted the land concession to the Seminary of St. Sulpice of Paris in the fall of 1717, and the grant was confirmed by Louis XV the following spring. In 1733, the Sulpicians asked for a second land grant, to compensate for the unforeseen expense of moving and building a new settlement, and to provide a greater land base for the Indians, who were "frequently in the habit of changing their place of habitation." The second grant was confirmed in 1735. In the case of both grants, the land was turned over to the Sulpicians for the use and benefit of the Indians of the mission, on the express condition that title would revert to the Crown if the Indians vacated the mission. By 1736, about sixty Mohawk warriors were living at the Lake of Two Mountains, along with about fifty Nipissing and twenty Algonquin warriors and their families.

In keeping with the Iroquois tradition of marking important events and treaties with belts of shells called wampum, the Mohawks fashioned a wampum belt to cement their agreement to settle at the Lake of Two Mountains. It depicted men on either side of a cross — a symbol of their adherence to the faith of the Sulpicians. A long white band in the background was meant to symbolize the limits of their territory. At each end of the belt was the figure of a dog, who was to stand guard over the seigneury, barking warnings to the Mohawks if anyone disturbed them in their lands.

However, the Sulpician promise to give the Indians a written deed to the seigneury was forgotten or ignored, and nothing in the King's grant expressly recognized the Indians' property rights. While the Sulpicians gave land to individual Indians to allow them to build homes and grow crops, the Indians were not permitted to sell either the land or the wood, or the hay and crops they harvested on that land, without the approval of the director of the mission. The Mohawk wampum belt, presented to the Superintendent of Indian Affairs in 1781 as proof of their title to the land, was rejected by the government as worthless. The priests had power and influence on their side, as well as an unshakeable belief that the seigneury was Sulpician land and that without their strict tutelage, the "Savages" would return to their "slothful and apathetic ways" and the lands and forests of the seigneury would be ravaged by indiscriminate tree cutting. This theme was repeated by the Sulpicians in response to the countless petitions the Indians brought before successive governments, beginning soon after the British conquest of New France in 1760.

The Sulpicians complained that from the very start, they could not rid the Indians of their "fanciful idea" that they were masters of the seigneury. That "fanciful" notion became even more firmly implanted in the minds of the Indians after the defeat of the French by the British.

With the Act of Capitulation of Montreal, the Indians who had been faithful to the French were guaranteed the right to stay on the lands they then inhabited, without fear of being disturbed. Those guarantees — that Indians were to be protected in their lands unless those lands were formally surrendered to the Crown — were confirmed in the Treaty of Paris and in King George III's Royal Proclamation of 1763, the document that is still considered by native people across Canada to be a kind of charter of their land rights.

The Royal Proclamation renewed the hope of the Indians of the Lake of Two Mountains seigneury that at last their rights to the territory would be recognized, especially since by that time other Mohawks were already being granted their own lands elsewhere in the province. The Mohawk reserve of Akwesasne was created in 1759. Three years later, the Mohawk title to the land at Kahnawake — then the Jesuit seigneury of Sault St. Louis — was recognized by the courts after the Mohawks successfully sued the Jesuits over their attempts to sell some of the land to French Canadian settlers.

Legal questions surrounding the Sulpician land grants at Lake of Two Mountains and elsewhere were the subject of several government inquiries in the years following the British conquest. Then, in 1840, after the Sulpicians helped the British quell the Rebellion of 1837-38, the matter was settled to the satisfaction of the Catholic order when the government passed an act confirming the seminary's titles. The Ordinance of 1840 imposed on the Sulpicians the same obligations to the Indians that were contained in the original grant. Nonetheless, by explicitly recognizing the Sulpician titles, the government dealt a huge blow to the Indians of the Two Mountains seigneury in their quest for legal recognition of their land claim.

Over the years, the government was petitioned separately by the Algonquins of Oka and the Mohawks of Kanesatake, who lived in separate villages on either side of the Sulpician church and presbytery, each group with its own chief and council. Algonquins and Mohawks both insisted on their right to cut wood on the seigneury and sell it in Montreal and in the white settlement of Vaudreuil across the lake. The profits they gained from this business were essential to their survival. In the summertime, the Mohawks could sustain themselves from their crops and their gardens, but in the winter, they had no other means of earning a living. The situation was even worse for the Algonquins. By tradition, they were hunters, not farmers, and they had never settled in one place for long. The best efforts of the Sulpicians to force them to take up farming failed. With the encroachment of white settlements, the animals they hunted fled the once-fertile hunting grounds of the seigneury, and more and more often, Algonquin hunting parties came home empty-handed.

The Indians were reduced to utter poverty, and they blamed the Sulpicians for their situation. They complained that the priests did not provide them with enough land to sustain themselves and that they arbitrarily confiscated their land without compensation. Their meagre income was further reduced because they were forced to pay for the upkeep of the church and presbytery through tithes. And according to the Mohawks, those tithes were of little benefit to the widowed and sick in the villages, whom the priests treated harshly, even taking away their wood if it had been cut without permission.

In one petition, sent in 1848 to Lord Elgin, the British colonial governor, the Mohawks tried to underline how the priests kept defeating their efforts to earn a living. "The government tells us: Imitate the white man and become farmers, and you encourage us to do so," the Mohawks said. But farming and commerce were impossible because of the constraints imposed by the missionaries.

In response to this petition, the seminary reminded Lord Elgin that its right to the seigneury had been established by the Ordinance of 1840. It maintained that the actions of its priests were for the good of the Indians. If the Indians were poor and misfortunate, it was due to their "natural laziness." Besides, the mission provided them with bread, meat, wood, and money. The seminary added "... it could be said with truth that thanks to the charity of the Missionaries ... one doesn't find at the Mission the great miseries that are found almost everywhere else."

The trouble was, the Indians did not want to be charity cases, subject to the paternal care of the missionaries. They demanded to be treated with respect, arguing that they had helped to defend Canada from the Americans in times of war. Despite that, they had been deprived of their ancestral lands. In one petition, sent to Parliament in 1851, the chief of the Algonquins at Lake of Two Mountains said the Indians were "often led to believe that the religious and humanitarian principles that civilized men professed were not well-rooted in their hearts." They claimed they had been victims of fraud because of their inexperience in transactions and games of diplomacy.

To weaken the Indians' case, the Sulpicians fostered divisions among them. A short time after the Mohawks submitted yet another petition to Lord Elgin in 1851, some of the chiefs who were faithful to the Sulpicians protested that they had not known about the petition and did not support it. Finally, after holding numerous councils to try to resolve their differences, the Mohawks stripped five of their chiefs of their titles, accusing them of being unduly influenced by the "black robes." The factionalism between the few Mohawks who remained faithful to the missionaries and the majority who wanted to sever links with the priests began a schism that still divides the community today.

The steadfastness of the Indians in their fight for their lands was interpreted as insolence by the missionaries. In 1852, the Bishop of Montreal excommunicated eleven Mohawks and four Algonquins for showing lack of respect for their priests. To be excommunicated from the Church was a severe punishment, but some colonists warned the bishop that the move could backfire, creating more dissension and driving the Mohawks into the arms of Protestant missionaries. "I don't know if my Lord has been advised of all that's happening here," wrote Joseph-Jean Giroir, a notary from the nearby settlement of St. Benoit, "but the state of exasperation that the Savages now find themselves in is extreme."

In 1853, the government set aside land at Maniwaki, about three hundred kilometres northwest of Oka, in western Quebec, for the Algonquins and another tract of land at Doncaster, one hundred and ten kilometres northeast of Oka, in the Laurentians, for the Mohawks of the Lake of Two Mountains and Kahnawake. But the new reserves remained vacant. The Indians chose to stay and continue their fight.

For a few years, the excommunications and a threat by Lord Elgin to strip the Mohawk and Algonquin chiefs of their titles seemed to have the desired effect, and life was peaceful in the seigneury. But the priests recognized that the peace those punitive measures had bought would not last for long. In 1863, one of them wrote that he saw in the hearts of the Indians "something that resembled burning embers hidden beneath the ashes, that sooner or later would once again catch fire."

Bitterness and resentment were indeed smouldering. In 1867, one of the Mohawks in the seigneury, a merchant named Petit Cri, was caught selling liquor to other Indians. As punishment, the priests refused to honour the vouchers that were handed out to the Indians to be exchanged for goods at Petit Cri's store. The merchant's business depended on those vouchers, and when he learned of the decision, he showed up at the presbytery in a rage. When he informed the missionary, Antoine Mercier, that nobody could stop him from selling liquor to his fellow Indians, Mercier replied that the Mohawk merchant was not acting out of love of his nation, but only because he wanted to make money. To that Petit Cri replied, "Nowadays everybody wants to make money, including you. What interest did you have in bringing the Savages here? If you don't know, I'll tell you." He then accused the priests of stealing the land of the seigneury from the Indians and treating them like slaves, for their own profit.

Mercier threatened to take Petit Cri to court for having called the missionaries thieves and liars. "Let them take me to prison," Petit Cri replied. "We'll see which of us goes, you or me. This is our land here." An Indian faithful to the priests also overheard him saying, "The Iroquois, our ancestors, massacred the priests ... and they did the right thing; the devil take me if I don't do the same."

The clash between Petit Cri and Mercier showed the growing frustration of the Indians at Lake of Two Mountains, their despair over their total dependence on the priests, and their increasing willingness to take the law into their own hands.

Meanwhile, the Indians continued to maintain their unwavering claim to the lands of the seigneury, and in 1868, they found a sympathetic ally. The new Superintendent General of Indian Affairs, William Spragge, could find no evidence that the rights of the Indians to the seigneury had ever been extinguished: he could see no difference between the land grants made to the Sulpicians and those made to the Jesuits at Kahnawake. In the case of Kahnawake, the courts had ruled that the priests were not the absolute owners of the land, but administrators on behalf of the Kahnawake Mohawks. Spragge suggested that the government negotiate with the Sulpicians to have the land of the seigneury transferred to the Crown to be held in trust for the Indians of the Lake of Two Mountains.

Within a day of Spragge's meeting with the Indians, word spread like wildfire throughout the Indian settlements that Spragge believed the land was theirs. The priests of the mission were mortified, and they demanded that Spragge set the record straight. But it was too late. Spragge's encouraging assessment of the Indian claims resulted in a flurry of new petitions from the Algonquins and the Mohawks. This angered the Sulpicians even more, and a priest announced that all who signed the documents would have to report themselves or be excommunicated.

This time the Mohawks refused to be intimidated. In the fall of 1868, without waiting for a reply to the latest appeal to the government, Chief Sose Onasakenrat appeared at the mission accompanied by other chiefs and warriors, and announced that he, as chief, was distributing the lands of the seigneury among his people. He had already staked out parcels of land and given them to individual Mohawks.

Sose Onasakenrat — or Joseph Swan, as he was known in English — had been a protégé of one of the Sulpician priests. Groomed for the priesthood, he was sent to school at the Sulpician college in Montreal where one of his fellow students was a young Métis from the Red River settlement named Louis Riel. After his formal schooling, he was hired to work as a secretary back at the mission. But in 1868, at the age of twenty-three, he was asked to serve as chief of the Mohawks. Despite the objections of the priests, he left the seminary and immediately threw all his intellectual training and energy into the fight to claim the lands of the seigneury for his people. Later he became a Methodist minister and translated the New Testament and a hymnbook into Mohawk. He died in 1881 at the age of thirty-five in mysterious circumstances, succumbing to an apparent case of food poisoning after a banquet in Montreal hosted by the Sulpician order.

That day in 1868, the priests had no intention of giving into their former protégé's demands; instead, they sought the intervention of a local judge, Charles Coursol. After failing to dissuade Chief Joseph and the other chiefs of their conviction that the land was theirs, Coursol wrote the secretary of state, Hector Langevin, asking him to meet the Mohawks and make it clear to them that the Sulpicians were the rightful owners of the seigneury. The Mohawks went to Ottawa eagerly, only to be told once again by Langevin that they had no rights to the land.

The Algonquins had received the same reply in December 1868, and in 1869, they finally gave up — departing *en masse* for the lands set aside for them at Maniwaki.

But Chief Joseph refused to give up, despite threats of excommunication and imprisonment. In late February of 1869 — four months after his failed bid to redistribute the lands of the seigneury — he again appeared at the presbytery of the Catholic mission, this time accompanied by forty armed Mohawk men. He informed the director of the mission that he was speaking on behalf of the entire Mohawk nation and warned him that the Sulpician priests had eight days to leave the mission because the Mohawks were claiming the land for themselves.

The same day, the chief sent a letter to the Governor General and the Secretary of State, advising them of what he had done. He informed the government that his nation would no longer tolerate the conduct of the priests, and "in default of having justice rendered to us, the chiefs, on behalf of the nation, will adopt such means as will ensure the removal of these priests."

A few days later, a posse of police arrived at the seigneury at three o'clock in the morning, accompanied by a judge. They arrested Joseph and two other chiefs in their beds and took them to the school house to have their charges read against them. A fourth Mohawk, who had hurled insults at the police, was also arrested.

As the four Mohawks were being taken away to jail at Ste. Scholastique, Chief Joseph appealed to the crowd gathered there. "My people, stay calm," he told them. "It's not the Queen who had us arrested, it's the priests, and the judge who has condemned us is not the Queen's judge but the judge of the priests."

The Mohawk leaders were freed on bail after promising to keep the peace and adhere to orders set out in a letter from the undersecretary of state, which required them to obey the law and respect the property rights of the Sulpicians.

"You must understand," the letter read, "that to act otherwise would be contrary to the law, and that the best method for you to obtain favours from the Government, or from the gentlemen of Saint-Sulpice, is to submit, unreservedly, to the law, and this without distrust. The Government has your welfare at heart and hopes that you will listen to the good advice which is given to you, and reject the evil ones which strangers of your nation may offer you ..."

The "strangers" the government referred to were, in all likelihood, influential English Protestants in Montreal, who were organizing to protect the rights of the Indians. Within weeks of their release on bail, the Mohawk chiefs sought advice from these supporters, including a schoolmaster from Kahnawake. By the late spring of 1869, most of the Mohawks had left the Catholic church. On May 15, 1869, they blasted their cannon in celebration to mark the arrival of a Methodist missionary in the seigneury.

They set out immediately to build a church, but six Mohawks, including the merchant Petit Cri, were arrested for cutting wood to build it. The Sulpicians did not want the Methodist church to go up in the seigneury, since they viewed the Protestants as troublemakers who encouraged the Mohawks to rise above their station in life and emboldened them in their pursuit of their land claim. The church was built anyway, in 1872. The seminary successfully prosecuted the Mohawks for erecting the church without permission and for using wood from the seigneury. In December 1875, three years after the church was built, it was torn down by court order.

The persecution of the Mohawks by the priests grew worse after the majority of them became Protestants. Now they were denied the right to cut down wood on common lands even for their own fuel and timber. The Mohawks complained about bullies hired by the seminary to harrass and threaten them, and the Sulpicians often called in the newly established provincial police force to arrest any Mohawk caught cutting wood. Chief Joseph himself was sentenced to six months in jail for claiming a larger tract of land than the Sulpicians had allowed him to cultivate. Between 1870 and 1873, over a third of the adult male Mohawks in the seigneury had criminal charges brought against them, all related to their stubborn refusal to seek permission from the Sulpicians when they used the lands and forests of the seigneury.

"The Indians would cut wood for making lacrosses or snowshoes or baskets for sale," wrote Amand Parent, the Methodist missionary who arrived in Oka in 1871. "They would be arrested, and dragged twenty miles for trial. There they would be bailed out. Some months after, they would be heard before the court. The juries would disagree or acquit them. They would hardly arrive home again before another arrest, and the round would be followed once again."

The government had tried several times to convince the Mohawks to move to the lands set aside for them years before at Doncaster, but they resisted the pressure. In late 1869, the Mohawks gathered to discuss the offer seriously, and after long debate, Chief Joseph sent word through Judge Coursol that "they were not inclined to leave, that they had too much attachment for their birthplace, which constantly recalled to their minds the glorious deeds of their ancestors, to consent to go."

By this time the Sulpicians were selling large tracts of land to white settlers, despite the objection of the Mohawks, and the town of Oka was being populated by a growing number of French Canadians who had settled on the lands vacated by the Algonquins. In 1875 there were so many settlers in Oka that it was incorporated as a municipality. Finding themselves more and more confined to the tiny plots they had received "at the pleasure" of the Sulpicians, the Mohawks became convinced that the priests were trying to force them out of the seigneury.

In December 1875, a Protestant Defence Association was established in Montreal to raise funds for the Mohawks to support their civil rights and their land claim. A war of words over the "Oka Question" began in Montreal's newspapers, and public meetings were held all across the country to raise funds for the cause of the Oka Indians. A federal government Indian agent who was responsible for the Mohawks of the seigneury complained that the whole affair had turned into "a stiff contest between the Protestants and the Roman Catholics."

By 1877, tensions in the seigneury were nearing the breaking point. Police continued to arrest Mohawks for cutting down wood and fencing off common lands. After Chief Joseph was once again imprisoned, this time for appropriating another piece of land in 1876, tempers flared. The few Mohawks who had remained faithful to the priests were threatened by some of the Protestant Mohawks, who warned that the settlement was on the verge of war and that those who sided with the seminary would be exterminated.

A group of white citizens of Oka appealed to the lieutenant-governor of Quebec, urging him to restore order in the municipality. They complained that armed Mohawks were roaming the streets, firing off their weapons, and threatening their property. The government replied that it was up to local authorities to preserve the peace. It was all an eery foreshadowing of the Oka crisis of 1990.

After the pre-dawn arrests of the Mohawks and the burning of the Catholic church that followed, the federal government realized something had to be done to settle the land question at Oka. The Mohawks were seen as troublemakers and criminals, and the Sulpicians, backed by French Canadians in the growing white settlement, wanted them to leave. The government decided to offer the Mohawks land elsewhere. They had already rejected the reserve set aside at Doncaster, partly because the land there was, in the sarcastic words of one of the Mohawk supporters, a "paradise of sterility, rock and frost." After the events of 1877, however, the Mohawks seemed willing to consider leaving the seigneury. The Mohawks had fixed their sights on land near Nipissing in northern Ontario, but the government decided that the Nipissing land was "too good for Indians."

Before they would agree to move anywhere, the Mohawks demanded that the government examine yet again their rights to the seigneury, in the highest court of the Commonwealth if necessary. They also sought compensation from the Sulpicians in exchange for their rights and privileges to the seigneury and for improvements they had made to their individually-held lands. If all else failed, the Mohawks said they would agree to accept half of the lands of the seigneury, which would then become a reserve.

The government commissioned more legal reports on the rights of the Mohawks to the lands of the seigneury, but once again the Indian claim was rejected.

The non-native Mohawk supporters — now going by the name of the Civil Rights Alliance — tried to help negotiate the terms of a move to a new reserve. They recommended land on Manitoulin Island in Lake Huron, but the white settlers on the island objected. Another island was offered, but the Mohawks felt it was too small and unsuitable.

In the meantime, the Sulpicians had stepped up their campaign of prosecution and persecution. They even demolished some Mohawk homes that had been built with local timber obtained without their permission. The Mohawks, accustomed to poverty, were now living in even worse squalor, without fuel to heat their homes or timber to repair old dwellings and build new ones. The Sulpicians carefully scrutinized each request for timber, and anyone not considered a good and obedient Indian was refused permission to cut wood in the seigneury.

In October 1878, the federal Indian agent in Oka warned his government that the Mohawks were no longer willing to tolerate the situation and were preparing to take up arms if necessary. Just a couple of months earlier, the French Canadian citizens of Oka had sent another petition to the government, complaining that the Indians were "threatening to commit new felonies." They demanded that a special constable be posted at Oka to maintain the peace.

In 1879, the Mohawks once again sought new territory in Ontario and compensation from the priests. This time, the government offered them twelve thousand acres south of Lake Temiscaming, in northern

Ontario. But the Mohawks concluded that the land was too far north, the soil poor, and the amount of land not adequate compensation for their territory at Two Mountains.

Two years later, the government set aside 25,500 acres of land at Gibson, in the district of Muskoka, Ontario. The seminary, eager to get rid of the recalcitrant Mohawks, agreed to buy the land and pay $9,000 in compensation to the Mohawks for improvements they had made to individual lots in the seigneury. Each family would receive 100 acres in the new location, as well as a log house, paid for by the seminary.

Thirty-five of the 120 Mohawk families made the move to Gibson in the fall of 1881, assured by the government's promise to provide them with provisions for one year. But when they arrived, they found no food or supplies waiting. Worse yet, with winter only weeks away, there were few jobs to be had and the log houses they were promised by the seminary had not been built. They also found many white squatters already living on the reserve; neither group welcomed the presence of the other.

The government in Ottawa and the Sulpicians pointed the finger of blame at each other. The government demanded an explanation from the priests. They replied that it had proved impossible to bring in materials to build the promised houses, because there was no road into the new reserve. After the snow fell, the supplies were carted in by sled and the first homes were built. In late December 1881, the Mohawks at Gibson wrote an Indian Affairs official that they were "pretty comfortable now as far as houses go. But the trouble is, we haven't anything to eat."

By the following spring, the squatters had left, coaxed away from their homes by $5,000 in compensation from the government. But the trials of the Gibson Mohawks were not over. Contrary to what they had been promised, the land was greatly inferior to the land they had cultivated at Oka, and several families decided to return there — only to discover that the Sulpicians had already sold their homes and property to French Canadian settlers. The federal government and the Sulpicians renewed their efforts to encourage the rest of the Mohawks to leave Oka, but the disastrous results of the move to Gibson convinced the remaining Mohawks to stand their ground.

"The Seminary authorities ... have a great project on hand to turn the reserve into a fine town site and populate it with French Canadian families once the Indians have gone," the *Toronto Daily Mail* reported in 1887. "Plans have already been prepared for this, and the Seminary only awaited the decision of the Indians to put it on foot."

But the Sulpicians would leave Oka without ever seeing their dream realized. The Mohawks never left Kanesatake.

CHAPTER 5
Bulldozers in the Pines

Oka Gets Its First Nine Holes

"Chief Kennatosse's Wife Hints that there will be Bloodshed"; "Detectives Hot on Trail of Chief Kennatosse: Indians Purchase Arms." It was the spring of 1902, and the Mohawks of Oka were making headlines again — in Montreal, and across the Atlantic in London, England. Once again, a Mohawk had been charged with cutting timber in the seigneury without the permission of the Sulpicians. The difference this time was that the chief — Joseph Kanawatiron Gabriel, known as Chief Kennatosse — decided to bypass the Canadian courts and take his case directly to the King of England.

With his American wife, Chief Kennatosse set sail for England in March 1902 and went directly to Buckingham Palace to lay the two-hundred-year-old Mohawk grievances at the foot of the throne. He was a strapping man who cut an imposing figure in the streets of London, and his arrival at the Palace without appointment caused a stir in the London papers. He was not received by King Edward VII, but he was invited to the British House of Commons to meet Gilbert Parker, a novelist and member of Parliament. Curious newspapermen reported their meeting word for word.

"Well, Chief, you have come a long way," Parker said.

"I have come to tell the King the troubles of our people," Kennatosse replied.

Parker listened to Kennatosse's story of the dispute over the seigneury, but he said there was nothing the King could do. Kennatosse refused to believe him.

"You say the King has no power. Is he not the King? It is to him that I come, to the King of all of us, the great King Edward VII. He can do everything."

Kennatosse returned to Kanesatake empty-handed, but he refused to admit defeat, threatening war against the federal government if the Mohawk land claim was not recognized. As the police were still trying to arrest him for stealing wood, he went into hiding. The authorities staked out every known haunt in the region and thousands of dollars were offered for his capture, but he somehow managed to elude his pursuers. The *Montreal Daily Star* followed every twist and turn of the manhunt, and its reporter went to great lengths to arrange a secret interview with the chief on May 27, 1902.

"They will never be able to gain their ends, unless it is over my dead body," Kennatosse told the reporter. He recounted again the Mohawk grievances. "I remember how my father was sent to gaol for three months for cutting three small logs in the woods to repair his house. I remember how others of my relations ... when they went out in the winter time to cut wood to keep their wives and children warm, were arrested in the bush and carried off to gaol, while their shivering wives and children, not knowing what caused the prolonged absence of their husbands and fathers, vainly waited for the fuel to warm their half-frozen bodies."

By June 1902, tensions were running so high in Oka that people living across the lake were afraid to visit the town. The Mohawks bought every pistol and revolver on the shelves of a store in nearby St. Placide, and the province, fearing an uprising, swore in special constables in Oka. French Canadian townspeople renewed their appeals to Ottawa to do something, but federal officials said they did not want to be dragged into the dispute. Meanwhile, from his hiding place in the hills near Oka, Chief Kennatosse was sending out messages that he planned to return to England to appeal once more to the King for help. The police raided a pow-wow where funds for his trip were being raised, but Kennatosse eluded them again. Hearing a report that he was on his way back from the United States by steamship, the police boarded a boat on Lake Ontario and searched it but did not find him. His descendants recall that the police were under orders to shoot Kennatosse on sight — even though the only charge against him was theft, for stealing wood.

Chief Kennatosse stayed in hiding for years, emerging every so often to rally his followers. Seven years after he first made headlines, he and forty armed Mohawks rode on horseback to Pointe Calumet, where workers for the Canadian Northern Railway were building a track that would cross over 250 metres of the seigneury. The Sulpicians had given the railway company their permission to pass through the territory, but the Mohawks had not.

"Indians Threaten War against Railroad Men," the headlines proclaimed. "Canadian Northern construction gang at Oka Stopped by Band of Forty Armed with Revolvers, Shotguns and Bludgeons. 'Chief' Kennatosse Gabriel Their Leader — Threaten Serious Trouble if Their Land is Crossed."

The proof that Kennatosse accomplished his mission still exists today: the railway track ends abruptly at the edge of the highway at Pointe Calumet. After the confrontation, Kennatosse went back into hiding, but a few years later, at the urging of his lawyer, he gave himself up. He had been on the run for fifteen years. By then, thousands of dollars had been spent in the hunt for the elusive Mohawk chief. In the end, the charges laid against him were dropped, but his children and grandchildren say he was harassed for the rest of his life. He was jailed for refusing to send his nine children to residential schools and was eventually forced into poverty by his refusal to give up the fight for the land.

"He was a hard-working man, who did everything for his family, to leave the land to future generations," his grandson, Richard Gabriel, says. "He died a poor man. He had to sell all his farm machinery and his animals to pay his lawyer's bills. But he left his family rich in history."

Perhaps because of the uproar created by Chief Kennatosse, the Seminary of St. Sulpice tried to settle the question of Mohawk rights to the seigneury once and for all in 1905. The Sulpicians offered to sell the federal government the remnants of the seigneury, including the forest, the common lands, and the lands already occupied by the Mohawks. But the Mohawks still demanded that all the original land grants be honoured, and they appealed to the government to test their claim again in court.

Their claim was brought before the Court of King's Bench by three Mohawk Chiefs — Angus Corinthe, Baptiste Gaspé and Peter Oka, and after wending its way through the appeal courts, it reached the Privy Council in London in 1912. The Privy Council rejected the Mohawk claim, ruling that the Ordinance of 1840 and subsequent legislation placed beyond question the Sulpicians' title to the seigneury. But the Lords of the Privy Council left the door open to the government for some kind of settlement with the Mohawks, suggesting that the Sulpicians did have obligations to the Mohawks that could be enforced by federal legislation.

This made no lasting impression on the government, which did nothing to protect the Mohawk settlement from further encroachment. A senior Indian Affairs bureaucrat merely accepted the assurance of one of the Sulpicians' lawyers that the seminary would not interfere with the lands the Mohawks were inhabiting and using. That promise was broken in 1936, when the Sulpicians sold the remnants of the seigneury — the pine forests of the Commons, Calvary Mountain, and the nearby farms — to a wealthy Belgian, Baron Empain. The Mohawks were using the Commons as pasturelands and woodlots, and they launched vehement protests against the sale. Undaunted, Empain hired another Belgian, one René Dourte, to manage the pine forests, and he proceeded to plant saplings in the clearing in the Pines, right in the middle of the traditional Mohawk gathering place. A few days later, a Mohawk named Barnard Gabriel rode into the Pines with his workhorses and swather and mowed the young trees down. Dourte and another man rode up on horseback and, brandishing their guns at Gabriel, demanded that he stop what he was doing. Gabriel's wife presented Dourte with a document from the Indian Affairs Minister of the day, stating that the common lands were for the use of the Mohawks. The foresters did not press any charges.

A few years later, in 1945, in an attempt to at last resolve the land question, the federal government purchased from the Sulpicians the lands that the Mohawks were still occupying. One hundred and thirty-two lots, scattered throughout the town of Oka and the farmlands west of the town, were all that remained of the vast tract of land granted for the mission in 1718 and 1735. It amounted to about four square kilometres — one per cent of the size of the original Two Mountains seigneury. The patchwork of lots did not become a reserve, but remained Crown land. The Mohawks were given "certificates of possession," and were permitted to stay on the land they occupied — in most cases, land passed down through each family from generation to generation — and the federal government made agreements with the parish and the town of Oka to pay annual property taxes on the Crown lands.

The purchase did nothing to solve the problem. The government did not consult the Mohawks about the transaction, and it made no attempt to secure the Commons, the land most important to the Mohawks, despite the fact that the government had previously recognized the Commons as traditional Mohawk land and the Mohawks had not given up their claim to it. Two years later, in 1947, the provincial government authorized the town of Oka to expropriate some of the Baron's land, including the Pines and the land now occupied by the nine-hole golf course.

By 1950, the Baron's lands had been sold again, and a sawmill had been set up in the forest near the present-day golf course, just west of the dirt road that now bisects the Pines. One of Chief Kennatosse's daughters, Lena Nicholas, was enraged when she saw loggers cutting down trees in the pine forest. On July 12, the fifty-four-year-old woman walked down to the sawmill and confronted the workers, reading them the Royal Proclamation of 1763, which promised that the Indians would not be "molested or disturbed" in the lands they occupied unless they had signed treaties to surrender the land. Lena Nicholas told the men they were on Mohawk land and they had no right to be there.

The workers stopped the sawmill temporarily, but they warned that they would return with the police. Nicholas went back to the Pines and confronted René Dourte, who was still managing the forest for the new owners. She insisted that he shut down the sawmill, but he refused.

"The next thing I knew we were striking one another and I fell to the ground three or four different times," she recalled later. "Each time I fell to the ground he hit me. I got right up and hit him right back. Twice I hit him and pushed him against a pile of logs. That was when he hit me on the left side of my face. I fell to the ground. He pulled my hair and struck my head ... then he ran off and got a long chain. I guess he was trying to scare me. He told me to get off the grounds."

When a police officer arrived from the town, Lena Nicholas showed him a copy of the Royal Proclamation. The officer told her she could not take the matter into her own hands, that she would have to fight the issue in the proper way.

"I know that," she told him. "That's what I'm trying to do."

She refused to go to the town with the police officer. The next day, the police showed up at her brother's house, where she was staying, with a warrant for her arrest, but again she refused to go with them. Later, three plainclothes officers returned to the house, and one of them, who was brandishing a gun, read her the warrant.

"Shoot me if you're man enough to do it," she challenged the officer. He did not fire the gun; he only asked what all the trouble was about. She explained that the Pines belonged to the Mohawks, and she again brought out her copy of the Royal Proclamation and demanded to know if the officer was loyal to the King. By now her sister-in-law and the children were in tears and her brother was fighting with the other police officers.

"I picked up a plank and swung that," she recalled. "I would not let anybody come near me ... I was watching two men, one in front of me, the other from the back. That's when they got me, dragged me into the car and took me to a jailhouse at St. Jérôme."

It took two days for her family to raise the $950 bail that was set for Lena's release. At her trial the following December, she refused to swear on the Bible because of her belief in the Longhouse religion. The proceedings were all in French, which she did not understand, but she was nevertheless found guilty of assaulting Dourte and fined $200 plus court costs.

The sawmill was dismantled soon afterwards and moved to a new location, and the incident was forgotten by most people. René Dourte, now an eighty-seven-year-old widower who still lives in Oka on the edge of the forest, has no memory of the confrontation with the Mohawk woman, but the children and grandchildren of Lena Nicholas have never forgotten. They still visit her grave in the tiny Mohawk cemetery, wedged between the Pines and the golf course. Throughout the summer of 1990, the descendants of Lena Nicholas called on their grandmother's fighting spirit to help them in the long stand-off with the Quebec police and the army.

The government had hoped to put an end to the land claim of the Kanesatake Mohawks in 1945 by purchasing the last remnants of the seigneury from the Sulpicians. But the Mohawks continued their fight — now against private landowners and the municipality of Oka. In the 1950s, when the municipality drew up plans to develop the disputed land which it expropriated in 1947, the Mohawk claim to the forests of the Commons was ignored. In 1959, the Mohawks protested against the municipality's plans to raze part of the Pines just west of the town to lease to a private, non-profit corporation, the *Club de golf Oka Inc.*, for a nine-hole golf course.

Outraged that the Mohawk claim to the Commons had once again been ignored, a young Mohawk named Jeffrey Gabriel — inspired by the memory of his father who had tried to protect the Pines from the Belgian foresters in 1936 — solicited the advice of two prominent Montreal lawyers, Émile Colas and Frank Scott, in 1959. When he asked them to try to block a private member's bill put before the Quebec National Assembly confirming the municipality's title to the property, they agreed to take on the case for free.

"Émile Colas tried everything with the Indian Affairs Department," Jeffrey Gabriel's younger brother Harvey recalls. "He told them, 'You have the power to stop this Quebec legislation before it becomes law.'" But the department claimed there was nothing it could do.

It was March 1961 before Jeffrey Gabriel was able to scrape together $50 to allow Émile Colas to travel to Ottawa, where he appeared on behalf of the Kanesatake Mohawks at a joint Senate-Commons committee on Indian Affairs. Already, bulldozers were ploughing through the Mohawk territory, and the golf course was almost completed.

"In order that the white man may have more opportunities for recreation, what was once reserved for Indian use and profit is now reserved for golf," Colas told the committee. "Is this truly fulfilling the intention of the original grant of the seigneury of the Lake of Two Mountains? ... We are not blindly opposing the inevitable adaptations to modern conditions that must take place. But why must these changes benefit the white men more than the Indians?"

After listening to the historical account of how the Mohawk territory had been whittled down to a mere one per cent of the original land grant, one of the committee members concluded, "They certainly did get gypped, did they not?"

The committee recommended a swift settlement of the 240-year-old Oka land question, urging the government to set up an Indian Claims Commission and naming the Oka claim as one of the priorities for the Commission. But the advice went unheeded.

"It was like crying in the desert," Colas recalls. "The people of Oka were ruthless. 'The savages haven't got anything to say about it,' they said. It was not fashionable then to speak up for Indians. We looked like people who had a chip on our shoulder, who wanted to oppose progress."

The Mohawks were not opposed to progress, but they were desperate to save their land base from being whittled down to nothing. They had pleaded their case endlessly, refusing to stand by while the Sulpicians sold off, piece by piece, most of the twelve parishes of the original seigneury. Their fears that no one would ever listen to their case were well founded. A decade after the Senate-Commons committee urged a quick settlement of the Kanesatake Mohawk claim, the federal government went ahead with the construction of the Montreal International Airport at Mirabel, on disputed Mohawk territory that was part of the original Lake of Two Mountains seigneury. The airport was built on prime agricultural land, and the feeble complaints of the Kanesatake Mohawks were drowned out by the louder protests of farmers in the region, whose families, in many cases, had tilled the soil there for several generations.

In 1975, the Mohawks of Kanesatake, Kahnawake, and Akwesasne submitted a comprehensive land claim to the federal and Quebec governments, asserting their right to lands along the St. Lawrence and Ottawa rivers, including the Lake of Two Mountains seigneury. Four months after it was submitted, the Department of Indian Affairs rejected the claim, saying that the Mohawks could not prove they had occupied the territory from time immemorial. Any aboriginal title that may have existed, the Department said, had been extinguished by the French Kings when they made their seigneurial grants and later by the British Crown when it opened the lands to settlement.

In 1977, the Kanesatake Mohawks submitted a specific claim for the original seigneury of the Lake of Two Mountains. They set out to prove that the royal grants of 1718 and 1735 had indeed been intended as a reserve for the Indians who settled there and that their rights to that land had never been extinguished.

That same year, a scrappy team of Mohawk women challenged the municipality's right to use a softball diamond located on the northeastern edge of the golf course, behind the town. The softball field was part of the Commons, and the Mohawks still considered it their land. But their defiance had by then dwindled to Mohawk children picking up stray golf balls in the field and taking aim at golfers on the greens.

Denise David-Tolley was a young mother in 1977. She remembers driving past the softball diamond where she had played in her youth and noticing that there were no longer any Mohawk children playing there. "I said, what's going to happen? My children are going to want to play there and they won't be able to." David-Tolley decided to do something about the situation. She went from house to house throughout Kanesatake and asked all the women — children, mothers, and grandmothers — to form a softball league to take back possession of the playing field.

"Some of them said, 'I have no children.' I said, 'Do you have nieces and nephews? Then get your asses down here!' I got forty-six people together, and we made two teams. Some of them couldn't play ball worth nothing, but I said, it doesn't matter, as long as you're here."

At first, the rag-tag Mohawk league was willing to share the field with people from the town. But then one evening, when the diamond had been set aside for the Mohawk women to practise, the Oka boys' league showed up to play. David-Tolley remembers the scene: "One of the women said, 'That's it. Now they're using little kids against us. We're not taking this.' They stood right out there on the field and said, 'Take your little kids home before they get hurt. This is our practice night.'"

A town councillor who was there claimed that the ball diamond belonged to the municipality and the women had no right to be playing on it.

"Go down to your municipal office, go get the documents, show us that you own this land," the women told him. David-Tolley says he drove down to the town and returned half an hour later without any documents, fuming with anger.

The women won their softball diamond — but the Mohawks lost their land claim. In 1986, after almost a decade of deliberations and appeals, the federal government decided that the claim did not meet its narrow criteria for "specific claims." While the government ruled that it had no legal obligation to the Kanesatake Mohawks on the land issue, it recognized that the Mohawks faced a serious land shortage and offered to consider other ways of resolving the Mohawk grievances. The Kanesatake band council was provided with funds to hire a consulting firm to study the settlement's land needs — but by then the land issue was overshadowed by political in-fighting over the system of government in the settlement.

The divisions that split the Mohawk settlement at Lake of Two Mountains date back over a century, to the days when one group of Mohawks was allied with the Catholic priests and the majority had converted to Protestantism in an attempt to drive the Sulpicians out of the seigneury.

The traditional spiritual and political institution of the Mohawk people, the Longhouse, had all but disappeared by this time, with the overwhelming influence of Christianity. Suppressed by both Church and government, Longhouse people were forced underground, to conduct their religious festivals and council fires in secret. The old ways were forgotten or rejected by the majority of the Kanesatake Mohawks. As time went on, however, people began learning the old beliefs again when they travelled to Onondaga and Akwesasne and other territories of the Iroquois Confederacy where the traditions still flourished. Over the past several decades, some families have renewed their faith in the Longhouse, discarding the Christianity they had once adopted. This return to the old ways reaffirmed the ancient principle of the Two Row Wampum. Enshrined in a treaty between the Iroquois and the Dutch in 1645, this principle held that the Iroquois and the Europeans could co-exist peacefully, without interfering in each other's traditions, just as a birchbark canoe and a European sailing vessel could share the same waterway. Inherent in this concept was the idea that anyone who tried to keep one foot in the canoe and another on the ship — calling himself a Mohawk while practising a European religion or submitting to a European-based government — would come to a disastrous end.

Although their practice was not obvious, the Longhouse people of Kanesatake had always kept some of the old ways alive in their settlement. An ancient war dance song still sung in other Confederacy territories mentions Kanesatake, and Kanesatake is named in the

Confederacy's condolence ceremonies, in which titles are bestowed on new chiefs and clan mothers. Muriel Nicholas, a seventy-eight-year-old Kanesatake Mohawk, remembers that her father was condoled as a Longhouse chief in a traditional Mohawk ceremony around 1920. Chief Kennatosse, too, was known as a traditional chief, although he was a practising Methodist. (His rival and the brother of Chief Sose Onasakenrat, the elected chief Angus Corinthe, counselled everyone to ignore Kennatosse's claims to speak for the Mohawks.) In 1964, the Mohawks constructed a Longhouse at Kanesatake and condoled eight chiefs and clan mothers in a spring ceremony.

People who were raised in the Longhouse tradition in Kanesatake remember the persecution they suffered in a settlement where the majority was Christian. They were condemned as pagans and witches and they were sometimes physically threatened. Linda Gabriel, whose two sisters were condoled as clan mothers, remembers watching Chief Frank Moses and other traditional people walking up the road towards their new, unfinished Longhouse building on the day of the condolence ceremony in 1964. "They were almost run off the road by somebody who said, 'I wish I had a machine gun — I'd line them all up and gun them down.'"

Linda Gabriel was married in a Longhouse ceremony in Akwesasne, but the wedding, like that of her parents, was not recognized as legal because it had not been conducted in a church or a courtroom. Younger Longhouse people, like Joe David and Allen Gabriel, recall being teased and taunted by other Mohawk children because they were "different."

But there was something special about being a follower of the old ways, something that made it possible to withstand all the teasing. Joe David remembers going to the Longhouse for festivals, when traditional people from other Mohawk territories would come into the community. He and boys his age would sit together, listening to the drums and rattles and the traditional Mohawk songs, and sometimes the same children who had taunted them would be outside, peering wistfully through the open doorway.

"You could tell that they wanted to come in, but they thought their parents wouldn't approve. Still, their curiousity drew them, brought them right to the door."

The most traditional of the Longhouse followers were strict adherents to the Two Row Wampum. They refused to recognize the jurisdiction of the Indian Act, to accept social assistance from the provincial government, or take any jobs that required them to swear an oath of allegiance to the Canadian government. But in a community where they were only a tiny minority, the Longhouse people had little influence over Kanesatake's affairs. Official power was vested in the band council, which conformed to the rules and regulations of the Indian Act.

Although the Christian Mohawks did not participate in Longhouse ceremonies, they did not discard their culture and customs completely. In the late 1960s, they began lobbying for a form of government that more closely resembled the old ways. They pressured the elected chief, James Gaspé, and forced him to resign in 1969 to make way for a return to a "traditional" political system. At a meeting in the fall of 1969, attended by about seventy people, the community approved the adoption of that system, in which three clan mothers were chosen by members of each of the Turtle, Bear, and Wolf clans, and they, in turn, were given the responsibility of appointing three chiefs from each clan for life. The system was based loosely on the model of the Iroquois Confederacy, laid out in the centuries-old doctrine known as the Great Law of Peace. The new band council called itself the Six Nations Traditional Hereditary Chiefs of the Iroquois Confederacy, much to the indignation of the Longhouse members of the true Confederacy, who saw the band council under any name as merely the administrative arm of a foreign government, since it accepted the authority of the Indian Act.

The system of government adopted by the band council was meant to be a grassroots democracy, relying on the advice of the members of each clan. It was hampered from the start, however, by the fact that many Kanesatake Mohawks had lost their clans through intermarriage with whites (clans are traditionally passed down through the mother) and therefore had no say in clan meetings. Because it operated under Indian Act authority, the band council also defied the principle of the Two Row Wampum and was rejected by Longhouse followers.

The federal government agreed to recognize the new system under provisions in the Indian Act for "custom" band government, but that recognition proved to be premature. Almost immediately, a rival group, called the Kanesatakeron Indian League for Democracy, challenged the new band council's legitimacy. It asserted that since elections were no longer required and since so few people had approved the change, the new system did not have the support of the majority of the community. It was also undemocratic. In 1973, the Department of Indian Affairs conducted a survey to ascertain the extent of support for the band council. The custom system drew the most support, by a slim majority, and the government confirmed its recognition of that council.

The survey did not put an end to the dispute over the best way to govern Kanesatake. In 1977, the group in favour of council elections — the Kanesatakeron Indian League for Democracy — filed a suit against the band council. At the same time, a group of chiefs who had been dismissed by the clan mothers refused to step down. By the spring of 1977, there were two sets of traditional chiefs and two sets of clan mothers, all claiming legitimacy, plus the rival faction seeking a return to the elective system. After a flurry of petitions arrived on the desks of the bureaucrats at Indian Affairs, one of them concluded: "This whole affair is a result of people not knowing what their custom is." And he was probably right. After three centuries of having one form of government or another imposed on them and their own clan system of government suppressed, it was not surprising that the Mohawks were having difficulty resurrecting old customs and modifying them to comply with both the regulations of the Indian Act and the expectations of the community for a modern-day government.

These problems were compounded by religious and linguistic divisions that dated back to the time of the Sulpicians. The Mohawks who had remained faithful to the priests were Catholic and French-speaking, but the majority spoke English and were Protestants. The dispute became even more complicated in the mid-1980s, when Bill C-31 was passed, giving back Indian status to hundreds of Kanesatake Mohawks who had lost their treaty rights through marriage to non-Indians. The band list nearly doubled, and it included many people who had lost their ties to Mohawk culture and traditions.

In 1983, a federal court ruling upheld the "custom" band system at Kanesatake but failed to quell the concerns of the Kanesatakeron League for Democracy and another group, called the Group for Change, which had joined the lobby for a return to an elected system of government. This committee included disaffected former chiefs who had lost power after they were ousted for one reason or another by the clan mothers.

Petitions and appeals continued to pile up on the desks of federal bureaucrats and politicians. In the three years leading up to the crisis of 1990, clan mothers shuffled the chiefs six times, culminating with the dismissal, in January 1990, of Grand Chief Clarence Simon on allegations of conflict of interest, related to his co-ownership of an ambulance service that had a contract with the band council. Simon was replaced by George Martin, an inarticulate man in a community of skilled orators, who had no political experience. Martin's appointment left many Kanesatake Mohawks incredulous and cemented their opposition to the "custom" band council. Meanwhile, Clarence Simon had refused to accept the decision of the clan mothers, and once again, through the winter and spring of 1990, two sets of "traditional" chiefs and two sets of clan mothers vied for control of the band council office.

As a result of the internal feuding, few public meetings were held in Kanesatake to discuss issues important to the community at large, and those that did take place often disintegrated into shouting matches. The Mohawk tradition of giving every person a turn to speak and reaching decisions by consensus was all but forgotten, and many people became thoroughly disenchanted with band politics.

But there was one issue on which virtually everyone in the settlement was united: the land that they had claimed as their own for over two and a half centuries. By 1990, Kanesatake was still not recognized as a Mohawk territory (as the Longhouse people claimed it was) nor as a federal Indian reserve (as those who accepted federal jurisdiction wanted it to be). The land question had a unifying effect because it touched almost every sphere of life in Kanesatake. The jurisdictional dispute with Oka froze economic development projects, for example. In March 1990, a proposal to construct a steel-manufacturing plant in Kanesatake was stymied by Indian Affairs' refusal to approve the project unless the Mohawks obtained municipal permits from the parish of Oka, thus implicitly acknowledging that the land belonged to Oka. The lack of recognition of the Mohawk land claim also meant that the Kanesatake Mohawks had no power to stop other parties from putting developments on disputed territory. They were not consulted about a marina project, a planned hotel-resort complex, new housing developments nor — as the world learned in 1990 — a project to expand the private Oka Golf Club into an eighteen-hole course.

In 1985, when Kanesatake reached an agreement with the federal government to open a native drug and alcohol treatment centre on Highway 344 near the Pines, a group of Oka citizens (supported by Mayor Jean Ouellette) fought tooth and nail to block the project. Residents living near the chosen site feared the Treatment Centre would lower their property values and threaten their security. But their greatest concern, according to an interview that the citizens' group gave to a local newspaper during the dispute, was that the opening of the Treatment Centre would be a "springboard" for further Mohawk claims to municipal land. The group collected seven hundred signatures from Oka citizens opposing the Treatment Centre, and they obtained the support of the local member of Parliament, Lise Bourgault. Despite the efforts of the Oka citizens' group, the centre was opened in 1987.

At the time of the controversy over the Treatment Centre, the municipality's plan to expand the nine-hole golf course next to the Pines was still in its infancy. But already the stage was set for another confrontation over the land issue. And again — as in 1877 — the warning signs went unheeded until the hidden embers of resentment and frustration were ignited by another police raid.

CHAPTER 6

Cowboys of the Sky

A Portrait of Kahnawake

On a blackboard on the classroom wall, Harley Delaronde is writing a new word for his grade nine students to learn. The word is "expropriate." Most of the Mohawk teenagers at the Kahnawake Survival School already know what it means, but they are puzzled by today's history lesson. They cannot understand how their parents and grandparents could have permitted Mohawk land to be expropriated during the construction of the St. Lawrence Seaway in the 1950s. "Why did they let the seaway go through?" the students demand to know. "How come they didn't block it? Why didn't they just step in front of the trucks?"

Two of the eight Mohawk teenagers in Delaronde's social studies class are wearing the distinctive camouflage jackets of the Mohawk Warrior Society. When the teacher holds up a map of Kahnawake to illustrate the location of the seaway, one of them points out the location of the barricade he helped defend in the summer of 1990. The students are proud, militant, battle-hardened, and imbued with a defiant Mohawk nationalism.

Delaronde asks his students to pretend they were Kahnawake residents in 1954 when the federal government was bargaining to purchase Mohawk land for the seaway. The students are supposed to re-enact a community meeting where the federal offer was debated.

Delaronde is trying to demonstrate that some Mohawks would accept the offer and others would reject it, leading to a divided and weakened community which was unable to defeat the seaway. But the role-playing doesn't work. The students cannot imagine any Mohawk bowing to the federal pressure. "Call in your goons, I'll never move," one of them declares.

Another student, Carl, is instructed to play the role of a Mohawk who is married to a non-native woman. "I wouldn't marry a white girl," he objects. But eventually he agrees to accept the federal payment for his land. The other students immediately turn against him. "What a sell-out," they chorus. They call him a traitor who must be punished.

While the teacher proceeds with his lecture, some of the students are secretly writing something on a piece of paper. A few minutes later, they give it to Carl. "Eviction notice," the paper says. "You and your white family have thirty minutes to leave our land."

The mood of Kahnawake has been radically transformed in the past thirty-five years. When the seaway was rammed through the Mohawk community in the 1950s, its residents were deeply divided. Some tried to fight the seaway, but most bowed to the authority of the federal government. They were bitter but fatalistic, and the possibility of blocking the seaway was never seriously considered. Only a handful of Mohawks refused to move when construction began, and even they were pushed aside by the bulldozers.

In the eyes of the federal government, Kahnawake is officially categorized as just another Indian reserve under the jurisdiction of the federal Indian Act. But its residents have always refused to call it a reserve. To them, it is a Mohawk territory, belonging to the Mohawk nation. Today, it has become a hotbed of Mohawk nationalism, and it is unquestionably the most rebellious native community in Canada. Over the past two decades, Kahnawake has fought for its independence in dozens of fierce conflicts with police officers and government officials. And despite the pressures of constant warfare, the vast majority of Kahnawake's six thousand residents are united in a fundamental belief in Mohawk sovereignty.

The youngest generation at Kahnawake is the most militant of all. Many of the Mohawk youths have cut their hair into the traditional scalplock of an Iroquois warrior. From an early age they have absorbed the ideology of Mohawk nationalism. In many cases, their parents have abandoned the Catholic church and converted to the Long-house, the national religion of the Mohawks and other Iroquois na-tions. A large percentage of Kahnawake's children have attended Mohawk language immersion programs in elementary school, and they are fluent in the language of their forefathers. When they enter grade seven, about two-thirds of them attend the Kahnawake Survival School, which is entirely controlled and supervised by Mohawks from the community. "It gives them the backbone of their identity," says Alex McComber, principal of the Survival School.

The warrior movement is not an official subject for classroom lec-tures at the Kahnawake Survival School, but the place has become a breeding ground for warriors. On a desk in the science classroom, one student has carved a popular slogan: "Long Live the Warrior Society." Many of the students picked up guns to defend the barricades at Kahnawake and Kanesatake during the summer of 1990, and students and graduates of the Survival School were among the final group of Mohawks who were besieged by the Canadian army at Kanesatake at the end of the summer. One seventeen-year-old warrior returned to the Survival School after he was arrested by the soldiers at Kanesatake.

At the entrance to the school's gymnasium, there are photographs of the seventeen-year-old warrior as a three-time champion of Mon-treal wrestling tournaments. He is just one of many young men from Kahnawake who have dominated the sport of wrestling in Montreal for many years. The gymnasium is the largest building on the 154-acre cam-pus of the Survival School. One of its inside walls has been converted into a climbing wall where students can practise rock-climbing skills.

About 230 students from grades seven to eleven are enrolled in the Kahnawake Survival School today. Most of the students are from Kahnawake, but a few are Kanesatake Mohawks who endure a long journey by bus every day to attend the Survival School. Although the school is financed by the Kahnawake Education Centre and the fed-eral Indian Affairs Department, its curriculum is entirely controlled by the school staff and a committee of Mohawk parents. From grades seven to nine, the schoolchildren study from a unique textbook, *Sev-en Generations*, which documents the history of the Mohawk people strictly from a Mohawk point of view. Published by the Survival School in 1980, it is the key source of information for Mohawk students in social studies classes at the school. Unlike other history books, it gives the Mohawk perspective on every major event in North American history. Despite this point of view, the textbook gives a generally accurate portrait of the Mohawk people and the historical loss of their land and their rights as a nation. The facts alone are enough to fuel a nationalist fervour in the students who read the textbook.

The textbook refers to the Mohawks by their original name, the Kanienkehaka (the Flint People). It describes the early European explorers and settlers as treacherous and duplicitous people who were motivated by greed to steal Mohawk land, and it portrays the Canadian government as an oppressive enemy of Mohawk sovereignty. The purpose of the Indian Act, for example, was "to weaken the power and prestige of traditional native government, to remove women of the nations from positions of power, to give native people Canadian citizenship, and to gradually terminate all claims of native people to lands in Canada."

An entire chapter is devoted to the controversy surrounding the construction of the St. Lawrence Seaway in the 1950s. It describes how the Kahnawake Mohawks lost their traditional connection to a great river, and it portrays the seaway's construction as a major setback for the Mohawk community. "The seaway was a defeat for the Kanienkehaka," the textbook says. "It reminded people of the kind of treatment that native people can expect from the Canadian and American governments."

For most of the twentieth century, the children of Kahnawake were forced to leave the reserve to attend schools which were controlled by Catholic or Protestant school boards. Then, in 1970, the Mohawks walked out of the Protestant high school in Châteauguay where most of them were enrolled, demanding Mohawk language classes and cultural studies. A temporary compromise was reached with the high school, but the Mohawks were dissatisfied. They still wanted their own school at Kahnawake. Their anger deepened in 1976 when Quebec passed Bill 101, which required Indians to get special permission if they wanted an exemption from the new requirement that all children within Quebec's borders be educated in French. Finally, in September of 1978, the Mohawk students in Châteauguay walked out of class and marched back to Kahnawake, accompanied by eight hundred Mohawk supporters. Within a few days, operating on a shoestring budget, a committee of volunteers had established the Kahnawake Survival School. They taught classes with volunteer teachers until Ottawa agreed to provide funding.

The school's founding committee was made up of Mohawk parents who stubbornly fought the federal and provincial bureaucracy for years while the school struggled to establish itself. Among the leaders of the school committee were Joe Deom, Lorna Delormier, Lorraine Montour, Nancy Deer, and Shirley Scott. A decade later, in the summer of 1990, all five were active supporters of the warrior movement. Joe Deom was a key negotiator for the warriors, Lorraine Montour was the mother of two young warriors, and all four of the women provided help to the warriors at their Kanesatake headquarters.

Over the past twenty years, an entire system of Mohawk-controlled schools has developed at Kahnawake. Children as young as five can enter a Mohawk language immersion program at the Karonhianonha Elementary School on the reserve, which has more than two hundred students enrolled. From grades one to three, all classes are taught entirely in Mohawk. After students become fluent in their mother tongue, a limited amount of English is introduced in later grades.

When they reach grade seven, students can enter the Survival School, where Mohawk language classes are compulsory and Mohawk culture and traditions permeate every aspect of school life. The student council, for example, is based on the rules of the Longhouse and the Iroquois Confederacy. Every student is a member of the student council, and their meetings are organized as if the students were members of clans or nations at a traditional Longhouse or Confederacy meeting. Meetings can last for an entire day. School administrators consult the students on every major policy question, from disciplinary decisions to the scheduling of tobacco-burning ceremonies and traditional feasts. School rules, which must be ratified by the students, are based on the Great Law of Peace, the law that the Iroquois Confederacy established to guide their spiritual and political life. Under the Great Law, there must be three warnings before any punishment is given.

Many of the Mohawk school children are as young as seven or eight when their parents begin to teach them about guns. Some become warriors at the age of thirteen or fourteen. A young boy named Rorhare, for example, is the son of Kahentiiosta and her husband, a Kahnawake warrior. He is only seven years old, a chubby boy with long black hair, but already he wears camouflage pants, just like his father. Soon he will be ready for his first gun. His mother says she is ready to start him on a .22-calibre rifle.

Rorhare is planning to become a warrior when he turns thirteen. Throughout his young life, he has watched his father get up in the middle of the night to put on his camouflage gear, pick up his rifle, and go out to confront the police. "My father is a warrior," he explains. "The warriors are my father's friends. They protect the Indians. If you're nice to them, they'll be nice to you. But if anybody takes a gun and tries to shoot them, they'll shoot back."

Even without any formal training, the Mohawk children soon absorb the military atmosphere at Kahnawake. The warriors conduct patrols of the reserve to guard against police incursions, and whenever there is a crisis — a police raid or a confrontation with the riot squad — the Mohawks are instantly mobilized on two-way radios. Hundreds of them can jump into their cars and race to the scene of a conflict within minutes. Hundreds of homes in Kahnawake are equipped with a police scanner and a CB radio or a two-way mobile radio. It is a sophisticated system of communications that keeps everyone on twenty-four-hour alert.

After the summer of 1990, when the barricades were dismantled, the Quebec police and the RCMP gained control of half of the Kahnawake territory. But the Mohawks prevented the police from entering the village at the heart of the reserve, where the majority of the six thousand residents live. They established a checkpoint at each entrance to the village, and they planted nails on the highways as booby traps for the police vehicles. Today, the warriors man the checkpoints around-the-clock, sitting in small huts and watching for any sign of a police incursion into the village. All non-residents are required to stop at the checkpoints to state their business. At the main checkpoint, on Highway 207, a blinding white spotlight is directed at every motorist who enters at night. A pile of rocks is stacked on a table near the hut in case the Mohawks need ammunition. The warriors keep their guns inside their homes in the village, but the weapons are readily available if necessary.

The signs of war are visible everywhere in Kahnawake. The Mohawks hold parades through the centre of their village whenever a warrior is released from prison. Warrior flags flutter over the checkpoints at the entrance to the village. The Mohawks often wear camouflage gear in the summer, and they switch to arctic camouflage clothing in the winter. Many of the warriors have gas masks to protect themselves from tear gas attacks. At the Mohawk flea market on Highway 138, several booths sell camouflage gear and warrior sweatshirts. A full outfit for a child is selling for thirty dollars. One booth specializes in military surplus equipment, including gas masks and billy clubs.

The embers of the militant nationalism now blazing at Kahnawake have smouldered in the community for more than three hundred years. Kahnawake was born in the seventeenth century as a French Jesuit settlement for Mohawks who had been converted to Catholicism. They were known as the "praying Indians" because of their loyalty to the Jesuit missionaries. In 1716, after several relocations, they ended up at the present-day site of Kahnawake (called Sault St-Louis by the French) on the south shore of the St. Lawrence River near the Lachine Rapids. Despite their conversion to Catholicism, they never abandoned their belief in the Mohawk nation. They retained the traditional Mohawk structure of three clans (the Turtle, Wolf, and Bear clans) and continued to respect their Longhouse faithkeepers and war chiefs.

The Kahnawake Mohawks were successful as fur traders and warriors in the eighteenth and nineteenth centuries. But as the city of Montreal grew rapidly around the Mohawk community (which was officially regarded as a reserve after the Indian Act of 1876), Kahnawake began to suffer the pressures of urbanization and assimilation. By the twentieth century, Kahnawake was hemmed in by the skyscrapers of Montreal to the north and the fast-growing suburb of Châteauguay to the south. The reserve was soon criss-crossed with railways and highways, built on expropriated Mohawk land. The Mohawk territory was whittled down from its original 17,800 hectares to just 5,260. The Longhouse religion remained alive in Kahnawake, but it was an underground movement, scorned by the Christian churches and harassed by the police.

In the early decades of the twentieth century, the Longhouse was forced to hold its meetings in secret locations because of the danger of raids by federal Indian agents and RCMP officers. Political decisions in Kahnawake were dominated by the elected council. Imposed on the Mohawks by federal edict, the elected council had a monopoly on federal money and official power under the authority of the Indian Act.

Lacking any natural resources on their reserve, the Mohawks of Kahnawake began catering to tourists who wanted to see the Hollywood image of a western frontier Indian. They entered the entertainment industry in a big way, adopting the look of Sioux Indians and joining white-owned "Wild West" shows that travelled across the United States and Europe. Working for commercial shows with names like Texas Jack's, the Mohawks learned the Sioux dances and horseriding tricks that the tourists wanted to see. They performed in vaudeville exhibitions, holiday pageants, and at conventions.

Many of the Mohawks had ramshackle booths in their front yards to sell souvenirs, mostly made in Japan, to tourists who visited the reserve. One entrepreneur, calling himself Chief Poking Fire, built a fake Indian village at Kahnawake to attract tourist dollars. His performers, dressed in the beaded buckskins and feather headdresses of the Sioux, put on "rain dances" to please the customers. Another Mohawk, who called himself Chief White Eagle, built two totem poles and an elm-bark teepee in his front yard. "Stop! & Pow Wow With Me," the sign on the teepee said. "Chief White Eagle. Indian Medicine Man." In reality, teepees and totem poles were completely foreign to the Mohawk culture, but the phoney image was a money-making enterprise in a community that had few other economic opportunities.

For most of the twentieth century, the spirit of Mohawk nationalism was suppressed, kept alive only by the Longhouse and a handful of militant traditionalists. Too divided to mount any effective resistance to the construction of the St. Lawrence Seaway in the late 1950s, the Kahnawake Mohawks lost about five hundred hectares of land in the federal expropriation, and dozens lost their homes when a deep trench for the seaway was dynamited and bulldozed through the edge of the reserve. Six of the Mohawks refused to move, but they were eventually evicted. The most stubborn of the evicted Mohawks was

Louis Diabo, who stayed in his home even as dynamite blasts rocked the surrounding area. He refused to leave until he was offered a $70,000 settlement.

The seaway expropriation, which was bitterly resented by the Kahnawake Mohawks, helped revive the nationalist movement and rebuild the popularity of the Longhouse. In the 1960s and 1970s, a growing number of young Mohawks abandoned the Catholic or Protestant faith of their parents and converted to the Longhouse religion. They were searching for their roots, and the Longhouse gave them a sense of cultural identity and meaning. It also gave them a political purpose: the fight for Mohawk nationhood. By the early 1970s, the Longhouse had become a powerful rival to the elected council which had dominated Kahnawake's political system for most of the twentieth century. The Longhouse followers began to criticize the elected council as a puppet of Ottawa. At the peak of the rivalry, there was violence. Molotov cocktails were thrown onto the porch of the council office in 1971, and log cabins built as tourist attractions were burned to the ground.

Today, the seaway's massive ocean-going freighters are a symbol of the defeat suffered by the Mohawks in the 1950s. The freighters loom up suddenly, just a few feet behind some of the houses on the edge of the reserve. Vibrations can be heard and felt in many Mohawk homes whenever a freighter slides past. "It shakes the whole house," says Wendell Beauvais, a Longhouse chief at Kahnawake. "It's a constant reminder."

In the Mohawk language, Kahnawake means "by the rapids." But because of the seaway, the Mohawk community has lost its traditional connection to the Lachine Rapids. "Hell, we're not even by the river now," Beauvais says. "We're by the seaway."

During the summer of 1990, about two weeks after the warriors seized the Mercier Bridge, the people of Kahnawake held a community meeting near the seaway to discuss the barricades. One man pointed to the site of his childhood home, which had been destroyed to make room for the seaway. "I wish we had the Warrior Society back then," he told the meeting.

The roots of the violent confrontations between the Mohawks and the Canadian government go back to the early decades of this century.

Although the battles have seldom been noticed by outsiders, this long-running guerrilla war has been bitterly fought for years. At first, the Mohawks clashed with the RCMP, which was the primary police force on all Canadian Indian reserves. Many of the Mohawks regarded the RCMP as a foreign authority, illegally trying to control Mohawk territory and suppress Mohawk sovereignty. In 1922 two Mohawk chiefs at Kahnawake were shot in a struggle with the RCMP during protests against a federal construction project that would have restricted Kahnawake's access to the St. Lawrence River. Throughout the 1920s and 1930s, the RCMP helped the federal government impose the Indian Act on rebellious Mohawk communities. And the RCMP sometimes raided Longhouse meetings to harass and intimidate Mohawks who followed the traditional religion.

During World War II, many Mohawks refused to be drafted into the Canadian army because they considered themselves a sovereign people who were not subject to Canadian laws. The RCMP was ordered to enforce conscription on the Mohawks, and police entered the reserve to arrest any Mohawk who was eligible for the draft. The Mohawks resisted the police, and there were frequent brawls between the RCMP and the Mohawks.

After the war, the Mounties continued to raid Kahnawake — this time for liquor violations, since the Indian Act made it illegal for Indians to drink. Violent confrontations often occurred in dance halls and nightclubs when the police tried to arrest Mohawks for drinking. In one incident in March of 1948, an RCMP officer was surrounded by a mob of sixty Mohawks at a restaurant on the reserve, where he was trying to make arrests. "The officer was struck with a chair and bottles and finally subdued, and a 20-foot-long wooden counter in the restaurant was placed on top of him," a Montreal newspaper reported. In another incident a few months later, a group of Mohawks confronted two Montreal detectives who were investigating an offence in Kahnawake. Their investigation report was ripped up and the Mohawks threatened to beat the detectives unless they left the community.

Kahnawake's elected council formed its own police force in 1969. It was the first Indian-controlled police force in the country, and it eventually won official recognition and government funding. But the Mohawk police were not legally permitted to handle serious crimes, and the RCMP and the SQ continued to roam freely through Kahnawake. There were further battles between the Mohawks and the outside police forces, including an armed confrontation between the Kahnawake Warrior Society and the Quebec police in 1973 when the warriors evicted non-native residents from the reserve.

Beginning in the 1970s, much of the resistance to the police was organized by the Longhouse and the Kahnawake Warrior Society, which were the most militant defenders of the concept of Mohawk sovereignty. But they were not alone in their defiance of outside authority. The vast majority of the community's six thousand residents, including the Christians and the elected councillors, were increasingly opposed to the presence of outside police agencies on Mohawk territory. As the mood of Mohawk nationalism grew stronger, almost everyone in Kahnawake agreed that the community should have its own system of policing, controlled only by Mohawks.

After the clashes of 1973, the Quebec provincial police realized the growing strength of the Mohawk resistance movement at Kahnawake. In an informal recognition of the community's right to police itself, the SQ began to stay outside Kahnawake — but they retained the right to enter the reserve at any time. The simmering feud finally came to a boil in 1979 when an SQ officer shot and killed David Cross.

Cross, a twenty-eight-year-old Mohawk steelworker from Kahnawake, was chased onto the reserve on October 20, 1979, by provincial police who had caught him speeding. The chase ended at his home in Kahnawake, where the police arrested his brother Matthew, a passenger in the car. David Cross rushed into the house, but he came back outside with a wooden stick when he saw his brother arrested. He smashed the windshield of the police vehicle and tried to rescue his brother from the back seat. A few moments later, Constable Robert Lessard grabbed a .38-calibre revolver and fired two or three bullets into David Cross's upper chest, wounding him fatally.

At the inquest, Lessard testified that he had shot Cross because he felt his own life was in danger. He said Cross had yanked open the front door of the police car and was lunging at him. But the inquest heard testimony from nine Mohawk witnesses who said Cross had made no effort to open the door. They said Lessard shot the Mohawk three times at point-blank range without any warning. They also testified that Cross had been beaten by the provincial police in a previous incident.

At the end of the inquest, the coroner ruled that Lessard was criminally responsible for the death of David Cross and concluded that the police could have arrested Cross without firing a gun. The shooting was an "abusive use of force," and Lessard's handling of the gun was "negligent, unskillful and acting without thinking," the coroner said. Lessard was charged with manslaughter in 1980, but he was acquitted after lengthy deliberations by a Quebec Superior Court jury.

The people of Kahnawake were infuriated by the shooting of David Cross. It was a grim reminder of their constant clashes with the Quebec police. The shooting had an enormous psychological impact on the Mohawks. One of the angriest of the Mohawks was a cousin of David Cross, a young man named Ronald Cross who eventually became the notorious warrior known as Lasagna.

After the David Cross shooting, the Mohawks could not tolerate the presence of the Quebec police any longer. The provincial police realized they would be risking a huge battle with the Mohawks if they entered the reserve, so they carefully avoided Kahnawake (except for their regular highway patrols on Highway 138). Although the SQ never struck any formal agreement with the Mohawks, they allowed the reserve to be patrolled by a new agency, the twelve-member Mohawk Peacekeepers, who were established by Kahnawake's elected council to replace the old Mohawk police force.

Few outsiders realized the fundamental reason for the Mohawk conflicts with the Quebec police. The Mohawks are not inherently a lawless people. Their traditional culture, in fact, was built on the strict rules of the Great Law of Peace. But they have always been strong believers in Mohawk sovereignty and nationhood, and the presence of the provincial police on Kahnawake territory was a bitter insult to them. They saw the police as a symbol of Quebec's refusal to accept Mohawk sovereignty. The police, in their view, were a foreign agency on Mohawk territory.

Even after the provincial police had withdrawn from Kahnawake, the Mohawks were worried that they might again invade the community. Their fears were heightened in 1981 when the SQ launched a brutal raid on Micmac Indians who were salmon fishing at the Restigouche reserve in eastern Quebec. Many of the Micmacs were clubbed and beaten by the police, who had been ordered to enforce provincial fishing regulations on the Micmacs. The Kahnawake Mohawks feared a similar attack on their community, and so the elected council, in co-operation with the Longhouse, devised a secret plan to defend Kahnawake from police attack.

The council spent about $10,000 to purchase a dozen rifles and semi-automatic weapons, including M-1 rifles and Ruger Mini-14 assault weapons. The guns were quietly distributed to key community members who were considered mature and responsible — including some members of the Warrior Society. Earl Cross, a prominent warrior leader, was given two of the guns. An internal security force, organized in secret cells, was established to serve as a civil defence network. Every major group in the community — the Longhouse, the Warrior Society, the elected council, the Peacekeepers, and the private business sector — had representatives in the defence network.

Today, almost all of the dozen guns are still held by Mohawks in the community, though the elected council tried to recall them several years ago after one of the weapons was fired into the air by a drunken Mohawk. It was seized by the Peacekeepers, and eventually the elected council decided to ask for the remainder of the weapons to be returned to the Peacekeepers — but only one gun was turned in.

The civil defence network was just one example of the increasing cooperation between the Longhouse and the elected council. Until the late 1970s, the community was badly split between Longhouse followers and council supporters. But as the mood of Mohawk nationalism grew stronger in Kahnawake, the two factions began to resolve their differences.

Inspired by the creation of the Survival School, the Mohawks held a series of community meetings in the late 1970s to debate Kahnawake's political future. The culmination of this debate was a huge meeting in the summer of 1979, attended by six hundred people from all of Kahnawake's factions. It was a pivotal moment. The Mohawks heard speeches from Longhouse chiefs and warrior leaders who urged the community to move toward the traditional system of government. One of the most emotional of these came from Tom Porter, the eloquent Longhouse chief from Akwesasne. "He mesmerized everyone in that room," recalls Richard White, a veteran member of the elected council. "If he had walked out of that hall and into the St. Lawrence River, six hundred people would have followed him."

A consensus quickly emerged at the 1979 meeting, and the community decided to support the move to traditional government. The process was never clearly defined, but the general direction has been repeatedly endorsed by the people of Kahnawake, and the elected council is now working towards an unofficial merger with the Longhouse. The two factions have agreed to work together on most issues. Within the next six years, the council hopes to have a new government in place, free from outside control and based on traditional concepts of Mohawk government.

Self-government is already well-advanced at Kahnawake. The community controls not only its own schools and peacekeeping force, but also its own administrative machinery for welfare and social services and its own criminal court for summary offences and highway traffic violations. The two Mohawk justices employed by the court hear as many as eight hundred cases a year.

These advances are on the cutting edge of Indian self-government in Canada — but they have still been made within the authority of the federal Indian Act, since the criminal court and the Peacekeepers operate under the control of the elected council. Many people in Kahnawake, especially the traditionalists, want to go much further. For example, they want to adopt the traditional concept of collective decision making by consensus to replace the Indian Act's system of elections.

In this traditional system of Iroquois government, no elections are held. Instead the community holds meetings and discusses each issue until a consensus is reached. This, in essence, is the procedure that was followed during the crisis of 1990. Community meetings were held in Kahnawake throughout the summer to confirm decisions about the barricades on the Mercier Bridge and the other local highways.

The consensus approach is not necessarily anti-democratic. It is, in fact, an alternative form of democracy, which offers certain advantages over the formal system of elections in a parliamentary democracy. After an election, there is always a disgruntled minority, and the losing parties are poorly represented in the government if they are represented at all. But in a consensus system, divisions like this are minimized.

All viewpoints are considered, and anyone can influence the final outcome.

Although about half of the Mohawks (primarily the Christians) support Kahnawake's elected council, even these moderate Mohawks are unwilling to give any support to the Canadian government. Almost nobody in Kahnawake votes in federal elections. In the 1988 election, for instance, more than five thousand Mohawks from Kahnawake were eligible to vote, but only four cast ballots. "It's not our system," a Longhouse leader explained.

There is another reason for Kahnawake's refusal to participate in the federal system. Under the Great Law of Peace, any Iroquois who chooses to "submit to the law of a foreign people" is considered to be "alienated" from the Iroquois Confederacy and automatically loses all birthrights in the Iroquois League of Six Nations. This has been interpreted as a strict prohibition on voting in Canadian or American elections, which are considered foreign jurisdictions. Some leaders of the Kahnawake Longhouse believe that anyone who participates in a foreign election cannot regain their Iroquois citizenship unless they are reinstated in a special Longhouse ceremony.

The Longhouse itself is a simple wooden structure on Highway 207, southeast of the village of Kahnawake. The building is about thirty metres long and fifteen metres wide, with old-fashioned log walls and pine floors, heated by two wood stoves and lit by gas lights. The eastern door of the Longhouse is the men's entrance and the western door is for the women. On the eastern side, the chiefs sit with their clans in tiers of wooden benches. Each of the three clans has a front bench for its three chiefs, and the men of the clans sit behind their chiefs. On the western side, the clan mothers sit on the front benches with the women members behind them.

At each end of the Longhouse, there is a wood stove, a symbol of fire. Whenever the chiefs or the clan mothers discuss an issue, the matter is symbolically passed "over the fire" from one clan to the next, until a consensus is reached.

The clan mothers still choose the nine Longhouse chiefs at Kahnawake, following the strict rules of the Great Law of Peace. It can take years for the clan mothers to groom and select the proper candidates for chief. The Kahnawake clan mothers say they look for a man who knows the ceremonies and traditions of the Longhouse, who is moral and honest, and who is calm enough to withstand the pressures of the job. "The thickness of their skin shall be seven spans," the Great Law of Peace says. "With endless patience they shall carry out their duty, and their firmness shall be tempered with a tenderness for their people."

Adjacent to the Longhouse, on Highway 207, is the official base of the Kahnawake Warrior Society. Its location next to the Longhouse is not accidental. In effect, the Longhouse and the Warrior Society are inseparable. From the viewpoint of most traditionalists in Kahnawake, the warriors are simply the men's society of the Longhouse.

From the outside, the warrior headquarters is anonymous and nondescript. Inside, there is a warrior flag, weight-lifting equipment, a room for radio communications, another room for weapons storage, a color TV, a refrigerator, a kitchen, and mattresses on the floor for homeless warriors. There is also a shelf full of trophies for warrior sharpshooters. Each of the three clans has its own marksmanship trophy.

When the police gained control of the eastern half of the Mohawk reserve at the end of the summer of 1990, the warrior building became vulnerable to police raids. For security reasons, the warrior headquarters was moved into the Mohawk Nation Office located in an old two-storey building at the centre of the village. The Nation Office, which is the administrative arm of the Longhouse, contains the usual office paraphernalia: telephones, photocopier, fax machine, and a bulletin board for newspaper clippings. On the bulletin board is a photocopy of the Webster's dictionary definition of Mohawk: a tribe of Indians who were "feared by neighboring peoples for their prowess in warfare." Tacked up on a wall is another quotation about the Iroquois. "I know I would not treat them as subjects," says the quotation from a British general, Thomas Gage, in 1772. "I believe they would, on such an attempt, very soon resolve to cut our throats."

Until recently, the bulk of the funds for the Nation Office came from a profit-sharing arrangement with Kahnawake's discount cigarette outlets. The illicit cigarette trade had begun in Akwesasne in the mid-1980s and quickly spread to Kahnawake. The Mohawks purchased Canadian-made cigarettes which had been legally exported, tax-free, to the United States for sale in that country. Then they smuggled the cigarettes back into Canada (usually through the Akwesasne reserve) and sold them at discount rates to customers who stopped at "smoke shacks" in Akwesasne, Kahnawake, and elsewhere. The Mohawks believed that they were allowed to transport cigarettes across the border because of the Jay Treaty of 1793, which guaranteed Mohawks the right to take personal goods across the international border. But the Canadian government disputed the validity of the Jay Treaty, and it argued that tax-free cigarettes could not be sold to non-Indians.

At the peak of the cigarette trade in early 1990, there were sixty retail stores at Kahnawake, employing seven hundred people in direct and indirect spin-off jobs. The industry pumped as much as $75 million into the local economy each year, creating a booming community as the Mohawks built new houses, bought new cars, and started new businesses.

The biggest donors to the Kahnawake Longhouse and the Nation Office were the community's two tobacco tycoons, Phillip Deering and Selma Delisle. Because of their donations, the Nation Office could afford to pay its employees a salary of seven dollars an hour. Of course, there were no deductions for provincial or federal taxes or unemployment insurance, but a percentage was deducted and set aside in a special bank fund to help the Mohawk employees if they became jobless in the future. Before the cigarette revenue ended abruptly in the spring of 1990, the Nation Office was working on a life insurance plan for its employees.

The cigarette donations also financed a wide range of community projects: more than $12,000 in medical equipment for the Kahnawake hospital, a Zamboni for the hockey rink, a business fund which gave interest-free loans of up to $5,000 each to Mohawk entrepreneurs, about $30,000 in Mohawk-language tapes and books, as well as funding for the construction of a new Longhouse, a Mohawk language immersion program for pre-school children, an anti-pollution program, and an alcohol and drug counselling program. Some of these projects were personally financed by Selma Delisle, who became a kind of godmother for the community. When one Mohawk family lost their home in a fire, she built them a new one. "We never turn anyone away," she said.

Selma Delisle, who is the sister of Kahnawake elected chief Joe Norton, insists that she spent little of her vast profits on herself. "I'm not into big cars, I'm not into condos, I'm a down-to-earth person," she says. She claims that she didn't even keep any accounting books for her cigarette revenue. Instead, she juggled all the numbers in her head.

The cigarette industry also provided financial support for a territorial patrol to keep watch for police raids and other threats to the community. About thirty warriors were hired to patrol the reserve at a salary of seven dollars an hour (about $335 a week for those who worked four shifts of twelve hours each). As many as ten vehicles were employed on the patrol, which operated twenty-four hours a day. To finance the patrol, the Longhouse collected $500 a week from large cigarette retailers and $100 a week from small retailers.

The territorial patrol, which was organized by the Longhouse after a massive RCMP raid on Kahnawake's cigarette industry in 1988, was a logical extension of the civil defence network that had begun in 1981. It was yet another step in the gradual militarization of the community, and it expanded the powers of the Longhouse and the Warrior Society. The territorial patrol had twice as much manpower as the Mohawk Peacekeepers, who were officially responsible for policing the reserve.

In the spring of 1990, the cigarette industry began to collapse. Barricades and police intervention at the Akwesasne reserve soon made it almost impossible to smuggle cigarettes to Kahnawake. The salaries of the Nation Office employees and the warriors on the territorial patrol were cut from seven dollars to five dollars an hour and then eliminated entirely when the Oka crisis began on July 11

Today, the Nation Office is staffed by volunteers, mostly Mohawk women, who answer the telephones and type letters for Longhouse projects. Throughout the day, members of the Kahnawake Warrior Society come and go, arriving for meetings or pouring themselves a cup of coffee in a back room. One of the Mohawks who can often be spotted in the Nation Office is a mild-mannered fifty-one-year-old man in jeans and a sweatshirt. He wears a baseball cap with a picture of a dog on it. His name is Allan Delaronde, and despite his unassuming manner, he is an influential leader in Kahnawake. He is the war chief of the Longhouse.

The position of war chief is one of the most important in the Kahnawake Longhouse. During meetings, he serves as a kind of chairman, ensuring that the rules are followed and the debate is orderly. He also relays information and requests from the ordinary Longhouse men to the council of chiefs who make the final decisions.

In addition to these duties, the war chief is the head of the men's society of the Longhouse — the warriors. He coordinates the activities of the Warrior Society, which include economic development projects (such as the Kahnawake super-bingo and the local flea market), as well as political and military activities. His office, which operates out of his home in the village, is responsible for radio communications among the warriors. If a Longhouse member needs help in an emergency, his first call is usually to the war chief.

Under the supervision of the war chief, the Kahnawake Longhouse has created its own system of justice and policing. Most of Kahnawake's traditionalists refuse to recognize the legitimacy of the local criminal court and the Mohawk Peacekeepers because they are financed and controlled by the elected council, under the authority of the Indian Act. So the Longhouse holds its own trials, based on traditional Mohawk concepts of justice. And it employs the warriors (especially those on the territorial patrol) as a police agency for traditionalists who refuse to seek help from the Peacekeepers. In domestic disputes or other incidents, Longhouse members call Allan Delaronde and ask him to send someone from the territorial patrol to intervene. "If they're drunk or fighting, we'll arrest them," Delaronde says.

The Longhouse has a policy of "zero tolerance" towards alcohol and drugs. Warrior leaders have declared that alcohol and drugs are "slow death" for the Mohawk people. But sometimes the policy is enforced with excessive harshness. In one case, when the warriors caught a cocaine pusher at Kahnawake, they tied him up and blindfolded him and demanded to know who he was. When he refused to say, they beat him with a stick and an electric cattle prod. He eventually confessed his identity, but the torture continued. One of the warriors took an empty handgun, put it to the head of the terrified pusher, and pulled the trigger several times. As he pulled, he told the drug trafficker there was a bullet somewhere in the chamber. Finally they handed the man to the Mohawk Peacekeepers.

In another case, dozens of warriors surrounded the house of an admitted cocaine pusher and forced her to leave the community. The

Mohawk woman was permanently expelled from Kahnawake after a Longhouse trial in which evidence was presented from "undercover" warriors who testified that they had purchased cocaine from the woman.

The Longhouse wants to have responsibility for policing all of the traditionalists on the reserve, leaving only the Christian Mohawks to be policed by the Peacekeepers. But the Peacekeepers refuse to accept the arrangement — they believe they have jurisdiction over the entire reserve. The situation is further muddied by Mohawks who switch their allegiances between the two systems. They sometimes call both the Peacekeepers and the war chief, hoping for a response from either one.

Joseph Montour, the head of the Mohawk Peacekeepers, says he is trying to maintain "lines of communication" with the Longhouse and the Warrior Society. The warrior territorial patrols can be "very useful" to the community and have sometimes helped the Peacekeepers by providing information on vehicles that the police force was seeking, he says. Montour views them as a kind of "neighborhood watch" and a warning system when criminals are on the streets.

However, Montour complains that the warriors have sometimes obstructed police investigations and threatened or intimidated Peacekeepers at the scene of an incident. "They have some members who they can't control," Montour says. He rejects the idea of a separate Longhouse system of justice and policing, which he says would create "two systems of justice" in the same community.

There are only twelve full-time certified Peacekeepers in Kahnawake, and they are vastly outnumbered by the warriors. The Peacekeepers make no attempt to enforce the arrest warrants on the dozens of Kahnawake Mohawks who are sought by the SQ or the RCMP in connection with the barricades and the cigarette-smuggling operations. Indeed, the elected council has specifically instructed the Peacekeepers to refrain from enforcing the arrest warrants on Selma Delisle and the other Mohawks who have been wanted for cigarette smuggling since the 1988 police raid. The council knows that any arrests would spark a huge riot.

In recent years, trials have been introduced at the Longhouse on an experimental basis. A justice committee of the Longhouse administers the system, which in some ways resembles the European model: witnesses are called, evidence is presented and sentences are handed down. But no lawyers are permitted, and the final verdicts are given by a group of Longhouse chiefs and community leaders who are appointed to hear the case.

Under the traditions of the Longhouse, those convicted of an offence are never jailed. In extremely serious cases, they could be expelled from the community. In other cases, they are given curfews or community work orders. Sometimes the warriors have surrounded the Kahnawake court building or police station to prevent a Longhouse Mohawk from being sent to an outside jail. "Who the hell benefits from incarceration?" Allan Delaronde asks. "All you get is more hatred."

Allan Delaronde has been at the centre of the Longhouse revival for the past thirty-five years. His father is Eddie Delaronde, the patriarch of the warrior movement. His brother, "Parr" Delaronde, was the war chief of Kahnawake for three decades. In 1982, because of ill health, his brother handed the title to Allan, who had been an assistant to the war chief for many years.

Delaronde has a long history of involvement in Mohawk conflicts with the police, and he has been arrested in several clashes from the 1950s to the 1970s. Today, as a result of the barricades of 1990, he is again wanted by the law. To avoid the police, he rarely ventures beyond the warrior checkpoints at the entrance of the village, but he remains an active leader of the Warrior Society, playing a key role in all its projects. "The warrior is in the heart of the person," he says. "It's what makes you want to do things. It gives you the 'go' power."

Allan Delaronde is not the only Mohawk wanted by the police. Close to one hundred of the Kahnawake Mohawks are named on arrest warrants in connection with their battles with the police and the army in the past three years. A few, such as Selma Delisle, are wanted for refusing to appear in court in 1988 after being arrested for cigarette smuggling. The godmother of Kahnawake has not dared to set foot outside Mohawk territory for the past three years.

Despite their status as fugitives from the law, the Mohawks feel secure in the village at the heart of the reserve. The checkpoints ensure that they will have plenty of warning if the police try to enter, and the village is an easy place to hide. It is an old town with winding streets and narrow lanes. The streets have no names and the houses have no numbers. Anyone who lives in Kahnawake knows where everyone else lives, but outsiders have difficulty finding the Mohawk residents in the maze of streets.

To help fulfill his duties as war chief, Allan Delaronde has three assistants — one from each clan. His assistant from the Turtle Clan is Mark "Cookie" McComber, a thirty-nine-year-old Vietnam War veteran. A short, taciturn man with sunglasses and a moustache, McComber served in Vietnam and Cambodia for eleven months, leading reconnaisance patrols on the Ho Chi Minh Trail and sometimes engaging in firefights with the Viet Cong. After he left the U.S. Army, he studied the Mohawk culture and worked as a teacher at the Survival School. He has lectured on native education and native culture in universities all over North America — including one lecture at Harvard. He was a front-line leader on the barricades in 1990, and after the barricades were dismantled he was arrested and charged with several weapons offences.

The assistant war chief from the Wolf Clan is Donnie Martin, a thirty-four-year-old folksinger who has travelled across Canada as a teacher of Iroquois culture and philosophy. He is half Micmac and half Mohawk and speaks both languages fluently. Martin is a gregarious man with a penchant for cryptic comments about the philosophical basis of the warriors. He sometimes refers obliquely to the Japanese and Chinese philosophies of war, and he talks mysteriously about "manipulation of thought" and "creating reality." By this, he means that the warriors have created an image in the minds of their enemies that has given them a psychological edge.

The assistant war chief from the Bear Clan is Michael Thomas, a thirty-two-year-old ironworker and veteran of the U.S. Marines. At the barricades, he is known by his codename — Omega Man. He wears his hair in a short ponytail, and one of his thumbs is horribly twisted from an ironworking accident in which three tons of steel landed on it. He grew up in the Longhouse religion, but drifted away and eventually became a heavy drinker and pot smoker. Six years ago, he kicked both habits and began to study the Great Law of Peace again. Now he is a strong crusader against drugs and alcohol. After the barricades were dismantled in 1990, he fled to Florida, but he was ambushed and arrested there by dozens of police snipers. He posted bail and returned to Kahnawake, where he resumed his warrior duties.

Another key warrior leader is a Vietnam vet who goes by the codename Windwalker. He still has nightmares from his days in Vietnam, where he served in the air mobile division of the U.S. Infantry. Every second day, he went on airborne assaults by helicopter. Because of his military expertise, he was a squad leader on the barricades in the summer of 1990; now he is a fugitive from the police. He vows that he will never be arrested. His home is guarded by a mean-tempered Rottweiler dog, and when he travels outside the checkpoints, he carries a gun. When asked about the police presence on the reserve, he pulls out a loaded Colt .357 revolver. "If they try to stop me, I'll blow away four or five of them," he says. "I did it before [in Vietnam] and I'll do it again."

Windwalker's family has become as militarized as the rest of Kahnawake. His seventeen-year-old daughter has served on the warrior territorial patrol. His eleven-year-old son races home from school every afternoon and rushes off to the checkpoints, wearing camouflage clothing and carrying a two-way radio. His youngest son, who is five, plays with a miniature warrior flag and a toy replica of a semi-automatic weapon as he scans the nightly television newscasts for stories about the Mohawks.

Windwalker and his family seem to be fully prepared for a shootout with the police. When they drive off to a community meeting outside the checkpoints, they know they could be stopped by the police at any time. As their car roars away, Windwalker's wife comes out of the house and yells a reminder. "Careful with my kids," she tells her husband. "Make them lie on the floor."

On a cold winter evening, a dozen Mohawks in white outfits are sweating under the gas lights of the Kahnawake Longhouse as they kick and punch each other. A sixty-three-year-old Longhouse chief is kicking a younger Mohawk in his chest protector as an instructor yells at them. A large Korean flag is pinned to the wall of the Longhouse, where the Mohawks practise the art of Tae Kwon Do almost every night.

The extraordinary alliance of Mohawk warriors and Korean martial arts instructors has been blossoming since the spring of 1990, when the Kahnawake Longhouse established its own official Tae Kwon Do society. Michael Thomas, who had studied Korean martial arts in his training in the U.S. Marine Corps, worked with Cookie McComber and other warrior leaders to organize the Tae Kwon Do society. After obtaining the formal approval of the Longhouse, they hired a Korean master to supervise the program. About two hundred Mohawks signed up. Some were as young as five years old — including Windwalker's son, who is a blue belt in Tae Kwon Do. In the spring of 1991, the Mohawks won two dozen medals in a province-wide competition. Their Korean master, Oh Jang Yoon, is intrigued by the Mohawks. He says they have a character he has never seen in the years since he left his home country. "They are very similar to the Koreans," he says. "They have a hot temper and they're aggressive. Mentally, they are very tough. They have a very strong spirit."

McComber and Thomas say they started the Tae Kwon Do program to help develop discipline and pride among the Mohawks and to provide an alternative to booze and parties. But they admit the skill can be useful in conflicts with the police or the army, as well. When the Mohawks brawled with Canadian soldiers at the end of the summer of 1990, some of the soldiers found themselves the victims of surprisingly accurate kicks from Mohawks who had studied Tae Kwon Do.

The martial arts training is only one more dimension of the traditional toughness and machismo of the Kahnawake Mohawks. For hundreds of years, they have thrived in some of the most dangerous occupations in the continent. Before they settled in Kahnawake, the Mohawk men were warriors and hunters. Later, in the eighteenth and nineteenth centuries, they were among the voyageurs who travelled across Canada in great fleets of canoes in the boom years of the fur trade. Then they switched to the timber rafting industry and became skilled boatmen, mastering the hazards of the Lachine Rapids. Because of their legendary prowess as canoemen, the Kahnawake Mohawks were often recruited to lead British and Canadian explorers in Africa and the Arctic, and one group of Mohawks was hired to lead an expedition up the Nile River in 1885 to try to rescue General Charles Gordon from an armed siege by rebellious Moslems.

By the twentieth century, the Mohawks had become legendary as high-steel construction workers and ironworkers in the big cities of the northeastern United States. It all began in the late nineteenth century, when the first railway bridges were constructed over the St. Lawrence River. Curious about these new structures, the Mohawks swarmed all over the bridges, showing little fear of heights. "It was quite impossible to keep them off," an official of the Dominion Bridge Company recalled. "If not watched, they would climb up into the spans and walk around up there as cool and collected as the toughest of our riveters, most of whom at that period were old sailing-ship men especially picked for their experience in working aloft. These Indians were as agile as goats. They would walk a narrow beam high up in the air with nothing below them but the river ... and it wouldn't mean any more to them than walking on the solid ground."

The Mohawks were soon hired to work on the railway bridges, where they specialized in high-steel construction. According to one Mohawk, they preferred not to work at the simple task of laying track because "it wasn't dangerous or interesting enough." Eventually they began working on skyscrapers, travelling from city to city and thriving on their freedom of mobility. They helped construct hundreds of skyscrapers (including the Empire State Building in New York City), often working in Manhattan all week, then jumping into their cars for the six-hour journey back to Kahnawake on Friday night. By the 1980s, about 70 per cent of the employed men of Kahnawake were ironworkers. Hundreds of them rented apartments in Brooklyn, which became the "downtown" of Kahnawake. One ironworker from Kahnawake, Albert Stalk, became a celebrity when he scaled the Eiffel Tower without any safety equipment in a television commercial for running shoes.

Ironworkers, sometimes called "the Cowboys of the Sky," have always endured the highest accident and mortality rate of any in the construction trades. Proud of their ability to walk along a six-inch beam with nothing to protect them from the ground eighty stories below, they have developed their own subculture. "Only men of great strength and courage became skyscraper men," one writer said. "Putting their lives in daily danger as they did, they developed a psychology of recklessness and violence that people in less hazardous occupations may have difficulty understanding."

The cemeteries of Kahnawake are full of the graves of ironworkers who fell to their deaths. Their graves are marked with distinctive iron crosses. On the main street of Kahnawake, two large crucifixes stand as a constant reminder of the great disaster of 1907, when thirty-three Mohawk ironworkers plunged to their deaths in the collapse of a bridge at Quebec City. After that, the Mohawk women forced the ironworkers to agree that they would never again work together at the same site, to minimize the risk of a similar disaster to the community.

But ironworking is still a rite of passage for young Mohawk men. It is a symbol of manhood, a way of proving their nerve and agility. "You can't put into words the feeling you get up there," says Michael Thomas. "It's a euphoria. You're a warrior of the sky. You have to come to terms with your fears. There's not many men in the world who can go to such heights, stand on the edge, and suck it all in."

Stories of their adventures in ironworking have become a popular chapter in the oral history of the Mohawks. Some anthropologists have suggested that ironworking is the modern equivalent of warfare for the Kahnawake Mohawks. It provides the same dangers and physical challenges that were once a part of daily life for the early Mohawk warriors.

In recent years, the young men of Kahnawake have developed another rite of passage. For many of the young Mohawk men, the U.S. Army has become the test of their manhood. An estimated thirty to forty of the Kahnawake Mohawks fought in Vietnam, and another twenty-two served in the U.S. Army in Saudi Arabia during the Persian Gulf War in 1991.

Very few of the Kahnawake Mohawks have served in the Canadian Armed Forces. For a variety of reasons, the U.S. Army is much more fashionable. "Better equipment," one Mohawk explains. "Better training," another says.

The military mentality has permeated Kahnawake — through the influence of the warrior leaders and the Vietnam veterans, and through the civil defence network that mobilizes the community against the police. Military jargon is popular. When the warriors refer to the possibility of a gunfight with police officers, they say simply: "We will engage." When they talk about the July 11 police raid at Oka, they discuss the police tactics knowledgeably, referring to an "envelopment attack" in which the "main assault team swept through the defensive perimeter." The military style of the warriors is increasingly becoming an accepted part of the Kahnawake community, just as the

Longhouse traditions are becoming an accepted part of the territory's government.

Joe Norton, the grand chief of the elected council, has been trying to co-operate with the Longhouse and the Warrior Society in recent years. Unity in the community is his biggest priority. He has regular contacts with the Longhouse, keeping it fully briefed on his negotiations with Quebec officials on policing issues and other matters. He often organizes joint news conferences with Longhouse leaders, and he has worked closely with the Longhouse to establish a lobbying office in Ottawa and a Mohawk "embassy" in Europe.

Norton is a popular leader in Kahnawake, and most of the elected council supports his co-operation with the Longhouse. But some have criticized him. Richard White, a member of the elected council for the past twenty-one years, says Norton is "sucking on an opium pipe" if he thinks he can move toward a merger with the Longhouse. He complains that the Longhouse justice system is "a farce" because its sentences are sometimes not fully enforced.

The Warrior Society also has its detractors among some disgruntled Longhouse followers. In recent years, two factions have broken away from the original Longhouse, criticizing the Warrior Society and establishing their own versions of the Longhouse. But both are hampered by tiny memberships — only about fifteen or twenty people attend their meetings.

One of the most prominent opponents of the Mohawk warriors is Myrtle Bush, a former member of the elected council and a defeated candidate for the grand chief's office. She is active in a group called "Good Minds" — a coalition of Christians and Longhouse followers who are strongly anti-warrior. About two dozen Mohawks regularly attend its meetings, although it claims a membership of about three hundred.

Bush argues that the illicit cigarette trade has been "a great corrupter," which has created a handful of "instant millionaires" in the community. But she does not totally oppose the cigarette industry — she feels it would be acceptable if its profits were shared among everyone in the community. Even the high-stakes bingo hall would be legitimate if the community benefited equally from its revenue, she says.

Myrtle Bush was baptized as a Christian, although she now describes herself as a Longhouse follower. The basic concept of Longhouse trials is sound, she feels, as long as the chiefs have authority from the community. But she criticizes the current chiefs as self-serving and lacking in true authority. Despite its professed belief in the Great Law of Peace, the Kahnawake Longhouse fails to follow the principles of its own religion, she says. "It's like the Devil quoting scriptures."

Many other community leaders, however, are strong supporters of the Longhouse and the warriors. June Delisle, the sixty-two-year-old administrator of Kahnawake's hospital, is widely respected as a political moderate and a former member of the elected council. Her father, brother, grandfather and great-grandfather were all council members. She is a peaceful person who has an instinctive dislike of guns, but in the summer of 1990 she supported the warriors at the barricades.

"I'm glad we had the guns, because otherwise we would have been overrun," she says. "When it was all over, I told the warriors to bury the guns, but keep them handy. This territory is all we have left. I have a great love affair with this community, and it will never end. Our territory is never to be given up."

Despite her past affiliation with the elected council, June Delisle now believes the traditional system of Longhouse government is superior. She supports the Longhouse trials and the territorial patrols. "I always felt there was something wrong with the elected system, but I didn't know what it was," she says. "I want to get rid of the elected system. It will take a long time. It's a gradual change."

Joe Norton has the same goal. He is working towards the elimination of the elected council — including his own job as grand chief. "We're working both administratively and politically with the Nation Office and the Longhouse people," Norton says. "A lot of people in the community want to see this continue. Some people don't like the relationship, but it's not a substantial number. They're never going to change their minds."

Nobody knows exactly how the elected council will merge with the traditional Longhouse system of government. None of the details have been worked out. But almost everyone agrees on the broad principles. The new system will be based on the traditional model of community consensus and clan-based meetings. "It is the intention of the Mo-

might say. In order to be independent, you have to do things that are considered illegal. There's no way we should be left defenceless in this day and age. Nobody else will defend us, so we have to defend ourselves."

CHAPTER 7
Romans of the New World

A Military History of the Mohawks

Hundreds of years before Europeans arrived in North America, the Iroquois people were already developing the art of warfare. It began as a deadly sport for idle men. In some ways, it was a byproduct of the unique organization of Iroquois society. Their farming economy (based on the cultivation of corn, beans, and squash) was controlled by the women, who harvested enough food to sustain the entire culture. The Iroquois men were therefore free to develop their own pursuits — hunting, politics, diplomacy, and warfare — travelling great distances, often leaving their villages for long periods of time. Their absence was tolerable because it was the women who sustained the economy and ultimately guided the matrilineal structure of Iroquois society.

Military conflicts among the Iroquois were originally a kind of masculine game, almost an athletic competition. The battles were undisciplined and casualties were low. But soon they degenerated into a ceaseless series of blood feuds. War parties were organized to settle scores — usually to gain revenge for the killing of a family member. Feuds, which often began with an accidental death, would mushroom into a chronic state of war. Cannibalism was one outgrowth of the feuds, and archeologists have found evidence that this practice existed among the Iroquois from the fourteenth to the sixteenth centuries.

It was in the darkest years of this troubled period that the great

Peacemaker emerged. His name was Deganawidah, and he was born in a Huron village near the Bay of Quinte on the northern shore of Lake Ontario. (The legendary site of his birthplace can be found today in the Mohawk community of Tyendinaga, west of the city of Kingston.) There are several different versions of the Iroquois legends about the Peacemaker, but they all describe him as the son of a virgin mother. When he grew to manhood, he carved a canoe from white rock and paddled off on a great journey.

Deganawidah crossed to the southern side of the lake and arrived in the land of the Iroquois, which was torn apart by violence and despair. They looked at him curiously because he carried no weapon. Deganawidah told the Iroquois that he was a messenger sent by the Creator to establish the Great Law among them. He described the Good Tidings of Peace and Power, and he promised that warfare would be banished among the Iroquois nations. The people were skeptical, and so he offered a test of his own powers. He climbed to the top of a tall tree, near a waterfall on the Mohawk River, and asked that the tree be chopped down. When he plunged into the chasm below the waterfall, the Iroquois thought he was dead, but the next morning they found him alive, sitting quietly by his fire in a cornfield.

The odyssey of Deganawidah was long and difficult. He travelled from settlement to settlement, trying to spread his message of Peace and Power. One day he came to the home of "the man who eats humans" — a notorious cannibal, feared by everyone, who lived alone because his wife and children had been killed in a blood feud. Deganawidah climbed to the roof of the house and waited. The man soon returned to his home, carrying a human body, and put his kettle on the fire. Deganawidah looked through the smoke hole into the house, and the cannibal saw a strange face reflected in the water of the kettle. He thought it was his own face, but he saw wisdom and strength and righteousness in the face. Amazed by the transformation, he decided he was a new man. "Now I have changed my habits," he said. "I no longer kill humans and eat their flesh."

According to some versions of the Peacemaker legend, this man was the first disciple of Deganawidah. His name was Hiawatha. (Centuries later, his name was mistakenly used by Henry Wadsworth Longfellow in his famous poem about the Ojibway Indians.) For many years, Hiawatha and Deganawidah travelled across the Iroquois territory, taking their message to the people. It was the Mohawks who finally became the first nation to accept the Great Law of Peace. The chief warrior of the Mohawk nation was impressed by Deganawidah's strength and power. The two prophets were adopted into the Mohawk nation, and the Mohawks became the founders of the Iroquois Confederacy.

One by one, the Iroquois nations accepted peace and the confederacy grew. In the end, it consisted of five nations: the Mohawks, the Oneidas, the Onondagas, the Cayugas, and the Senecas. (A sixth nation, the Tuscaroras, joined the Confederacy in 1724.) The alliance of Iroquois nations held its first council at Onondaga Lake (in what is now New York State) to hear Deganawidah explain the terms of the Great Law of Peace. This marked the official creation of the powerful Iroquois Confederacy. Historians believe the Confederacy was founded in the fifteenth or sixteenth century.

The central symbol for the Great Law is a tall white pine, known as the Tree of Peace. Under the influence of the Peacemaker, the Iroquois took their hatchets and war-clubs and buried them beneath the Tree of Peace. At the top of the tree is an eagle, watching for enemies and screaming a warning if it detects any approaching evil. The branches of the tree symbolize the shelter and protection provided by the alliance. The roots symbolize the three main principles of Iroquois life: soundness of mind and body, justice and law for everyone equally, and military power to ensure self-defence and to enforce justice.

Fifty chiefs, often known as peace chiefs, or sachems, were appointed to the Great Council of the Confederacy. There were fourteen Onondagas, ten Cayugas, nine Mohawks, nine Oneidas, and eight Senecas, all of whom were "condoled" in an ancient ceremony which included a rite of condolence for the dead. The chiefs became the official representatives of the Iroquois people and were authorized to meet in the Great Council to decide important matters for the Confederacy. Local or regional matters were left to a council of Longhouse chiefs in each community.

According to some versions of Iroquois history, the Longhouse of each nation was led by a war chief as well as a council of peace chiefs. Regardless of their official status in the Longhouse, there is no question that an informal system of war chiefs has existed for most of the past five hundred years. They led the war parties, planned the military operations, and often exercised as much influence as the peace chiefs.

For centuries, the Iroquois Confederacy has followed the rules of the Great Law of Peace. Whenever a condoled chief dies or is removed from office because of misconduct, he is replaced by another chief in a condolence ceremony. It is the clan mothers who choose the chiefs and decide whether a chief should be removed from office. The clan mothers themselves are chosen by the women of their clan. The choice is confirmed by the women of the other clans, and then by the men of all the clans. Finally, the chosen women are condoled in a formal ceremony in the Longhouse.

The Great Council still exists today, and continues to meet at the Onondaga reservation in upper New York State. In recent decades, however, serious disagreements have arisen concerning the legitimacy of some of the condolence ceremonies. Condoled positions have been plagued by confusion and duplication, and some Iroquois communities have not held condolence ceremonies for decades. The authority of the Confederacy chiefs has been thrown into question. Much of the decision-making power has shifted to the village chiefs (also known as subchiefs) who serve as the local Longhouse council in each Iroquois community.

Because of the complex philosophy of peace and justice that underlies the Great Law, the Iroquois were sometimes called "the Romans of the New World." Benjamin Franklin was fascinated by the federal structure of the Confederacy, and it probably had some influence on his contributions to the American Constitution. Karl Marx praised the Great Law because it operated without any police, jails, monarchies or aristocracies.

Under this system, the people are the source of all power. The chiefs are simply representatives, chosen because it is impossible for all of the people to attend every Longhouse meeting. Decisions are made by consensus, and the principles of equality and individual autonomy are cherished. Nobody is permitted to rule an Iroquois community by coercion or divine right. In dramatic contrast to the Christian societies of Europe and North America, the Iroquois have no concept of hierarchy or blind obedience to authority.

To ensure that the chiefs do not abuse their position, the Great Law was based on a system of checks and balances. The clan mothers are always alert for any violations of the Great Law by the chiefs. "Women thus had great power, for not only could they nominate their rulers but also depose them for incompetency in office," the Seneca anthropologist Arthur Parker wrote in 1916. "Here, then, we find the right of popular nomination, the right of recall and of women's suffrage, all flourishing in the old America of the Red Man and centuries before it became the clamor of the new America of the white invader. Who now shall call Indians and Iroquois savages!"

Another crucial principle of the Confederacy is the concept of unity and strength. In Wampum 57 of the Great Law, the image of five arrows bound together is the symbol of this unity. Each arrow represents one of the five nations of the Confederacy. Because they are bound together, the five arrows are so strong that they cannot be broken.

The Longhouse is another symbol of the Confederacy. The five nations are perceived as a family, living together in the same lodge. The Mohawks, the farthest east of the five nations, are the Keepers of the Eastern Door of this symbolic Longhouse. The Senecas, who dwell the farthest west, are the Keepers of the Western Door, while the Onondagas are the keepers of the Central Fire because they are situated in the centre.

The Mohawks were always among the strongest and most powerful of the nations in the Confederacy. Although their population was relatively small and spread over a large territory, their military discipline and skill in warfare gave them a prominent role. Along with the Senecas and Onondagas, they were the "Elder Brothers" of the Confederacy. They held a veto over the decisions of the Great Council and had a tremendous influence on the Confederacy's decisions, especially those relating to war and foreign affairs. Because of their position at the eastern door, the Mohawks were also the first to experience any extended contact with Europeans: they enjoyed the most lucrative trade (and endured the fiercest battles) with the European intruders.

The Confederacy itself had a military purpose as well as a peaceful one. The Great Law contemplated the expansion of the Confederacy to bring peace and justice to neighbouring Indian nations, symbolized in the second wampum of the Great Law by the roots of the Great Tree of Peace growing and stretching to the surrounding territories. If a nation refused to accept a request to join the Confederacy, the Great

Law authorized the Iroquois to conquer their neighbour by military tactics, forcing it to join the Confederacy.

The establishment of the Great Law was successful in its objective of ending warfare within the Confederacy: the five nations ceased fighting each other. But at the same time it broadened the scope of Iroquois warfare, authorizing full-scale wars with foreign enemies. Organized warfare against outsiders became a substitute for the deadly rituals and blood feuds between individual clans and families.

"The Iroquois reputation for pertinacity and ruthlessness in fighting with their external enemies may be regarded as an indirect consequence of the blocking of the blood feud among the participating members of the League," anthropologist Anthony Wallace has written. "The *pax Iroquois* resulted in the displacement of revenge motivations outward, onto surrounding peoples, Indian and European alike."

When the Europeans first arrived in the St. Lawrence Valley in the sixteenth century, the Mohawks were primarily interested in trading with them to obtain European goods. However, that trade was controlled by other Indian nations — including the Algonquins and a little-known tribe of Iroquoians who lived in the villages of Hochelaga and Stadacona near the present-day sites of Montreal and Quebec City. Shortly after the European arrival, Mohawk war parties began to launch raids against the Algonquins and the St. Lawrence Iroquoians to plunder their trade goods and gain control of the region.

By the early years of the seventeenth century, the Mohawks and other Iroquois warriors were fighting the Algonquins, the Huron and the Montagnais in the St. Lawrence Valley. The Mohawks were experienced warriors and they posed a real threat to their enemies. But when Samuel de Champlain arrived in the St. Lawrence Valley to establish a trading post in 1608, he gave military help to his Indian trading partners in their war against the Iroquois.

In a famous battle that took place in 1609, Champlain and two other French musketeers helped an expedition of Algonquins, Hurons and Montagnais defeat a raiding party of about two hundred Mohawk warriors. Following the usual tradition, the Mohawks had arranged the combat in a formal meeting with the Montagnais chiefs a day earlier.

On the day of the battle, three chiefs led the Mohawk warriors in an orderly advance toward the enemy. Champlain simply raised his gun and fired at the chiefs, killing two of them and wounding the third, despite the arrow-proof armour they were wearing. When the battle was over, about fifty of the Mohawks had been killed. The Mohawks had never encountered guns before.

The battle of 1609 taught the Mohawks the importance of some new military tactics: mobility, ambushes, surprise attacks, and guerrilla warfare. Sometimes they would pretend to retreat, luring their enemy into a trap, then turning and charging at the Europeans with short spears and war clubs before any guns could be fired.

Eventually the Mohawks withdrew from the St. Lawrence Valley and began to trade with the Dutch, who had established a trading post at Albany on the Hudson River in 1615. Seeking control of the region around that post, the Mohawks fought a lengthy battle with the Mahican Indians. At first, the Dutch helped the Mahicans, but after four years of warfare the Mohawks won a decisive victory and forced the Mahicans to flee eastward. They refused to let any other Indians trade at Albany, and the Mohawks were so powerful that the Dutch were forced to accept this Mohawk monopoly.

In 1645, the Mohawks and the Dutch signed a treaty of peace and friendship, known as the Two Row Wampum Treaty because the Mohawks used the symbolism of two parallel rows on a wampum (a beaded belt) to represent their relationship with the Dutch. The two rows represented the Dutch and Mohawk nations, each independent and autonomous, never interfering with the path of the other. The treaty was often summarized by the symbolism of a canoe and a ship, the canoe representing the Mohawks and the ship representing the Dutch, both travelling side by side, each never steering into the other and always respecting the independence of the other.

The treaty of 1645 set down the principles of Indian sovereignty which were incorporated into subsequent treaties between the Europeans and the Iroquois. Each side — the Dutch and the Mohawk — agreed to respect the boundaries and political systems of the other and to refrain from meddling in the affairs of the other. By establishing the principle of non-interference, the Two Row Wampum Treaty was following a basic rule of international relations, implicitly recognizing that the Mohawks were a nation by international standards. The Iroquois have never abandoned this concept, even in the modern era.

In the early decades of the seventeenth century, the French and the Dutch had refused to sell guns to the Indians because they feared their own safety would be jeopardized if the Indians possessed muskets. But around 1639, the Mohawks succeeded in purchasing guns and ammunition from English traders in the Connecticut Valley. The Dutch quickly followed by selling their own guns to the Mohawks. By 1644, the Mohawks had enough muskets to equip four hundred of their eight hundred warriors, and the other Iroquois nations also had guns, although not nearly as many as the Mohawks. The new firearms gave the Mohawks and their Iroquois allies "a considerable psychological advantage over their enemies," historian Bruce Trigger has written. "It is likely that it was this psychological advantage, rather than any intrinsic superiority of guns over bows and arrows, that explains the success of the Iroquois."

The French responded to this development by supplying muskets to their Huron trading partners. But the Jesuits insisted that guns could only be sold to Indians who had been baptized, and thus the Hurons were never as well armed as the Mohawks. Within a few years, the Mohawks were conducting regular raids into Huron and Algonquin territory in the St. Lawrence Valley, seizing furs and European trade goods.

The raids were a natural outgrowth of Mohawk culture in this period. Although there was a total of only three thousand Mohawks in North America in the 1640s, warriors made up almost one-quarter of the population. The Mohawks had cultivated the skills of warfare, rather than the entrepreneurial skills that were well developed among the Hurons and other Indian nations. So they waged war, instead of trading furs and other valuables, to obtain European goods.

Throughout this period, the Mohawks won a series of military victories over the Hurons, ending with a campaign in 1649 in which a war party of a thousand Mohawk and Seneca warriors destroyed two Huron villages. This led to the defeat and dispersal of the Hurons, some of whom voluntarily joined the Iroquois and were adopted into Iroquois families. This became a pattern for many of the defeated enemies of the Iroquois. Thousands of Hurons, Eries, Petuns, Neutrals, Algonquins, Susquehannocks and other Indians were absorbed into Iroquois society during the second half of the seventeenth century, thus strengthening the Confederacy further.

After their victory over the Hurons, the Iroquois began to travel widely over a huge territory. In the winter of 1649-50, they raided and hunted in northern Ontario for the first time. They attacked the Nipissing Indians and then roamed the shores of Georgian Bay, engaging in battles with the Hurons and Algonquins. This region became an important source of beaver skins for the Iroquois, who traded the pelts to the Dutch. In the early 1650s, they attacked and dispersed the Neutrals and the Eries. This allowed them to raid and hunt in the Ohio Valley, far to the west of their traditional territory. They also roamed as far east as Tadoussac and as far north as Lake Mistassini in what is now northern Quebec.

By the middle of the seventeenth century, warfare had become a way of life for the Iroquois. Many of their ceremonies — including the war feast, the war dance, and the white dog sacrifice — reflected the continuing importance of warfare in their culture. As they became embroiled in military alliances with the colonial powers, the Iroquois war chiefs soon became more influential than the peace chiefs, who were unable to control the Iroquois warriors. The Europeans came to regard the war chiefs as the true leaders of the Iroquois nations, and it was normally the war chiefs, rather than the peace chiefs, who signed treaties with European officials.

The Iroquois gained a frightening reputation as bloodthirsty warriors. Centuries after the conflicts of the seventeenth century, French Canadian parents could still hush their children at night by warning them of the terrors of "*les Iroquois.*" And of all the Iroquois nations, it was the Mohawks who were the most widely feared. Their name, Mohawks, is itself an Algonquin term meaning "eaters of men." (The Mohawks preferred to call themselves the Kanienkehaka — the People of the Flint.) European settlers and neighbouring Indian tribes were equally afraid of the Mohawks. One historian described the reaction in New England: "As soon as a single Mohawk was discovered in their country, their Indians raised a cry from hill to hill, a Mohawk! a Mohawk! upon which they fled like sheep before wolves, without attempting to make the least resistance."

It appears likely that the Mohawks cultivated this fierce reputation because of its usefulness as a psychological weapon. With a small population and a large territory to protect, they needed psychological tactics to keep the enemy at bay. Even today, the Mohawks tell stories of how their ancestors would torture an enemy soldier while a second soldier watched. Then they would free the second soldier and send him scurrying back to frighten the enemy with tales of Mohawk cruelty. Three hundred years later, after the Warrior Society was created in Kahnawake, the Mohawks still used psychological tactics — including an exaggerated reputation — to intimidate their enemies.

At the peak of their power, the Iroquois — and particularly the Mohawks — were experts in guerrilla warfare and tree-to-tree fighting. If attacked by a stronger enemy, they simply withdrew from their communities and melted away into the depths of the forests. When engaged in large battles, they used a tactical line to co-ordinate their fire and their movements. First the archers and gunners fired their weapons, then the second line rushed forward, armed with clubs and tomahawks.

According to one scholar, John Price of York University, there were four basic reasons for the military success of the Iroquois in the seventeenth century: their greater use of firearms; their "strong determination and persistence in warfare" because of their desire to dominate the fur trade; their development of the new military tactic of "mass attacks on distant villages at any time of the year"; and the psychological effects of their devastating victories over the Hurons in the 1640s. The defeat of the Hurons created "a domino effect of falling societies, with greater strength on the part of the Iroquois and panic on the part of the other tribes of the region," Price wrote. It was another example of how the Iroquois had learned to exploit the panic of their enemies. "The Iroquois developed and used what military tacticians consider to be the basic principles of modern warfare," Price concluded.

By the mid-seventeenth century, the Iroquois were the dominant Indians in the vast territory east of the Mississippi River. Virtually all of their Indian enemies were defeated and absorbed into their own ranks. They reigned supreme over a huge empire — from the Great Lakes to Tennessee, from the Atlantic Ocean to the Mississippi, from the Ohio

Valley to Quebec. They enjoyed a strategic location at the centre of the fur trade, commanding the rivers northward and westward.

Their influence continued to grow. In the second half of the seventeenth century, the Iroquois gradually improved their weapons technology and built up their military manpower. With a huge population now under their control and easy access to firearms and ammunition at the Dutch trading post at Albany, the Iroquois armies grew larger and larger until finally they could put as many as two thousand warriors in the field. They controlled the balance of power in the colonial rivalry between the English and French and played a key role in determining the political fate of North America.

By the 1650s, the Iroquois were turning their attention toward the French for the first time in almost half a century, in an attempt to gain control of the trading routes that led to the French settlements. They wanted the French to promise to remain neutral, as the Dutch had, so that the Mohawks could raid and hunt in the entire territory without any French interference. They began by conducting guerrilla warfare against the French in the St. Lawrence Valley, killing French settlers and taking prisoners as far east as Quebec City. The Mohawks launched a surprise attack on Trois-Rivières in 1653, and after failing to capture the village, laid siege to it. They hoped to force the French to withdraw to Quebec City, leaving the Mohawks in control of the western half of the St. Lawrence Valley.

Because of the growing strength of the Confederacy and the comparative weakness of the French, the Iroquois were able to dictate the terms of a peace agreement with the French in 1653. This allowed the Mohawks to raid the Algonquins and Montagnais without any danger of French intervention. For several years, this uneasy truce held, but in the late 1650s the Mohawks started skirmishing with the French again. By then, after the defeat of virtually every other Indian nation, the French were the only enemy the Iroquois still faced.

In 1660, the Iroquois mobilized a large force of warriors and advanced toward Montreal Island. Along the way, they encountered a group of French soldiers led by Adam Dollard Des Ormeaux, who took shelter at an abandoned Indian fort near the Long Sault Rapids of the Ottawa River. In a bloody battle, most of the French soldiers were killed and the remaining handful were taken prisoner.

A few years later, the French were ready for a counterattack. In the winter of 1665-66, they sent an expedition against the Mohawks, but they were ambushed and forced to retreat. Another expedition of French soldiers was dispatched to attack the Mohawks in the fall of 1666. This time they succeeded in burning five Mohawk villages and the Mohawks were forced to flee. Finally they agreed to a peace treaty with the French in 1667, the terms of which were much less favourable than the terms of the treaty of 1653.

Despite this military defeat, the Iroquois continued to act as middlemen in the fur trade between Albany and the western Indians, forming military alliances with the British in the 1670s and 1680s. But in 1687 another French expedition conducted a raid into Iroquois territory and destroyed a Seneca village. In retaliation, about 1,500 Iroquois warriors attacked the Lachine settlement near Montreal, destroying the village and slaughtering its inhabitants. The incident became widely known as the Lachine massacre, and it has become a staple of history courses in Quebec schools.

The massacre was followed by a series of attacks and counterattacks by both sides. Throughout the 1690s, the Iroquois raided and pillaged French communities along the St. Lawrence and Richelieu rivers, preventing any furs from reaching the French trading posts in Montreal and Quebec for several years. But in 1693, French soldiers destroyed several Mohawk communities, capturing three hundred Mohawks. Three years later, the Iroquois suffered a massive attack by 2,200 French soldiers who destroyed several Oneida and Onondaga villages. Finally, in 1701, the Iroquois reached another peace agreement with the French.

Throughout the intercolonial wars of the eighteenth century, most of the Iroquois nations stayed neutral. In the 1750s, when the British and French were struggling for control of the northern half of the continent, both of the European powers sought the assistance of the Iroquois Confederacy, knowing that the Iroquois warriors would be a formidable force if they entered the war. At first, the Iroquois remained neutral. But in the final stages of the conflict, they decided to join the British side. It was the final blow for the French, and it was a crucial factor in determining the fate of what is now Canada.

During the American Revolution, the Mohawks supported the British. They were led by Joseph Brant, an influential Mohawk war chief who became a colonel in the British army and persuaded most of the Iroquois nations to support the British forces. When the British gave up their campaign against the American rebels in 1783, however, Brant's loyalty brought no reward: the peace negotiations failed to make any provisions to protect the Iroquois territories in the new United States.

Faced with the devastating loss of traditional Iroquois territory, Joseph Brant negotiated an agreement with Britain to give the Iroquois a vast parcel of land along the Grand River in what is now southwestern Ontario. Eventually the 570,000 acres were occupied by people from each of the six Iroquois nations, and it became known as the Six Nations reserve. (The size of the reserve was later drastically reduced by Brant's policy of selling land to white settlers.)

Brant tried to persuade the remaining Iroquois in upper New York State to migrate to the Six Nations reserve, but his efforts failed, and a split developed between the New York chiefs and the Grand River chiefs. Abandoning their policy of co-operation, the two Iroquois groups became rivals and created two parallel Confederacy structures, each with its own set of condoled chiefs. One of the Confederacies was centred at Onondaga in New York State and the second was centred at the Six Nations reserve at Grand River. The division still exists today.

Meanwhile, hundreds of Mohawks had moved northward to the new community of Kahnawake (then known as Caughnawaga), which had been established by Jesuit missionaries near Montreal in the late seventeenth century. After several relocations, the Kahnawake settlement came to its present location in 1716. Because of their strategic location, the Mohawks acted as middlemen in a contraband fur trade between Albany and Montreal. It was a lucrative business, and it helped the Kahnawake Mohawks avoid the economic decline of the Iroquois to the south.

Military organization was still an important tradition for the Mohawks of Kahnawake in the eighteenth and nineteenth centuries. Despite the influence of the Jesuit missionaries, the people of Kahnawake retained their warriors and their war chiefs, and they continued to be allied with the Iroquois Confederacy. In 1716 there were an estimated two hundred warriors at Kahnawake. The same number of warriors, along with one thousand guns, were reported to exist at Kahnawake in 1751. The French were forced to build a stone fort near the community to protect themselves from the warriors.

The Mohawks of Kahnawake refused to become officially aligned with the British or the French during most of the wars of the eighteenth century. They maintained their independence, dealing with both sides in the conflict, and ultimately helping to tip the balance toward the British. In 1760, a group of warriors from Kahnawake helped pilot the boats of a British army through the Lachine Rapids as the soldiers advanced on Montreal. But after the British captured Montreal, the Mohawks resumed their policy of independence. Because of their military influence and their strategic location, the British respected their autonomy.

During the War of 1812, the British tried to persuade the Kahnawake Mohawks to join the battle against the Americans. However, the Mohawks continued to assert their sovereignty and refused to accept British command over their warriors. Instead they remained neutral until American troops invaded Mohawk territory in their advances on Montreal. Then the Mohawks mobilized their warriors and fought the Americans at the battles of Châteauguay and Beaver Dam. There were an estimated 350 Mohawk warriors at the Battle of Châteauguay and a further 400 warriors at Beaver Dam, and they were largely responsible for the victories over the Americans in both battles. According to a British lieutenant at the Battle of Beaver Dam, the Mohawk warriors "beat the American detachment into a state of terror."

By the late nineteenth century, the Iroquois territory had diminished and their power was waning. The Canadian government was now ready to assert its dominance over the entire Indian population, including the Iroquois. The federal Indian Act, which came into effect in 1876, was the primary instrument of the government's attack on Indian sovereignty. The Act created a system of elections, alien to the Iroquois tradition, and imposed this system onto the Iroquois nations. It was designed to strip away the power of the Longhouse chiefs and the clan mothers and to destroy the matrilineal structure of Iroquois society. Under the new system of elections, Iroquois women would not even be allowed to vote.

If the Iroquois had accepted the elected system, they would have submitted to the authority of the Canadian government and abandoned the principle of Iroquois sovereignty — a principle they had fought to defend for centuries. So the Iroquois staunchly resisted every attempt by the Canadian government to impose this foreign system on their nations. When federal bureaucrats organized a meeting in Sarnia in 1871 to discuss the elective system, the Iroquois refused to attend, but the federal government went ahead with its plan, and elections were held at several Iroquois communities, including the Mohawk community of Tyendinaga at the Bay of Quinte in eastern Ontario. Most of the Iroquois boycotted the elections.

Throughout the 1880s and 1890s, the elective system was strongly resisted by the Warriors Party, a group of traditionalists at Grand River led by Seth Newhouse, an Onondaga writer and scholar who sought to codify the Great Law of Peace in written form. In 1890, the Longhouse chiefs of Grand River sent a formal petition to the Governor General of Canada, complaining that the Indian Act was a violation of ancient treaties between the Iroquois and Britain. Similar petitions were sent to Ottawa by the Mohawks of Kahnawake, Kanesatake, Tyendinaga and Akwesasne. All of them rejected the Indian Act. The Mohawks of Tyendinaga, for example, had held a meeting in 1887 and overwhelmingly endorsed the traditional Longhouse system of government. "We therefore do not want our Council Fire extinguished, because it was the custom and manner of our forefathers," they told the federal government.

In their petitions, the Mohawks reminded the Canadian government that the British Crown had signed treaties with the Iroquois, recognizing the sovereignty of the Iroquois people. "What is your power and authority to rule our people?" one petition asked. Another petition, signed by more than one thousand Mohawks, said: "The Indian Act breeds only sorrow, contention, hatred, disrespect of family ties, spite against one another, and absence of unity among us Indians. It also creates two distinct parties at the elections. The law was never authorized in its adaptation among Indians."

All the petitions were flatly rejected by the federal government, and a law was approved in 1890 which authorized the Indian Affairs Department to impose the elected system without the consent of the

Indians. But the Mohawks continued to assert their sovereignty. The conflict soon turned into a violent struggle between Canadian police and Mohawk warriors.

In 1898, when the federal government tried to organize an election on the Canadian side of the Akwesasne reserve, the Mohawks refused to permit it. "We have considered the elective system as not being intended by us Indians, and we would therefore return to our old methods of selecting our life chiefs, according to our Constitution Iroquois Government," the Akwesasne clan mothers wrote in a petition to Ottawa. Then they went ahead and appointed a new council of Longhouse chiefs and advised Ottawa of the names of the chiefs.

The Department of Indian Affairs was enraged by the rebelliousness of the Mohawks. "The Department is determined not to allow any of the Indians to set its authority at defiance," a senior official wrote to the federal Indian agent at Akwesasne. "They might as well look for the falling of the sky as to expect recognition of their claim to hold the position of a practically independent state," another official wrote.

The department sent police officers to Akwesasne in 1898 and 1899 to force the community to hold an election, but twice the Mohawks forcibly prevented the election from being held. In the spring of 1899, another election was scheduled. Two police officers accompanied the Indian agent, George Long, to a school house where the election was to occur. "They found it surrounded by about 200 aborigines," the *Montreal Star* reported. "They were refused admittance and a general riot took place. The police were badly assaulted and Indian Agent Long was seized and locked up in the school house. A guard was placed over him, and the Dominion Police were driven away. At six o'clock at night, Mr. Long was still caged up."

One of the police officers said Ottawa might be forced to call out the 43rd Battalion of the Canadian army to force the Mohawks to hold an election. The newspaper said the Mohawks had "fought like demons" with "visions of the warpath before them." If the police officers had tried to use their weapons against the Mohawks, it said, "they would have been scalped by the frenzied mob."

A few weeks later, on May 1, 1899, the police set a trap for the Mohawks. Pretending to be representatives of a construction company, they sent a message to the Longhouse chiefs, asking for a meeting at the Indian agent's office to discuss the possible purchase of some stone for a bridge. When the chiefs arrived at the agent's office, they were seized and handcuffed by the police. One of the chiefs was hurled to the floor. His brother, variously identified as Jake Ice or Jake Fire, rushed to the agent's office when he heard the news. He burst through the door and tried to free the chief, but he was intercepted by a police officer. There was a struggle, and the Mohawk was shot and killed.

Over the following weeks, fifteen Mohawks were arrested and jailed, including five chiefs who were imprisoned for almost a year. After a trial in the spring of 1900, they were given a strong warning and released. Finally, after all this intimidation, a small group of Mohawks was persuaded to hold an election. The vote was held in Cornwall to avoid the wrath of the people of Akwesasne. In its report on the election, the government admitted that there was "only a small attendance." The Akwesasne Mohawks say the voters were plied with alcohol to ensure their cooperation.

Meanwhile, the Iroquois of the Six Nations reserve were embroiled in their own struggle to resist the elective system. Because of their large population, they were somewhat more successful, and as late as the 1920s they still refused to allow any elections on the reserve. The Six Nations Iroquois were led by Levi General, a fiery orator known as Deskeheh. During the controversy over conscription in World War I, he had led an Iroquois delegation to Ottawa to explain that the federal government had no authority to impose the draft on the Iroquois.

After the war, Deskeheh and the Six Nations Iroquois hired a lawyer to research a court case to confirm their sovereign status. They were alarmed when they saw the signs of increasing federal encroachment on their sovereignty. In 1921, Deskeheh travelled to London, England, to present a petition to the British Colonial Office. He gained a lot of publicity from Fleet Street newspapers, but the British government refused to intervene in the dispute.

The Longhouse chiefs of the Six Nations reserve insisted that they were a sovereign people, not subject to the laws of Canada, and they urged their people to resist any police officers who entered the reserve. When several constables raided the reserve in 1922 to search for liquor manufacturers, a group of armed Indians forced them to leave.

Shots were fired, although it is not clear who fired them. In response, the federal government sent in the RCMP and ordered them to set up a permanent detachment on the reserve. The RCMP jailed a number of Mohawks and raided the home of Deskeheh, who had hastily fled to the United States. This show of brute force temporarily quelled the rebellion, but the Iroquois regarded themselves as an occupied nation, and they described the RCMP as the "armed forces" of a foreign power.

In 1923, Deskeheh went back to Europe to campaign for international recognition of Iroquois sovereignty. A group of Mohawk chiefs and warriors had raised thousands of dollars to fund his campaign, which took him to London and Geneva. He lobbied diplomats at the League of Nations in Geneva and persuaded a Dutch diplomat to present an Iroquois petition to the League's secretary-general.

Meanwhile, Ottawa had appointed Andrew Thompson, a lawyer and former military officer, to investigate whether the Six Nations reserve should have an elective system. The Longhouse chiefs refused to testify at the inquiry because they did not recognize Ottawa's jurisdiction. In his final report, Thompson acknowledged that the Longhouse chiefs saw themselves as sovereign people. "The separatist party, if I may so describe it, is exceptionally strong in the Council of Chiefs, in fact it is completely dominant there," Thompson reported.

"There can be no doubt that some of the people cling to this ancient form of government," he added. "The Six Nations Indians have a wonderful history, and they are surprisingly well acquainted with its main features. They know that their confederacy, though numerically small as compared with the total Indian population, dominated America from the Great Lakes almost to the Gulf of Mexico, and from the Mississippi to the Atlantic ... Today they find themselves confined to a territory the size of a township, and with a total population less than that of a small Canadian city. They feel bitterly their fallen state. Their greatness and their influence are gone. Their history alone remains to them."

Thompson quoted one Indian who proudly described the Longhouse system as "the oldest form of government on the American continent." But he concluded that the Longhouse government had "long outlived its usefulness" and recommended that an elective system be inaugurated "at the earliest possible date."

In October 1923, a new Indian superintendent was appointed at Brantford, near the Six Nations reserve. He was Colonel C.E. Morgan, a Boer War veteran and a former South African colonial administrator who frequently wore a pistol. He urged Ottawa to use the police to tighten its grip on the Iroquois.

By the spring of 1924, Deskeheh had won the support of diplomats from Persia, Estonia, Ireland and Panama, who presented the Iroquois case before the League of Nations. The British, resorting to a campaign of backroom arm-twisting and threats of serious diplomatic consequences, persuaded these countries to abandon their efforts, but the entire incident was annoying to Ottawa. And so in September of 1924, the federal government passed an order-in-council requiring the Indian Act to be fully applied to the Six Nations reserve.

A few weeks later, Colonel Morgan arrived at the Six Nations council house to enforce the order. Accompanied by twenty police officers with guns, he interrupted a meeting of the Longhouse chiefs and announced that the Longhouse government had been abolished. The police expelled the traditional chiefs, broke open their safe and seized the legal records of the Iroquois, including their wampum belts — the symbols of Iroquois government. And the police burst into homes on the reserve to remove loose wampum which might be used to make new wampum belts.

An election was finally held in October of 1924, but few of the Iroquois participated. Several months later, Deskeheh fell sick and returned to North America. In his final speech, in a radio broadcast on March 10, 1925, he remained defiant. "An enemy's foot is on our country," he said. "The governments of Washington and Ottawa have a silent partnership of policy. It is aimed to break up every tribe of Redmen so as to dominate every acre of their territory. Over in Ottawa, they call that policy 'Indian Advancement.' Over in Washington, they call it 'Assimilation.' We who would be the helpless victims say it is tyranny. If this must go on to the bitter end, we would rather that you come with your guns and poison gases and get rid of us that way. Do it openly and above board. Do away with the pretense that you have the right to subjugate us to your will."

Within three months, Deskeheh had died. At his funeral, Iroquois leaders urged their people to continue his work. The RCMP monitored the funeral and interrogated some of the participants later to get translations of the speeches.

The Six Nations Iroquois did continue to lobby for recognition of their sovereignty, and in 1928, three years after Deskeheh's death, they hired lawyers and issued a declaration of independence. The Mohawks held secret meetings to plot a strategy for asserting their sovereignty, but the RCMP planted a spy at their meetings and monitored their tactics.

Elections were held regularly at the Six Nations reserve and other Iroquois communities in Canada, but few people ever voted. Ottawa began funding the elected councils and allowing them to control all federal grants and financial programs on the reserves, yet the elected councillors failed to gain any legitimacy. It was the Longhouse chiefs who continued to exercise authority on the reserves, since most people regarded the elected councils as puppets of the federal government. At the Akwesasne reserve, as few as 20 people voted in elections where several thousand people were eligible to cast ballots. At Six Nations, only 53 of 3,600 eligible voters participated in an election in 1957. In other elections at Six Nations, no more than a few hundred of the Iroquois have cast ballots.

Throughout the twentieth century, the Iroquois consistently asserted their sovereignty. Time and time again, they petitioned Ottawa and London to remove the elected system and restore the Longhouse system of government. They issued their own Iroquois passports, which were eventually accepted by more than twenty countries around the world. In 1926, a judge in Philadelphia declared that the Iroquois had the right to travel freely across the border between Canada and the United States because they were "a nation within a nation." In 1930, an Iroquois delegation travelled to Britain and appeared before a parliamentary committee to argue their case for sovereignty. And in 1945, another Iroquois delegation made a submission to the United Nations. "As a nation, we appeal to the conscience of the democratic nations for action to correct the deep injustice under which we are suffering," the Iroquois told the United Nations.

Their efforts were largely unrewarded, however, as the Canadian government still refused to recognize the authority of the Longhouse government. So the Iroquois decided to take matters into their own hands. On March 5, 1959, a group of about 1,300 Iroquois people — led by a group calling itself the Mohawk Warriors — marched to the council house at Six Nations. The elected councillors, who were holding a locked-door meeting at the time, fled out the back door while the Iroquois were removing the front door from its hinges.

After seizing the council house, the group called a community meeting. About five thousand people, including Christians as well as Longhouse followers, came to hear the speeches. One of the most powerful speeches was given by Mad Bear, a famous Tuscarora leader who travelled frequently to Iroquois reserves across the continent. After the meeting, the Iroquois drafted a proclamation and nailed it to the door of the council house. It abolished the elected council, restored the Longhouse council, and appointed a 133-member Iroquois police force to replace the RCMP. The new police force began patrolling the reserve and arresting motorists for traffic infractions.

Six days later, the federal government ordered the Iroquois police to stop making arrests. "I must further inform you that steps will be taken without delay to restore and maintain peace and order on the Six Nations reserve," Citizenship Minister Ellen Fairclough told the Iroquois in a telegram. The warning was ignored. "She can go and jump in the lake," Mad Bear told a meeting on the reserve.

A day later, at three o'clock in the morning, sixty RCMP officers attacked the council house, where about 130 people had gathered to resist the expected raid. A riot quickly developed, led by the Iroquois women, who tried to push the police out. As television cameras recorded the scene, the police clubbed the Iroquois and dragged them out of the council house.

The events of 1959 were proof that the warrior tradition was still alive. For almost a century, the federal government had been trying to extinguish the threat of Iroquois nationalism. The government passed special laws to destroy the Longhouse system, installed puppet governments to replace the traditional chiefs, and ordered the RCMP to crush the Iroquois rebels with brutal tactics. Yet the Iroquois never surrendered their sovereignty. With the Mohawks at the vanguard of the battle, the nations of the Iroquois Confederacy stubbornly fought any attempt to restrict their independence, and they defended their territory and their political institutions with every possible tactic —

including violence when it was considered necessary. Although few Canadians were aware of it, a war of independence was being waged in the Mohawk communities of Ontario and Quebec. Over the next several decades, the mood of Mohawk militancy would continue to intensify, and a new generation of warriors would revive the military strategies and psychological tactics that their ancestors had introduced so successfully.

CHAPTER 8

The Psychology of Fear

The Rise of the Warrior Society

The scene on the bridge was chaotic. Dozens of provincial police and RCMP officers were fighting with a hundred angry Mohawks who had seized the Seaway International Bridge on Cornwall Island. The Mohawks were throwing their bodies in front of trucks that were trying to clear away the blockade. At the centre of the pandemonium was a fifteen-year-old Mohawk youth, a short kid with long blond hair. When the Mohawks seized the bridge, he had driven a station wagon into the middle of the bridge to block traffic. Now he was lying on the floor of the vehicle as the police officers tried to push it away. Every time the cops pushed the station wagon, the youth pulled on the emergency brake. Then he would release the brake as the crowd of Mohawks shoved the vehicle back toward the cops. The police kept pleading with the blond kid to get out of the car, but he refused to leave. The Mohawks tried to convince the police that the teenager was deaf. It didn't work. The blond kid was arrested and hauled away.

It was December 18, 1968, and the history of Mohawk militancy had shifted to a new level of intensity. From now on, the Mohawks would not wait for the authorities to attack their communities. They had decided to go on the offensive, to assert their sovereignty by setting up barricades and repossessing their traditional land. The takeover of the Seaway International Bridge, which crossed the Akwesasne reserve as it connected Canada and the United States near Cornwall, was a crucial event in modern Mohawk history.

The blockade, designed to protest Canada's decision to levy customs duties on goods carried across the international border by Mohawks, had been carefully planned for weeks in advance. It finally ended when the RCMP and the Ontario Provincial Police stormed onto the bridge and arrested forty-eight Mohawks. But the arrests failed to quell the rebellious mood. The bridge incident was quickly followed by a series of other confrontations between Mohawks and legal authorities in both Canada and the United States.

The blond kid on the bridge was a young firebrand named Paul Delaronde. His arrest that day was the first in his life, and the first in a long series. Over the next twenty-three years, he would be arrested so often he would lose track of the number.

Delaronde and two of his Mohawk buddies had walked and jogged for sixteen hours to reach the Seaway International Bridge. They were among a contingent of young militants from Kahnawake who had joined the crowd of Akwesasne Mohawks in the seizure of the bridge. Though he was still only a teenager, controversy seemed to follow Paul Delaronde everywhere. At a high school in Châteauguay, where most of Kahnawake's teenagers went to school in 1968, he was the only Mohawk who refused to cut his hair and wear the school uniform. All the other Mohawks were amazed at his acts of defiance. The teachers kept sending him home from school because of his challenges to their authority, but the punishment had little effect.

Delaronde was always arguing with a history teacher who tried to deliver the standard version of local history, laced with tales of the savage Iroquois and their brutal massacres of innocent whites. The teenager kept trying to give the Iroquois point of view. Finally the teacher exploded at the rebellious kid: "I'm the teacher, you're the student!"

"Yeah?" the teenager responded. "Well, I'm the Iroquois."

He was eventually sent to the office of the school principal, who prohibited him from attending any more Iroquois history classes.

The blond kid was the grandson of Eddie Delaronde, a Longhouse chief who became the patriarch of a huge family of activists and militants. Eddie had seven sons, seven daughters, and countless grandchildren and great-grandchildren, almost all of whom became prominent in the warrior movement at Kahnawake. Two of his sons became war chiefs at the Kahnawake Longhouse, and many of his other descendants became warriors. If anyone can be called the father of the Warrior Society, it is Eddie Delaronde. He is still alive today, a ninety-year-old man who lives quietly at the repossessed Mohawk territory of Ganienkeh in upper New York State.

As a child, Paul Delaronde was surrounded by Longhouse old-timers. He listened to their stories and peppered them with questions. When he was sent to bed, he would sit at the top of the stairs so he could keep listening to the conversation of the elders.

For a while, Paul was worried that his skin and hair were too light-coloured. Was he perhaps a white person? But the elders assured him that he was definitely a Mohawk.

The Delaronde family got its first exposure to radical action in 1957 when they joined an unsuccessful attempt to repossess a parcel of traditional Mohawk land in New York State. The move was led by Standing Arrow, a charismatic Mohawk chief from Akwesasne, who established an encampment of two hundred followers on private farmland in the Mohawk Valley near the town of Amsterdam. Many of his followers were ironworkers from Kahnawake who had been constructing a new bridge on a nearby state expressway when they learned of the move. Others were Mohawks who complained that they were "blasted from their homes" when the St. Lawrence Seaway was pushed through Kahnawake and Akwesasne. For almost a year, the Mohawks lived in poverty in an abandoned school bus and a handful of shacks on the land they were trying to repossess.

Standing Arrow had obtained a copy of a 1784 treaty which appeared to confirm that the land was Mohawk territory, and he showed the treaty to anyone who challenged the encampment. But eventually his followers drifted away and the farmers obtained an eviction order. The move to the Mohawk Valley, which had begun in a mood of optimism, ended in complete failure.

Standing Arrow returned to Akwesasne, but he was a beaten man. He was criticized and disowned by some Longhouse leaders, who were not yet ready to accept militant tactics. Soon he disappeared from the political scene.

When the Delarondes drove back from the Mohawk Valley, they

refused to pay a toll on a state expressway, citing their rights under old Iroquois treaties. Their argument was rejected, and two of Paul's uncles were arrested. For the next decade, the people of Kahnawake and Akwesasne subsided into silence.

By the late 1960s, however, a revival of Indian militancy was sweeping across North America, and the Mohawks were at the forefront of the movement. The American Indian Movement (AIM) was founded in Minnesota in 1968, and it began to gain influence among urban Indians across the continent. Other events soon followed — including the seizure of the Seaway International Bridge by the Mohawks. Then, in 1969, a group of Indians jumped off a boat in San Francisco's harbour and swam out to Alcatraz Island, the site of the famous penitentiary which was now abandoned. They announced that they were "reclaiming" the island "by right of discovery" — in a deliberate imitation of the early European explorers.

Eventually about eighty Indians occupied Alcatraz Island. Their leader was Richard Oakes, a Mohawk from Akwesasne who had travelled to California after eleven years as an ironworker.

The takeover of Alcatraz generated huge publicity in the United States, where it was seen as the first major event in the new era of "Red Power." The Indians, who succeeded in gaining a resolution of support from the U.S. Congress, occupied the island for nineteen months. Then in 1970, the White House ordered the Coast Guard to cut off electricity and water supplies to the island. After a long stalemate, the few remaining Indians were arrested and removed from the island in June 1971.

Richard Oakes was shot and killed in an unrelated incident in 1972. His legacy, however, is still alive today. One of his cousins, Harold Oakes of Akwesasne, was a leader of the Mohawk warriors who defended the barricades at Oka in the summer of 1990. Harold Oakes, who went by the codename Beekeeper, was one of the most senior of the Mohawk warriors who remained at Oka to the bitter end.

The political and cultural revival of the Mohawks that began to build momentum in Kahnawake in the late 1960s was fuelled by a new generation of young Mohawks, including Paul Delaronde. They had seen Mohawk dances in their childhood, especially during the takeover at Mohawk Valley, and now they wanted to learn the traditional songs of their culture. One of Paul's uncles borrowed some tape recordings from an elder at the Onondaga reservation in New York State, and after raising enough money to buy a tape recorder, the Mohawks began to study the songs. In 1968 they formed a Mohawk Singing Society, with Paul Delaronde and one of his brothers as the lead singers. It was the first organized group among the young militants, who were determined to rebuild the fighting spirit of the Mohawk nation and bring back its former glory. Over the next few years, the Singing Society evolved into the warrior movement at Kahnawake, and many of the traditional singers became the founders of the Mohawk Warrior Society.

There were seven young Mohawk men, including Paul Delaronde, who emerged as the strongest activists in the cultural and political revival at Kahnawake. By the late 1960s, they were already calling themselves the warriors. Soon they decided to describe themselves as the Warrior Society. Although the term "warrior society" had never been used before in Iroquois history, there was a long tradition of warriors in all the Iroquois nations. There was also a long history of Iroquois secret societies, including medicine societies and false face (mask) societies, which kept their cultural traditions alive in ceremonies and rituals. The Warrior Society combined these two traditions.

Some of the young men preferred to call themselves the *rotiskenrahkehteh*. Usually translated as "warriors," the literal meaning of the Mohawk word is "the men who carry the burden of peace." This phrase captures the original sense of the warriors' role, as embodied in the Great Law of Peace. According to the Great Law, all able-bodied men had a responsibility to help defend their people.

Others argued that the complex Mohawk word was meaningless to outsiders. They wanted a simple name, easily understood in English, and they wanted to gain a psychological edge on their opponents. By calling themselves the Warrior Society, they could create a frightening image for their organization. The warriors needed every psychological advantage they could find. Their organization had a small membership, and they did not want outsiders to realize how weak they might really be. "We capitalized on their fear," Paul Delaronde says.

Weapons were not a significant part of the warrior movement in the early days. However, virtually every Mohawk family in Kahnawake owned a shotgun or a hunting rifle, and the warriors were no different. Sometimes they carried those guns in their cars and trucks when they travelled to confrontations or blockades in the late 1960s and early 1970s.

The earliest incidents were relatively peaceful. In 1970, the young warriors from Kahnawake helped a group of activists from Akwesasne who had reclaimed two islands of traditional Mohawk territory in the St. Lawrence River. The Canadian government had given the islands to wealthy cottagers on long-term leases for as little as six dollars a year. Inspired by the Alcatraz takeover in California, the Mohawks seized Stanley Island and Loon Island in the spring of 1970.

Paul Delaronde was one of sixteen young Mohawks who helped occupy Stanley Island. "We played mind games with the cottagers," he recalls. "We built huge bonfires and yelled and scared the hell out of them."

Three weeks later, more than a hundred Mohawks climbed into a barge and invaded Loon Island. "Some were punching the air with clenched fists and as the barge approached the shore, all burst into a Mohawk battle song," one newspaper reported. "Minutes later the barge tied up at the island's community dock and the Indians swarmed ashore, carrying tents, cooking pots, and two signs that said they were reclaiming the island for the Mohawk nation."

The Akwesasne island takeovers were led by Mike Mitchell, a young activist who later became the elected chief of the Canadian side of the reserve. Mitchell was not a warrior, but many of those who occupied the islands (such as Paul Delaronde) were members of the Warrior Society, and the success of the Akwesasne takeovers helped build their reputation.

As their reputation grew, the Kahnawake warriors received pleas for help from other Iroquois reserves. In the summer of 1971 it was the Onondagas of New York State who made an urgent late-night telephone call to Kahnawake. New York State authorities were trying to expand Highway 81, an interstate route that passed through the middle of the Onondaga reservation, south of Syracuse. Longhouse activists had blocked the construction workers, refusing to surrender an inch of Iroquois land. "The United States ends here," Chief Leon Shenandoah told the state authorities.

The state had tried to resume construction, however, and it was then that the Onondagas called for help from the Kahnawake warriors. Paul Delaronde, Eddie Delaronde and Richard Oakes were part of the contingent that rushed down to join the battle. They drove all night, arriving at Onondaga in time for a Longhouse ceremony at dawn. Before long, the state troopers arrived to serve a court injunction against the protesters, and there was a tense confrontation between the troopers and the two hundred Indians who had come to oppose the construction. Many of the Mohawk warriors had guns in their cars, but they kept the weapons out of sight. When the troopers finally left, the warriors helped to occupy the construction site for several weeks until an agreement was reached.

As the warriors continued to gain strength, some of the older and more moderate chiefs at Kahnawake began to resent the challenge from these young militants. Paul Delaronde and most of his supporters were still just teenagers. "We were outspoken and we weren't diplomatic," Delaronde recalls. In 1972, when one of the older chiefs complained about their conduct, the warriors went to the Kahnawake Longhouse to get an official stamp of approval for their organization — which they received after a brief discussion among the chiefs of the three Mohawk clans.

At the time of its sanctioning as an official society of the Longhouse, the Warrior Society had about thirty members at Kahnawake. Most were teenagers and young adults from the Longhouse, which itself was enjoying a rapid growth in popularity. After decades as an underground organization, holding secret meetings to avoid police raids, the Longhouse was now openly supported by a large percentage of the community. And it was bitterly feuding with the Kahnawake band council, the elected body which was legally recognized by the federal government as the sole legitimate government on the reserve. Unlike the Longhouse, the band council accepted the authority of the Indian Act. The warriors and the Longhouse rejected the Indian Act and defied its rules wherever possible.

In 1973, a year after they became a sanctioned society, the warriors at Kahnawake engaged in their first pitched battle with the Quebec police. The conflict, which began as an eviction campaign and turned into an armed siege at the Kahnawake Longhouse, brought the Warrior Society to the attention of the mainstream media for the first time.

It all began when the warriors discovered that a white family had obtained a quarter-acre of land on the Kahnawake reserve and had begun to build a home on the site. The family said they had legal permission to own the land, but the legality of white ownership had never been fully clarified in the courts, and many Mohawks were angered by the presence of non-native residents on the reserve. There was already a severe shortage of housing at Kahnawake and many of the younger Mohawks were unable to find a home on the reserve. So in early September 1973, the warriors sent eviction notices to hundreds of non-native "trespassers" who were living on the reserve. The warriors, backed by the Longhouse, told the non-natives to leave their homes within two weeks. "If you fail to comply with this request, physical action will be taken by the Warrior Society," the notices said.

Soon the warriors were travelling from house to house, urging the non-natives to leave. Paul Delaronde, accompanied by another Mohawk militant named Art Montour, rode on horseback at the head of the warriors. Six members of the American Indian Movement, who had participated in the famous siege at Wounded Knee, South Dakota, just a few months earlier, joined the small band of warriors in the eviction campaign, and hundreds of ordinary Mohawks helped the warriors.

Ron Kirby, the chief (or mayor) of the elected council, said the warriors were moving too fast. The council set its own deadline, October 15, for the eviction of the non-natives, emphasizing that its own evictions would follow the rules of the Indian Act. When the warriors continued with their forcible evictions, Kirby went to court to charge six of the warriors (including Paul Delaronde) with intimidation, threatening, and mischief, among other charges. The warriors pleaded not guilty, arguing that the Quebec courts have no authority over Mohawk territory.

By the middle of October, almost all of the non-natives had agreed to leave the reserve. Some acknowledged that they shouldn't have been on the reserve in the first place; others were afraid of the warriors. But one white resident still refused to go. On the afternoon of October 15, a dozen warriors arrived at his doorstep and forced him to leave. The warriors, including Paul Delaronde and several of his relatives, took over the house and occupied it.

Before long, the SQ were on the scene. Quebec has always insisted that Kahnawake is within the jurisdiction of the provincial police, and police officers had been patrolling the reserve for weeks because of the increasing tensions. When they arrived at the house, they smashed windows and threatened to fire tear gas canisters into the building. In the end, the warriors agreed to leave — but they fought with the police officers who tried to arrest them for break-and-enter. One of the warriors set the house on fire as he left. Paul Delaronde, who suffered three broken ribs in the brawl with the police, was among a group of warriors who were arrested and taken to a police station on the reserve.

The police station was immediately surrounded by hundreds of enraged Mohawks who believed the Quebec police had no right to arrest people on Mohawk territory. They demanded that the warriors be released within an hour. When the deadline passed with no warriors released, a riot erupted. The Mohawks injured three police officers and overturned three police cars. "Their roofs [were] crushed like cardboard, window glass spilled on the street like crushed ice and gasoline poured from their tanks," a Montreal newspaper reported. The police tried to use tear gas to disperse the mob, but the wind blew the gas in the wrong direction and the police fled. The Mohawks climbed on top of the overturned vehicles and delivered angry speeches denouncing Kirby and the police. Eventually a police riot squad, equipped with helmets and riot sticks, arrived in Kahnawake to clear the crowd.

Dozens of warriors retreated to the Longhouse, where they armed themselves with hunting rifles and dug foxholes and military-style bunkers for protection. Kahnawake itself was transformed into an armed camp, with about 150 SQ officers patrolling the reserve, stopping Mohawk motorists and searching their vehicles. The armed standoff, which continued for a week, had a radicalizing effect on the people of Kahnawake. Embittered by the massive police presence in their community, many of the Mohawks — including some Catholics and Protestants — became Longhouse supporters for the first time in their lives. Some picked up guns to help defend the community.

After a week of fear and tension, the Quebec police agreed to withdraw — but on one condition. Convinced that the six members of AIM were the ringleaders in the riot, they said they would withdraw from Kahnawake as long as the AIM activists would agree to leave the reserve. An agreement was struck and the siege ended on October 23. But it was not the AIM members who were the source of all the trouble at Kahnawake. It was the Mohawks themselves. Their militancy could not be suppressed by police intervention because it sprang from their fervent belief in Mohawk sovereignty and their willingness to fight for that belief.

During the siege at the Longhouse, the warriors had plenty of time to sit inside the building and discuss their future. They realized that their bunkers and foxholes were defending a tiny site — barely a hectare of land on the fringes of the Longhouse. Yet the traditional Mohawk territory, now contained within the borders of Vermont and New York State, amounted to 3.6 million hectares. "Why don't we take back some of our land?" one of the warriors asked.

After lengthy discussion in the weeks that followed the siege, the Longhouse approved a secret plan to repossess a parcel of land in the traditional Mohawk territory. During the winter of 1973-74, the warriors planned their strategy. Four warriors — including Paul Delaronde and Art Montour — were dispatched to Vermont and New York State to scout for the perfect site. Recalling the confrontations with farmers who owned the site of the Mohawk Valley encampment in 1957, the warriors decided that this time they should find land owned by the state. Their battle, after all, was aimed at government policies. It was not a fight with private landowners.

In the end, the scouts chose a mountainous 248-hectare site in the Adirondacks of upper New York State. The area, known as Moss Lake, was an abandoned girls' camp that had recently been purchased by the state. It had no telephones and no electricity — but it had other advantages if the police tried to dislodge the warriors. "Moss Lake was an excellent place for a war," one Mohawk recalls. "It was very hilly, and there was lots of tree cover." Another described it as a "mountain stronghold" for the warriors. "There were huge trees," he said. "It was like a jungle." For the first time, military considerations were entering the warrior strategy.

Although the warriors were convinced that they had found the best site, they held a tobacco-burning ceremony at Moss Lake to seek confirmation of their choice from the Creator. Soon they spotted a hawk, an eagle and a deer — animals with a special significance in the

Mohawk tradition. These were the signs they were waiting for.

To ensure the success of the takeover, the warriors maintained absolute secrecy about the location of the site. As a diversion tactic, they started a rumour that they would be occupying a site in Vermont. Then, in the spring of 1974, they began shipping food and supplies to Akwesasne, where they prepared for the final move.

Late on the night of May 13, 1974, about forty carloads of Mohawks drove from Kahnawake to Akwesasne, accompanied by a school bus carrying their children. Police officers were waiting at the Vermont border — but the Mohawks never showed up. Instead, leaving Akwesasne quietly in the middle of the night, they drove to Moss Lake. It was still dark when they arrived and took over the camp.

About eighty people, including women and children, were in the first contingent of Mohawks who settled at Moss Lake. They issued a manifesto, declaring that they were repossessing a small part of their ancient homeland and that they would "live off the land" in a co-operative farming economy. The manifesto said the Mohawks had a right to control their territory "with no interference from any foreign nation or government." The territory would be called Ganienkeh — "Land of the Flint" — the traditional name for the Mohawk homeland.

On the first day of the occupation, a pair of forest rangers arrived at the gate. But when they tried to enter, they were met by thirty warriors with shotguns and high-powered rifles. They quickly retreated. All of the Mohawk men had guns. "You had to carry a gun everywhere," one recalled. "You even had to sleep with your gun."

State authorities postponed any official action against the Mohawks, but the local residents soon became resentful of the new community. On several occasions, motorists drove past and fired shots into the Mohawk encampment. Finally, on October 28, 1974, the Mohawks returned the gunfire and two whites were injured, including a nine-year-old girl.

The police insisted on entering Moss Lake to investigate the shootings, but the Mohawks refused to give permission, and an armed standoff began. One police officer warned the Mohawks to remove their women and children from the site within two hours because the police were about to attack. The women held a meeting and unanimously decided to stay in the encampment.

Hundreds of Indians — including veterans of the 1973 Wounded

Knee siege — rushed to Moss Lake to help defend the community. Carrying guns, they crept through the woods to get past the roadblocks the police had set up. They dug bunkers, planted "booby traps" of boards with nails in them, and prepared for the expected assault by the state troopers.

The police, however, had recently gone through a bloody assault on rioting convicts at Attica Penitentiary and were not anxious for another battle — especially against a well-organized group of armed warriors. One police commander said it would have been "a bloodbath to end all bloodbaths" and it would have "made Attica look like a Sunday school picnic." The Mohawks confirmed that they were prepared to repel any police invasion. "It would have been just like a shooting gallery," one Mohawk said later.

Five weeks later, a district attorney obtained a search warrant to authorize police entry into the encampment. But when the police warned it would take three hundred troopers to enforce the search warrant, he announced that he would not try to carry it out. No arrests were ever made in connection with the shootings.

Shortly before the October shootings, a softspoken Shawnee Indian from Oklahoma had arrived at Moss Lake. He had been given a Mohawk name, Tronnekwe, but everyone knew him by his nickname — Cartoon. An AIM member and a veteran of the Vietnam war, Cartoon had helped the Kahnawake warriors in 1973 in the siege at the Longhouse, giving them advice on the construction of military bunkers. Now he was ready to provide the same tactical advice at Moss Lake.

The warriors asked Cartoon to organize a security force to protect the Moss Lake encampment. He taught the warriors how to conduct a military patrol, how to dig foxholes, how to strip a gun in the dark and put it back together. And he taught the warriors how to kill.

"They weren't accustomed to taking someone's life," he recalled in an interview. "I trained them to take a man out, any way you can. I made soldiers out of them. I taught them to be commandos. Any military unit would have been proud to have these guys. They knew that if there was a shooting war, they might not come back alive. But they were willing to pay the price."

A few of the Mohawks had served in the U.S. military, but none of them had Cartoon's combat experience. The Mohawks acknowledge that Cartoon played a crucial role in training the warriors. One of them described Cartoon as the unofficial war chief of Moss Lake.

"How does it feel to kill someone?" the warriors would ask Cartoon.

"It all depends on the man who does the killing," he always replied with a quiet smile.

He used the standard psychological tactics of a marine sergeant to train the warriors, terrifying them with warnings of what he would do to any warrior who ran away from a gunfight. "I'll be right behind you," he told them. "I'll see the first man run and I'll shoot him myself. That's not a promise, that's a guarantee."

Even the Mohawk children were given military training. Mark "Blackjack" Montour became a warrior at the age of thirteen when he was given a gun to help defend the Moss Lake encampment. "They tell you three things when they give you a gun," he recalls. "You've got to keep it clean, you protect your people and your territory, and you only return fire and never initiate it."

In the mid-1970s, the warriors were still using shotguns and hunting rifles. They had not yet acquired any semi-automatic weapons. One day, they asked Cartoon what kind of gun he recommended. He said he preferred the AK-47. "You can put it in dirt, snow, mud, give it a good shake, and it still operates," he said. "I've seen one with bullet holes in it and it still operated." Within a few years, when the warriors acquired their first semi-automatic weapons, they followed Cartoon's advice and chose the AK-47.

Although the warriors were outnumbered by the state troopers, they used the mountainous terrain to their advantage. "We were in an ideal position, geographically," Cartoon remembers. "We only had a small number of men, but a lot of them were born and raised in the woods. The troopers didn't know how many we were. A good military man will make the enemy think you have something you don't."

For months, the non-native residents near Moss Lake had been trying to evict the Mohawks with legal action, but they failed to convince the courts to order the Mohawks removed. Eventually the Mohawks entered into negotiations with New York officials, and in 1977 an agreement was reached. The Mohawks agreed to abandon Moss Lake in exchange for two parcels of land in Clinton County, near the town of Altona, just south of the Canadian border.

The new site, which soon came to be known as Ganienkeh now that the old Ganienkeh was abandoned, was not as defensible as Moss Lake because it was not in a mountainous region. But it had one distinct advantage: it was much closer to Kahnawake and Akwesasne. Now reinforcements could reach the community within an hour if a crisis arose.

The land at Moss Lake had been too rocky to allow much farming. The land at Ganienkeh was much better, but life in the new encampment was still harsh. There was no electricity and there were few modern conveniences. The Mohawks built their own log houses and kept a few cattle and chickens. Economic self-sufficiency proved difficult to achieve, and some of the Mohawk men were forced to hold jobs as ironworkers to get enough income for their families.

As much as possible, the Mohawks of Ganienkeh followed the rules of the Great Law of Peace. The Longhouse was the official government for the community, as well as the focus of its spiritual life. Alcohol and drugs were strictly prohibited and anyone violating that rule could be banished from the community. Indeed, some Mohawks came to live in Ganienkeh temporarily to break their dependency on alcohol or drugs.

The Reverend Richard Campbell, a local clergyman who developed a friendship with the Ganienkeh residents, has suggested that there are parallels between the birth of Ganienkeh and the birth of the state of Israel in 1948. "Both are examples of devout people who returned to their ancestral land for largely religious and spiritual reasons," he wrote in 1985. There are other parallels as well, it might be added. In both cases, military training and confrontations with hostile neighbours were a routine fact of life.

As the situation in Ganienkeh began to stabilize, the warrior movement was relatively quiet for several years — until an armed conflict erupted in 1979 at Akwesasne. The incident began at Raquette Point, a small chunk of Akwesasne territory on the U.S. side of the St. Lawrence River. The man at the centre of the armed standoff was Loran Thompson, a young Longhouse chief and faithkeeper who had a reputation as a spellbinding speaker in his Mohawk tongue. Thompson was a good-humoured man with a wolfish smile. He was utterly uncompromising in his belief in Mohawk sovereignty, and perhaps as a result he became one of the most controversial figures in

Akwesasne: a man who inspired loyalty from his followers and hatred from his enemies.

In the spring of 1979, Thompson found a gang of workers cutting down trees near his home on Raquette Point, in preparation for the installation of a fence that the elected council on the U.S. side of Akwesasne had ordered. The Longhouse was strongly opposed to the fence project because it weakened their claim to their traditional territory outside the reserve, so Loran Thompson confronted the workers and confiscated their chainsaws. A few hours later, an Akwesasne police officer and several state troopers arrived at Thompson's home with a warrant for his arrest. Since the Longhouse does not recognize the state's jurisdiction over Mohawk territory, Thompson resisted arrest and skirmished briefly with the police until he was subdued and taken away.

The next day, Longhouse members told the Akwesasne police that their arrest of Loran Thompson was a violation of the Great Law of Peace. The Mohawk police, controlled by the elected council of Akwesasne, were acting as agents of a foreign government and they must resign and disband, the traditionalists announced. The police refused to resign. After three warnings, a crowd of several hundred Mohawks and other Longhouse supporters marched to the police station. The Mohawks rushed in and fought with the police for several minutes. They disarmed the police and took over the entire building, which included the headquarters of the elected council.

Three weeks later, Thompson was charged with larceny and resisting arrest. He ignored the charges. Then, in August, a further twenty-one Mohawks were named in sealed indictments in connection with the battle at the Akwesasne police station. This meant that they were subject to arrest at any time. Those who feared arrest began to gather at Thompson's home at Raquette Point.

Two weeks later, in a massive show of strength, the state troopers invaded Akwesasne. Assisted by a police airplane and a SWAT squad, the troopers arrested three Mohawks, but they did not dare to enter the Thompson property, where a gunfight would probably have ensued. Instead they blockaded the roads and sealed off Raquette Point.

The Mohawks, including Art Montour and Paul Delaronde and a number of other warriors from Ganienkeh, built emergency housing and dug bunkers to defend the Thompson property. A few Mohawks began carrying AK-47s and other semi-automatic weapons for the first time. The police eventually withdrew their roadblocks, but the Mohawks remained behind the bunkers at Raquette Point because they feared arrest. Armed vigilantes, mostly Christian Mohawks who supported the elected council, threatened to invade Raquette Point to capture the wanted men.

The stalemate continued through the winter of 1979-80 and into the spring of 1980. Tensions reached a peak in early June when there were mounting rumours of an attack by the police or the vigilantes. Finally, on June 13, telephone lines at the Thompson property were mysteriously cut and a crowd of vigilantes set up a barricade at the entrance to Raquette Point, threatening to storm the Mohawk fortress, which still contained seventy people. State troopers arrived on the scene, but they made no effort to disperse the mob. At several points in the afternoon, the troopers threatened to enter Raquette Point. A bloody gunfight seemed possible at any minute.

Ganienkeh and other Iroquois communities were in close contact with the people of Raquette Point, and the Onondagas and Tuscaroras issued warnings that they would cut all power lines and gas lines through their territories in upper New York State if the troopers invaded. The Mohawks of Ganienkeh issued their own threat: if the police attacked at Akwesasne, they would immediately launch a counter-attack against the state police in the Altona area, preventing them from deploying all of their forces at Akwesasne.

In the end, the crisis passed without incident. Tensions began to ease, and in August the vigilantes agreed to take down their barricade at Raquette Point. In 1981, a judge dismissed the indictments against Loran Thompson.

Meanwhile, the warrior movement was evolving separately at Akwesasne. Although they did not begin to call themselves the Warrior Society until the 1980s, a group of Longhouse militants at Akwesasne had participated in most of the warrior projects, from Loon Island to Moss Lake. "It was a cultural movement in those days," recalls Mike Mitchell, the Longhouse activist who became the grand chief (elected chief) of the Canadian side of Akwesasne. "It was a movement for cultural survival. It was commonly known as the warriors."

By the 1980s, as many as a hundred Mohawk men and women were attending monthly Warrior Society meetings at a variety of Mohawk communities and neutral locations such as hotels. "It was not an underground operation," recalls Francis Boots, the war chief at Akwesasne. Indeed, the Akwesasne warriors scarcely bothered to maintain any secrecy. When they met in hotels, the signboard in the lobby would read: "Warrior Society caucus."

Throughout this period, the Longhouse was gaining followers on the Akwesasne reserve. Eventually it came to be perceived as a threat by the Akwesasne elected councils, and the community was split between those who supported the Longhouse and those who were loyal to the councils. The split was worsened by the conflict at Raquette Point. In addition, there were deep religious differences between Christians and Longhouse followers, there were political divisions caused by the international border that bisected the reserve, and there were family feuds that sometimes led to violent disputes. Perhaps most important, the Akwesasne Longhouse was itself split into opposing factions.

Into this divided community came the lure of cigarette smuggling and casinos. The Mohawks of Akwesasne discovered that they could make tremendous profits by selling discount cigarettes, taking advantage of their tax-free status. They also discovered that they could attract customers from all over the northern United States and southern Canada by setting up super-bingos and casinos with slot machines on the U.S. side of the reserve. Bingos and casinos were legally permitted on Indian reservations in New York State if certain conditions were met. Slot machines were illegal, but the Mohawk casino operators believed the state had no right to intervene in sovereign Mohawk territory. The casino operators were supported by about half the Akwesasne Longhouse members, including the warriors, who believed that Canada and the United States were foreign countries with no authority to regulate the cigarette and gambling industries on Akwesasne territory. They regarded the cigarette stores and casinos as a desperately needed source of economic development in a community with a high unemployment rate and few natural resources.

However, another Longhouse faction, which was supported by many others in the community, opposed the gambling industry. They saw it as immoral, illegal, and divisive, and they believed the super-bingo and casino operators were corrupting the community by introducing an element of greed and materialism.

Despite this controversy, Loran Thompson wanted the Akwesasne Longhouse to share in the profits generated by the gambling industry. He argued that the Longhouse had already sponsored mini-bingos in Akwesasne, and he could see nothing in the Great Law of Peace that prohibited gambling. In 1987 he negotiated an agreement with an investor from Tell City, Indiana, who was willing to establish a super-bingo in Akwesasne and split his profits with the Longhouse. The anti-gambling faction in the Longhouse told Thompson to scrap the project, but he gained support from three clan mothers and decided to proceed with it.

By the second half of the 1980s, huge profits were being earned from cigarettes and gambling at Akwesasne. At the peak, the casinos and super-bingos were employing 450 people and generating millions of dollars in profits. The split within the Longhouse grew worse, and violent confrontations began to occur. Members of the anti-gambling Longhouse faction were joined by Christians and elected council supporters who opposed the casinos. Roadblocks were erected, brawls erupted, and casinos were attacked by anti-gamblers who smashed the slot machines and fired gunshots into the walls.

At Kahnawake, the gambling and cigarette industries provoked less controversy because the community was more unified. There were never any casinos or slot machines on that reserve, and when the Kahnawake Longhouse began planning a super-bingo in 1986, the operation was supported by most community members. Those who opposed the project did not voice their opinions as bitterly, and no violence occurred.

The discount cigarette business — supplied by Mohawks who smuggled U.S. cigarettes across the international border at Akwesasne — was first established at Kahnawake in 1985. The first tobacco tycoons, Phillip Deering and Selma Delisle, were both Longhouse supporters. Although there was some opposition from the community, most of the Kahnawake Mohawks supported the industry, and dozens set up their own "smoke shacks" on the highways that bisected the reserve. Many of the cigarette entrepreneurs were warriors or supporters of the warriors.

Before long, the cigarette industry was generating a steady flow of money for the Kahnawake Longhouse and the warriors. Some of the cigarette retailers at Kahnawake, including Phillip Deering and Selma Delisle, gave a percentage of their sales to the Longhouse. In 1986 and 1987, for example, some retailers gave seventy cents to the Longhouse for every carton of cigarettes they sold. Almost half of this percentage went to the Warrior Society. According to internal Longhouse documents, the warriors were given a total of about $350,000 in payments by cigarette retailers over those two years.

Flush with this money, the Warrior Society of Kahnawake became better organized and its guns became more expensive. A code of conduct for the warriors was drafted on August 24, 1987. It prohibited any consumption of alcohol or drugs, prohibited any theft of property, and required the warriors to follow the Great Law of Peace. "The warriors will, at all times, be a defensive and peace-keeping force and not an offensive force," the code said. "We will never initiate an action unless so directed by the War Chief or Council of Chiefs with the War Chief in attendance."

The secret document also outlined the military structure of the Warrior Society. "In times of emergency, the warriors will form into squads," the code said. "In every squad, one warrior will be designated squad leader and he will be responsible for the squad and communications with the War Chief. Every warrior in a squad will take orders from the squad leader unless his conscience dictates otherwise. The squad leader will choose one of the squad to be his assistant."

The Warrior Society purchased dozens of portable two-way radios to ensure that the warriors would have rapid mobilization and instant communications in an emergency. The warrior code gave strict rules for communication on this network of two-way radios. The radios are required "for information and direction from the warriors' office and the War Chief," the code said. "No personal names will be given over the air. Codes and code names will be used at all times."

Finally, the warrior code contained a detailed set of rules to govern the use of weapons. It gave a long list of recommended guns, including pump-action shotguns and semi-automatic weapons such as the Ruger Mini-14 and the Colt AR-15. These weapons, which can be fired repeatedly without reloading, can be legally purchased from gun retailers at a cost of $600 to $1,200 each. The code specified that each warrior must have 100 rounds of ammunition for every gun in his possession.

"No weapon is to be discharged while on duty except at a target," the code said. "Weapons will be kept out of sight at all times, except during emergency situations. All weapons will be carried pointing up or down, the chamber empty and the safety on. No weapon will have a round in the chamber except in an emergency situation. Any violation of this rule may lead to confiscation of the weapon."

By 1988, the cigarette trade was flourishing at Kahnawake and the Warrior Society was stronger than ever. The federal and provincial governments were losing millions of dollars in unpaid taxes and duties from the bootleg tobacco. When the Mohawks heard rumours of an impending police raid at Kahnawake, the Longhouse warned that any police raid would be regarded as an invasion of sovereign Mohawk territory.

On June 1, 1988, two hundred RCMP officers swarmed onto the Kahnawake reserve in a massive raid on six cigarette stores. Backed by helicopters and riot squads, the police wore bullet-proof vests and carried semi-automatic weapons as they arrested seventeen people and seized $450,000 in cigarettes. Selma Delisle was among those arrested in the military-style operation. When she arrived at her cigarette store, the RCMP grabbed her by the ankles and dragged her out of her car. One of the police officers held a gun to her head until she was handcuffed and taken away.

It was not just the military overtones of the invasion that angered the Mohawks. They also viewed the raid as a serious threat to their sovereignty. No outside police force had entered Kahnawake in such massive numbers since 1973. The RCMP raid seemed to jeopardize the hard-won autonomy of the community.

Within an hour of the police raid, the warriors had seized the Mercier Bridge. They mobilized trucks and bulldozers to close every highway that passed through the reserve and dumped gravel on the roads to ensure that motorists could not get through. Armed with semi-automatic weapons and baseball bats, the warriors kept the bridge closed for twenty-nine hours, creating traffic chaos in all of Montreal's south-shore suburbs. The Mohawks finally lifted the blockade when provincial and federal officials agreed to negotiations on the cigarette issue.

Although the warriors were at the vanguard of the Mercier Bridge blockade in 1988, they were supported by hundreds of ordinary Mohawks who were infuriated by the massive police raid. Even those who had opposed the bootleg cigarette industry were disturbed by the police invasion. The events of 1988 gave new support and legitimacy to the warriors, who were now regarded as defenders of the community.

It was a spontaneous reaction to the RCMP raid, but the seizure of the Mercier Bridge became a dress rehearsal for the blockade of the bridge in 1990. The takeover went smoothly, without a hitch. From then on, it became an unspoken emergency plan. If the Mohawks were attacked, the bridge could be seized again.

A year after the first seizure of the Mercier Bridge, the warriors of Akwesasne established their own territorial patrol to guard against police raids. For these warriors, the greatest threat was the possibility of a police crackdown on the lucrative casinos and super-bingo operations on the U.S. side of the reserve. State troopers had raided seven of the casinos in June of 1989, hauling away slot machines and laying charges against the owners. Shortly after those raids, the warriors held a meeting at the Bear's Den, a restaurant and casino on the U.S. side of Akwesasne, and decided to establish an armed patrol to keep an eye out for state troopers who might be raiding the Mohawk territory.

They called it the Mohawk Sovereign Security Force (MSSF), but it was essentially the Warrior Society of Akwesasne. Its headquarters was the Akwesasne warrior base, and its ideological justification, once again, was the principle of Mohawk nationhood. Any police raid at Akwesasne would be regarded as a violation of Mohawk sovereignty.

The members of the patrol were paid about $300 a week, financed by regular donations from the casinos and cigarette retailers. The patrol had eight vehicles, each painted white and marked with MSSF signs. When the troopers needed to enter the reserve to investigate an accident or a criminal offence, they telephoned the MSSF office and requested an escort from the patrol.

Early in 1990, the casino dispute at Akwesasne escalated to the brink of civil war. The anti-gambling faction put up barricades on a number of Akwesasne's highways in March of 1990 to try to keep customers away from the casinos. Violence flared at the barricades over the following weeks, leading to an all-out gunfight which killed two Mohawks on May 1, 1990. Within a few hours of the shootings, hundreds of New York state troopers and Canadian police officers took control of the reserve. The police effectively ended the MSSF security patrols — but the Akwesasne Warrior Society remained alive.

As the Akwesasne civil war was raging, another armed confrontation was taking place at Ganienkeh. A military helicopter, flying over the community on an emergency medical mission, was hit by three rounds of AK-47 gunfire on March 30, 1990. One of the bullets wounded a civilian doctor on the helicopter. Another damaged the helicopter's hydraulic line, forcing it to make an emergency landing near Ganienkeh.

The state police set up roadblocks on the highways around Ganienkeh. They asked for permission to enter the Mohawk territory to investigate the shooting, but the Mohawks refused. It was the same policy they had followed for sixteen years — no foreign agencies were permitted to set foot on their territory.

Warriors from Kahnawake rushed down to Ganienkeh to help their sister community. Arriving within a few hours of the helicopter shooting, they helped establish a set of checkpoints and barricades to defend Ganienkeh against any attempt by the state troopers to enter the territory. The Mohawks denied they had fired any shots at the helicopter and Mario Cuomo, the governor of New York, hinted that the gunshots might have been fired by local residents who were trying to discredit the Mohawks.

Cuomo had developed a good working relationship with the Ganienkeh Mohawks over the previous fourteen years. As the New York secretary of state, he had negotiated with them when they were still at Moss Lake. A number of the warrior leaders — including Paul Delaronde and Art Montour — were invited to Cuomo's inauguration when he became governor.

Despite the Mohawk denials and the hints from the governor, the state police insisted that the gunshots had come from a building in Ganienkeh. They gave deadlines and ultimatums to the Mohawks who manned the barricades, but the warriors refused to comply. "The potential for violence was very high," one warrior said.

Finally, after eleven days, the Mohawks agreed to let the police enter the territory — but only to search one building for a two-hour period. The troopers seemed to find little evidence at the site, and no charges were laid in connection with the shooting.

However, warrants were issued for the arrest of sixteen Mohawks in connection with the barricade activity at Ganienkeh. They were charged with illegal use of firearms, assaulting police officers who were executing a search warrant, and resisting the execution of a search warrant. Only a small handful of those warriors were apprehended. Some of them remained at Ganienkeh, refusing to leave the territory. Others quietly slipped back to Kahnawake and Kanesatake to help the warriors at the barricades in the summer of 1990.

Today, the Mohawks of Ganienkeh are more secretive and militarized than ever. Their Longhouse is too small to support a full council of chiefs, but they do have a war chief. Everyone in Ganienkeh has a gun. They use cellular telephones and two-way radios for communication, and they have stockpiled enough food to allow them to survive for years if they are blockaded. To prevent any threat of government control, they refuse to accept welfare or government grants.

After almost two decades of confrontations with state troopers, the Mohawks are convinced that police spies are trying to infiltrate Ganienkeh. They refuse to permit any outsider to venture past the outskirts of their territory, and they investigate anyone who requests permission to visit the community. To protect themselves from police raids, they conduct regular patrols of their territory. "We're very familiar with the land here," says Darryl Martin, a warrior who has lived in Ganienkeh for fourteen years. "Our intimate knowledge of the land gives us an advantage. If the troopers come in, they'd have to walk through heavy bush for miles."

After the armed siege at Ganienkeh in the spring of 1990, a warrant was issued for the arrest of Paul Delaronde. By then, he was beyond the reach of the police, behind the barricades at Kahnawake, where he remained a key strategist for the Mohawks during the summer of 1990. Although he was not a military leader at the barricades, he spoke forcefully at Kahnawake community meetings throughout the crisis.

Whenever he spoke, the warriors fell silent and listened closely. He was only thirty-seven, but he had become a respected elder statesman among the warriors.

Early in 1991, Paul Delaronde continued to elude the police. Taking careful precautions, he travelled back and forth to Kahnawake, where he could sometimes be spotted with his four adopted children at the Kahnawake flea market on Sunday mornings. He was still a striking figure — a handsome man, unshaven, his hair long and light brown. The young warriors, teasing him about the motorcycle he sometimes drove, called him "Peter Fonda." But he preferred a different nickname. As he cuddled an infant daughter, he called himself "Mr. Mom." He was weary of the limelight, fed up with the police investigators and media hounds who saw him as the ringleader of the warriors.

For the past two decades, the story of Paul Delaronde has been inseparable from the story of the warriors. It has become a life of almost permanent conflict — a life of barricades and weapons and bunkers. For him, and for the warriors he has inspired, the dangers of an armed standoff are scarcely noticed anymore. They are simply viewed as a normal risk in the gamble of daily life.

The barricades at Kanesatake and Kahnawake in the summer of 1990 were just the latest in a twenty-two-year series of tense standoffs between warriors and police forces. But there was one crucial difference in 1990. Until the events of July 11, the police had always backed away from the ultimate confrontation. Until the raid at Oka, they had never dared to attack.

CHAPTER 9
Food Smugglers and Gun Runners

Behind the Barricades at Kanesatake

A tall white pine loomed over the warriors as they peered up into the thick foliage. "If you're up there, you're coming down with the tree," a warrior named Apache yelled. He yanked the cord on the chainsaw, and it sputtered to life. The saw chewed into the bark of the tree. A police sniper, perched on the branch of the tree next to it, hurled himself to the ground ten metres below, then picked himself up and fled towards the town of Oka.

The atmosphere in the Pines was electric. Just a couple of hours earlier, the Sûreté du Québec's tactical intervention team had launched an attack on the Mohawks occupying the Pines. The warriors, hidden in the dense forest, had exchanged gunfire with the police. As soon as the SQ realized one of their men had been hurt in the exchange, they beat a swift retreat, right behind the ambulance that sped off to a hospital in St. Eustache with the fatally wounded Corporal Marcel Lemay. The Mohawks were convinced that the police were preparing for a second attack. Already hundreds of police reinforcements were massed in the town of Oka, and the police were setting up checkpoints on every road leading into Kanesatake. An SQ helicopter circled in the sky overhead. One Mohawk, who had been allowed to pass police blockades to go to work in Montreal, called back to warn his people that at least one hundred police cars had gathered at Parc

Paul Sauvé, a provincial park just east of Oka. It seemed as if every SQ officer in the province was being dispatched to the Oka area.

In Montreal, Jacques Lacaille, the lawyer for the Kanesatake band council, received a call from the SQ at mid-morning, warning that the police were indeed ready to mount a second attack. They gave Lacaille half an hour to get in touch with the band council to inform the chiefs. Instead, Lacaille called the premier's office. He had already been on the telephone since 6:30 that morning, trying to reach someone — anyone — in Quebec City with the authority to call off the police operation. He made forty-five calls in four hours, but none of the low-level bureaucrats he reached seemed to believe the situation was that serious. Finally, after the SQ warning, he was put directly through to the premier. He told Robert Bourassa that a police officer was dead. Lacaille was not entirely certain that this was true, because the SQ had not yet released any details of Corporal Lemay's condition, but the calculated risk appeared to pay off. The second raid was cancelled.

Meanwhile, the people of the Pines, unaware of Lacaille's intervention, resorted to desperate threats to ward off a second assault. "If our people get hurt, the Mercier Bridge will fall," Ellen Gabriel told reporters. Other Mohawks assured journalists that the Kahnawake warriors holding the Mercier bridge had the technology to blow it up.

Ellen Gabriel was acting as the chief spokesperson for the people of the Pines. Though she was a recent convert to the Longhouse and had no previous experience in Mohawk confrontations, she was articulate and passionate and spoke French reasonably well, so she was chosen to go before the TV cameras and microphones to explain the Mohawk demands. Within a day, the image of the petite, softspoken fine arts graduate had been beamed all over the world, and for thousands of people, that image came to symbolize the Mohawk struggle. In reality, Ellen Gabriel did not exercise much influence over the other Mohawks, but the public image stuck. When government negotiations collapsed at the end of August, the Quebec negotiator feared Gabriel might well become a Mohawk martyr. "You will never, never be able to explain that to the world," Alexander Paterson warned government officials. "She has become the heroine of an oppressed people. All the problems of the native people are in that woman's soul."

Mohawk men who had never set foot in the Pines throughout the spring's occupation — including some who had opposed the protest camp from the start — now stood in the Pines with their hunting rifles, ready to back up the warriors if the police attacked again. Plumes of black smoke and acrid fumes rose from piles of tires that lay smouldering on the highway as a commandeered front-end loader rumbled down the dirt road in the Pines and cut onto the golf course. Its shovel tore a gaping hole in the neatly manicured lawn. Some of the Mohawks cheered and clapped; others zipped around the golf course and through the Pines in stolen golf carts.

A few had broken into the golf clubhouse and gone on a rampage. Years of pent-up rage were vented in a few short hours. Chairs were overturned, flowerpots were smashed, shards of glass lay on the floor. Someone broke into the wine cellar and went on a shooting spree. Upstairs, a group of women helped themselves to drinks at the bar. They were not supporters of the Pines occupation and their drinking infuriated other Mohawk protesters. A couple of the Mohawks spent most of the afternoon pouring bottle after bottle of liquor down the sink, getting rid of everything in sight so it would be out of temptation's reach.

Most of the warriors stayed in the Pines, trying to get the situation there under control. The area was overrun with people, and no one was paying any attention to the warriors' order to clear out in case the police returned. Children, elderly men and women, teenagers looking for a piece of the action — everyone from Kanesatake was in the Pines. If the police attacked again, there was certain to be a bloodbath.

Some of the warriors wanted to retreat. "We'll hide out in people's houses in Kanesatake," one of the men suggested.

"They're going to hit every house," argued Kahentiiosta, a woman from Kahnawake who had come to the Pines with her two children. She made an impassioned plea to stay. "If the men here aren't ready to stand up again, they can leave. But I'm staying here. What happened this morning shows there are other things in the universe helping us. It's not just us, the two-legged that are here. The trees are here. Look how long they've been here. Now we're going to stand up and protect them."

There were about twenty men from other Mohawk communities and double that number from Kanesatake who were prepared to stay — a fighting force of sixty or seventy men, plus a couple of women prepared to carry arms — and more warriors were on their way. Already, more Mohawks had arrived from Kahnawake by boat.

By mid-afternoon, Dan David had reached Kanesatake. He was living in his wife's community of Maniwaki, a three-hour drive away in western Quebec, but as soon as he heard about the police raid, he jumped into his beat-up Dodge Dart and headed for home. The thirty-eight-year-old journalist knew that his entire family had been involved in the occupation of the Pines, and he wanted to find out if they were all right.

At English Point on the western edge of Kanesatake, about twenty police cars were parked along the highway, turning traffic away from the settlement. As soon as they spotted Dan David behind the wheel of the car, several officers rushed towards him, their rifles levelled at his head. It took several minutes of argument before the police let him through.

Dan David drove on into Kanesatake, only to find the place deserted. Unlike Kahnawake, where warriors had already set up barricades at every entrance to the reserve, Kanesatake was completely unprotected except for a kilometre-long stretch of highway adjacent to the Pines. David drove to the back barricade at the north end of the Pines, where he found scores of people from Kanesatake, their cars parked on the shoulder of the road. He was standing around talking to a couple of reporters when he caught a glimpse of his brother on the edge of the golf course. He did a double-take.

His brother Joe had never carried a gun in the long months leading up to the police raid and he had argued against the decision to allow arms into the camp. Now he had a black scarf pulled over his face and an AK-47 in his hand. The two brothers looked at each other in silence. Finally Joe David said to him, "I know. I don't believe it either." Like so many others who had been opposed or indifferent to the Mohawk warrior movement in the past, Joe David had suddenly become a warrior. For the rest of the summer, he would go by his code-name, Stonecarver.

In the afternoon, Ellen Gabriel phoned the elected chief at Kahnawake, Joe Norton, who informed her that Quebec Minister of Native Affairs John Ciaccia wanted to talk directly to the Mohawks occupying the Pines. Ciaccia had been given no advance warning of the police assault. The previous day, he had assured the Kanesatake band council that there would not be a raid and that he would personally intervene to negotiate a settlement to the land dispute as soon as he came back from a scheduled visit to the Soviet Union. Quebec Public Security Minister Sam Elkas, who was on holiday in Quebec's Eastern Townships when the raid occurred, claimed he had only received official word of the operation from a senior official in his office at seven o'clock that morning, after the SQ operation was already underway. The moment Elkas learned that Corporal Lemay had died, he flew to Quebec, where Premier Robert Bourassa met him and several other key ministers and deputy ministers to discuss how to resolve the crisis. During that meeting, Ciaccia was given the go-ahead to negotiate directly with the Mohawks in the Pines.

Ellen Gabriel reached Ciaccia by cellular phone late that afternoon. He agreed to cross the barricades to meet the Mohawks the following day and gave Gabriel his home phone number, assuring her she could call him at any time of the day or night if another crisis arose.

Few people slept that night. The warriors received word that six men from Akwesasne and Kahnawake were trying to find a way into the settlement by road, but the police had every route sealed off tight. Crazyhorse slipped into an eighteen-foot canoe and paddled out on the Lake of Two Mountains, making his way silently past the police who were staked out at the ferry docks at Oka, and going on to Pointe Calumet, a few kilometres farther east. He picked up the six stranded warriors and all their guns and gear and paddled back to Kanesatake. They scarcely breathed as they glided past Oka in the murky darkness. "It was real risky," recalls Crazyhorse. "But we had no choice. We were expecting really bad shit up there. We needed everybody we could get."

The east barricade — by now known as "Main Gate" — was left virtually unguarded. Strategically, the Mohawks had the advantage of being at the top of a hill, and the warriors did not expect police to try to come straight up the highway and past Main Gate. They suspected that the police would try to enter the Pines by sneaking through the woods and across the golf course, or from the north entrance to the Pines, now called "Sector Five." Most of the warriors spent the night on patrol or dug into bunkers at Sector Five and China Beach, a hastily built bunker on the eastern edge of the Pines, overlooking the golf course. Two young Mohawks were hunched down in sleeping bags near the overturned vehicles on the highway, jumping up to peer over the barricade whenever they heard the slightest noise from the lines of police stationed below.

At dawn, a half dozen police cars sped up to the police roadblock on the highway below Main Gate. The warriors at the barricade leapt to attention. Two-way radios crackled to life. But it was a false alarm — a change of shift on the police line.

Most of the homes on the south side of Highway 344 across from the Pines were deserted. Within a couple of hours of the police retreat on July 11, armed warriors had escorted three frightened families out of their houses. Some of them had reason to be fearful. They had pressured the Oka municipal council to clear the Mohawks out of the Pines and had lobbied hard in support of the golf course expansion project.

Lise Tardif, a middle-aged woman who lived across from the Mohawk cemetery, right next to the barricade, refused to leave. She was outraged by the police attack and did not believe she had anything to fear from the Mohawks. Her greatest concern was for the safety of her four prize-winning poodles, one of whom died from the effects of the tear gas soon after the raid. Tardif buried Sasha under a pine tree on her front lawn and placed a wreath over his grave. "The second victim of the Sûreté du Québec raid," Tardif told reporters. The journalists laughed, but the heartbroken woman was not joking.

Lise Tardif got up early on Thursday, the day after the raid, and brought out coffee for the journalists who had camped near Main Gate overnight. Then she dressed for work and walked down the hill between the Mohawk and police barricades, insisting on her right to pass the police line. She submitted to searches each time she passed the police; they even examined the inside of her shoes. Of the scores of non-Mohawks living behind the barricades, few others dared to make the trek down the hill. Each time anyone appeared in the no-man's-land between the Mohawks and the police, the officers on duty jumped to attention and took up position with their weapons.

July 12 was a long, blistering-hot day. Some of the Mohawks dragged a couple of junked cars across the highway at the west end of the settlement, not far from the police stationed there. Men from the community took turns keeping watch. Halfway through the afternoon, four police cars cruised into the settlement from the north, down the highway, and toward the western barricade.

"Son of a bitch," yelled the lone sentry at the barricade, a middle-aged Mohawk man from the community, who was armed with nothing but a shotgun. His eyes went wide with fright. But the police appeared to be just as shocked to see him and the barricade of trashed cars. The lead car slammed on its brakes, pulling a U-turn in the middle of the highway. The other cars followed suit, almost smashing into each other in their haste to turn around.

The incident made everyone acutely aware of how vulnerable the settlement was to another police raid. Later that day, two more old cars were dragged out to an intersection north of the settlement. But the warriors had trouble finding anyone willing to take up sentry duty at that post, which became known as North Pole. Surrounded by cornfields and pastureland, anyone posted at North Pole was wide open to attack.

Stocks on the shelves of the two convenience stores in Kanesatake were already depleting rapidly. One of the Mohawks, Joyce Nelson, decided to try to leave the encircled settlement to buy groceries. She piled her three youngest children in the back of the car and headed for Oka. Under normal conditions, it was a five-minute drive from the Nelson household to the town, but now, with the east end of the settlement blockaded, the only way out of Kanesatake by car was to travel north for two kilometres, then east, doubling back onto Highway 344 east of Oka, passing three police checkpoints along the way. At each checkpoint her car was searched. It took Nelson ninety minutes to get to Oka, buy her groceries, and make her way back. At the police checkpoint closest to Kanesatake, her car was searched again.

"You and your children can go," the officer said, "but you'll have to leave your groceries here. You'll have to dump them."

The officer was polite but insistent. He told Joyce Nelson that the police at the checkpoints had received new orders not to allow any food into the settlement. Nelson had just spent one hundred dollars and she was not about to leave her food in the ditch. While she argued, other police officers trained their guns on the car. Her children, who had been chattering away in the back seat, grew silent. They were petrified. "How much longer are we going to have to wait here, Mommy?" her son whispered. At last, Nelson relented and took her groceries to a friend's hairdressing shop twenty kilometres away.

That's when it first dawned on the Kanesatake Mohawks that the SQ's strategy was to starve them out of the settlement. The Quebec Human Rights Commission later confirmed the Mohawk version of events. On July 13, an SQ officer told a Commission official that there was no question of allowing "individuals of native origin" to cross the police barricades with provisions. At the same time, the SQ refused to permit the Commission's representative to enter Oka or Kanesatake to investigate the situation — in defiance of the Quebec Charter of Rights and Freedoms.

The police had the same orders for medical supplies. One pregnant Mohawk woman spent several minutes convincing an SQ officer that the pills she was carrying were not illicit drugs, but iron supplements. There were several diabetics behind the barricades, including one of the Kahnawake warriors in the Pines, and many elderly people were on medication. A couple of days after the raid, the head of the Kanesatake emergency medical service, Ronny Bonspille, arranged for a sympathetic pharmacist to meet his son Bobby outside Oka with twenty-one prescriptions he had phoned in. Heading back to Kanesatake with the medication, Bobby Bonspille's ambulance was stopped and the young driver was detained, accused by police of smuggling drugs. After four hours, he was released and allowed to return home with the medication.

The human rights abuses by police at the checkpoints multiplied as the summer progressed. One young Mohawk couple was strip-searched in full view of the road. A Mohawk man complained that the interior of his car was ripped apart during an arbitrary search. The behaviour of the SQ officers at the checkpoints was unpredictable: often, Mohawks were treated politely; at other times, they had guns pointed at their heads, and the officers — their badge numbers obscured by the bullet-proof vests they wore over their uniforms — refused to divulge their identities on request.

A day after the police raid, Sam Elkas asked for help from the Canadian army. Military officers, wearing civilian clothes to disguise their identities, were secretly dispatched to Oka and Kahnawake to help the

SQ. The army quietly sent a supply of C-7 rifles, night-vision devices, and bullet-proof vests to strengthen the SQ's weaponry. Armoured vehicles were surreptitiously sent to Montreal from the Canadian Forces Base at Valcartier in case the SQ needed them.

John Ciaccia arrived in Kanesatake late in the afternoon of July 12. Ellen Gabriel, Denise David-Tolley, Eba Beauvais, and some of the other Longhouse women gave him a tour of the Pines. They showed him the scars in the trees where bullets had ripped through the bark, and they pointed to the empty tear gas canisters that still lay strewn about the clearing. Then they brought him to the green tent in the Pines that was serving as their temporary Longhouse.

Ciaccia assured the women that the golf course would not be built. "You got what you wanted," he told them. Once the immediate crisis was dealt with, Ciaccia said, he would be prepared to intervene with the federal government to resolve the Kanesatake Mohawk territorial claims.

"We still need protection for our people from the Sûreté du Québec," Ellen Gabriel told him. "We need a guarantee of safety for our men to leave." Gabriel was angry because already it was apparent that every Mohawk was under suspicion for Lemay's death. Earlier that day a couple of Kanesatake men had been arrested while drinking in a bar in Oka. They had been roughed up by police, and no one knew where they were being held. After the women confronted Ciaccia about that incident, he made a fast call on a cellular phone to someone in the office of the Minister of Public Security.

"What the hell are you guys doing?" one of the women overheard Ciaccia asking the official. "Do you want me to get shot up here?"

"What I heard in his voice was frustration, dejection, and fear all rolled into one," says Susan Gabriel, an aunt of Ellen Gabriel, who was in the Pines that day. "The government left him out on a limb, and the SQ were cutting the limb from underneath him."

The talks on July 12 broke off at sunset, in keeping with a Mohawk tradition not to carry on negotiations after dark. But Ciaccia assured the Mohawks that the Sûreté du Québec would not mount another attack as long as the talks continued. The warriors seemed reassured by that commitment. For most of that night, the second night of the siege, there was no one on guard at Main Gate. The only people on the barricade were the journalists, who peered over the makeshift roadblock at the line of police at the bottom of the hill and joked about the absurdity of the situation. Where were the warriors? Most of them were catching up on sleep, a luxury they had not had for the past thirty-six hours. Until then, adrenalin had been keeping most of them going, although a couple of the warriors admitted to taking amphetamines to stay awake.

Each afternoon for the next two days, John Ciaccia returned to the Pines. Despite angry calls from the Mohawks for federal Indian Affairs Minister Tom Siddon to play a role in the talks, Siddon refused all overtures. He said the crisis at Kanesatake and Kahnawake was a police matter that fell under Quebec's jurisdiction. Not until the barricades were down would he deal with the land issue that had sparked the confrontation.

Ciaccia, too, called for the federal government to live up to its responsibilities, although behind the scenes, Ciaccia and Siddon had agreed that the Quebec Cabinet minister would play the lead role in settling the dispute. As he repeated often in the weeks that followed, Siddon did not want to go behind the barricades to negotiate with armed warriors. Privately, Ciaccia welcomed Siddon's stance; he thought his federal counterpart's cool, distant demeanour and the lack of mutual respect between Siddon and the Mohawks would only hamper negotiations in the tense atmosphere of the Pines.

On Friday, July 13, Ciaccia met the Longhouse negotiators for five hours. Again, he listened sympathetically to their complaints of police harassment and their fears that they would be attacked once more. At one point, a tear slipped down his cheek.

"He showed he was human," says Eba Beauvais. She wanted desperately to trust him, but John Ciaccia was working against three hundred years of history that had taught the Mohawks never to trust the government.

Few people in the Quebec Cabinet supported any negotiated deal with the Mohawks — which gave Ciaccia little room to manoeuvre. But he made what gestures he could. He helped one Mohawk return to Kahnawake to avoid being arrested for breaking his bail-imposed curfew. He helped bring in a Red Cross team to examine the leg of a wounded Mohawk, Psycho, and he agreed to allow advisors from other Mohawk communities to come to Kanesatake to help with the negotiations.

The Longhouse people in the Pines had already asked several Iroquois communities to send their leaders to Kanesatake to help resolve the situation. Walter David Sr., the secretary of the Kanesatake Longhouse, had talked to Iroquois leaders in Onondaga, Six Nations and Akwesasne. The senior chiefs at Onondaga, Leon Shenandoah and Oren Lyons, were both away in Australia. Jake Swamp, a Mohawk chief and Confederacy representative at Akwesasne, was an avowed anti-warrior and refused to help Kanesatake as long as warriors were there.

Walter David Sr. believed it was imperative that the entire Iroquois Confederacy unite behind the people of the Pines, regardless of their attitude toward the warriors. "The boys that are here are only helping to defend us," David Sr. argued. "They are not here for gambling or cigarettes." But Jake Swamp could not be persuaded.

In the end, most of the advisors came from the Kahnawake Longhouse. Among them were Joe Deom, Laura Norton, and Lorna Delormier — three of the Mohawks who had pulled their children out of provincial schools in the late 1970s in defiance of Quebec's language law. After years of fighting to establish the Kahnawake Survival School, they had plenty of experience in standing up to governments. With them was Loran Thompson, the militant and charismatic Longhouse follower from Akwesasne who had been at the centre of a two-year standoff with police and vigilantes at his home on the reserve in 1979 and 1980. Thompson was a fiery and compelling orator who inspired the warriors to keep fighting for the Mohawk cause.

The arrival of the staunch traditionalists from Kahnawake and Akwesasne alarmed some people in Kanesatake. They were seen as too militant and uncompromising. "There was a general panic," says Maurice Gabriel, a Kanesatake Mohawk who initially shared that sense of distrust towards the Kahnawake advisors. "What are these people talking about? We didn't really understand that we are a nation, we are sovereign ... You're looking at several generations of people who have only been exposed to the Indian Act, who believed that was the only alternative out there for native people."

Some Kanesatake Mohawks were concerned that what had sparked the confrontation — the golf course expansion plans and the lack of a recognized land base in Kanesatake — was quickly becoming a side issue in negotiations, replaced by the traditionalists' demand for recognition of Mohawk nationhood. They demanded a role in the talks.

It was not clear who in the community should be in charge, if not the Longhouse people who had led the occupation of the Pines. Grand Chief George Martin and the band council were gone. The doors of the band office had been locked since the morning of the raid, and the chiefs were staying in a hotel in Montreal, where they and their lawyer, Jacques Lacaille, had met separately with John Ciaccia and other officials.

With the council's departure, the split between it and the Longhouse people in the Pines was now almost complete. The council continued to conduct its affairs from an office in nearby St. Eustache, but the lack of community support made it politically ineffectual for the duration of the crisis.

With the band council gone, the rest of the non-Longhouse Mohawks in Kanesatake called a meeting in the school gym on the afternoon of Saturday, July 14, and appointed their own representatives, Mavis Etienne and Maurice Gabriel, to participate in the talks in the Pines. Mavis Etienne was a devout Pentecostal who hosted a weekly gospel music show at the Kanesatake radio station and worked as a drug and alcohol counsellor at the Treatment Centre. Although she was not a member of the Longhouse, she held a deep respect for Mohawk traditionalists and shared their absolute belief in the Mohawk right to the Pines. Maurice Gabriel was a cousin of Ellen Gabriel, a quiet, restrained man in his early thirties who was well liked by almost everyone in the community and who could be counted on to assess the situation calmly and rationally. Both Etienne and Gabriel proved to be willing students of the more experienced Kahnawake negotiators and accepted their approach to settling the conflict, an approach based on the principles of Mohawk sovereignty and the Mohawk right to defend their land.

When talks resumed with John Ciaccia on July 14, the circle of Mohawks involved in negotiations had widened to include Ellen Gabriel and the rest of the Kanesatake Longhouse women, Loran Thompson, Joe Deom and the other advisors from the Kahnawake

Longhouse, plus Mavis Etienne and Maurice Gabriel. Others, including non-Longhouse members of the community and some of the warriors, were present as observers. That evening, the tradition of breaking off negotiations at sunset was set aside. The situation was becoming urgent. Tensions in Châteauguay, the suburb that neighbours Kahnawake, were at a breaking point, and Ciaccia was under extreme pressure to secure a commitment from the Mohawks to open the Mercier Bridge. But the bridge was the only real bargaining chip the Mohawks had, and they wanted assurances that the police would not sweep through Kanesatake the moment the Kahnawake barricades came down.

After six hours, they reached a tentative agreement. The roadblocks on the Mercier Bridge would be cleared. Independent observers would monitor the dismantling of the barricades, and no one in Kahnawake would be prosecuted for events related to the bridge blockade. The Mohawks in the Pines would co-operate in a police investigation into Corporal Lemay's death.

The agreement hinged on the withdrawal of a significant number of police from the territory around Oka. John Ciaccia did not have the power to authorize that withdrawal, but he left the Pines late Saturday night filled with optimism, telling reporters it was just a matter of time before the Mercier Bridge re-opened. Only a few "technical details" had to be worked out, he said. As a sign of good faith, Ciaccia left one of his officials in the Pines to spend the night.

But there was no evidence that the police were prepared to back off. Through the night they filled and stacked sandbags, fortifying their barricade at the bottom of the hill. Once again it appeared to the Mohawks that the police were preparing to launch an assault. It was clear to the warriors that John Ciaccia had no control over the Sûreté du Québec — it appeared to them that *no one* in the Quebec government did. "The police will be up the hill in no time," Lasagna told the Mohawk women.

John Ciaccia was supposed to return to the Pines by 2:00 p.m. the next day, July 15. But he spent most of the day in discussions with senior politicians, trying to convince Premier Robert Bourassa and other members of the provincial Cabinet to accept the terms of the agreement worked out the previous night. From the start, most members of Cabinet were opposed to any deal with the Mohawks. They viewed the events at Kanesatake and Kahnawake as a purely criminal matter that should be left to the police. The hawks among the Quebec ministers and their advisors were willing to contemplate an assault on the Mohawk barricades, even though such an attack would probably mean more bloodshed. "You can't make an omelette without breaking eggs," one provincial official kept repeating.

Because of the long arguments with his superiors, John Ciaccia did not arrive in Kanesatake until 6:00 p.m. As he walked up the hill, accompanied by clergy whom he had invited to act as observers, the skies suddenly opened up and the rain began to pour, drenching everyone. The sudden rainstorm after days of stifling heat should have come as a relief, but it was received as a bad omen. In the Pines, it was immediately obvious that the mood had changed drastically. Whatever good faith had existed the previous night was gone. The four-hour delay in Ciaccia's arrival had left the Mohawks suspicious and mistrustful. Warriors pointed to the police fortifications in the town below. They refused to believe Ciaccia's claim that there had indeed been a reduction in the number of police in and around Oka.

Earlier that day, an ambulance had suddenly appeared in Kanesatake. Its driver and four attendants claimed that they were on their way to replace another ambulance in Oka and that the police had waved them through the checkpoint and on into Kanesatake when they had taken a wrong turn. Skeptical of this story, the Mohawk men who had stopped the ambulance escorted it to the Pines to face the warriors. They searched the ambulance for weapons, but the only incriminating object they found was a camera. The warriors accused the frightened ambulance crew of being police spies, and the provincial official who had been left in the Pines overnight was called to check their credentials. Their story seemed to check out — they all had identification papers, and their employer, reached by cellular phone, vouched for them. The nervous driver and his passengers were escorted back out of the settlement the same way they came in.

As soon as the ambulance was out of sight of curious reporters, however, the warriors pulled the vehicle over again. They held a revolver to the head of one of the ambulance attendants, demanding to see his police badge. Terrified, the man confessed he and two more of the ambulance staff were police officers.

The undercover police were allowed to leave unharmed, but the incident left many of the warriors furious. The ambulance ploy was seen as a clear breach of the commitment Ciaccia had given them the previous day. Tensions grew even worse later that day when the people in the Pines discovered that the police were preventing their Kahnawake advisors from crossing the barricades. They waited at a police roadblock in Oka for five hours before they were finally allowed to climb up the hill to Kanesatake.

Inside the green tent in the Pines that had become the Mohawks' makeshift Longhouse, John Ciaccia faced angry accusations from all sides. He heard a litany of complaints about everything that had gone wrong since the tentative agreement had been reached the previous night. The Mohawks reminded him of his promise that the Mohawks would no longer have any trouble getting food into the settlement. But when three Mohawk women had walked down the hill towards Oka to buy groceries, the police had refused to let them into the town.

The Mohawks felt they could not trust Ciaccia anymore, and the tentative agreement fell apart. Ellen Gabriel stood up in the green tent and declared they had done enough talking for one night. The meeting was over.

When he had arrived in Oka at six o'clock, Ciaccia had told reporters that "measures [were] being taken to open the Mercier Bridge." When he left, three and a half hours later, he spoke of "procedural difficulties" that still had to be overcome. Ciaccia maintained there was still a tentative agreement to open the bridge, and he pleaded for the patience of south-shore commuters, but privately he realized that all hope of a quick settlement was gone.

Meanwhile, in Oka, Mayor Jean Ouellette had disappeared from sight. He was under police protection, the victim of anonymous death threats. The acting mayor, Gilles Landreville, told supporters he was not opposed to a second police assault on the Pines if it proved to be necessary. The pro-golf Oka citizens' group congratulated Ouellette and his council for their political courage. When Jean Ouellette re-emerged in the community a week later, still under police protection, he said he had no regrets about calling in the police. If he had to do it all over again, he said, he would have done the same thing.

The town of Oka was becoming increasingly isolated from the rest of the world. On July 15, the owner of the Oka ferry service suspended service for the first time in seventy-nine years, after police stopped allowing anyone except Oka residents to disembark from the ferry which crossed the Lake of Two Mountains from Hudson, a small town on the south side of the lake.

The streets of Oka were calm, almost deserted. About sixty Mohawk women and children who lived in the town, along with some of their non-Mohawk friends and allies, held an evening candlelight vigil behind the police roadblock on July 13. Those who opposed the Mohawks watched from their porches. Most people seemed anxious not to make the situation any worse than it already was. White townspeople and Mohawks eyed each other carefully, but kept their distance. The Oka townspeople were divided over Mayor Ouellette's decision to call in the police to raid the Mohawk barricade.

In the weeks that followed, petitions circulated around Oka — one calling for Ouellette's resignation, the other supporting the mayor's stand. As the summer dragged on, hostility grew worse between the Mohawk and non-native townspeople. One non-native who called for reconciliation with the Mohawks found a rock heaved through the plate-glass window of his antique store when he arrived at work one morning.

In another ugly incident in late July, about two hundred protesters — angry that their business losses and hardships were being ignored — had to be restrained by police from advancing on a native peace rally in a field outside the town. Elijah Harper, the Manitoba native politician who had helped to block the Meech Lake accord just weeks before, was the object of some of their taunts. He was protected by tight security when he appeared at the rally.

At first, journalists appeared to be as much the object of the police officers' wrath as the Mohawks themselves. On the day of the raid, three photographers who had chanced upon the police changing out of their riot and SWAT gear in Paul Sauvé Park on the outskirts of Oka were accosted by the police when they tried to photograph them. They were held at gunpoint, the film was ripped out of their cameras, and their equipment was damaged. "If you're not out of here in thirty seconds, I'll blow your head off," an SQ officer barked. Valuable photographs, including some taken at the site where Corporal Lemay had fallen, were destroyed, and the photographers lost thousands of dollars in potential revenue. That incident set the tone for an uneasy relationship between the police and the media throughout the summer.

From late July 11 to July 13, reporters who were not already in Oka or camped out behind the Mohawk line in Kanesatake were barred from passing the police roadblocks that ringed the region. Alarmed at the Sûreté du Québec's blatant attempt to censor news of the crisis by keeping journalists out of Oka and Kanesatake, senior managers of several media outlets met SQ officials in Montreal on July 13 and convinced the police to issue accreditation to journalists to allow them at least into the town of Oka itself.

Journalists were still not permitted to pass the police barricade at the foot of the hill on Highway 344 to get behind the Mohawk line, so they resorted to cloak-and-dagger tactics to get past the police. They sneaked along the beach and through private yards, up a steep hill and through more yards, to get to the highway behind the Mohawk barricade. Later, journalists discovered a much easier route, through the woods, and onto the golf course at the top of the hill. Police were obviously aware of it, but after a few days it became apparent they were turning a blind eye to the comings and goings of the reporters.

During the weekend after the raid, a fifteen-year-old white kid from the town appeared behind the Mohawk barricade. "Blondie" had watched the events of July 11 from the bottom of hill in Oka, and after the raid, had sneaked up through the woods and past the golf course to join the Mohawks. For a couple of days, he hung around the journalists, running videotape and film down the hill to their producers. He sat by the barricade of overturned police cars, swapping stories with a young warrior at the lookout post. When darkness fell, he sat at the campfire in the ditch next to the Mohawk cemetery. "I've lived in Oka for ten years," he told reporters. "I've been running in these woods a long time, so I want to fight for them." Within a couple of weeks, Blondie had proven himself to the warriors, and he was given a gun and a post on the barricades. Some of the Mohawks disagreed with that decision, but they were desperate for any help they could get. By the end of the summer, after his father had given him an ultimatum to abandon the barricades or move out of his home, Blondie became an adopted member of the people of the Pines.

On July 16, the funeral of Corporal Marcel Lemay was held in L'Ancienne-Lorette, just outside Quebec City. Lemay's colleagues on the tactical intervention squad acted as pall-bearers, carrying the coffin draped with the Quebec *fleur-de-lis*. Over two thousand people, including police officers from all across Canada, attended the service. Robert Lavigne, the director of the Sûreté du Québec, offered his condolences to Lemay's pregnant wife Lorraine and his two-year-old daughter, Catherine. He implored his men not to exhibit vengeance towards the Mohawks.

At precisely 1:00 p.m., the SQ officers guarding the barricade at the bottom of the hill stood at attention, silently honouring their dead colleague. In the Pines, the Warrior flag was lowered to half-mast. The Mohawks offered their condolences to Lemay's family, but none accepted responsibility for his death.

Later that night Grand Chief George Martin and his council returned to the settlement with Konrad Sioui, the Quebec vice-chief of the Assembly of First Nations. Mohawks from all the factions in the community gathered in the Pines for a meeting, and they pledged to work together to resolve the crisis. They held hands together in a great circle, then emerged from the Pines, whooping and hollering. A crowd of eighty Mohawks made their way to Main Gate, where they erected the blue and white flag of the Iroquois Confederacy and the red and yellow flag of the Mohawk Warrior Society. Some of the women had tears in their eyes. Eba Beauvais raised her fist in a gesture of defiance. "For my ancestors and for the future children of our nation!" she cried.

For several days, that unity held. Loran Thompson was beginning to emerge as an influential person in the Pines, and he was intent on persuading all the Mohawks, regardless of their political leanings, to support the Longhouse goal of gaining recognition for Kanesatake as sovereign Mohawk territory. Despite the skeptical reaction he received from Ellen Gabriel and some of the other Kanesatake Longhouse followers, Thompson cast his net wide, visiting people throughout the community, including Allen Gabriel and the other Longhouse people who had bowed out of the protest in the Pines a few days before the raid, and encouraging them to participate in planning the direction of the talks.

At first, people listened attentively to Thompson's fiery speeches. Only through sovereignty could the Mohawks regain control of their lives and their territory, Thompson told the Mohawks. But away from the Pines, the Kanesatake Mohawks who had never followed the Longhouse traditions were more doubtful about Thompson's militant philosophy. Many of them simply wanted the disputed land turned over to Kanesatake, and they resented the high-profile role that Thompson and the Kahnawake Longhouse people were beginning to play in the dispute. Nor did they want that role to be usurped by the band council, which was still trying, without success, to wrest control of the talks. But for the time being, most Kanesatake Mohawks kept their doubts and resentments to themselves, grudgingly acknowledging that their greatest hope for resolving the dispute lay in sticking together, as they had done on July 11.

By the second week of the siege, the immediate problem was finding a way to feed everyone behind the barricades. Linda Simon, the director of education in Kanesatake and the wife of former grand chief Clarence Simon, organized some of the adults and older children to help conduct a house-to-house survey to determine how much food was available behind the barricades. As she had suspected, the survey showed that a lot of cupboards in Kanesatake were bare. One old man had nothing but two slices of bread left in his house. His electricity had been cut off, and because he had an electric water pump, he had no water either.

Linda Simon gave the results of the survey to the Red Cross, and after obtaining written guarantees of safe passage from both the Quebec government and the Mohawks, the agency made its first trip behind the lines of an armed conflict in Canada since the war between Canadian soldiers and Métis warriors in Saskatchewan during the North-West Rebellion of 1885. At daybreak on July 17, a convoy of Red Cross vehicles arrived with medicine and food packages for 150 people who were identified as being in most urgent need of relief. Each package contained one loaf of bread, one litre of milk, two eggs, three carrots, one turnip, three bananas, two oranges, and two rolls of toilet paper. This was to feed a family with small children for three days. Linda Simon shook her head when she saw the Red Cross provisions, knowing it would not be enough.

That day the school gym was converted into an emergency food bank. The Quebec Native Women's Association had set up a food depot in Montreal and it was swamped with donations, but the problem was getting the provisions into the settlement. Already some food was being ferried by boat from Hudson. A "safe house" had been set up there, and a Mohawk who worked in Hudson was arranging the pick-up and delivery of food donations. Each night, as soon as darkness fell, a couple of boats from Kanesatake would venture out into the water, making their way past police boats patrolling the lake. They would pick up the food in Hudson, then head back to Kanesatake. The navigators of the little fleet of speedboats, which became known as the "Mohawk Navy," had a clear advantage over the police. They knew all the shoals and rocky places on the shallow lake, and they could safely navigate around them in the dark.

On July 19, the police at the roadblocks relented and allowed the entry of two Salvation Army trucks loaded with food from the Six Nations reserve near Brantford, Ontario. The Six Nations people had also sent a supply of gas and propane tanks, portable stoves, and sleeping bags. But those provisions were certain to raise the ire of police, so they were shipped in separately by boat.

For almost a week the SQ had prevented the Human Rights Commission from investigating complaints of human rights abuses in Kanesatake. A Human Rights Commission official had tried to enter Kanesatake on July 13, but was refused permission to cross the police roadblock by the Sûreté du Québec — in violation of the Quebec Charter of Rights and Freedoms. It had taken the authorization of the Quebec public security minister for the Human Rights Commission to obtain passage into Oka and Kanesatake on July 19; the next day, July 20, human rights officials were again refused access to the besieged communities by the SQ, because of a "change of philosophy." After a telegram to Quebec Premier Robert Bourassa from the Human Rights Commission was made public on July 21, Quebec Justice Minister Gil Rémillard personally intervened to make sure the SQ and all other authorities understood their obligations to co-operate with the Commission.

With the SQ's "change of philosophy" on July 20, the rules on bringing in food changed again, and even the Red Cross ran into obstacles in its attempts to bring food past the barricades. Its second trip to bring in food and medicine was delayed for twenty-four hours while Red Cross officials awaited police authorization.

The Quebec government's official position on allowing food into the communities appeared to depend on which minister was doing the talking on any given day. On a visit to Oka on July 21, a senior Cabinet minister, Claude Ryan, said the refusal to allow food into the Mohawk communities was official government policy, not police vindictiveness. A few days later, Ciaccia denied that efforts to get food into Kanesatake were being deliberately stymied. "There was never any question of depriving them of food," he told reporters.

Although every highway and sideroad into Kanesatake was blocked by police, the Mohawks soon realized that the Sûreté du Québec never ventured off the road. A restaurant in St. Placide, just west of Kanesatake, became a drop-off point for food donations from eastern Ontario and shipments of moose and caribou meat from the Algonquins in western Quebec. Runners picked up the food at the restaurant and backpacked it into Kanesatake, across fields and through the woods.

By the second week of the crisis, warriors in Kahnawake were asking for volunteers to go to Kanesatake to relieve the exhausted men at the Pines. They crossed the lake dozens of times over the course of the summer, often using a hydroplane donated by Dr. David Gorman, the stepfather of Mark and Hunter Montour, two Kahnawake warriors who spent part of the summer at the Pines. Police boats were patrolling the lake, and not everyone evaded detection. On some nights, shots rang out over the lake as police boats tried to intercept warriors and food smugglers. Early in the crisis, two men were caught, and their speedboat was torn apart by police before it was finally returned to the Mohawks. One of the men, a self-described "professional" warrior from Akwesasne named Dennis "Major" Lafrance, was released from custody after a few days. He found his way back to Kanesatake and made many more boat trips throughout the summer until he was apprehended for a second time on August 29.

The warriors had no problem obtaining ammunition and camouflage gear from gun stores and over-the-counter suppliers in Montreal. Sometimes they even presented their Indian status cards to pay for their purchases tax-free. At least one shipment of assault rifles and thirty cases of ammunition, probably from Akwesasne, was loaded onto a boat in Hudson while the police patrolled nearby.

With the exception of a very few warriors who had served in the U.S. Army, most of the Kanesatake warriors had no formal military training. Some had gone to a "summer school" at the militant Mohawk community of Ganienkeh in upstate New York, where they learned to dig bunkers and use AK-47s, but military manoeuvres were still foreign to most of them.

The lack of military experience in Kanesatake was evident in the fact that no one was actually in charge of the territory's defence. The organization of shifts was completely arbitrary. Hunched down in a bunker at Sector Five at the north entrance to the Pines, Stonecarver waited for three days for someone to show up to replace him during the first week of the siege. Some of the "homeboys," mostly young Mohawks in their twenties who had not joined the fight until the morning of the raid, took over a bunker on the eastern fringe of the Pines, looking out over the golf course, which became known as China Beach.

Those neophyte warriors had to be watched carefully because they were known to be hotheads and troublemakers who drank and did drugs, or, like Apache — the warrior who gesticulated defiantly with his gun from atop the barricade of overturned police vans on July 11 — they waved their guns around indiscriminately. "He was a hyper guy," Francis Boots recalls. "We almost put him under lock and key."

The older warriors worried that some of the young gun-slinging Mohawks would discredit the warrior movement. Within a couple of weeks of the siege, however, many of the young Kanesatake men on the barricades had drifted off, some of them angry or fed up with the stalled negotiations, a few of them more attracted to the idea of living in a police-free zone than in putting in long hours on duty in the Pines.

About a week after the siege began, some of the Kanesatake Mohawks who had not joined the warriors but were determined to stay in the settlement set up their own security patrol to help the warriors police activities behind the Kanesatake barricades. At first, the main reason for the patrol was to keep an eye on the beach. Some people suspected infiltrators were sending light signals across the lake to the police, to let them know when boats were crossing. But no one was ever caught doing that, and within a few days it became apparent the security patrol had other problems to deal with.

While the police were stopping groceries from entering the community, they made no apparent effort to prevent the Mohawks from bringing in alcohol. "It was just like the good old days," one Kanesatake woman said bitterly. "Let the Indians have their booze and they'll create their own problems."

On several occasions, tanked-up young Mohawk men in broken-down cars and trucks screamed through Kanesatake at breakneck speed. One night a couple of Mohawk kids and their white friends were caught with a houseful of booze and electronic equipment that had been stolen from white homes behind the barricades. After the kids tried to intimidate a warrior on patrol alone on Kanesatake's back roads, a group of warriors was sent to take care of the situation, and they entered the house with their weapons in hand, ready for a fight. But the kids were too drunk to put up any kind of defence. In a fit of rage, one angry warrior riddled the black Mustang the kids had been driving with bullets.

The warriors piled the teenagers into another vehicle and took them to Main Gate, where, protesting vehemently, they were sent down the hill to the SQ on guard there. Stolen goods found in the house were turned over to one of the members of the security patrol for safekeeping.

By late July, break-ins were growing more frequent, especially in houses along the lakeshore. The security patrol suspected that outsiders were responsible for some of them, probably with the help of some Mohawks. But there was only a handful of men on patrol, and no one was ever caught red-handed.

The deserted homes along the highway near Main Gate, owned by the most outspoken supporters of the golf course expansion, were vandalized soon after the siege began. The warriors regarded them as "liberated" territory. They slept in the beds and swam in the pool, and generally treated the places as communal property.

For Lasagna and a couple of his buddies, all of Kanesatake was now their turf. They believed they deserved an occasional night of "Rest and Relaxation," by which they mean all-night drinking binges. For a while, their drinking was tolerated as long as the guns were put away while they were partying. But after a vacated house was completely demolished and shot up, the women in the Pines insisted that the men responsible for the damage be disarmed and thrown out of the settlement. Three men, including Lasagna, were taken to Kahnawake.

The vast majority of warriors were there for only one purpose: to defend the land of Kanesatake until an agreement was reached. They were family men like Richard Two Axe, a Kahnawake Mohawk who was a born-again Christian and had never been part of the warrior movement until the protesters in the Pines called for help in early July. He was an ironworker who went by the name of Boltpin, a devoted father who would sing his three-year-old daughter in Kahnawake to sleep by phone.

Hundreds of Indians from across Canada joined the fight. Most made their way first to Kahnawake. Nine Micmacs arrived at Kahnawake on July 15, and the next day four of them went to Kanesatake. Among them was Tom Paul, a forty-eight-year-old pipecarrier — a spiritual leader — and a veteran of Indian protests and confrontations at Wounded Knee, Ganienkeh, Raquette Point, and Restigouche. He was the product of a residential school in Shubenacadie, Nova Scotia, where he had been beaten for speaking his language and for questioning the catechism taught by the priests. At fifteen, after ten years at the school, he ran away and started a life of heavy drinking and petty crime in Boston's skid row. In the mid-1970s he quit drinking and began his discovery of native spirituality, learning the ways of the pipe and the drum. On his first day in Kanesatake, Tom Paul stood at the main barricade, his waist-length black hair in two long braids, a fierce expression on his scarred face, refusing to identify himself to reporters except by his Micmac name — Mestaghuptaasit Kitpu, or Spotted Eagle. Within a day, he had picked up an AK-47 and donned the camouflage uniform of the warriors. Gradually, he became less fearsome as his quirky but easygoing personality emerged. He adopted the outrageous codename of General Fits-in-Tight and sometimes masked his face with a Groucho Marx nose and glasses instead of the obligatory camouflage scarf.

The General and his cousin Kevin Gould (a warrior who was codenamed Beaver) were both cousins of Donald Marshall, the Micmac who was jailed for eleven years in Nova Scotia for a murder he did not commit. Like so many others who went behind the barricades to join the warriors, their personal experience of injustice had motivated them to support the Mohawk cause.

There were brief respites from the tension of the armed siege. Warriors who were members of a Longhouse singing society would set up a circle in front of Main Gate, drumming and chanting for hours. Young people sat on the grass at the edge of the road and listened attentively, while women shuffled around them on the highway, dancing to the beat of the drum. Sometimes, when tensions were high, Donald "Babe" Hemlock, a Kahnawake Longhouse chief who had set aside his title to join the fight, would lead the warriors in a few verses of the War Song.

A few weeks into the siege, native spiritual leaders arrived from Micmac communities and from Mexico. The Micmacs built a sweatlodge in the Pines and prayed for the warriors. A Buddhist monk and a Filipina acupuncturist sneaked into Kanesatake and stayed at the Treatment Centre. Each morning, the monk would arise at dawn and walk up and down the dirt road, chanting and banging a gong. The Mohawks welcomed his prayers and support, although some jokingly complained about the rude morning awakening. The Mohawks conducted their own tobacco-burning ceremonies each morning. Occasionally they performed the powerful "hatui" ceremonies, in which the spirits of false face masks carved from century-old living trees were invoked for the protection of those living behind the barricades.

By the second week of the standoff, the Mohawk negotiators had set up their base of operations at the Onen:to'ken Treatment Centre, across the highway from the Pines. During the hot, windless days, they isolated themselves in the centre's stuffy basement and set out to draft a new plan of action.

Telephone calls went back and forth between the Mohawks at the Treatment Centre and Montreal native rights lawyer James O'Reilly, who was acting as an envoy to John Ciaccia. During the second week of the siege, however, most of the Mohawk efforts were concentrated on organizing a plan for renewed negotiations, beginning with the establishment of ground rules for all discussions. The Treatment Centre became an accelerated summer school in Mohawk culture and history, open to any Mohawk in Kanesatake willing to devote time to the cause.

The tentative agreement reached with Ciaccia on July 14 was still hanging by a thread. Joe Deom, Ellen Gabriel, and the other Mohawks at the Treatment Centre wanted to meet face to face with Kahnawake warrior leaders from the Mohawk Nation Office to discuss Ciaccia's proposals, but when the Kahnawake Mohawks arrived at Oka on July 17, the police held them for four hours. By the time they arrived in the Pines it was nearly dusk. The Mohawks interpreted the long delays at the police lines as further proof that the Quebec Cabinet was exerting no control over the Sûreté du Québec.

"That was the last straw," recalls James O'Reilly. "That's when the Mohawks decided they needed some preconditions to further negotiations."

On July 18, the Mohawks drafted the following revised list of demands: title to the lands slated for the golf course expansion and the rest of the historic Commons; the withdrawal of all police forces from all Mohawk territories, including Ganienkeh in New York State and Akwesasne, on the Quebec, Ontario, and New York borders; a forty-eight-hour time period in which anyone leaving Kanesatake or Kahnawake would not be subject to search or arrest; and the referral of all disputes arising from the conflict to the World Court at the Hague.

At the same time, the Mohawks insisted that three preconditions would have to be satisfied before any further negotiations with the government could take place. There had to be free access to food and other provisions; unhindered access to clan mothers, spiritual leaders and other advisors; and the posting of independent international observers in Kanesatake and Kahnawake to monitor the actions of the police.

The list of preconditions was sent to James O'Reilly, who passed them on to John Ciaccia before his morning Cabinet meeting on July 18. Ciaccia was expected to return to the Pines to discuss the demands that afternoon, but by mid-afternoon the Quebec government's strategy had changed. A Cabinet crisis committee, led by veteran minister Claude Ryan, was established. After the Cabinet meeting, Ciaccia told reporters that the Mohawks had cancelled the meeting in the Pines.

O'Reilly, however, had a different interpretation of events. "Ciaccia didn't have the authority to go back to the Pines without the authorization of that new committee," he says. "Quebec decided not to negotiate, and not to consider those three preconditions. Ciaccia chose to interpret my message (the list of new conditions) as a cancellation of the meeting."

The tentative agreement that was reached on July 14 had now fallen apart completely. John Ciaccia declared that the new demands of the Mohawks, particularly those concerning the withdrawal of state, federal, and provincial police in Akwesasne and other Mohawk territories, were completely out of his jurisdiction. And Premier Robert Bourassa was emphatic that there would be no negotiations on the question of possible criminal charges arising from the crisis.

The Mohawks' demand for a forty-eight-hour moratorium on all arrests was also considered unreasonable by Owen Young, another native rights lawyer who was advising the Kahnawake warriors. He suspected that the new hard-line position was inspired by the Mohawks' new adviser, Stanley Cohen. Cohen had arrived in the Pines on July 18, the same day as William Kunstler, a celebrated civil rights lawyer who had defended some of the key activists in the American Indian Movement following the events at Wounded Knee in the early 1970s. Kunstler did not stay long, but Cohen — the lawyer for the Akwesasne warriors — became a key advisor to the Mohawk negotiating team based at the Onen'to:kon Treatment Centre. The young, bearded lawyer and civil rights activist was an avowed supporter of the Mohawk cause, and he was every bit as uncompromising as Loran Thompson, Ellen Gabriel, and the other staunch idealists who made up the core of the Mohawk negotiating team. The Mohawks affectionately called him Takos ("cat"), and he was privy to most of the comings and goings in the Pines.

The circumstances were ripe for someone espousing a hard-line approach like Cohen to gain influence in the Pines. The corps of militant Longhouse people there had lost faith in Ciaccia, and the actions of the SQ gave them little reason to believe the government was prepared to negotiate in good faith. Few people in the Pines saw any reason to be accommodating towards the government any longer. But Owen Young felt that Cohen's unyielding approach to the negotiations was doomed to failure. He also suspected that Cohen was hampered by his lack of understanding of the Canadian and Quebec political scene, for willingly or not, the Mohawks were caught up in the charged climate of Quebec nationalism and uneasy English-French relations that followed the June 23 failure of the Meech Lake accord.

Around July 21, Young arrived in Kanesatake by motorboat to meet Cohen, but he never made it off the beach. After a brief conversation with the New York lawyer, it was obvious to Young that Cohen's radical fervour would pose serious problems. In Young's view, Cohen was interested less in helping the Mohawks negotiate an end to the dispute than in encouraging them to take no-win positions. He jumped back in the motorboat and left in disgust.

The Mohawks' new list of demands of July 18 was set aside while they waited for their three preconditions for negotiations to be met. For almost three weeks, there was a steady stream of faxes and telephone calls between the Mohawk negotiating team and Ciaccia's office. Five different drafts of an agreement were shuttled back and forth. In all of them, however, there was one consistent problem: the government's refusal to accept the Mohawk demand for independent international observers to monitor events in Kanesatake and Kahnawake. Although the federal government did not play a direct role in the talks, a senior provincial official revealed later that Ottawa insisted Quebec must not cave in to the demand for independent international observers. This federal stance was one of the greatest obstacles to negotiations in late July. Allowing an international team to oversee the negotiations was seen by Ottawa as an implicit recognition of Mohawk sovereignty.

Indian Affairs Minister Tom Siddon continued to sit on the sidelines, though his officials were working behind the scenes to purchase the forty hectares of land slated for the golf course expansion and the adjacent luxury housing development. Siddon's department had shown no urgent desire to negotiate the purchase of the disputed land in the months leading up to the crisis, but after July 11, it went to great lengths and astronomical expense to halt Oka's development plans in a belated attempt to try to defuse the crisis.

At the end of July, the federal government secretly flew land developer Maxime-Maurice Rousseau from his home in France to Montreal to complete the transaction. The town of Oka paid Rousseau the previously-agreed-upon price of $70,000 for eighteen hectares of land just west of the Pines. The federal government paid the developer and his brother, Jean-Michel, $1.44 million for the remaining twelve hectares, which were to have been subdivided for luxury houses, and offered Oka $1.34 million for the other twenty-eight hectares, including the land it had just purchased from Rousseau. Ottawa also paid the lawyer's fees for Rousseau and Oka, which amounted to another $53,000. The federal government was obligated to pay fair market value for the land transaction, but, as one federal official admitted months later, "under the circumstances, we were not in a position to bargain." The deal still had to be ratified by Oka's town council, but when it came before council at a public meeting on July 31, angry townspeople insisted that it could not be approved while the barricades remained in place.

"I'm insulted, I tell you, I'm insulted to think that you would sell these lands to the federal government and that tomorrow, the Indians are going to laugh through the nose at you and say, no, that's not good enough, we're not lifting the barricades," an angry taxpayer told Mayor Ouellette. The Oka resident was supported by thunderous applause from the packed council chambers.

The federal government made a second attempt to buy the land in early August, this time making it clear to Ouellette that the land would be expropriated if the sale was not approved by his council. On August 8, the stubborn Oka councillors regretfully accepted the windfall deal. They were paid a total of $3.84 million for the land, including $2.5 million in compensation for foregone taxes — plus one dollar for the tiny Mohawk cemetery.

The federal government seemed to view the Mohawk crisis primarily as a political problem that required a public relations campaign to neutralize the groundswell of support for the Mohawk cause. At a private briefing in Ottawa on July 23, the deputy minister of Indian Affairs tried to persuade a roomful of reporters that the Mohawk warriors were "a criminal organization" who had hijacked the communities of Kanesatake and Kahnawake. "It is a potent combination of cash, guns, and ideology," said deputy minister Harry Swain, who went on to describe the crisis as an "insurrection" by an "armed gang." Swain claimed that the warriors were opposed by most Mohawks and "not blessed" by the Longhouse. His allegations were highly misleading, however. The warriors were fully supported by the Kahnawake

Longhouse, and their stand in the Pines had the tacit, if not explicit, support of the Kanesatake Longhouse chief, Samson Gabriel. Although some Mohawks criticized the negotiating tactics of the people of the Pines, few residents of Kanesatake or Kahnawake wanted the barricades to come down if it meant their communities would be overrun by police.

Despite the federal government's public pretense of condemning the warriors as terrorists and thugs, Indian Affairs Minister Tom Siddon had secretly arranged to meet a representative of the Warrior Society in private. In early August, one of Kahnawake's assistant war chiefs, Donnie Martin, and veteran Mohawk politician Andrew Delisle Sr., were escorted to a guarded private room in a Montreal hotel, where they dined on prime rib with Siddon and the Minister of State for Indian Affairs, Shirley Martin. "He wanted to know who he was dealing with," Donnie Martin said later. "We gave him our view of history and our philosophy. We talked about the Warrior Society, the duties of women ... We talked about our aspirations as a people." But it was clear to Donnie Martin that Siddon was not about to look at creative solutions to the crisis, and so Martin reverted to his penchant for psychological tricks. "There's a simple solution to all this," Martin said, as the Cabinet minister leaned forward to hear his response. He paused. "But I'm not going to tell you what it is."

On July 27, John Ciaccia offered to withdraw most of the Quebec police from the barricades if the Mohawks agreed to deposit their weapons in a sealed container, pull their warriors away from the barricades, allow non-Mohawks to return to their homes in Kanesatake, and co-operate with the inquiry into Lemay's death. The Mohawks refused to respond to that offer until the preconditions they had demanded on July 18 were met. Ciaccia next proposed a "supervisory commission" to oversee a return to normalcy in the Mohawk communities, including one member from an international organization. That, too, was rejected by the Mohawk negotiators.

While the Mohawk negotiators at the Treatment Centre were doggedly pursuing an agreement on the preconditions to negotiations, the pressure of the long siege in Kanesatake was mounting and threatening to tear the community apart. In a desperate bid to hide the festering divisions from the public, the negotiating team and the warriors had confined all journalists to a tiny patch of highway directly in front of Main Gate.

Until then, there had been an uneasy camaraderie between the journalists and the warriors, whose duties included "babysitting" the media and accounting for all of them, lest some should stray into off-limits areas like the Pines. "What time would you like to tee off, sir?" a warrior posted at Hellhole, a sentry post near the golf club, would ask as he wrote down a reporter's name and credentials on a sign-up sheet stolen from the golf club. By August, however, that relationship had changed. *Montreal Gazette* reporters were completely banned from Kanesatake because of allegations that one reporter's harshly critical coverage of the warriors was fostering racism. After several more journalists were expelled for signing a petition decrying the restrictions, the press corps walked out of Kanesatake *en masse* on August 1. Later, an uneasy truce was negotiated with the help of a mediator from the Canadian Association of Journalists, but this did little to guarantee press freedoms behind the barricades. For an entire week, journalists were allowed to visit the community centre and other public areas in Kanesatake only when they were blindfolded and escorted by armed warriors.

Despite the restrictions, it was impossible to hide the growing divisions in the Mohawk community. By late July, some community members were exerting pressure on Chief George Martin and his band council to resign because of their failure to provide leadership throughout the crisis. The organizers of the Kanesatake emergency food bank accused Martin and his band council of holding back for the council's use thousands of dollars in donations that had been sent to Kanesatake and Kahnawake by four Western Canadian bands, who had asked specifically that the money go towards food and medical relief. On August 1, a warrior alleged that he was almost run over by one of the band councillors, Jerry Etienne, who had refused to stop at a roadblock the warriors had set up to try to prevent alcohol from coming into the community. Later that evening, several young Mohawk men from the community confronted Etienne at George Martin's house. They kicked in the door and assaulted Etienne, ordering him to get out of the settlement. Outside, warriors fired warning shots into the air.

Etienne and Martin left the reserve immediately and reported the incident to the Sûreté du Québec. They blamed the warriors. "That reserve is my reserve," Martin told reporters in Montreal. "The warriors have to get out of Kanesatake."

Ovide Mercredi, the Manitoba vice-chief of the Assembly of First Nations, visited Kanesatake on August 1. Chrystal Nicholas, Ellen Gabriel's uncle Harvey Gabriel, and some of the other Kanesatake Mohawks who had agreed to represent the concerns of non-Longhouse Mohawks when talks with the government resumed asked Mercredi to provide technical expertise to help in the negotiations. He obliged, requesting that the AFN send in two lawyers and a treaty expert. But the Mohawk negotiators at the Treatment Centre, dominated by the militant Longhouse followers, did not trust the AFN advisors, because of the AFN's affiliation with elected band councils, which recognized the Indian Act. The AFN team, accompanied by Chrystal Nicholas and other non-Longhouse people, arrived at the Treatment Centre on August 4 to meet the Longhouse negotiators, but the meeting turned into an angry confrontation. It ended when Joe Deom, who was emerging as one of the key strategists on the Mohawk negotiating team, accused the AFN advisors of being government spies.

The following day, August 5, the Kanesatake Mohawks who had asked the AFN to get involved held a community meeting to discuss their lack of influence over the negotiations. The Mohawk negotiators who attended the meeting, including Loran Thompson, Joe Deom, and Walter David Jr., persuaded some of the non-Longhouse Mohawks to continue supporting them, but other non-Longhouse Mohawks collected signatures to support the formation of an independent Kanesatake negotiating team.

The meeting ended in a blow-up. Some of the dissenting Mohawks demanded that everyone on the Longhouse negotiating team leave for Kahnawake.

"We almost boarded the boats that night," recalls Walter David Jr. "But then we decided, we can't allow these people to do this. After the tear gas, the concussion grenades, and the bullets of July 11, we can't allow these people to scare us out of here. We were still trying to negotiate those preconditions."

The split had little to do with the presence of the warriors. It had more to do with the resurgence of old personality conflicts and long-held resentments: the militant Mohawks who dominated the negotiating team, including Ellen Gabriel and the David family, were perceived as cliquish, and their insistence that the land at the heart of the dispute be vested in the Mohawk Nation was seen by some non-Longhouse Mohawks as a power grab by the Kanesatake Longhouse minority.

But as long as the SQ maintained their ring around Kanesatake, most Mohawks felt that the warriors were keeping the community safe. Some of those who had signed the petition to allow non-Longhouse community members to take over the talks included people whose sons were still on the barricade, like Ann Cross, Lasagna's mother, and others who, while not warriors, were working alongside them, ferrying people and food across the lake.

On August 5, the same day as the divisive meeting at Kanesatake, there was a new threat: Robert Bourassa gave the Mohawks forty-eight hours to reach an agreement to lift the barricades. The Mohawks remained intransigent. "We are one people, one nation, and we will not be brought to our knees before anyone," said Peter Diome, a spokesman for the Kahnawake warriors. The Kanesatake Mohawks opposed to the Longhouse negotiators had already been in touch with John Ciaccia to inform him of their willingness to take over negotiations. This led Ellen Gabriel to accuse Ciaccia of deliberately trying to divide the Mohawks by negotiating behind their backs with "people who do not represent the best interests of the Mohawk nation."

When they heard the ominous announcement of Bourassa's deadline, hundreds of non-native Oka residents began leaving their homes, accepting a long-sought promise of compensation from the provincial government. By the day of the deadline, August 8, about eighty Mohawk families — approximately one-third of the settlement — had fled Kanesatake as well.

On the day of the ultimatum's expiry, the warriors fortified their positions. One warrior in a front-end loader tore chunks out of the hillside on the edge of the golf course, piling up the dirt to build rows of new barricades between the Mohawks and the town of Oka below. After two hours of work, the warriors planted a small pine in the centre of the new three-metre-high roadblock. "It's the tree of peace," one of the warriors said in sombre tones.

Late in the afternoon of August 8, Robert Bourassa invoked the

National Defence Act and called upon the Canadian Armed Forces to replace the Sûreté du Québec on the police lines around Kanesatake and Kahnawake. At the same time, Brian Mulroney announced the appointment of a special mediator, Quebec Chief Justice Alan Gold, to try to reach an agreement between the Mohawks and the government on the question of the preconditions to negotiations.

The prime minister's office had consulted the Mohawks about Gold's appointment, and the Mohawk negotiators welcomed the move. They saw it as a sign that Ottawa was finally assuming its responsibilities in the crisis. Looking exhausted and relieved, Joe Deom sounded conciliatory as he put the best possible face on Quebec's decision to call in the Armed Forces.

"The army operates under a different set of rules than the Sûreté du Québec," Deom said. "They must follow the Geneva Convention, and therefore the U.N. Declaration of Human Rights. So as far as that's concerned, we're better off. The army doesn't have any vendetta to avenge. I kind of like the connotation of a peacekeeping force here — except I would have preferred perhaps the Swiss army."

CHAPTER 10
Buck Fever

Behind the Barricades at Kahnawake

The noise was deafening. The mob of Châteauguay residents had gathered at the front entrance of the IGA grocery store, and they were screaming and hissing at a frightened Mohawk woman who was trapped inside. To prevent the Mohawk woman from escaping, cars were parked in front of the entrance. The drivers were leaning on their horns, honking loudly and incessantly. The store manager was forced to lock his doors to prevent the mob from barging in.

It was late in the morning of July 13. The crowd had gathered at the Châteauguay shopping centre when they learned that the police were planning to allow some of the Mohawks, whose families were running short of food, to leave Kahnawake to buy groceries. But the first woman who set foot in the grocery store, just a few hundred metres past the southwestern border of Kahnawake, became a target for the fury of the Châteauguay residents. She finally escaped when the Châteauguay police helped her slip out by a rear exit. They instructed her to leave her groceries behind, to placate the mob. With the help of a sympathetic Châteauguay man, she made it as far as the SQ barricade on Highway 138, but the crowd gathered there spotted her, and angry youths pelted her with tomatoes. Soon after, another Mohawk woman and her two children tried to venture on foot into Châteauguay to get provisions. But as soon as they crossed the police line, they were met by yet another barrage of tomatoes, and they turned and fled back onto the reserve.

Early in the afternoon, a Mohawk ambulance was allowed past the police checkpoint on Highway 138. The mob rushed forward, blocking the ambulance and rocking it back and forth. They forced the driver to open the back door of the ambulance. Inside was a young boy with blood dripping from a gaping wound on his knee. There was a look of pure terror on his face.

Fewer than three days had passed since the Mohawks had seized the Mercier Bridge, and already the mood was turning ugly. For the sixty thousand commuters who used the Mercier Bridge every day, the barricades were a disaster. They were forced to take long detours, and the traffic jams were phenomenal. A drive from downtown Montreal to the south-shore suburbs that normally took twenty minutes had turned into an ordeal of three or four hours.

The forty thousand residents of Châteauguay, who lived just a few kilometres southwest of the Mercier Bridge, were suffering some of the worst headaches. Local businesses were losing an estimated $25,000 a day. The town's mayor, Jean-Bosco Bourcier, was trying to be patient. He knew the town depended on its Mohawk neighbours for millions of dollars in business each year, so he did not want to increase tensions between the predominantly French-speaking suburb and the six thousand English-speaking Mohawks who lived in the territory next door. But already Bourcier was being flooded with complaints from angry citizens. He fired off letters to federal and provincial politicians, demanding that they negotiate an immediate end to the Kahnawake blockade.

The police barricade on Highway 138, controlled by the Sûreté du Québec, with the support of the fifty members of the local Châteauguay police force, quickly became a gathering place for Châteauguay residents who wanted to vent their anger. People crowded onto the road to taunt the warriors, who were camped a few hundred metres farther up the highway. On July 13, when they heard that some Mohawks were being allowed to leave Kahnawake, hundreds of people from Châteauguay swarmed to the barricades. They spotted two young men in camouflage pants and, assuming they were Mohawks, they chased them and beat them up. Police officers moved in and dragged away the victims, sheltering them behind an empty store. A sister of one of the beaten men pleaded for his release while the crowd jeered. "I'm not Indian, OK?" she yelled at the crowd. "My brother is not a warrior."

The crowd threatened to boycott the grocery store at the shopping centre if it served any Mohawks. Later that day, the IGA pulled down a "Welcome" sign that was written in Mohawk in a store window. Then it took down the English version of the sign. Only the French welcome sign was left in the window.

By nightfall, the crowd at the barricade had swelled to two thousand. "*Le Québec aux Québécois!*" one of the men yelled. "Give the Mohawks a case of beer and they'll get out," a woman said. As the mood grew uglier, the police reinforced their checkpoint with a hundred officers in riot gear.

"Bring in the army," the crowd chanted. The idea of military intervention had already been advocated by Ricardo Lopez, the member of Parliament for Châteauguay who was notorious for his criticisms of Indians and who had once suggested that Canadian Indians be shipped to Labrador if they wanted their own country. He became a frequent visitor to the police barricade on Highway 138.

On the other side of the barricade, the warriors taunted the mobs. Some of the Mohawks pointed their weapons at the crowd menacingly, and the mobs dared them to shoot. One of the warriors burned a Quebec *fleur-de-lis*. They played Mohawk chants on loudspeakers at their own bunkers. A warrior on a motorcycle circled in front of the Mohawk barricade, holding aloft a Warrior Society flag.

Early in the evening, one young Mohawk girl crept through the woods to the shopping centre. The crowd spotted her and chased her, but the police formed a tight circle around the girl to protect her. "If we had caught her, she would have got a good beating," one young man boasted as he held aloft a skull-and-crossbones flag.

After the explosion of anger at Châteauguay, the police refused to allow Mohawks to cross the police checkpoint on Highway 138 except in emergencies. As a result, the food shortages at Kahnawake quickly grew worse. The reserve had only a handful of small family-run stores, and the Mohawks usually did most of their shopping in Châteauguay. Soon the stores in Kahnawake had no more stocks of bread, milk, or fresh fruit. Some shipments of food were brought into Kahnawake by boat, but the food was snatched up as soon as it landed on store shelves. One store began selling its provisions at highly inflated prices. After a few days, the Kahnawake radio station complained about the practice and embarrassed the merchant into reducing his prices, though he defended himself by saying he had been forced to raise his prices because of the high cost of gasoline and the runners who were hired to pick up provisions.

For the first two days of the crisis, Betty Coles was as angry as everyone else in Châteauguay. "Who the hell do these Mohawks think they are?" the forty-three-year-old homemaker asked herself as she got into her car to shop for groceries at the IGA on July 13. "They can't take the goddamned bridge every time they're mad about something."

A few minutes later, as she watched the mob besieging the Mohawk woman in the grocery store, she was shocked and disgusted. It was the worst mob scene she had ever encountered in her life. When she returned home from her thwarted shopping trip, she was determined to do something about what she had seen. She telephoned the Kahnawake radio station and asked what she could do to help the Mohawks who could not get food.

Betty Coles became part of a clandestine support network that worked tirelessly to bring food and other provisions into the reserve. The announcers at the radio station suspected that their phone lines were tapped, so they gave Betty Coles the Mohawk translation of the phone number for a secret contact in the supply network. She took down the unfamiliar words painstakingly and practised them for several minutes until she could pronounce the numbers reasonably well. Then she had to track down the father of a Mohawk acquaintance to translate the number into English. Finally she called the contact, known to her only by the codename "Number 50," who was ferrying supplies from a Châteauguay marina to Kahnawake.

Within a few days, the network had grown. A home near the reserve became a safe house for provisions. Slinging their grocery bags on a broomstick, the "food warriors" carted as many as two dozen bags into the reserve at a time, while one of the women stood on the road to make sure nobody spotted the runners. They hurried across the road, through the bush, across a field, through more bush, and finally onto a road, where a Mohawk would meet them.

Betty Coles made only one trek through the bush during the entire operation. Overweight and out-of-shape, she was frightened of the vanloads of Châteauguay vigilantes who were travelling up and down the sideroads near Kahnawake. If they caught her, she knew she could not outrun them.

One day as a woman was standing outside the safe house near the road, with a bag of groceries in each hand, a van whizzed around the corner. "We got one!" the occupants yelled. She raced into the bush, hoping the vigilantes would be afraid to follow her because of the danger of encountering a warrior there. She was right. There were no warriors hiding in the woods, but the vigilantes never took the risk of finding out.

There were many other Châteauguay residents who wanted to help the Mohawks in spite of being terrified of the vigilantes. One night Betty Coles got a call from someone who had a donation of groceries for the Mohawks. When she arrived at his door, the man shook his head. "We're not sympathizing with anybody," he told her gruffly. Then he asked her to come back in an hour. When she returned to the house, it was dark and all the curtains were drawn. Several bags of groceries were sitting on the side of the road, waiting to be collected.

As the summer wore on, the "food warriors" had to use all their ingenuity to find new ways to deliver food to Kahnawake. At one point, they had no means of transportation to take a large load of food to the river, where a boat was waiting for them. One of the "cell" members went to a car dealership near the police line and borrowed a van for a test drive. Then he picked up the food with the van, made his delivery, and returned the van to the dealership.

Meanwhile, the protests in Châteauguay were growing angrier and uglier. The daily "hatefest," as some of the reporters dubbed it, soon fell into a predictable routine. Each day, scores of people would show up at the barricades, setting up their lawnchairs, bringing coolers of beer and other refreshments. One elderly couple came every day to the same little spot in the shade, where they settled in comfortably for a few hours of barricade watching. Hawkers set up mobile canteens, selling coffee and snack food to the crowds. T-shirt vendors sold their wares. Parents brought their children. Teenagers brought their sweethearts. Young men stood on top of a bus shelter, binoculars to their eyes, watching the warriors on the barricade, who gazed back with binoculars of their own.

In the evenings, the crowd began to swell, and as more people arrived, the atmosphere became dangerous. The protesters, who had arrived at the barricades as ordinary people with their own individual frustrations, turned into a frenzied mob as darkness fell.

Just as the sun started to set, someone would bring out a megaphone and begin pumping up the angry crowd. Many of the people were drinking heavily. They hurled obscenities at the Mohawks and mocked the police for failing to do anything to free the bridge. Then someone would hoist up an effigy of a Mohawk warrior, and as it turned dark, the effigy would be set ablaze. The first effigy burning inspired other angry protesters to go home and make their own Mohawk dolls. Every night, someone would bring a homemade *"bon-homme"* to the barricades — at first, the basic Mohawk model, and later, as the standoff dragged on and the riots continued, effigies of Premier Robert Bourassa.

The first nights of riots erupted spontaneously. But within a few days, a few people became active organizers who worked to incite the crowd. One group of men had a Winnebago parked at a gas station near the barricade. They were equipped with walkie-talkies and a megaphone, and they brought coffee and doughnuts for each night's event. It was clear that they were well-organized agitators who had drawn up plans in advance.

"We're here to do the job for the police," one of the men told a reporter who inquired about their activities, but he grew circumspect when she pressed for more information. The man, known to his friends as "Rocky," kept a close eye on the reporter and monitored her reports on the radio. Early one morning, after she had spent a night on the barricades, he tracked her down and accused her of portraying the demonstrations as violent and racist. "If you want to live, you better back off," he told her.

Later in the week, when the same radio reporter tried to record an argument between Rocky and another journalist, Rocky knocked away her microphone and smacked her in the face with enough force to knock her to the ground. A police officer, who had witnessed the entire incident, stood by silently without taking any action. The reporter demanded that Rocky be arrested. But the police refused to take her complaint. They said the journalists would have to press charges themselves at the local Châteauguay station.

This was only one of countless incidents in which the mobs tried to intimidate journalists. TV cameramen were punched and photographers had their cameras damaged or broken. A crowd led by Rocky surrounded a TV station's satellite truck, rocking it and shaking it until the reporter emerged. The police told her to leave the barricade because they could not guarantee her safety.

All this anger was directed at journalists — particularly English-speaking ones — because the Châteauguay mobs thought they were being unfairly portrayed as violent racists and bigots. But screams of "*maudits sauvages!*" and the burning of effigies could not be interpreted as anything but blatant racism. Many people insisted that they hated the Mohawks not because they were Indians, but because they thought they were "above the law." Few people seemed aware of the Mohawk concepts of sovereignty and traditional law, nor did they consider the fact that the Mercier Bridge and the network of highways had been rammed through Mohawk territory with virtually no consultation.

The venom of the Châteauguay mobs came spewing forth in acts and statements that defied reason. "If I find out who you work for and if I hear you reporting that we are violent, I am going to find you and knock your head in," one man shouted at a reporter. Beside him, her little hand gripping his, stood the man's eight-year-old daughter. The reporter didn't know whether to laugh or cry.

The carnival atmosphere at the barricades drew all kinds of fringe groups. Motorcycle gangs roared around the boulevard, sometimes racing down the highway towards the police line. They surrounded reporters and others whom they wanted to intimidate. White "warriors" threatened to hire bulldozers to plough through the Mohawk barricades. One man who owned an eighteen-wheel semi-trailer boasted that he was planning to force his way past the police and knock down the Mohawk barricade.

After a few days of rioting, the Sûreté du Québec erected a metal barricade to separate themselves from the crowds. Over and over again, the mobs surged forward and knocked down the fence. One night, a man succeeded in breaking through the police line and kept on running toward the Mohawks. When he looked back, however, he discovered that nobody was following him, and hastily retreated.

On July 14, the night the first effigy was burned in Châteauguay, Michael Rice was rudely awakened from an early sleep. A call had just gone out over the Kahnawake radio station asking for reinforcements on the Highway 138 barricade. It was the worst night of rioting at Châteauguay since the crisis had begun, and the warriors were afraid the mob would break past the police line and storm the reserve. After two months of basic training in the Canadian militia, this was Rice's first weekend leave, and he was exhausted. But he jumped into his army gear and flagged down a school bus, which drove through the village fifteen minutes after the broadcast of the announcement to pick up volunteers. Hordes of men, wearing hard hats and lacrosse helmets, carrying bats, tire-irons, slingshots, and lacrosse sticks swarmed to the barricade, ready to club the Châteauguay rioters if they broke through the police roadblock and crossed into Kahnawake territory. The invasion never happened, but after that, whenever there was a threat from the Châteauguay mobs, an alert would go out on the portable radios. "We need a baseball team," the warriors would say, and hundreds of Mohawks would be mobilized within minutes.

The warriors watched the nightly spectacle with some amusement. Often they crouched down quietly in the bushes, just five or ten metres away from the fringe of the mob. "We had front-row seats," says Mark "Blackjack" Montour.

Inside the reserve, many Mohawks watched in horror as the nightly riots were broadcast on their television sets. The men and women in the mobs just outside Kahnawake were their neighbours. They were clerks at the Châteauguay stores where the Mohawks shopped, customers at the Mohawk discount cigarette stores, or parents of the classmates and team-mates of the Mohawk children. What the Mohawks saw on the faces of those who chanted beneath the burning effigies was pure racial hatred. The mobs helped to unify the Kahnawake Mohawks and solidify their support for the warriors at the barricades.

On the morning of July 11, Kahnawake's grand chief, Joe Norton, had been wakened by a call from the chief peacekeeper on the reserve,

Joseph Montour, who told him the warriors had blocked the Mercier Bridge and the highways. Montour was not yet sure why the bridge had been seized, but he thought the action might be linked to an incident early that morning. Just after 2:00 a.m., two Montreal Urban Community police officers had chased a couple of suspected car thieves over the Mercier Bridge from LaSalle and into Kahnawake. When the police tried to arrest the pair, they were surrounded by fifteen unarmed Mohawks. The Mohawk peacekeepers had asked the MUC officers to withdraw before there was any violence, and the police had complied. Montour suspected that the Mercier Bridge barricades might be a response to that incident. Or, he mentioned almost as an afterthought, it might have something to do with a dawn raid by the Sûreté du Québec in Kanesatake. There were reports that the SQ were using tear gas and concussion grenades to clear the roadblocks in the Pines.

By the time Norton had confirmed that the barricades were indeed a response to the police raid in Kanesatake, he was already being swamped by telephone calls from Ottawa and Quebec City — including calls from the Prime Minister's Office, from Tom Siddon, John Ciaccia, and Sam Elkas, and from Premier Robert Bourassa himself. Bourassa demanded that Norton carry out his "responsibilities" as a leader, insisting that Norton put down the revolt and get the bridge open. Norton explained that Kahnawake had not yet assessed the situation. When the premier kept pressing him, threatening to use the full force of the law on Kahnawake if the barricades did not come down, Norton told Bourassa that the conversation was over. Then he hung up on the premier.

The Prime Minister's Office took a different tack. Brian Mulroney's staff wanted to know what kind of help they could offer Kahnawake's elected council to help quell the uprising. They seemed to believe that the Mohawk community needed to be rescued from the warriors. But the grand chief had no desire to be "rescued" by anyone.

Norton still did not have enough details of what had happened in Kanesatake to judge whether the events of that morning justified the stand the Kahnawake warriors had taken. Eventually, he reached the people in the Pines by phone. He spoke to Ellen Gabriel, who urged him to back the warriors. The Mohawks in Kanesatake were certain that the SQ was planning a second attack and that the Kahnawake warriors' seizure of the Mercier Bridge was the only protection they had.

At first, the elected council and the Kahnawake community as a whole were divided over whether to support the warriors. At community meetings in the first few days, Norton and his council came under pressure from many Kahnawake Mohawks to persuade the warriors to take down the barricades. The warriors themselves showed no willingness to dismantle the barricades as long as hundreds of police officers were massed around Kanesatake — especially since they believed the Mercier Bridge was the only bargaining chip the Kanesatake Mohawks had. Norton and his council had to weigh their options carefully. The grand chief was anxious to preserve unity in Kahnawake, and if he ordered the warriors to dismantle the barricades and they refused, the councillors and the Kahnawake peacekeepers would be forced to confront their own brothers, uncles, fathers, and children on the barricades. "If that fails, what are we going to do?" Norton asked. "Are we going to fight?"

The memory of the civil war in Akwesasne in the spring of 1990 was still fresh in everyone's minds. In the conflict over Akwesasne's gambling casinos, Mohawks had fought Mohawks and two men had died. "We did not want to see the same thing happen here," Norton says. "There would have been internal fighting, and the SQ and the RCMP would have taken advantage of that situation and come in. Seeing disunity, seeing that there wasn't popular support for the elected system — that would have been the signal for the police to come into the community."

On July 13, there was a funeral for a young Mohawk man who had died of an inoperable brain tumour in a Montreal hospital. He was one of six sons of Shirley Goodleaf, a political moderate who worked at the Kanienkehaka Raotitiohka Cultural Centre in Kahnawake. It was the start of a hellish summer for Goodleaf. Her husband was also in hospital, suffering from a stroke, and she could not get out of Kahnawake to visit him. Despite her personal hardships, she decided to remain inside the reserve as long as the blockade lasted. She said she finally knew how her ancestors felt when they were being forced off their traditional land, describing it as a feeling of helplessness — "like someone has his foot on your neck." She was not a Longhouse follower, but she supported the warriors, and her surviving sons served on the barricades throughout the summer.

After her son's death, the Mohawks had great difficulty getting his body back to the reserve. On the day of the funeral, two of the Goodleaf brothers went to the main barricade on Highway 138 to collect the flowers from a delivery truck waiting there, and they were stoned by the Châteauguay mobs.

At the funeral, the Mohawks discussed the crisis with Joe Norton and other councillors. At first, some of them had hesitated to support the barricades in Kahnawake and Kanesatake, but then they recalled how an older generation of Kahnawake leaders had allowed the St. Lawrence Seaway, the Mercier Bridge, and other bridges and highways to be pushed through their territory. "We had always said we would never let them do what they did to our fathers and grandfathers," one Kahnawake Mohawk recalls. This was their opportunity to show that they could fight the government instead of letting the government win by default.

A few days after the police raid on the Pines, Ellen Gabriel and Denise David-Tolley took a boat to Kahnawake to meet with the community to describe the crisis in Kanesatake and to try to convince the Kahnawake Mohawks who still questioned the warriors' stand that it was important that the barricades remain in place on the Mercier Bridge. "Some of them didn't believe we had been shot at," says Ellen Gabriel. "We had to tell them what had happened, and thank them for putting the barricades up."

Norton knew that if he and his council decided to support the barricades, they would alienate some Mohawks who opposed the warriors. But the elected chief had his finger on the pulse of the community, and it quickly became clear to him that the majority of the Mohawks were ready to defend Kahnawake and Kanesatake. On July 15, four days after the barricades were erected, the elected council voted unanimously to back the warriors and keep the barricades up. Hundreds of Mohawks attended a community meeting at the Knights of Columbus Hall that day and ratified the decision to support the barricades.

From that day forward, the elected council worked closely with the Mohawk Nation Office, the Kahnawake Warrior Society's political arm, and the councillors agreed to attend meetings at the Kahnawake

Longhouse. "There was a coming-together," Norton says. "There was an effort at unifying the leadership in the community to deal with this issue."

The Kahnawake Mohawks who supported the elected council insisted that their grand chief should not leave negotiations with the Quebec and federal governments to the warriors alone. As a result, Joe Norton told the warriors that in exchange for his support, he wanted a role in the talks. The Mohawk Nation Office complied, entrusting Norton with a dual mandate to negotiate on behalf of both the Kahnawake Longhouse and the elected council.

Meanwhile, Joe Deom, Laura Norton, Lorna Delormier, and the other clan mothers and advisors from the Kahnawake Longhouse had gone to Kanesatake in response to a request for assistance from the people in the Pines, and they were settling into their role as negotiators and strategists. Some of them balked at the idea of allying themselves with Joe Norton, since they refused to recognize the authority of anyone elected under the federal Indian Act. But Norton reminded them that even the most militant of the Kahnawake Mohawks, the warriors at the Mohawk Nation Office, had agreed to work with him and his council. In the end, they accepted the arrangement, and Norton became a key negotiator throughout the summer.

Norton and one of his senior councillors, Chief Billy Two Rivers, made several trips to Kanesatake to discuss negotiating strategy with the people in the Pines. Two Rivers was a former professional wrestler who used to enter the ring decked out in an Indian feather war bonnet when he had travelled around the world as an exotic attraction on the wrestling circuit from 1955 to 1976. The two men were experienced negotiators, and they exerted a moderating influence on the Longhouse people in the Pines.

At first, the Kahnawake chiefs went by car to Kanesatake, but they were constantly delayed at the SQ checkpoints, so they started making the journey by boat. Even then, they were almost always stopped on the water by the SQ or the RCMP. On more than one occasion, Norton had a gun pointed at his head while the police checked his identification.

Norton was unflappable. "The longer you hold me up," he told one nervous SQ officer who was pointing an M-16 at him, "the more difficult it becomes to settle this."

Once they understood that the issue was the defence of Mohawk territory, the Kahnawake Mohawks rallied to the cause with a singular sense of purpose. Even some of the strongest critics of the warriors picked up guns and joined the warriors on the Kahnawake front lines. Some of the Mohawks went to the Longhouse for the first time in their lives. Men who usually wore three-piece suits showed up on the barricades in camouflage gear. Mohawks as old as sixty-three became warriors. Young men who usually spent their days in an alcoholic stupor sobered up and stayed sober. They had their territory to fight for, and helping in that fight restored their pride.

Even Joe Norton's sixteen-year-old son joined the men on the barricades. "He's not a terrorist, he's not a murderer, he's not a criminal," Norton told the hundreds of people who thronged to a peace rally on the outskirts of Oka on July 29. "My wife and I did not raise that boy to be any of those things. But he knows what his duty is. And how could I stop him?"

Andrew Delisle Jr., the son of a longtime elected chief, was a thirty-two-year-old artist and construction contractor who had never been politically active before July 11. He walked into the Nation Office on July 12, got a tour of the barricades from a warrior, and immediately joined the Nation Office as a full-time volunteer. "People took a stand for what they believed in, and that's what drew me in," Delisle says.

Delisle's father, Andrew Delisle Sr., joined the Nation Office a few days later. For most of the 1960s and 1970s, he was Kahnawake's top elected chief, and he was a bitter rival of the Longhouse leaders. But the crisis of 1990 brought him into a strong alliance with the Longhouse for the first time.

Delisle Sr.'s sister is June Delisle, the administrator of the Kateri Memorial Hospital in Kahnawake. A former elected councillor and a political moderate, she walked into the Mohawk Nation Office for the first time in her life after she learned of the police raid on July 11. She talked to Ken Deer, an activist in the Nation Office, and then she talked to Joe Norton at the council office. "If you need me, I'm here," she told both of them.

June Delisle was placed in charge of bringing food into Kahnawake. She co-ordinated the efforts of the Red Cross, the Native Women's Association and the Native Friendship Centre in Montreal, and the network of church groups and individuals who collected food for the Mohawks, including Betty Coles and her "cell." In late July, she helped arrange for a Red Cross airplane to land in Kahnawake to bring in food and medicine.

For more than a decade, Delisle has been confined to a wheelchair because she suffers from muscular dystrophy. But she insisted on staying in Kahnawake throughout the crisis, despite her medical condition. She picked up a handful of earth. "This is mine, and I'm not giving it up," she said.

Delisle was proud of how the crisis unified the Mohawk community and engendered a stronger feeling of Mohawk identity. "It brought a sense of knowing who we are," she said. "There were people at the barricades who you'd never expect to see — docile people who never say too much. I was so ecstatic when I saw it."

Seven Mohawks, including June Delisle, met every morning to evaluate the situation in Kahnawake. They became known as the "Group of Seven." They were the emergency team, representing the care providers and officials from various sectors of the community. Within a few days a food bank was established at a community hall within walking distance of most people in the village of Kahnawake. When provisions arrived, they were divided between the food bank and the cookhouse at the Longhouse, where women organized and cooked meals for the men at the barricades. At the food bank, elderly Mohawks and other volunteers divided the donations into family-size rations. Fresh fruit was always in short supply, and it was set aside for diabetics and other people with medical conditions.

Kahnawake's restaurants became communal kitchens. Women volunteered to cook food for the warriors, and men made trips from kitchen to kitchen in all-terrain vehicles, picking up the meals and driving them out to the barricades. Within a few days of the beginning of the standoff, gasoline was in such short supply that it was rationed. By the end of the first week, it was "for official use only," limited to emergency vehicles and warriors on duty. That meant the people in the community could not get out to the barricades to visit the men posted there. So a school bus was requisitioned, and it made trips several times a day from the village to the barricades so that the women and children could visit their husbands, fathers and brothers on duty. Most people rode bicycles, or sometimes horses, to get around the reserve.

"It was so peaceful," says Helen Cross, who lives a stone's throw

Mohawk women moments after shoot-out in the Pines.
July 11, 1990.

Photo Credit: John Kenney, Montreal Gazette

Warrior in commandeered SQ cruiser.
July 11, 1990.

Photo Credit: John Kenney, Montreal Gazette

Warriors perched atop front-end loader on Highway 344.
July 11, 1990.

Photo Credit: John Kenney, Montreal Gazette

"Sunshine" with crying child and box of bullets. July 11, 1990.
Photo Credit: John Kenney, Montreal Gazette

Quebec Native Affairs Minister and aides climb Highway 344
toward Mohawk barrricade, SQ road-block in background.
July, 1990.

Photo Credit Shaney Komulainen

Ellen Gabriel with warrior

Photo Credit: John Kenney, Montreal Gazette

Warriors at "Main Gate." ("Blackjack" at far right.) August, 1990.

Photo Credit: Shaney Komulainen

"Stonecarver"

Photo Credit: John Kenney, Montreal Gazette

17-year-old warrior at the razor wire

Canadian soldiers stand at original barricade in the Pines.
September, 1990.

"Mad Jap" confronts military police at razor wire.
September, 1990.

Photo Credit: John Kenney, Montreal Gazette

Micmac warrior "Beaver"

Photo Credit: John Kenney, Montreal Gazette

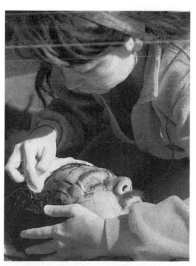

Cathy Sky attends to beaten "Spudwrench."
September 8, 1990.

Photo Credit: Shaney Komulainen

"Lasagna" with arsenal inside Treatment Centre compound.
September 23, 1990.

Photo Credit: John Kenney, Montreal Gazette

Rorhare waves Mohawk Warrior Flag inside Treatment
Centre compound, military helicopter hovers over
Lake of Two Mountains.
September, 1990.

Photo Credit: Sylvain Julienne

Aniatariio looks beyond razor wire.
September, 1990.

Photo Credit: John Kenney, Montreal Gazette

Mohawks and supporters at Treatment Centre burn tobacco together for
the last time, September 26, 1990

Photo Credit: Shaney Komulainen

"Lasagna" disposes weapon in fire during final moments at Treatment Centre.
September 26, 1990.

Photo Credit: John Kenney, Montreal Gazette

Mohawks and their supporters leave Treatment Centre.
September 26, 1990.

Photo Credit: Shaney Komulainen

Oneida faithkeeper Bruce Elijah with sacred objects
(false face mask or "hatui" and eagle wing.)
September 26, 1990.

Photo Credit: Shaney Komulainen

14-year-old Waneek Horn-Miller, with sister
Ganyetahawi, tries to break free of soldier's grip.
September 26, 1990.

Photo Credit: John Kenney, Montreal Gazette

away from Highway 132. "For the first time, I didn't have to worry about my kids playing close to the highway."

The Kahnawake radio station, CKRK, became a key information centre for the Mohawks. Every day the station let people know whether gasoline was available, what hours the medical clinic and the food bank would be open and when the "tour bus" would be leaving for the barricades. Thousands of non-Mohawks listened to the station and called in on its popular hot-line shows; the station was swamped with faxes of support from as far away as British Columbia and the Virgin Islands. But the CKRK announcers inadvertently played into the hands of the Mohawks' opponents. Media outlets such as the popular French-language radio station CJMS monitored CKRK and relayed information to its wide audience about the evacuation plans for Kahnawake's women, children and elderly in late August. That allowed the white vigilantes who were glued to CJMS for its up-to-the-minute details of the crisis to know exactly where to assemble to block the Mohawks' departure.

Complicated arrangements had to be made for Mohawks who required chemotherapy or other medical treatment in Montreal, which meant that patients at the Kahnawake hospital were reluctant to leave the reserve for X-rays or other treatment unless it was absolutely necessary. "People took enormous risks with their personal health for fear of leaving the community," says Dr. Louis Montour, who is the hospital's medical director and a Mohawk. The SQ refused to guarantee that Kahnawake's two ambulances would be allowed back into the community once they left, so patients had to be transferred to provincial ambulances at the police line, where the waiting mobs often jeered and harassed them.

Every time they entered Kahnawake, the non-Mohawk staff of Kateri Memorial Hospital were also forced to endure long identification checks by armed police officers while the mobs taunted and harassed them. "They would try every means they could to dissuade me from coming on (to the reserve)," said Dr. Sue Tatemichi. "They were trying to terrorize me." Dr. Ann MacAuley, a doctor who worked several weekends at the hospital, had her car rocked by angry crowds at Delson, east of Kahnawake. They threatened to roll her car into the ditch.

Later in the summer, after the Mohawks had obtained permission from John Ciaccia's family to set up a landing dock on Ciaccia's lakeshore property in Dorval, some of the doctors and nurses travelled into Kahnawake by boat. "It was an act of great humanitarianism," says Dr. Montour. But three days after the dock went up, vigilante groups began patrolling the lakeshore, and gangs gathered on Ciaccia's Dorval property with sticks and baseball bats. On one occasion, a doctor had to be flown across the St. Lawrence River by chartered helicopter, at a cost of $650. The hospital asked the Armed Forces to fly in medical staff, but they refused.

Amanda Jacobs, a twenty-one-year-old Mohawk woman who was expecting her first baby, did not want to take the risk of crossing the barricades and being harassed by the mobs, so when she went into labour early in the morning of July 27, her mother called Amanda's aunt, Selma Delisle, who was a midwife. She also called Helen Cross, who had given birth to her eleven-year-old son Skahionhati behind the barricades at Akwesasne during the siege at Raquette Point in 1979. "It felt so good for all of them to be there with me," Amanda Jacobs recalls. At 7:54 a.m., she gave birth to a girl. The baby's father buried the placenta in the ground, in the old Mohawk way, giving thanks to Mother Earth for the baby's life.

Amanda Jacobs' daughter was the first of four babies to be born at home behind the barricades in Kahnawake during the standoff. Selma Delisle, Kahnawake's midwife and the "godmother" of Kahnawake's cigarette trade, helped all of them into the world. One baby was named Liberty, and Amanda's daughter was given the Mohawk name Iontateweni:io, which means "freedom."

A few days after the police raid on the Pines, the Kahnawake warriors asked for help from the military veterans of their community. The Legion branch at Kahnawake had about 120 members, including thirty Vietnam vets, two of whom were key warrior leaders: Mark "Cookie" McComber and a warrior codenamed Windwalker. They asked a fellow Vietnam veteran, codenamed Little Marine, to recruit help from the Legion. An infusion of army veterans was needed because some of the younger warriors did not know how to dig proper bunkers or conduct military-style patrols. A meeting of Legion members was called, and everyone volunteered their support — even the older vets, who drove ambulances, delivered food to the barricades, and did whatever they could to help.

Gerald "Slim" Marquis, a thirty-two-year-old construction worker, had never been a member of the Kahnawake Warrior Society. "But I was always there if they needed me," he said. He described himself as "on call." Marquis, who served in the U.S. Army in Germany from 1976 to 1979, was appointed a squad leader at Highway 138 because of his military experience. He gave briefings to his five-man squad to help them learn about the weaponry of the police and the army, and he taught some of them how to use a gun.

The warriors got help from some surprising sources. A number of Kahnawake Mohawks were in basic training in the U.S. Army, in North Carolina and elsewhere in the United States at the time of the crisis. Each was allowed a seven-day leave, and they took advantage of their free time to return to Kahnawake, where they picked up guns and helped to man the barricades. They were still wearing their U.S. Army uniforms when they passed through the SQ lines on their way back to Kahnawake.

Twenty-one-year-old Michael Rice was in training with the Canadian militia at the Longue Pointe military base in Montreal when the crisis began. On July 12, a contingent of soldiers from the famed 22nd Regiment — the "Van Doos" — arrived at the base, where they were ordered to remain on standby close to the Mohawk communities in case the army was called to respond to the crisis. Rice overheard a couple of them joking about the possibility of "killing a few Indians." He called his mother in Kahnawake, and, speaking in Mohawk so the other soldiers could not understand, he warned her of the army's plans. The next day he left the army base, returned to Kahnawake, and joined the warriors. Soon a dozen other Mohawks quit the Canadian militia, returning to Kahnawake to help the men at the barricades.

Around the middle of July, the Kahnawake Longhouse sent a "request-for-assistance" wampum to the Oneidas of southwestern Ontario, the closest allies of the Mohawk warriors. About one hundred Oneida warriors from Ontario, New York State, and Wisconsin came to help. Most went to the Kahnawake barricades. A dozen Micmacs from Nova Scotia, some of whom eventually moved on to Kanesatake, also volunteered to help man the barricades. Kahnawake became the main gathering point for warriors from Akwesasne and other Indian territories who were sent to Kanesatake to relieve the men on duty there.

White sympathizers, too, tried to help the warriors. When they opened some of the bags of groceries that had been smuggled into the reserve from non-native supporters, the Mohawks were surprised to find revolvers and other handguns. A number of the Mohawk sympathizers were virulently anti-French white anglophones who offered their services in order to vent their anger against their French-speaking neighbours. But the Mohawks wanted no part of a language war, and they refused to associate with the anti-French bigots.

Later in the summer, two young white "Rambo" types crept past the police and the army and onto the reserve to join the men on the barricades. They were already wearing camouflage gear and carrying guns. The warriors said they appreciated the offer of help, but they could not be sure whether the two volunteers were trustworthy — so they asked the two young Rambos to leave.

For the first few days, there were no organized shifts at the Kahnawake barricades. Slim Marquis spent three days at his post, sleeping in the bush. Breaks were so infrequent that if the Mohawks had not organized the "tour buses" to the barricades, some of the men would have seen their families only rarely. Once shifts were established, the situation improved, however, and at the peak of the summer, the warriors had two squad leaders and as many as forty warriors per shift at each highway.

As support for the barricades in Kahnawake grew, as many as five or six hundred men took turns on duty. "It was everyone's father, son, brother or uncle on the barricades," says Trish Delormier, a Mohawk law student from Kahnawake. Indeed, it would have been nearly impossible for the four highways and the bridge to be constantly barricaded and for the warriors to be sustained with food and supplies for six weeks unless there was strong support from the community.

Even some of the Longhouse chiefs joined the warriors. One of the younger ones, Donald "Babe" Hemlock, picked up a gun on July 11 and went to the barricades. Because Longhouse chiefs are supposed to be peace chiefs, he had to step down temporarily from his Longhouse position to become a warrior. Two other Longhouse chiefs did the same thing.

"I had to go where I felt I was needed the most," Hemlock said.

When he was first appointed to the Longhouse by clan mothers in 1988, he had warned them he would probably be at the barricades if trouble happened. The clan mothers said they understood.

Like the warriors at Kanesatake, the Kahnawake Mohawks believed they had one significant advantage over the army and the police. For most of the summer at least, the warriors were willing to die for their cause, whereas most Canadian soldiers had never expected to see combat duty when they joined the army. "The army and the police are fighting for a paycheque," one Mohawk remarked.

There were many moments during the summer when the warriors believed they would die. Twice, when tensions were high, Little Marine was scared enough to say his final goodbyes to his wife.

Wendell Beauvais, a Longhouse chief with close connections to the warriors, believes the warriors were so highly motivated and disciplined that they could have repelled the first thrust of a military attack, even though it was inevitable that the army would eventually win because of its superior technology and manpower. "I think we had more combat experience than they did," he said.

Beauvais was appointed as the main messenger at Kahnawake during the summer. On his daily rounds to the fourteen bunkers and barricades where warriors were located — a tour which took six hours to complete — Beauvais answered questions and provided the latest bulletins on the state of negotiations. He gave updates on the food situation and he passed on sensitive information that could not be transmitted on the two-way radios. Wild rumours often swept through the reserve, so rumour control was one of his main tasks.

The headquarters of the Kahnawake Warrior Society was moved to a secret location inside the village during the summer, since the official WS base, adjacent to the Longhouse, was too obvious a target for the SQ and the army.

Allan Delaronde, the war chief in the Kahnawake Longhouse, played an important role in the summer's events, but ironically he was not a military commander. He had less influence than the squad leaders, because he had no direct control over the non-Longhouse Mohawks, who made up the majority of the men at the barricades. Delaronde opened and closed the community meetings at the Longhouse, where the barricade strategy was debated, and he conducted tobacco-burning ceremonies at the bunkers each morning at dawn, asking for "good minds" for the warriors to help them protect the land and the people. Each morning he travelled to the four major barricades, dropping off tobacco at each one. Then he would conduct the thanksgiving ceremony at the final barricade while other Longhouse members conducted ceremonies at the other roadblocks.

Legion members provided most of the brains for the organization of the Mohawk defences at Kahnawake. The Vietnam veterans advised the warriors to put bunkers on either side of their barricades to prevent ambushes. Some of the bunkers were decoys, designed to lure the police or the army into attacking an empty bunker. Later in the summer, the warriors dug a series of "tank traps" at their barricades in case they were attacked by armoured personnel carriers. The traps were carefully designed to be big enough so that the front end of the APC would fall downward, but too short for the armoured vehicles to crawl out.

The warriors at Kahnawake had two different lines of defence, known as Plan A and Plan B. The first line of defence, Plan A, consisted of the original barricades on each highway at the edge of the reserve. The warriors knew they couldn't hold the original barricades if the police or the army attacked. The "Plan A" locations were poor strategic positions because they were surrounded by miles of open highway. Plan B was the fallback position, on the outskirts of the village, including sites with natural defensive advantages such as a tunnel underneath a railway line on the northern edge of the village, known as "Hole in the Wall." If the army got past the Plan B positions and into the village, the warriors would wage guerrilla warfare from house to house.

Psychological warfare was a crucial element of the Mohawk strategy. After the army listed the technical names of the machine guns they claimed the warriors possessed, the warriors began using those names in their radio communications — to intimidate the army into thinking they really had the hardware.

Taking their psychological advantage a step further, the Mohawks used a variety of homemade devices to imitate the high-powered weapons the army thought they had. A circular cutting tool used in ironworking became an imitation M72 rocket launcher. An ordinary black plumbing tube was placed in the back of a pick-up truck and camouflaged so that it resembled an anti-tank missile launcher. The ruses worked. When the army distributed a press kit on warrior armaments in late August, it included a photo of an M72. The warriors roared with laughter when they saw the photos on TV that night.

The warriors called the army's reaction "buck fever" — a psychological syndrome that afflicts deer hunters who are overanxious to find a deer. They look for their quarry so intensely that they sometimes assume a cow or a horse must be a deer, and shoot the wrong animal. Wanting to see high-powered weapons in warrior hands to confirm their intelligence reports, the army persisted in believing that the Mohawk decoys were weapons. Even in their negotiations with the warriors in late August, the army commanders referred to rocket launchers and anti-tank weapons, and they called the Mohawks liars when they insisted that they had no such armaments.

"We played on their fears and let their imaginations play games with them," said Cookie McComber, one of the assistant war chiefs. "It was their paranoia. They took themselves so seriously."

The warriors covered empty shoe boxes in black, strapped them to their backs, and clambered over the Mercier Bridge to make the SQ think they were planting explosives on the bridge. They used welding torches on old scrap iron, behind a blind, to make it seem as if they were cutting the anchor bolts of the bridge to weaken it. And they wandered around an empty field, looking at a map, to pretend they were picking their way through a minefield. It was all part of a deliberate strategy to keep their enemies off guard and confused. "It was like a chess game," said Little Marine. "They didn't know who we were, they didn't know what to expect," added Michael Thomas, another warrior leader.

Psychological warfare is an old Mohawk tactic. In 1988, the first time the warriors seized the Mercier Bridge, they put a .50-calibre machine gun on the structure to intimidate the police — but the gun was just for show. It was actually an old World War II relic, and it had cement in its barrel.

In reality, the warriors had very few of the deadliest weapons. They did have a .50-calibre semi-automatic machine gun, capable of firing 450 to 600 rounds per minute, which was eventually seized by the army in a raid on the Kahnawake Longhouse. Its bullets were half an inch thick and four inches long, and they could penetrate an armoured personnel carrier at 800 metres. However, the warriors claim it only had a five-bullet clip and was legally purchased for $9,000 at a gun shop. After the summer, the Kahnawake peacekeepers found another large machine gun, mounted on a tripod. The gun had been hidden by the warriors, and a group of children eventually stumbled upon it.

Contrary to the assumptions of many outsiders, the warriors did not have a large number of illegal automatic weapons. Semi-automatic guns such as AK-47s can be easily converted to fire automatically. But the warriors disliked the converted weapons because their accuracy is significantly reduced. Automatic guns fire so rapidly that they are difficult to hold steady. And they tend to waste ammunition. "That automatic stuff is the Hollywood image," says Cookie McComber. The warriors preferred the AK-47 because it is compact and lighter than a hunting rifle. "It's really ugly, cheap wood," McComber says. "It's got no artistic value."

Some newspapers claimed that the warriors had as many as six thousand guns. In reality they had about five to six hundred. At the beginning of the crisis, there were not enough guns for every Mohawk man at the barricades at Kahnawake. Because of the shortage of guns, most of the warriors were forced to rely on shotguns, 22-calibre hunting rifles, baseball bats and wooden sticks. If a Mohawk had two or three guns, he shared them with other Mohawks. The vast majority of the weapons, including the semi-automatic weapons, had been purchased legally before July 11 by warriors who obtained firearms acquisition certificates from the second floor of the SQ headquarters on Parthenais Street in Montreal. In most cases, the SQ mailed the firearms certificates to the warriors within two weeks.

The AK-47s were divided among the groups of warriors, so that each patrol had one or two semi-automatic weapons. One of the warriors had only a .303 hunting rifle with twenty rounds of ammunition at the start of the summer, but he soon succeeded in purchasing an AK-47. Despite the presence of the police and the army, the warriors continued to buy weapons and military supplies throughout the summer. In the third or fourth week of the crisis, a shipment of about eighty AK-47s was smuggled into Kahnawake to ease the weapon shortage. All summer the warriors were freely obtaining military gear, camouflage clothing, and ammunition. Most gun stores in Montreal were quite happy to sell weapons to the warriors, even when they produced their Indian cards to get a tax exemption.

Despite their bluffs, it is unlikely that the warriors went so far as to wire the Mercier Bridge with explosives. However, it would not have been a difficult task if they had chosen to do so. The Mohawks had enough explosives in their local construction companies to blow up dozens of bridges.

To ease the boredom of the long stalemate, the warriors spent many hours planting boobytraps in the bush around Highway 138. It was the only location where the SQ or the army could outflank the Mohawks. They dug holes in the bush, put four-inch nails in wooden boards, put the boards at the bottom of the holes, and covered the holes with branches. It was a trick they had learned in Vietnam, where they used bamboo instead of nails.

In another old Vietnam trick, the warriors put fish hooks on tree branches in the woods. The hooks would not seriously injure anyone, but if they caught an eye or a limb they would put a soldier or police officer temporarily out of action.

Eventually the bush was so full of boobytraps that it was dangerous even for the warriors to enter it. "We couldn't even go on patrol any more because we had forgotten where we put the traps," Little Marine admits.

As the summer dragged on, the stress of the situation at Kahnawake took its toll on many of the Mohawks. Rhonda Horne, the eighteen-year-old daughter of one of the warriors at Kanesatake, suffered a nervous breakdown in late July after weeks of worrying about her parents in the Pines. She had to be taken by ambulance to a Montreal hospital after she began hyperventilating.

By early August, a growing number of Mohawks were fed up with the armed blockade. There had been no negotiations between the Mohawks in the Pines and the government in more than three weeks. The riots in Châteauguay were growing uglier and more violent, and some Kahnawake Mohawks feared the militant position of the Mohawk nationalists was starting to wear down the sympathies of the Canadian public. They began to question the usefulness of continuing the standoff.

"A lot of people felt the point had been made," says Don Horne, who was the executive director of the band-controlled Kahnawake Social Services. "They wanted the negotiators to take a more rational approach. We had the greatest opportunity to achieve something while the attention and sympathy were with us, but we allowed that to be lost."

Some Mohawks, like Reena Diabo, who also worked for Kahnawake Social Services, had never supported the barricades. After one angry community meeting in early August, in which opponents to the barricades felt their complaints were being ignored, she decided to leave Kahnawake with her three children. She wanted to be sure that her two-year-old son, who suffered from a medical ailment, could get the regular treatment he needed. From a high school in Pointe Claire, she continued to work closely with Kahnawake Social Services and provincial civil protection authorities, arranging accommodation and help for the hundreds of other Mohawks who began an exodus from Kahnawake.

Those who left the community had many different reasons for going. People who were sick found it difficult to get the food they needed for their special diets. Others had to get to jobs outside Kahnawake and it was almost impossible to make the daily trek through the police lines and the mobs. One Mohawk, Madeleine Montour, took the risk of slipping off the reserve with her grandchildren for what she thought would be a day trip to the city. She was allowed past the police checkpoint on one of the back roads without any problem, but when she returned that night she found the mobs had blocked off the road. The police advised her to turn back. "I can let you go through," an officer told her, "but they'll throw rocks at you. It's not good for the kids to see that." For the next two days, Montour tried to return to Kahnawake, but each time the mobs blocked her route. She ended up moving into a hotel with the children for the next three weeks. The police did little to stop the mobs from blocking exit routes from the reserve, and some leaked information to the vigilantes to help them cut off those routes. One officer complained that hundreds of Mohawks were getting past police checkpoints on Highway 207 because there were no mobs to stop them. "This barricade is a veritable sieve," he told a reporter. "I wonder why the Châteauguay people don't come here to demonstrate their frustration?" Sure enough, the mobs soon swarmed to Highway 207 with their sticks and baseball bats.

For several days at the end of July, the mob activity subsided a bit; many residents of Montreal's south shore had left their homes for Quebec's annual ten-day construction holiday. But when the construction holiday ended on August 1, thousands of workers returned from vacation to face a brutal reality: the barricades were still blocking their path to work.

By then, the angry Châteauguay residents had a leader. He was Yvon Poitras, a forty-seven-year-old retired SQ officer and an aspiring politician who hoped to replace Châteauguay Mayor Jean-Bosco Bourcier in the next municipal election. Now a real estate agent and small businessman, Poitras was well connected in Châteauguay and had little difficulty obtaining the backing of frustrated merchants and businesspeople to organize Solidarité Châteauguay — a pressure group intended to mobilize the people of Châteauguay in a more organized campaign. Solidarité Châteauguay had the encouragement and support of the local member of Parliament, Ricardo Lopez, who lent its organizers the resources of his riding office to produce flyers urging people to participate in demonstrations.

On August 1, Poitras led ten thousand people in a march through the streets of Châteauguay, stopping at the offices of local politicians and demonstrating in front of city hall, where they demanded Mayor Bourcier's resignation. They also called for immediate intervention by the army and made it clear that they were ready to do whatever was necessary — including blocking the highways and bridges themselves — to force the government to take decisive action.

On August 3, the citizens of Châteauguay staged the next phase of their revolt. It began at 5:00 a.m. at the St. Isidore station, where a special commuter train had been operating for the previous two weeks to relieve the congested traffic on the south shore. Fifty cars showed up. They tried to block the train, but failed. Then the convoy headed towards St. Constant, southeast of Kahnawake. Passengers leaned out of their cars, waving baseball bats and urging other vehicles to follow them. The caravan stopped at a major highway intersection in Candiac, east of Kahnawake, where motorists blocked the highway and persuaded several sympathetic truckers to reinforce the blockade with their massive semi-trailers. Other demonstrators blocked the Champlain Bridge. It was morning rush hour, and a colossal traffic jam soon developed. One doctor had to be ferried from the south shore by SQ helicopter to the Royal Victoria Hospital in Montreal.

It took most of the afternoon for the police to negotiate with the demonstrators and break up the roadblock. They towed away one of the semi-trailers and arrested five of the principal agitators. But by evening, more chaos had forced the traffic to grind to a halt again. Three hundred angry citizens from Ste. Catherine, on the eastern border of Kahnawake, had stormed out of a Chamber of Commerce meeting, heading first toward the St. Lawrence Seaway to try to capture the locks. When that failed, they blocked Highway 15 again, near the intersection of Highway 132. A carload of American tourists was surrounded and nearly forced into the ditch when it tried to crawl past the parked cars. Angry demonstrators lit fires along the roadside. Many people were drinking, and the highway was littered with empty bottles and broken glass.

The unhappy citizens of Châteauguay had their own cult hero — Gilles Proulx, host of a popular phone-in program on Montreal's CJMS radio station. He was a cheerleader for the Châteauguay demonstrators and openly intolerant towards the Mohawks. Before long, Proulx had become a key actor in the drama unfolding in Châteauguay. When he and his crew parked their mobile studio at the Châteauguay barricades in August, they wore "Solidarité Châteauguay" T-shirts. Proulx was loved by thousands of south-shore listeners because he professed to understand the frustrations of the Châteauguay mobs and was not afraid to verbally pummel and abuse the Mohawk warriors on the air. His mere presence at the barricades drew hundreds of additional people to the site.

Proulx was also an outspoken Quebec nationalist, and he often reminded his listeners that the Mohawks could not speak French. In the climate of fervent Quebec nationalism that followed the failure of the Meech Lake accord in June, any reference to the language issue was bound to evoke a passionate response, and many of the people in the mobs resented the fact that the Mohawks had sided with the English for hundreds of years.

As in any mass movement, radical fringe groups started getting in on the act — in this case, white supremacists, who spotted a hungry audience for their tracts. By late July, Châteauguay police acknowledged that there were members of the Aryan Nation and other ultra-right-wing groups in the mobs that gathered nightly in Châteauguay. Volunteers from the Canadian Centre on Racism and Prejudice, a group that monitors the actions of the ultra-right movement, spotted and photographed one prominent white supremacist, Michel Larocque, in the mobs in early August. Larocque was the leader of Longitude 74, a Quebec nationalist branch of the Ku Klux Klan. Other KKK members moved around the crowd, distributing flyers and tracts with messages designed to stir up Quebec nationalist fervour. "We, Québécois, are inhabitants and builders of la Belle Province," said one. "For more than 400 years we have been masters here. We make up the demographic majority. So are we going to be led by the country's cultural minorities? ... We greatly respect aboriginal people but we will not tolerate their use of a supposed 'historical excuse' to squeeze from us our money and our territories."

Another tract demanded that Quebec withhold all rights and services from the Mohawks, including social assistance, since the Mohawks do not recognize Quebec's jurisdiction over them. The tract boasted that the KKK would defend "the values and ideals of the white majority."

Solidarité Châteauguay distanced itself from the radical fringe groups, but the literature distributed by some of the group's own followers did not differ much in tone or content. One anonymous poem, printed under the banner of Solidarité Châteauguay, called the Mohawks "assassins" who "are worth nothing" and "have killed one of our own." The poem criticized Bourassa and the government for doing nothing to settle the crisis. It ended with a statement that was truer than its writers knew: "Don't you worry, the army is coming."

CHAPTER 11

War Songs and Black Wampum

The Theology of Violence

In every corner of the troubled territory of the Mohawk people, the most visible symbol of the Warrior Society is a red and yellow flag showing an Indian with a traditional Iroquois scalplock and a single feather in his hair. Behind the Indian, on a blood red background, is a stylized image of the sun — known as the mighty warrior in Iroquois mythology. Mohawk warriors have brandished the flag in every major confrontation with legal authorities in Canada and the United States over the past seventeen years. It fluttered defiantly over the barricades at Oka and Kahnawake throughout the summer of 1990.

While the warrior flag became a familiar sight on Canadian television screens during the Oka crisis, few people know the story of the fiery Mohawk ideologue who designed it. Louis Hall, an artist and writer from Kahnawake, created the flag in the early 1970s as a symbol of unity for North American Indians. It was quickly adopted as the unofficial flag of the Mohawk Warrior Society.

For two decades, Louis Hall was a key figure in the revival of the Mohawk warrior tradition. As a chief in the Longhouse of Kahnawake in 1972, he helped authorize the creation of the Warrior Society, and two years later he became a leader in the armed movement to repossess ancient Mohawk land at Moss Lake and Ganienkeh in upper New

York State. In 1979, he wrote the *Warrior's Handbook*, a slender volume of essays and sketches to inspire the militant young men who were gaining influence in every Mohawk community. And over the following decade he produced a series of provocative newsletters for the Warrior Society.

Today, at the age of seventy-two, he lives in a small trailer on a rutted gravel road in the woods of Kahnawake. (The trailer is owned by cigarette kingpin Phillip Deering, whose warehouses and trucks are protected by surveillance cameras at the end of the isolated road.) Although he is retired from Longhouse politics, Louis Hall continues to churn out warrior manifestos on an ancient typewriter in a cramped corner of the trailer. A replica of an eighteenth-century rifle used in the American War of Independence hangs on one wall; the other walls are covered with Hall's brilliantly coloured paintings and political slogans. "I want you for the Warrior Society," says one poster, which shows a Mohawk war chief pointing his finger at the viewer like Uncle Sam in the old American military recruitment posters.

Much of Louis Hall's writing and painting is tinged with bitter humour. "There will come a day when the Red man shall put the white man in a boat and send him back to Europe where he belongs and keep him there," one of his posters says. "A wall shall be built around Europe, not to keep people out but to keep the white man in. It's not good for the world to have the white man running around loose." When asked if he is serious, Hall admits it might be difficult to find a big enough boat for all the white people to get back to Europe. "It would be a hell of a job," he muses. "I was laughing when I wrote that. I imagine a lot of Indians enjoyed it when they read it. But it would be the solution to a lot of problems."

Although his advancing years have left him balding and slightly stooped, Hall is still muscular and mentally alert. He is toiling at his typewriter, trying to complete a new treatise about the horrors unleashed by the arrival of Columbus in the New World in 1492, when the telephone rings. "City Morgue," he barks into the phone. "The only time we smile at you is when you're dead. Do you have a stiff for us?"

Some critics have described Louis Hall as the father of the warriors, and they claim that his writing inspired the entire warrior movement, but Hall's alleged influence has been grossly exaggerated. Although he was one of the early leaders of the movement, his writing is simply a condensed version of the basic beliefs of the Longhouse militants who form the backbone of the Warrior Society. "His books aren't a driving force — they're more of a mirror," says Joe Deom, a Kahnawake Mohawk who became one of the key negotiators for the warriors in the crisis of 1990.

Most warriors, indeed, have never read the bulk of Louis Hall's written works. They do not need to study his books because they have already absorbed his ideas through the teachings of the Kahnawake Longhouse. Louis Hall is best understood not as the "father" of the warrior movement, but as an angry and eloquent spokesman for one hard-line faction among the Mohawks. His writing is a pugnacious summary of the doctrines held by the majority of Longhouse followers in Kahnawake, the most militant Mohawk community in North America. At its heart, the ideology of Louis Hall and the Kahnawake warriors is founded on a single document: the Great Law of Peace.

The Great Law is a unique document. Unlike most other religious doctrines, it provides a complex combination of spiritual and political rules, with no separation of church and state. It is the rulebook for an entire way of life, containing regulations for spiritual ceremonies, political leadership, warfare against external enemies, justice, international relations, funerals, adoptions, and the resolution of internal disputes. The Great Law extends far beyond religion, entering realms of political action that are normally taboo for churches. It forms the basis of a modern theocracy.

Originally preserved in oral recitals by Iroquois chiefs, the Great Law was never written down until the twentieth century. This created a serious problem. When the Great Law was finally put to paper, several different versions emerged, and leaders of the Longhouse disagreed as to which of the written versions was more authentic. Some chiefs argued that only the oral versions of the Great Law were genuine.

One faction of the Longhouse — the faction that is most active in endorsing and supporting the Warrior Society today — has followed a written version of the Great Law that emerged in the early years of the twentieth century. It interprets this version as literally as possible, with only a few concessions to the realities of modern society. Louis Hall is a prime spokesman for this faction, which has a strong following in Kahnawake.

Another Longhouse faction, which opposes the Warrior Society, relies entirely on oral recitals of the Great Law and is heavily influenced by the teachings of Handsome Lake. This Seneca visionary and reformed alcoholic became a prominent leader in the Iroquois communities of upper New York State in the early nineteenth century and established a code that revived many of the dying traditions of the Longhouse. However, some of the most important ideas in Handsome Lake's essentially pacifist code were borrowed from Christian and Quaker religious thought. It forbade alcohol and gambling, endorsed the concepts of heaven and hell, called for the confession of sins and the achievement of salvation through repentance, and strongly opposed all forms of warfare.

By the time of his death in 1815, the teachings of Handsome Lake had gained widespread acceptance among the six nations of the Iroquois Confederacy. Most of these nations, weakened and demoralized by military defeats, turned to Handsome Lake in a desperate bid for cultural survival. But the Seneca prophet never travelled to the Mohawk communities in Canada, and his evangelistic message never spread to the people of Kahnawake. Even if the code had been taught to the Mohawks, they might not have accepted it. Because of their role as middlemen in the fur trade, they were relatively prosperous in the early years of the nineteenth century and were not as vulnerable to the feelings of desperation that haunted the other Iroquois nations in this period. As a result, Kahnawake was never a fertile breeding ground for the Handsome Lake code.

Moreover, because the people of Kahnawake had been under the control of Jesuit missionaries for many decades, the Christian elements of the Handsome Lake code represented domination and oppression to them. They felt no desire to adopt the teachings of a Christian-influenced prophet.

Of all the Iroquois nations, it is primarily the Mohawks of Kahnawake (and its sister community at Ganienkeh) who still refuse to follow the code of Handsome Lake today. The other Iroquois nations — the Seneca, the Cayuga, the Oneida, the Tuscarora, and the

Onondaga — have largely embraced his teachings. Even among the Mohawks, the Handsome Lake code is popular at the Akwesasne reserve, where a pacifist faction led by chiefs Tom Porter and Jake Swamp gained control of the Longhouse headquarters after 1986.

Three different Longhouse factions are active at Kahnawake today, but an overwhelming majority of the Kahnawake Longhouse people have rejected the pacifist teachings of Handsome Lake. Instead they follow an interpretation of the Great Law that they regard as older and more authentic. In their view, they are following the original Great Law, without any taint of Quaker influence. It is this interpretation that found its most vocal advocate in Louis Hall. And among its most devoted followers are the members of the Mohawk Warrior Society.

There is some evidence that the Kahnawake Longhouse people are indeed following the original version of the Great Law. Their interpretation of the law — edited by Louis Hall and distributed by the Mohawk Nation Office in Kahnawake — is remarkably similar to the versions documented by early anthropologists and Iroquois writers such as Arthur C. Parker and Seth Newhouse. One of the earliest known translations of the Great Law, published by Parker in 1916, is essentially the version followed by the Longhouse people of Kahnawake and Ganienkeh today. This version is also accepted by perhaps half the Longhouse people at Akwesasne and by a significant number of traditionalists at Kanesatake and at the Six Nations reserve near Brantford in southwestern Ontario.

This early interpretation of the Great Law holds the key to understanding the motivations of the Mohawk warriors who manned the barricades in the summer of 1990. Its 117 articles (known as wampums) establish a harsh and sometimes brutal set of rules for maintaining peace and justice among the six Iroquois nations. There is beauty and richness in the law's descriptions of Longhouse ceremonies and thanksgiving rituals, in its discussion of the role of clan mothers and chiefs, in its elaborate metaphors of the Tree of Peace and the eagle who watches for danger. But there is also a clear acceptance of violence and warfare as legitimate methods to protect peace and social harmony within the Confederacy.

More than one-quarter of the 117 wampums refer to warfare, warriors, or the duties of the war chief. Wampum 37, for example, specifies that one of the duties of the Iroquois war chiefs is "to take up arms in case of emergency"; Wampum 91 authorizes the warriors to "resist invasion" by launching a war "in defence of the territory"; and Wampum 80 authorizes a declaration of war on any foreign nation that refuses to accept the Great Peace, thus allowing the Confederacy to extend the Great Peace "by a conquest of the rebellious nation."

Other wampums give detailed instructions on how a war chief should conduct warfare. "War must continue until the conquest is won," says Wampum 88. Another wampum gives the lyrics of the War Song to be sung by the war chief "until his scouts have reported that [his] army is near the enemy lines" — at which time the war chief "shall approach with great caution and prepare for the attack." (A small group of Mohawk warriors, led by Akwesasne war chief Francis Boots, actually sang the War Song several times in the Pines at Kanesatake as they awaited a possible confrontation with the Quebec police in the summer of 1990.)

One of the most famous legends of the Iroquois Confederacy is the story of how the Peacemaker persuaded the Iroquois to uproot the tallest tree and cast all weapons into the hole created by the uprooting. The weapons were then buried forever to safeguard the Great Peace among the nations of the Confederacy. According to modern-day pacifists in the Longhouse, this story is proof that warfare cannot be waged by the Iroquois today. But the warriors point to Parker's 1916 version of the Great Law, which clearly specifies that the prohibition on weapons applies only to warfare within the Confederacy. Weapons could still be picked up by warriors as a defence against external enemies.

Parker's interpretation of the Great Law also allows for the use of extreme violence in administering justice. If a treasonous chief refuses to mend his ways, for instance, he is given three warnings by the clan mothers and the war chief. If he refuses to heed those warnings, he is called to a meeting at the Longhouse, where the war chief will hold a bunch of black wampum strings in his outstretched hand. If the treasonous chief still refuses to submit, the ultimate punishment is imposed on him. "At this point, the war chief shall drop the bunch of black wampum and the men shall spring to their feet and club the erring chief to death," the Great Law says.

Many warriors still believe that the execution of traitors is an appropriate form of justice today; some are even willing to identify "treasonous" leaders who should be executed. Most warriors reluctantly admit, however, that executions are an impractical solution in modern North American society because criminal charges would likely be laid against anyone who organized an execution.

Despite the restrictions imposed by modern-day realities, the warriors try to interpret the Great Law as literally as possible. In 1975, for example, the Mohawks of Moss Lake were faced with a resident who refused to obey the community's ban on alcohol and drugs. After he ignored several warnings, he was brought before a community meeting, where he was told that he had to touch the black wampum before it fell to the ground. If he failed to touch the wampum, it would signify his continued defiance of the community's wishes. The black wampum was dropped, he refused to touch it, and the warriors instantly sprang to their feet. According to two Mohawk warriors who witnessed the event, the defiant resident was punched in the face and then escorted out of the community.

The Mohawks often summarize the message of the Great Law in three interwoven concepts: peace, power, and righteousness. Power is necessary to enforce the peace and to protect the righteousness of the law. "Power means authority, the authority of law and custom, backed by such force as is necessary to make justice prevail," the Peacemaker told one of his earliest followers in Iroquois legend. According to Paul Wallace, an American scholar who has studied the Great Law, the Iroquois realized that "peace will endure only if men recognize the sovereignty of a common law and are prepared to back that law with force."

In that respect, the 1916 translation of the Great Law fits into the mainstream of North American political philosophy. Like the political leaders of the United States during the Cold War era, the Longhouse people of Kahnawake believe in "peace through strength" and they use the threat of violence and warfare to deter foreign aggression. They see circumstances under which violence and capital punishment are legitimate and justifiable to preserve the security of their community. And they view the warriors as a domestic army to protect peace in their territory. The barricades and weapons of the summer of 1990 were regarded as a war "in defence of the territory" — authorized by Wampum 91.

Some questions of interpretation still remain, however: How often should the Great Law be applied to the realities of North American society in the 1990s? How far should the warriors go to enforce peace and defend their territory from outside invasion? Here, the works of Louis Hall offer some insight into the thinking of the most militant Longhouse faction in the Mohawk nation.

"To get peace, you must first fight a ferocious, ruthless battle," Hall wrote in a Warrior Society newsletter. "The meek and humble get pushed around. It's the strong who achieve peace. The Indians shall have to fight for peace to achieve it."

Mohawk sovereignty will never be achieved through quiet negotiations, Hall argues. "When the peaceful Indians fail at the conference table, they'll find it necessary to turn the matter over to the Warrior Society who will do it the way the world understands. The Indians shall have to be just as hard and tough as the rest of the world to regain their lost sovereignty, national independence and self-government. Every nation that ever achieved sovereignty and self-government got it by themselves. They asserted it. They fought for it. It was never a gift."

According to Hall, the Mohawks must revive their "fighting spirit" to prevent themselves from being assimilated into white society. He recommends that they perform the War Dance as often as possible, to lift their spirits in their "psychological war" with Canadian and American governments. "Let us shatter the night by our wild yells and war whoops," he wrote in the *Warrior's Handbook*.

Above all, he recommends the establishment of warrior societies in aboriginal communities across the continent. "Only fear is respected," he writes. "Fear inspired by the strong. Indian nations without a Warrior Society are in a weak position. They do not struggle. They decrease in number, die out and become extinct."

The Mohawks will never have any bargaining power unless they possess "the ability to destroy the peace of the opposition," Hall writes. "An Indian nation with no Warrior Society presents no threat to the white man's peace ... Not having an army is unthinkable to any nation. They would be speedily overcome."

A warrior society is not, however, the only necessity for a strong nation, Hall argues. He recommends new business enterprises to help finance the Mohawk nation and its defence. Many warriors, in fact, have pored over the Parker version of the Great Law and concluded that it contains nothing to prohibit casinos or tax-free cigarettes as a source of money for the Warrior Society.

"Indians did not need money when the great Iroquois Confederacy was all-powerful," Hall writes. "Now, Indians need money to achieve power. So let's go after money. Not just some money, but a lot of money."

Much of Louis Hall's anger is reserved for the code of Handsome Lake. He blames Handsome Lake for the downfall of the Iroquois Confederacy and says the pacifist code made it easy for the early white settlers to seize land from nations in the Confederacy.

"To bury the weapons is to bury the fighting spirit," he writes. "People need fighting spirit to survive. Because of their religion, the Handsome Lake followers cannot fight to protect and defend themselves ... Handsome Lake followers would allow themselves to be killed without raising a hand in self-defence. They had buried their weapons and with it their fighting spirit. It's something like a death wish. When a people lose their fighting spirit, they also lose their will to live and their population declines until they are no more."

Louis Hall's defence of violence can sometimes lead him into dangerous territory. In a speech to an audience of Indians in Oklahoma in 1984, he appeared to advocate terrorism. "What can the warrior societies do?" he asked. "They can dump bridges into rivers which are now sewers, and into the seaway, cancelling all traffic; knock out powerhouses [and] high-tension power lines; punch holes in the reactors of nuclear powerhouses."

In an interview, he refuses to back down from those controversial words. "Jack Dempsey said the best defence is a powerful attack," he says. "There are times when you have to take desperate measures."

Despite this call to action, other Mohawk leaders have rejected any form of terrorism. According to Joe Deom, the Mohawks realize that Louis Hall sometimes resorts to excessive rhetoric to make a point. "They won't take it seriously because they know Louis," says Deom. "They laugh about it. Who would act on it?"

At the same time, however, many of the Mohawks share the same frustrations that led to Hall's suggestion of bombs and terrorism — particularly when they see bridges and power lines and waterways rammed through their territory. "We've had that feeling for years," says Deom. "It's been a sore point for everyone."

Hall's manifestos are often deliberately designed to infuriate people, Deom says. "He says things that he knows will make you mad." But there is a serious side to Hall's writing, Deom adds. "The point he makes is that the time for talking is over. It's time to get busy."

When the Mohawk warriors captured the national spotlight in the summer of 1990, there was a brief flurry of newspaper stories about Louis Hall. He was portrayed as a terrorist who kept a secret "hit list" of traitors to be executed, and some newspapers said he was the founder of the entire warrior movement. He responded with a sarcastic letter to the *Montreal Gazette*. "You are making me into a celebrity," he told the newspaper. "Up to now, my life has been dull and meaningless. Thanks to your tall tales about me, the final period of my life has become happy and exciting."

Louis Hall's life story, in fact, could never be described as dull. He was born in Kahnawake in 1918, the son of Tom Hall, an ironworker who later became an Indian dancer in a Wild West show for tourists. Louis was raised a Catholic and attended a Catholic school in Kahnawake, where the priests regarded him as one of their best students. "They wanted me to be a priest," he recalls. "I was Number One in catechism and religious studies."

Rejecting the suggestion from the priests, he dropped out of school at the age of fifteen and became an amateur wrestler and a construction worker. Then he entered a technical school in Montreal and studied to be an electrician. But people refused to hire him. "I was already controversial," he says. "I'm naturally controversial, I guess. I was a rebel even when I was young."

Hall embarked on a series of jobs — as a butcher, carpenter, ironworker, and commercial artist. He became a voracious reader of history and philosophy texts, including the works of Plato and Aristotle. But the pivotal event in his life took place in 1955, when the people of Kahnawake were consulting lawyers about the federal expropriation of their land to make room for the St. Lawrence Seaway. In a Montreal law office, Hall met a Jewish lawyer and struck up a conversation. The lawyer explained that the Jews had survived persecution for thousands of years because of the strength of their religion. He asked whether the Mohawks had a national religion. Hall replied that the Longhouse was the national religion of the Mohawks. When the lawyer asked how many Mohawks belonged to the Longhouse, Hall was too embarrassed to reveal the small number of people who were still following the traditional religion in the 1950s. So he exaggerated the number and told the lawyer that about half the Mohawks belonged to the Longhouse. "You'd better get the other half to join, because a national religion is a force for unity and national survival," the lawyer said.

Hall thought it over and decided the lawyer was right. "It was the best advice I've ever heard," he says. Within four years, he had officially abandoned Catholicism and joined the Longhouse, where he quickly became a leader.

Hall has always admired the Jews for their "fighting spirit" and their battles to create the state of Israel in a hostile territory. "The meek and humble Jew suddenly turned tiger and even killed a lot of Arabs to set up Israel," he wrote later. They are "an example of success" for the Mohawks to follow, he said.

At a Longhouse ceremony in 1963, Louis Hall was given a Mohawk name, Karoniaktajeh, which means "close to heaven." He became a chief in the Longhouse, and he was one of the first chiefs to promote the Warrior Society after it was established in Kahnawake in the early 1970s. A few years later, he was a key leader of the Mohawks who moved to Moss Lake to repossess a parcel of their traditional land. In 1977, after lengthy negotiations with New York State, he helped the Mohawks move to their new site at Ganienkeh, near Plattsburg.

He finally returned to Kahnawake in 1983 because his doctor told him his health was so poor he could die at any moment. He wrote up a will, then resumed writing books and newsletters for the Warrior Society. When the Quebec police attacked the Oka barricade in the summer of 1990, four days went by before Hall discovered what had happened. "I saw it on television," he recalls. "I said, hey, what's going on?" Throughout the crisis, he went to the barricades at Kahnawake only once, and that was to deliver food. "The doctor told me: no excitement. He said if I had any excitement I'd drop dead."

Today he lives almost like a hermit, surrounded by paintings and boxes of books in his crowded little trailer. "Sometimes a whole month goes by and I don't see anyone," he says. "I just don't draw people. If I have any influence, it's from my newsletters, because I never do any preaching. Anything I know, I write it down and spread it around. I guess it gets around."

Despite his modesty, it is clear that Louis Hall is the most senior ideological spokesman for the warriors. His posters are framed on the walls of the Mohawk Nation Office, and his books are sold by the staff there. The Nation Office also distributes his annotated edition of the Great Law as their official version of the law.

Doug George, a thirty-five-year-old Mohawk journalist and former law student, is probably the leading ideological opponent of the warriors. George churns out his own manifestos at the offices of two Mohawk newspapers in Akwesasne, where he has become the anti-warrior faction's counterpart to Louis Hall. He has travelled across Ontario and Quebec to denounce the warriors as a violent gang of criminals and terrorists. By cultivating contacts at newspapers and television newsrooms across the country, he has gained tremendous influence over the media's coverage of the Warrior Society. Often he is portrayed as an objective observer of the Mohawk scene. In reality he has been deeply embroiled in Mohawk politics for many years.

In 1979 and 1980, during the bitter siege at Raquette Point on the Akwesasne reserve, Doug George was an ally of Loran Thompson and others who later became key leaders of the warrior movement. He spent ten days in a jail cell in 1979 after he helped a crowd of Longhouse activists disarm the Akwesasne police, and when the siege began at Raquette Point, he joined the gunmen who were fighting to defend Thompson and the other Longhouse followers.

By the second half of the 1980s, however, the Akwesasne Longhouse had split into two camps. The fierce debate over gambling was the official reason for the internal divisions, but much of the dispute was simply a result of personality conflicts and family feuds. Doug George, along with his four brothers, began to clash openly with Loran Thompson's faction. A violent brawl erupted between the Georges and the Thompsons in 1986, and Loran and his brother Larry were severely beaten by the five George brothers. In retaliation, Loran got a gun and fired a shot in the direction of the George brothers. Shortly afterward, the Akwesasne Longhouse held a meeting and removed Loran Thompson from his position as a Longhouse chief. (The warriors maintain that the Akwesasne Longhouse failed to follow the proper procedure for deposing a chief, but they acknowledge that Thompson has been effectively ostracized by the faction led by Tom Porter and Jake Swamp, who now control the Akwesasne Longhouse.)

When the gambling issue exploded into violence in 1990, Doug George was in the thick of the action, helping set up the highway barricades that prevented customers from reaching a strip of casinos on the American side of the reserve. When the warriors attacked the barricades, his car was among those destroyed by bulldozers. Soon he was leading the anti-gambling faction against the warriors in a series of gunfights, which finally ended when two Mohawks were shot dead. Police swarmed onto the reserve to restore order, and Doug George was eventually charged with murder in connection with one of the shooting deaths. After a six-day preliminary hearing, he was freed.

In his speeches and newspaper articles, George maintains that the Mohawk Warrior Society is illegal under the Great Law of Peace. "As far as every legitimate Iroquois government is concerned, there can be no such thing as the Warrior Society," he tells audiences. "This organization operates outside Iroquois law, without the sanction of Iroquois government. It is, by its essence, illicit."

Like the other Longhouse people who oppose the warriors, Doug George rejects Arthur Parker's 1916 interpretation of the Great Law. Instead he relies on oral recitals of the law by Longhouse elders who appear to be following the Handsome Lake code. He argues that the Peacemaker banned warfare forever when he established the Great Law of Peace in the pre-European era. George describes the Peacemaker as "a messenger of God," who preached pacifism to the Mohawks. Before the arrival of the Peacemaker, the Mohawks were controlled by bloodthirsty warlords, he says. "They were a cruel and merciless people. Their reputation for cruelty was unsurpassed. It was to them, the cruelest people, that the Peacemaker went first. He managed, after a great deal of work, to convince these cruel people to put aside the weapons of war and pursue the principles of peace and universal justice. He worked a miracle."

In his ideological attack on the warriors, Doug George sometimes makes a secondary point to support his main argument. "We are a people who cannot logically hope to win a war against the government of Canada," he says. "We just can't do that. There are 25,000 Mohawks. How can you possibly hope to win an armed conflict with a far greater power? You can't do that — you have to use alternatives, and that's what we're looking for."

Doug George is closely linked to the Longhouse faction that is headed by Tom Porter and Jake Swamp, two of the longest-serving chiefs at Akwesasne. For many years, Porter and Swamp were united with Loran Thompson in their struggle to revive the traditions of the Longhouse; all three fought on the side of the traditionalists in the Raquette Point dispute. Although they never carried guns, Porter and Swamp remained at Thompson's barricaded fortress during the long siege at Raquette Point, and by their presence alone, they seemed to condone the carrying of weapons by the armed traditionalists who defended the Thompson property. Today, however, they denounce the use of weapons. "They went from guns to roses," says Loran Thompson.

In an article written in 1984, Tom Porter said the Peacemaker was sent to North America by the Creator "to stop war and the evilness and sadness that come about when there is war and killing." The Peacemaker "introduced a law to ban Indian warfare," Porter went on. "Our chiefs cannot go to war; they would forfeit their claims to be peace chiefs. If they do go to war, they must give their leadership back to the clan mother while the war goes on. If they kill someone in that war, they will never get their leadership back because they are peace chiefs."

Jake Swamp, who has been a Longhouse chief for twenty-one of his forty-nine years, was a follower of the Parker version of the Great Law for most of his life. But eventually he abandoned the Parker version and began to accept the interpretation of the pacifist chiefs. "I suddenly realized, hey, the weapons were done away with," he recalls. "If anyone picks up a weapon, he's breaking the Great Law, because all the weapons were buried. If people truly believe in peace, they will never pick up weapons."

Historical records show that the Longhouse has never officially endorsed the actions of any warriors, Swamp says. "We're peace leaders. We have no right to tell them to go to war. We tell them the weapons were buried."

Swamp recognizes that the Kahnawake Longhouse has strongly supported the warriors for the past nineteen years, but he argues that the Kahnawake Longhouse is not officially recognized by the Iroquois Confederacy. "The Confederacy has determined that they're still in the learning process," he says. "They're still on trial. We cannot work with that Longhouse." Swamp acknowledges that the Kahnawake Longhouse has plenty of followers, but he claims that its adherents are motivated by greed. "When you have money, you have a lot of followers," he says.

Swamp and Porter refuse to accept many of the wampums in Parker's version of the Great Law. They insist, for example, that there is no such thing as a war chief. And a treasonous chief, they say, should not be executed. "The worst you can do is remove him from the community," says Swamp.

Some Mohawks have reminded the pacifist chiefs that the Iroquois have a long history of warfare and armed conflicts, from the seventeenth century to the 1990s. However, Swamp maintains that Iroquois warriors from the earliest days were acting without the approval of the Longhouse. Individual bands of warriors would resist the European settlers, but their actions were unauthorized, he says.

During the armed conflict at Raquette Point in 1979 and 1980, the Akwesasne Longhouse officially supported Loran Thompson's refusal to submit to the jurisdiction of New York State. But when the traditionalists asked the Longhouse to authorize the carrying of guns to defend themselves from vigilante attacks, Swamp says the Longhouse refused. Instead it was left to individuals to decide whether or not to pick up weapons. The Longhouse assigned Joe Swamp, a brother of Jake, to try to prevent bloodshed during the lengthy siege at Raquette Point. "It was his job to ensure the weapons were safe and not displayed in front of people," Jake Swamp says.

There are some inconsistencies in the position of the pacifist chiefs. Despite his opposition to weapons, for example, Swamp has defended the carrying of guns in certain situations, and he supported the actions of anti-gambling activists such as Doug George who picked up weapons in the battles of 1990. "It's justifiable in his case because he was attacked by fifty warriors," Swamp says. "If someone is coming after you, it's always natural to defend yourself. An animal will defend itself if it's cornered. Even though it's wrong to pick up weapons, people have to defend themselves sometimes when the chips are down. You cannot help but respect them."

Swamp says the Akwesasne Longhouse never investigated the Oka dispute to see whether it was justifiable to pick up guns at the barricades, but he adds: "I can understand why some people would react in that way." Swamp admits that many of the warriors at Oka and Kahnawake, including some of the leaders, were motivated by a desire to protect Mohawk land and sovereignty. "Some truly believe they are building a nation," he says. "Those are the ones I really respect. They made a stand for the right reasons — to defend the land and the people. But the ones in command took advantage of those people."

The pacifist chiefs have never produced a written version of the Great Law because they believe that problems arise whenever the oral version is translated into writing. Followers of the Longhouse who want to hear the complete version of the Great Law must wait for an oral recital, an elaborate event which occurs only once every four or five years. "It requires a tremendous memory on the part of the reciter and his audience," says Louis Hall. "How can we remember all that the man said? Or did the man remember to say all the laws? The reciter could 'forget' to recite certain parts so that the chiefs and the people will miss out on what they should know ... Why should anyone not be permitted to read his own law?"

According to the Kahnawake Mohawks, the followers of Handsome Lake put too much emphasis on the religious aspects of the Great Law. "It's become evangelistic," says Ken Deer, a chief in the Kahnawake Longhouse. "It's super-fundamentalism."

The warriors of Akwesasne are equally critical of the pacifist interpretation of the Great Law. "It's silly for a nation to remain defenceless because of a spiritual interpretation," says Francis Boots, the war chief of Akwesasne. "The Mohawk nation would have disappeared a long time ago ... Power has to be used. It's useless if it's never used."

Because of its support for the Warrior Society, the Kahnawake Longhouse stands outside the mainstream of the Iroquois Confederacy. Almost all of the nations in the Confederacy are faithful to the Handsome Lake code. Only the Longhouses of Kahnawake and Ganienkeh, along with the Oneidas of Ontario and the followers of Francis Boots and Loran Thompson in Akwesasne, have strongly rejected the pacifist philosophy. As a result, they have been effectively barred from participating in key decisions at Confederacy meetings, and the Confederacy refused to support the warriors who established the barricades at Oka and Kahnawake in the summer of 1990.

The split between the pacifist chiefs and the Mohawk Warrior Society is ultimately a disagreement over the best methods to achieve justice for the Mohawk people. Both sides believe in Mohawk sovereignty and land rights, but they are divided over the question of tactics. The split is similar to the divisions within the Third World national liberation movement and the U.S. civil rights movement. It resembles the debate between the followers of Martin Luther King and Mahatma Gandhi, who opposed violence in all its forms, and the followers of Malcolm X and Nelson Mandela, who accepted some forms of violence as a necessary measure in the battle for social justice. The debate has no easy answer, since each side can claim a certain moral legitimacy for its position. Among the Mohawks, both sides can point to their own versions of the Great Law of Peace.

For the past decade, Mohawks have been forced to take sides in this theological and tactical debate. The conflicting philosophies have influenced all the recent battles in Mohawk country, from Akwesasne to Oka. And the outcome of this debate will shape the future of the Mohawk people for many years to come.

CHAPTER 12
Shock Waves

Reverberations across Canada

Brad Larocque can remember the days when he was just another kid in a Prairie farm town. He grew up in Weyburn, Saskatchewan, and had a typical middle-class childhood. His father was a teacher. His mother was a nurse. Like the other kids in Weyburn, he played hockey and baseball and went waterskiing in the summer. It was a comfortable life.

Brad knew, however, that he had something different in his blood. His parents and his brother and two sisters were white, but he was dark. He eventually discovered that he was an Ojibway Indian who had been adopted by a white middle-class family when he was still a toddler.

At the age of eighteen, he enrolled at the Saskatchewan Indian Federated College in Regina. He knew little about his roots, but for the first time in his life, he was making friends with other Indian people. He began going to sweat lodges and meetings with native elders, and little by little, started to learn about Indian ways.

Over the next couple of years, Larocque met people who knew his Ojibway relatives, and through them he was able to piece together the details of a life he didn't remember. He discovered that he had been born on the Poor Man reserve, an Ojibway community about 120 kilometres north of Regina. He was one of a family of nine children. At a dance in 1988, he met his younger sister Lisa. "We just sat there and looked at each other," he recalls. "It was strange. I was floored for a long time."

Larocque was a hard-working student of economics and politics at the Indian college in Regina and an increasingly active participant in native student politics. In 1988, he joined a group of student activists who went to Calgary to demonstrate in support of the Lubicon Indians during the Winter Olympics. On the day the Olympic torch was carried into the city, people threw snowballs at the protesting Indians and elbowed them aside. It was his first experience with blatant racism.

He knew nothing of the Mohawk Warrior Society until the spring of 1990, when he read a magazine story about the gambling casinos of Akwesasne. The story described how violence had broken out in the dispute between anti-gamblers and warriors, and how two men had been killed. "My idea of the Warrior Society was pretty well the same as everybody else's," Larocque says. "Pretty negative."

But when the Quebec police attacked the Mohawk barricade at Oka on July 11, Larocque and his native friends were angered by the action. They tried to block a bridge in Regina in a gesture of support for the Mohawks, but dozens of police cars and helicopters swarmed around them. Instead they held a legal demonstration, and later about a hundred of the students and other native activists occupied the local offices of the Indian Affairs Department.

In late July, the Canadian Federation of Students invited Larocque to travel to Ottawa to help prepare a policy paper on the Oka crisis. He arrived in Ottawa on July 29, joining about fifteen other native students who were chosen because of their reputations as activists. Three days later, the students travelled to Montreal and took a boat across the river to Kahnawake to begin their research.

On his first night in Mohawk territory, he watched a mob of thousands of people rioting on the other side of the police barricade in Châteauguay. The student federation and its policy paper soon seemed trivial in comparison with the Mohawk cause, and most of the students decided to stay with the warriors. They never did complete their policy paper.

After a couple of days in Kahnawake, the Mohawks told Larocque that they needed reinforcements for the small band of warriors in Kanesatake. He volunteered to go. Along with three other students, he travelled by boat around the Island of Montreal and across the Lake of Two Mountains to the Mohawk side of the barricades in Kanesatake. As soon as he arrived, the Mohawks gave him a supply of camouflage gear, an AK-47 rifle, and a codename — Freddy Krueger. He had become a warrior.

"It just became really clear that this was what I had to do," says Larocque. "The decision wasn't hard to make at all. I knew I'd be there until the very end, no matter what."

All of his peaceful protests and demonstrations in Alberta and Saskatchewan had seemed futile. They were always ignored by the government. Now, finally, he had found a group of Indians who were willing to take action. "This was something that was really solid," Larocque says. "All those years of demonstrating, holding signs, speaking loudly — we didn't really have the answer. It never really got anything accomplished."

Later in the summer, a masked warrior was immortalized in the most famous photograph of the entire crisis. He was staring down a fresh-faced soldier in a tense standoff as the army advanced into Mohawk territory. The photograph of the nose-to-nose confrontation was published in newspapers and magazines around the world and soon became a symbol of the Oka crisis. The soldier, Private Patrick Cloutier, was later rewarded for his unflinching courage. The warrior remained anonymous. Some people thought it was Lasagna, the most notorious of the Mohawks. In reality, it was a twenty-three-year-old Ojibway from Weyburn, Saskatchewan, who quietly returned to university in Regina when the crisis was over.

Brad Larocque was just one of a large number of Indians from all over North America who converged on Kanesatake and Kahnawake to help the warriors after the July police raid. Among them were a hundred Oneidas from New York, Wisconsin, and southwestern Ontario, an Algonquin from northwestern Quebec, and Indian women from several regions of British Columbia and the Yukon. There was also a group of nine Micmacs from Nova Scotia, including a cousin of Donald Marshall Jr., the Micmac who was jailed for eleven years for a murder he never committed.

Thousands of aboriginal people across Canada had the same reaction when they saw the Mohawk warriors on their television screens in that hot summer of 1990. "They saw it as the last stand of one people," said Georges Erasmus, national chief of the Assembly of First Nations from 1985 to 1991. "They saw a people prepared to stand up and defend their rights, virtually to the end. That's when so many people decided to support them, to stand up and be counted. The whole issue was emotional, from beginning to end."

Most aboriginal people were not yet prepared to risk their lives by picking up guns. But they understood and sympathized with the Mohawk warriors. By supporting the Mohawk cause, they thwarted the federal government's strategy of splitting the national Indian movement into several conflicting camps.

After the shootout at Oka on July 11, the Mohawk warriors posed a serious political problem for the federal government. Under the existing rules, Indian bands with land grievances were supposed to wait patiently for a solution from Ottawa. They were told to file an official claim and join the long line of bands waiting for a bureaucratic decision, which could take a decade or longer. By refusing to follow the established rules, the warriors became a dangerous threat to the status quo. They exposed the weaknesses of federal land claims policies, dramatized the frustrations of aboriginal people, and generated enormous public sympathy in much of the country. Day after day, the warriors focused an embarrassing amount of attention on Ottawa's failings in aboriginal issues.

For the federal strategists, controlling the Oka crisis soon became a question of public relations. If they portrayed the Mohawk Warrior Society as a fringe group with no support from the mainsteam of native society, the warriors could be discredited and public support for them would dwindle. And so, at a news conference on July 19, Indian Affairs Minister Tom Siddon appealed to Indian chiefs across the country to condemn the warriors and "abide by the rule of law." Both publicly and privately, Siddon and other Cabinet ministers begged for help from prominent aboriginal leaders such as Georges Erasmus and Ethel Blondin. They were the mainstream Indian activists — the socalled "moderates" — who had regular contacts with federal officials through the standard lobbying channels. If the moderates criticized the warriors, Ottawa would have succeeded with its traditional strategy of "divide and conquer" — splitting the native movement into conflicting factions.

A few surprises were in store for Ottawa, however. Despite the guns and masks of the warriors, the vast majority of Canada's native leaders refused to condemn them. To the amazement of the federal government, Oka sparked the greatest display of Indian unity in recent Canadian history. All across the country, natives rallied to support the warriors. The events at Oka struck a deep chord of sympathy in thousands of aboriginal people. They had experienced the same kinds of frustrations, the same bureaucratic obstacles and political neglect that had motivated the warriors to take up arms. They felt the same burning anger.

"If you are pushed around for a hundred years or two hundred years and you run out of patience and finally there's nothing left and you're in the last corner of your home and there's nowhere to move, then it's a legitimate reason to take up arms," said Gary Potts, chief of the Bear Island Indians of Lake Temagami in northern Ontario. "There comes a time when it's necessary to take up arms. We've been pushed back far enough. Instead of living a life like a living death, we were prepared to take steps to ensure that we don't fade into history."

Potts was applauded by a roomful of aboriginal people when he made those comments on a TV program at the end of the Oka crisis. He was voicing the frustrations of a new generation of natives who are more willing and able to fight for their rights than their forebears. That militancy has increased over the past decade as native leaders have grown weary of lengthy and often futile negotiations. Blockades, protests, sit-ins, barricades, and hunger strikes have been used frequently in every region of the country in recent years. Guns were simply the next logical step. After decades of banging their heads against a wall of bureaucratic indifference, Indian leaders in every corner of Canada could imagine themselves reaching the same conclusion as the Mohawk warriors.

"Oka could have happened anywhere," said Georges Erasmus. "It was something that everyone identified with. The only difference between us, in the end, was that some people had barricades with guns and we had barricades across the country without guns. In essence, we were doing the same thing."

Erasmus was a prime target of the federal government's arm-twisting campaign because of his high-profile position at the Assembly of First Nations, which represents about six hundred chiefs from Indian bands across the country. "The pressure was from people like Tom Siddon and others, both publicly and privately," Erasmus recalled.

But the pressure had no effect on the national chief. Even though he disagreed with the Mohawk warriors' violent approach, he understood their intense anger. The expansion of the Oka golf course became a symbol of the daily encroachment of outsiders on Indian lands across the country.

"It's what we see every day," Erasmus said. "We know we've never given up those mountains or forests, and yet they're being mined every day. We see those big trucks running by, taking the logs out, and we know there's no benefit to our people. We know our treaties have been signed, but they're not fulfilled yet. Oka was an opportunity for people to remember the empty promises. When we saw people deciding to stand up and be counted, deciding to end this kind of abuse and non-recognition, there was a real outpouring of support."

Other aboriginal leaders experienced the same shock of understanding when they saw the masked warriors on television. They had tried to follow the path of non-violence, they had tried to obey the rules of the game, but they had gotten nowhere. For the first time, they were beginning to suspect that the guns of the warriors were the only tactic that might bring justice to their people. "Everything else has collapsed and failed," said Ethel Blondin, a Dene Indian and Liberal MP from the Northwest Territories. "I could never denounce the warriors. They symbolize something I believe in — the struggle to defend our land and our rights."

Alanis Obomsawin, an Abenaki Indian from southern Quebec and an acclaimed film-maker at the National Film Board, is a soft-spoken woman who hates violence and feels uncomfortable around guns. Yet she refused to condemn the tactics of the Mohawk warriors. Aboriginal people were consistently ignored until they picked up weapons, she said. "For hundreds of years, our people tried everything. Nobody listened until now."

For aboriginal people across Canada, the Mohawk battle against the Oka golf course was symbolic of their constant struggle to protect their land and regain their lost territory. One of the central factors in the Oka crisis was "the continuing failure of Canadian society to grasp the implications of natives' profound attachment to land and their willingness to sacrifice anything for it," wrote Rudy Platiel, a *Globe and Mail* reporter who has specialized in aboriginal issues for more than twenty years. "Canada was settled by immigrants who left their homelands for a new piece of land here. But for Indians, that kind of transplanted attachment is completely foreign ... Indians see themselves personally as only a link in a continuous, unending circle of life, stretching back through distant ancestors and ahead through unborn generations. The land is the connecting element."

For the past two decades, the militancy of Canadian Indians has been fueled by the constant frustration of their efforts to resolve their land claims. Until 1973, the federal government did not even recognize the concept of aboriginal land title. Only after a long and protracted court battle by the Nishgas of British Columbia did Ottawa admit that Indians might have a right to their traditional homelands. The Nishgas fought for almost a hundred years — including five years in court — before they persuaded the federal government to change its land claim policy.

After the 1973 court decision, Ottawa agreed to recognize two kinds of land claims: comprehensive claims, which can be filed in regions where an Indian band has never signed a treaty to surrender its land rights, and specific claims, where a government has violated a treaty by seizing Indian land or failing to provide the land it had promised. The federal claims process was intended to replace the complex and expensive process of court challenges for each claim.

Despite this new policy, however, progress in resolving land claims has been agonizingly slow. Legal complexities, bureaucratic delays, narrow interpretations, and restrictive regulations have conspired to frustrate almost every Indian band that has tried to follow the new rules of the land claim system. According to the Assembly of First Nations, claims are usually filed in Ottawa "only out of desperation and for lack of any other forum." Only a few claims are resolved each year, and a new claim must wait up to seven years before the Justice Department issues an opinion. Some claims have languished in the federal bureaucracy for more than a decade while private companies continue to take minerals and trees from Indian homelands. Some lawyers have advised Indian bands not to bother filing a claim with the federal government. The courts, despite their tremendous expense and delay, are still cheaper and faster than the federal system.

An estimated one thousand specific land claims have been filed or prepared by Indian bands across Canada. Fewer than fifty of these have been settled to the satisfaction of the bands. Dozens of comprehensive claims have been filed, but only one group of Indians — the Crees of James Bay — have achieved a successful resolution.

The experience of the Kanesatake Mohawks is typical. When they filed a comprehensive land claim in 1975, federal bureaucrats rejected it almost immediately because the Mohawks couldn't prove they had occupied the land since time immemorial. When the Mohawks filed a specific claim in 1977, the government pondered it for nine years, and then rejected it again.

Long before the introduction of Ottawa's land claims policy, Kahnawake had suffered the loss of a large percentage of its traditional territory. Its land was expropriated by the federal government to make room for three provincial highways, a railway, two bridges, and a seaway for ocean-going freighters. When the Mohawks finally seized the Mercier Bridge, it was a symbolic protest against all the bridges and highways and railways that had ever been rammed through Indian territory across Canada without adequate compensation or consultation. The financial payments could never really compensate for the loss of their traditional land.

When the new land claims policy was created in 1973, it was imposed on aboriginal people without any significant consultations. And the weaknesses in the policy were aggravated by the fact that, throughout the 1970s and 1980s, the government refused to negotiate any more than six comprehensive claims at a time. In 1985 a federal inquiry estimated that it would take one hundred years to resolve all the outstanding comprehensive claims at the current rate of settlement. The situation for specific claims is equally grim. Because of the heavy backlog, it will take an estimated forty years to resolve the existing claims, let alone the new claims that will likely be filed.

"The process is heavily weighted in favor of the government," the Canadian Human Rights Commission concluded in a special report on federal aboriginal policy in 1990. "A claim may be rejected solely on the legal advice of the Department of Justice and without any opportunity for aboriginal people to test the validity of that advice. This is a clear conflict of interest."

Under the existing policy, Ottawa is the judge and jury for Indian land claims — yet it is also the adversary of the Indians when they go to court to assert those claims. There is no independent assessment of land claims, no arbitration or mediation process, and no right of appeal if a claim is rejected. The Assembly of First Nations views the federal reaction toward Indian land claims as one of "denial, avoidance, intimidation and intransigence."

This attitude was reflected in the federal budget for specific land claims, which was frozen at about $15 million annually for most of the 1980s. Taking inflation into account, the budget actually declined.

Federal officials admit that hundreds of Indian claims are morally valid, yet they are rejected for narrow technical reasons. Comprehensive claims, for instance, are crippled by federal policies that require the Indians to extinguish their aboriginal title in exchange for federal money — a tradeoff that is strongly resisted by most bands because it would jeopardize their fundamental belief in their inalienable land rights.

Many claims do not even proceed that far, however, since the federal government requires an Indian band to prove it occupied the land "from time immemorial." If the traditional homeland was once occupied by a different (but related) Indian band, as in the case of the Kanesatake Mohawks, the claim is rejected. Even if a band has always occupied the same land, it can be difficult to find absolute proof of that fact.

"The first thing you have to do is you have to prove that you use the land," Georges Erasmus says. "My God, people come here and claim your land, virtually claim your living room, which you've been living in for tens of thousands of years, and you've got to prove to the intruder that you've actually lived there and owned it and all the rest of it — before you even get to the land claim. So everybody has frustrations."

After the Oka crisis, Tom Siddon promised to settle every Indian land claim by the year 2000. Indian leaders were skeptical. They remembered that the federal inquiry of 1985 had recommended a broader and fairer set of criteria for land claims, but that Ottawa had rejected most of the recommendations.

Peter Russell, a University of Toronto political science professor who served on the 1985 inquiry, says that the federal stonewalling on land claims was "a classic recipe" for the outbreak of violence. The land claim submitted by the Kanesatake Mohawks in 1975 was rejected, he says, because of Ottawa's narrow criteria for acceptance of claims. "You close off the channels of peaceful and legal negotiation and change and you provoke violence. That's what we've got here."

The deep flaws in the federal land claims policy were a key reason for the outpouring of support across Canada for the Mohawk warriors in the summer of 1990. At an emergency meeting at Kahnawake in mid-July, about 150 Indian chiefs from across the country passed a resolution in support of the warriors. "We endorse the right of self-defence of aboriginal peoples in response to the violation of aboriginal and human rights of the Mohawk Nation and other aboriginal people of Canada," the resolution said.

In Manitoba, a conference of three hundred native leaders applauded the chiefs who supported the warriors. One chief, Louis Stevenson of the Peguis band, called for a violent response if the police or the army tried to attack the Mohawks on the barricades. "When lives are threatened, one has to defend oneself," added Phil Fontaine, leader of the Assembly of Manitoba Chiefs.

In Alberta, a Blackfoot chief said the warriors should keep their guns until the police withdrew. "Throughout history, whenever there were confrontations, it was always the Indians who laid down their arms first," Chief Strater Crowfoot said. "And we know what happened to them. So this time, we are saying No."

In Quebec, the Grand Chief of the Quebec Crees said the warriors were forced to protect their community from a non-Mohawk invasion. "The real issue is land," Matthew Coon-Come asserted. "The Mohawk Nation has been pushed to the brink and reacted accordingly in defending the remaining land of their nation."

Saul Terry, the president of the Union of British Columbia Indian Chiefs, praised the Mohawk warriors for pushing Indian issues to the top of the national agenda. "I salute your heroism and patriotism, which has been an inspiration to us all," he said in a message to the warriors. "You have successfully protected your territory and citizens. In doing this, you have forcefully asserted the Mohawk Nation's sovereign right of self-defence in the face of government propaganda, deception, manipulation and military power. You have shown First Nation citizens throughout Canada that direct action can speak louder than words, and that sometimes this is the only way our peoples' voice can be heard."

Throughout Canadian history, Indian militancy has surfaced sporadically — particularly among the Mohawks, but occasionally among other native groups as well. In 1974, for instance, a group of armed Ojibway warriors (inspired by the Mohawk warriors of Kahnawake) seized a municipal park in Kenora to draw attention to an unresolved land claim and to protest police harassment of Indians. A few months later, a pitched battle took place between hundreds of Indian protesters and riot police on Parliament Hill. Massive protests were launched by native leaders in the early 1980s when the federal government tried to exclude aboriginal rights from its amendments to the Canadian constitution. And in 1985, in one of the earliest examples of well-organized Indian barricades, a group of Haidas successfully blocked logging roads on their traditional homeland in the Queen Charlotte Islands.

But the militancy of Canadian Indians began to shift to a new level in 1987, after the failure of the final First Ministers Conference on aboriginal self-government. (The prime minister and the provincial premiers had promised to hold a series of conferences on aboriginal self-government after they amended the Constitution in 1982. Three conferences were held from 1984 to 1987, but each conference ended in failure because some premiers complained that the concept of self-government was too vague to entrench in the Constitution.)

When it became obvious that many of the most powerful politicians in Canada were simply not prepared to accept the basic principle of native self-government, Indian leaders gave up on the political process. They were convinced that the standard lobbying avenues led nowhere.

At a national meeting in 1987, chiefs from across Canada officially endorsed the concept of direct action to assert their land rights and sovereignty. A year later, Georges Erasmus issued a dramatic warning. Violence was brewing in the next generation of young Indians, he said, and violent conflicts would become inevitable if governments continued to ignore native issues. He did not realize how prophetic those words were.

In 1989, some of Canada's most militant Indian bands signed a mutual defence agreement, promising to support any band that became involved in a confrontation with the police or other authorities. By this time, barricades and occupations were becoming a widespread phenomenon in Indian communities across the country. Militant tactics were adopted by the Crees of Lubicon Lake, the Innu of Labrador, the Ojibways of Bear Island, and several bands in British Columbia. Logging trucks were blocked, military airports were occupied, and oil-drilling operations were halted.

Aboriginal leaders such as Georges Erasmus began to regret their past moderation. As leader of the Dene Nation in the 1970s, Erasmus had tried to negotiate agreements with Ottawa on land rights and self-government. Now, in hindsight, he acknowledges that the methods of the past were "overly peaceful." Instead of trying to persuade the government to sign a deal, the Dene should simply have followed their own laws, establishing their own government in their homeland without waiting for federal approval. They should have forced the federal government to go to court to challenge these Dene laws, Erasmus says.

The new attitude and innovative tactics of the Indian movement were symbolized in the spring of 1990 by the Meech Lake controversy. The constitutional accord, signed by the prime minister and ten premiers in 1987, perpetuated the myth that Canada had only two "founding races" — French and English. In its definition of the distinct characteristics of Canada, the accord made no mention of aboriginal people, and Indian leaders had been virtually ignored in the entire process of drafting the accord. By the early months of 1990, Canada's native people were determined to kill the accord, but they were still ignored by almost every government — until Elijah Harper intervened in the final days before the ratification deadline.

Harper, a New Democratic MLA from the riding of Rupertsland in northern Manitoba and a former chief of the Ojibway-Cree community of Red Sucker Lake, was an obscure backbencher when the controversy began. But with the adroit assistance of the Assembly of Manitoba Chiefs, he devised a strategy to block the accord in the provincial legislature. Carrying an eagle feather for spiritual strength, he quietly shook his head whenever the government asked for unanimous consent to introduce the accord in the legislature. When the Meech Lake deadline expired on June 23, Elijah Harper had defeated the accord, and he had become a national hero to Canada's aboriginal people.

The death of Meech Lake was hailed as a victory by Indians in every corner of the country. By strengthening the unity and militancy of aboriginal people, Harper laid the groundwork for the national support that the warriors enjoyed in the summer of 1990.

Within days of the SQ's July 11 attack on the barricade at Kanesatake, the warriors were flooded with support from Indians across Canada. On Indian reserves in British Columbia and Manitoba, barricades were thrown up on highways, logging roads, and railways to express solidarity with the warriors. Similar actions soon followed in Alberta, Saskatchewan, Ontario, Quebec, and Nova Scotia.

The earliest blockades were spontaneous responses by individual bands, but later roadblocks were established after the Assembly of First Nations sent a memorandum to Indian bands across the country, asking them to mobilize to support the Mohawks. It was probably the easiest campaign the assembly has ever launched. Dozens of sympathy barricades and protests were organized with breathtaking speed. "There was virtually an instantaneous response," Erasmus recalls. "It was very, very fast and very, very easy. It was extraordinary."

Hundreds of natives rallied at the Manitoba Legislature to support the warriors. Micmacs in Nova Scotia held protest marches and hunger strikes. Algonquins from western Quebec occupied an island in the Ottawa River. Ojibways in northern Ontario partially blocked the Trans-Canada Highway. Alberta Indians threatened to destroy hydro transmission lines if the Mohawk barricades were attacked. At the end of July, more than two thousand natives and non-natives from as far away as British Columbia and Prince Edward Island rallied at a park outside Oka to boost the morale of the warriors. "Things have changed; things will never be the same," said Graydon Nicholas, former head of the Union of New Brunswick Indians.

Of all the protests across Canada, the most intense took place in British Columbia, where native militancy has grown dramatically in recent years — largely because the B.C. government had consistently refused to negotiate Indian land claims. It was the only government in Canada that flatly rejected the entire concept of aboriginal land title.

By late July, Indian barricades had been set up on seven roads and railway lines in British Columbia, originally as gestures of support for the Mohawk warriors, but later as a negotiating tactic in a determined bid to seek justice from the provincial government. The blockades wreaked havoc on the tourism and forestry industries of central British Columbia, halted train traffic in the interior of the province, and brought losses of $750,000 a day to BC Rail.

The pressure soon had an effect on the government. On July 25, a provincial Cabinet minister acknowledged for the first time that Indians had "certain aboriginal rights and interests" in the province. On the same day, a report by the Premier's Council on Native Affairs recommended that the government immediately abandon its policy of refusing to participate in Indian land claim negotiations.

Twenty-four hours later, Premier Bill Vander Zalm visited the Seton Lake reserve — the scene of the railway blockade — and proclaimed that the St'latl'imx Indians were "nice people," whose demands he promised to take to Cabinet. A few days later Tom Siddon agreed to meet a group of B.C. chiefs. The federal minister predicted that the roadblocks and protests would have "a very positive and beneficial result" by accelerating government decisions on native issues.

After the premier's unexpected visit to Seton Lake, the St'latl'imx Indians temporarily lifted their railway blockade, but progress in negotiation was slow. On August 7, the B.C. chiefs warned that the province was "ready to explode" unless Indian land claims were resolved. In the middle of August, the Seton Lake band resumed its blockade of the railway line to support the Mohawk warriors. The B.C. Supreme Court ordered the Indians to dismantle their barricade, but they refused. Finally, on August 24, about sixty police officers stormed the blockade with clubs and dogs, arresting sixteen people and tearing down the barricade. A few hours later, a group of Lil'wat Indians blocked the railway at Mount Currie, about one hundred kilometres to the south. The RCMP broke up that blockade too.

Despite the dismantling of the barricades, the protests had a significant effect in British Columbia. According to Saul Terry of the Union of B.C. Indian Chiefs, the blockades produced "the first serious movement in 120 years toward settling the Indian land question in this province." He gave the credit to the Mohawk warriors.

In northern Ontario, the warriors inspired the political awakening of an obscure band of Ojibways on a tiny reserve near the town of Longlac. The reserve, known as Long Lake No. 58, had always been politically apathetic. The chief and councillors did little except distribute welfare cheques. But in the summer of 1990, the Ojibways were galvanized by the events at Oka.

The Long Lake reserve is a tiny patch of swampland, less than two square kilometres in size, which nevertheless houses more than eight hundred people. Residences are jammed together, and most families share a single shack with one or two other families. There is not even enough land on the reserve to bury the community's dead, and logging operations have destroyed much of their traditional trapping territory. Nearby lakes are poisoned by paper mills and tree-spraying programs. A railway bisects the reserve, taking the high land and consigning the Ojibways to the swamp. The Trans-Canada Highway runs through another chunk of reserve land. The band has never signed a treaty, yet the government has treated the Ojibways as if they were bound by a treaty signed by neighbouring bands in 1850.

In early August, the Ojibways of Long Lake took their first step toward militancy. Following the example of the Mohawk warriors, they blocked the Trans-Canada Highway and issued a four-page list of grievances. They demanded a treaty and a much larger reserve. "Never did our ancestors agree that this tiny plot of land was fair payment to allow outsiders free access to the immense resources in our traditional lands," the band said. "This bit of muskeg could not conceivably be considered as fair payment for the tremendous wealth taken out of our lands in recent decades."

The highway blockade gave the Ojibways enough courage to plan a more important action. On August 13, about one hundred band members seized the CN railway line that passes through their reserve. For a week, the Ojibways camped on the railway line and blocked all train traffic. It was a flimsy barricade of wooden ties and lawnchairs, but it forced the trains to grind to a standstill, causing a backlog across the country. Canadian National estimated that the barricade cost $2.6 million in lost revenue each day.

The barricade by the Long Lake Ojibways was soon followed by similar blockades on the nearby CP railway line by the Pic Mobert and Pays Plat bands. Whenever the railway companies obtained a court injunction to remove the Indians, another barricade was erected by another band. An injunction was served on the Long Lake Ojibways on August 18, but they insisted that it be translated into their own language. The next day, with two hundred police officers mobilizing in the nearby town of Longlac to enforce the court order, the Ojibways finally removed their barricade.

Without the example of the Mohawk warriors, it is unlikely that the Ojibways would have taken such drastic action. They had always known that they had been cheated out of their traditional territory, but they had never acted on that knowledge before. By blocking the railway line, they developed a sense of pride. "The community regained a sense of its own history," said Tony Hall, a native studies professor who acted as an advisor to the Ojibways.

One of Oka's legacies for aboriginal people across the country was a new willingness to consider militant tactics and even violence to overcome the wall of official indifference to their situation. Indians in Nova Scotia, Ontario, and Saskatchewan have begun to consider creating their own warrior societies.

In northern Ontario, for instance, Chief Earl Commanda of the Serpent River band has promised that an Ojibway Warrior Society will be established if the province tries to build a nuclear generating station on the northern shore of Lake Huron. In British Columbia, Chief Roger Adolph of the Fountain Lake band was wearing the traditional black face-paint of a warrior when he met the provincial premier at the Seton Lake barricade. "I'm the war chief, I'm the one that represents the warriors," he said later. "I have a heck of a time controlling them. In one sense, I don't believe in guns, in the other sense, we have a lot of frustrated young people, and angry young people."

And there are more indications that the tactics of violent resistance are spreading beyond the Mohawk communities. In late August of 1990, just a few hours after the RCMP used clubs and dogs to force an end to the Indian blockade of a railway line at Seton Lake in British Columbia, a blaze caused severe damage to the Seton Portage railway bridge. Arson was suspected. A week earlier, a railway bridge in northeastern Alberta had been set ablaze, and an Indian was charged with arson. And in early September, after the army advanced into Mohawk territory, five hydro transmission towers were damaged on a southwestern Ontario Indian reserve. Bolts were pulled from the transmission towers, which toppled to the ground. At another Indian reserve in the same region, a railway bridge was set on fire.

In southern Alberta, even before the end of the Oka crisis, a group of Peigan Indians resurrected an ancient clan known as the Lonefighters Society in an effort to block a half-constructed dam on the Oldman River. The Lonefighters, who were inspired by the Mohawk warriors, vowed to fight to the death to defend their river. They said the dam would destroy the river valley and flood their sacred burial grounds. A number of the Lonefighters were ex-convicts, and they were willing to contemplate bloodshed. "We started this without guns, but if it means we have to die to protect the situation, that's what we're going to do," said Milton Born With a Tooth, the thirty-three-year-old leader of the Lonefighters.

In early August of 1990, the Lonefighters got a bulldozer and began digging a diversion channel to render the dam useless. "We are trying to heal this river," Born With a Tooth said. Provincial politicians were contemptuous. One compared the Lonefighters to little boys "playing with their Tonka toys in the dirt." For several weeks, the government ignored the diversion work by the Lonefighters. But after twenty-eight days, the Lonefighters breached an earthen dyke and water began to flow into the diversion channel.

On the morning of September 7, dozens of RCMP officers arrived, intending to escort provincial employees and heavy equipment onto the Peigan reserve to repair the dyke. But the Lonefighters accused the police and provincial employees of trespassing and ordered them to leave the reserve. When the officers kept advancing, Born With a Tooth grabbed a hunting rifle and fired two warning shots into the air. The police scrambled for cover. There was a tense thirty-three-hour standoff. Eventually the police withdrew, but they returned a few days later and removed the bulldozer. Born With a Tooth was arrested and charged with dangerous use of a firearm and pointing a firearm.

One of the most probable locations of violent resistance by Indians in the future is the James Bay region of northern Quebec. For years, the James Bay Crees have been fighting the province's plans to implement the massive $62-billion second phase of the James Bay hydro project. The project would flood 4,400 square kilometres of Cree territory and devastate their traditional economy, poisoning the fish in their lakes and destroying their hunting and trapping industries. Despite strong objections from the Crees, the province seems determined to proceed with the hydro project. If it begins construction in defiance of the Crees, blockades and confrontations are likely.

Cree leaders have always maintained that they do not support violence, but they have warned that they cannot control the younger and more militant band members who are strongly opposed to the hydro project. These younger Crees were keeping a close watch on the tactics of the Mohawk warriors in the summer of 1990. "There is no doubt that what the warriors have done will inspire the youth to possibly resort to violence," said Grand Chief Matthew Coon-Come.

Some of the James Bay Crees have warned that hydro towers could be sabotaged and bridges destroyed. The province has taken those threats seriously. It has established an SQ headquarters in the James Bay region, and it has sent police officers into the Cree villages to search for information. "The young people, 65 per cent of our population, are fighting mad," said Billy Diamond, the most prominent Cree leader for the past twenty years. "Taking up arms has now become an option for many … I don't believe in violence. I don't believe in roadblocks. But there will be violence."

For most of Canada's aboriginal people, the lessons of Oka were simple. For hundreds of years, peaceful negotiations and polite discussions have led nowhere. When they followed the rules imposed by the federal government, Indians relegated themselves to a position of insignificance. Their land claims have taken decades to settle or been dismissed on technicalities. By refusing to obey the rules, however, they finally gained the attention of the nation.

Despite the federal government's insistence that it would not negotiate with armed warriors, it was obvious that the Oka crisis had forced Ottawa to put a higher priority on native issues. Even before the crisis was over, Prime Minister Brian Mulroney was promising a dramatic increase in federal money for land claims. "There were Cabinet ministers who had never dreamt they would be talking about native issues, and they had to deal with it," Georges Erasmus said. "Everyone started to talk about Canada's relationship with aboriginal people, treaty rights, land rights — and we're still talking about it, right across the country. The Mulroney agenda is being pushed by this issue. Whether they want to or not, they have to deal with it."

CHAPTER 13

Rolling Out the Razor Wire

The Army Moves In

The flags of the Iroquois Confederacy and the Mohawk Warrior Society fluttered in the breeze, strung alongside the flags of Canada and Quebec between two great pines. Seven men sat at a table set up in the clearing beneath them. Walter David Sr., was seated to the right of Alan Gold, the Chief Justice of the Quebec Superior Court. He wore a traditional ribbon shirt and a ceremonial head-dress, its three eagle feathers identifying him as a member of the Mohawk nation. The judge handed David Sr. the first of a stack of documents. Solemnly, the Kanesatake Longhouse secretary bent over the paper, signing his Mohawk name, Tehotenion, and beside it, making a stick drawing of a wolf to mark his clan.

It was a proud moment for Walter David Sr. All his life he had fought for the recognition of a sovereign Mohawk nation. He had raised eight children who pledged allegiance to no government but their own, the Mohawk nation, and the Iroquois Confederacy; he had made sacrifices and faced disagreements with his own people. But at this moment, those hardships were forgotten. Farther down the table sat John Ciaccia and Tom Siddon. The document in David Sr.'s hands was not a treaty — indeed, it was only a precursor to the negotiations that had been stalled for nearly a month — but that paper, and the very presence of the government officials in the Pines, encouraged the

Mohawks to believe that the government implicitly recognized the Longhouse people and the Mohawks as a nation.

Before two o'clock that morning, August 12, none of the Mohawks could have imagined this scenario in the Pines. When Chief Justice Alan Gold had left Kanesatake the previous evening, the Mohawk negotiators were despondent, certain that they had lost all hope of a peaceful settlement to the month-long standoff. They were convinced that the army would roll into Kanesatake at any moment.

Alan Gold had left the Pines equally worried. In all his years as a labour lawyer and skilled mediator prior to his appointment to the bench, Gold had seldom failed to bring two parties together to settle a dispute. When he was called in to mediate between the Mohawks and the government, it was yet another case in which he had interrupted a vacation to help resolve a national crisis. In 1973, he had returned home from California to settle the national rail strike. In 1981, he had left Vermont to mediate an end to a lengthy postal strike. The seventy-three-year-old judge was renowned for his diplomacy, wit, and affability. When he arrived in the Pines on August 9, the day after Prime Minister Brian Mulroney appointed him to try to bring the Mohawks and the government back into negotiations, Gold joked about how he was in a hurry to get a deal, because he wanted to get back to his vacation. But the Mohawks were in no mood to laugh.

"You have ice in your blood," Gold told them. The Mohawks had indeed been reluctant to trust Gold, and they were determined to show no weakness — refusing even to succumb to the judge's easygoing charm. Gold had won them over all the same, though they did not let him know it. He had dared to defy potential critics by crossing over the barricades to meet them face to face. He had taken walks by himself in the Pines, remarking on the tranquillity he felt in the cool shade of the trees.

Gold was meeting daily with the senior commander of the army, Lieutenant-General Kent Foster. Brigadier-General Armand Roy, Commander of the 5th Mechanized Brigade, who reported to Foster, had already begun making preparations to move his troops toward Oka and Kahnawake. Gold made no secret about the time constraints he was under to resolve the impasse in negotiations. But the Mohawks did not have to spend hours giving Gold an explanation of their fight for political recognition and cultural survival. Gold was Jewish, and many Mohawks had great admiration for the Jews, who, like the Mohawks, were a cultural minority who had fought tenaciously to keep their traditions and religion intact.

Gold's presence and his direct, honest style had defused the tense atmosphere in the Pines, but it had not resulted in an agreement on the three conditions to further negotiations — access to food and medicine, access to advisors, and the presence of international observers at Kahnawake and Kanesatake. After weeks of balking, the federal and provincial governments had eventually agreed to allow international observers. In fact, they were ready to meet all three of the conditions the Mohawks had first proposed on July 18 — but only if the Mohawks agreed to negotiate the dismantling of the barricades. The Mohawks refused to budge on that point. They wanted their preconditions met first, as a sign of the government's good faith, before they would talk about the dismantling. That was how the situation stood on August 11, when Gold left Kanesatake after the third day of talks.

When he arrived back in Montreal that evening, Gold called James O'Reilly, the lawyer who had been acting as the Mohawk envoy to the federal and provincial governments. A disheartened Gold told O'Reilly that he was on his way to meet the Quebec Cabinet crisis committee. "I don't know what I'm going to tell them," Gold said. "I haven't got a deal."

O'Reilly asked him to hold off on his report to the Cabinet committee until he had made a few more calls. While Gold waited, he talked to Peter Diome at the Mohawk Nation Office in Kahnawake, but Diome was unequivocal: the Mohawks wanted the preconditions met first, and they would not tag on an agreement to dismantle the barricades unless Quebec granted a moratorium on arrests until the Mohawks and the governments agreed on what should happen to the warriors.

"We wanted something that would give us some breathing space," says Owen Young, the lawyer who was advising Diome and the Mohawk warriors in Kahnawake. "If the barricades came down, what the hell were we to do with these guys?"

A flurry of phone calls and faxes ensued — between O'Reilly, the Cabinet committee, the Mohawk negotiators in Kanesatake, and the Nation Office in Kahnawake. At Kanesatake, Maurice Gabriel was chainsmoking nervously, waiting for the latest proposal to arrive at the Treatment Centre, which was the Mohawk negotiators' headquarters. Everyone was on edge.

"I have bad feelings," said Bill Sears, an Akwesasne Mohawk and Vietnam veteran who had arrived in Kanesatake a short time before. "They're the same feelings I used to get when the Viet Cong were about to overrun us."

"That's all we need, Bill, this kind of encouragement," Gabriel told him with a wry smile. After thirty days of continual meetings, phone calls, discussions, and stalled negotiations, Gabriel was exhausted and his nerves were frayed. When the proposal calling for a moratorium on arrests arrived from Kahnawake, Gabriel groaned. The last time they'd mentioned the word "moratorium" to government officials, the reaction had been furious. "They just flipped out, they just lost their minds," Gabriel recalls. "That was it, they were sending in the army."

Finally, Diome put forward another idea. The Mohawks would agree to issue a separate communiqué in conjunction with the agreement on the three preconditions. Once the agreement was signed, the Mohawks would undertake to negotiate, as the first item on the agenda, the terms by which the police and armed forces would be withdrawn and the barricades would be dismantled. The phrase "terms by which" was the key to that communiqué. Without explicitly naming those terms in their document, the Mohawks agreed among themselves that one of those terms would be some kind of protection from prosecution for the armed warriors once the barricades were down. (The Quebec government was also aware of how crucial this phrase was. In a French draft of the communiqué, the word "terms" had been translated as "*les modalités*," which left it open to being interpreted as "the means" by which the barricades would be taken down. The Mohawks insisted that the French translation be redrafted to reflect the communiqué's intent.)

O'Reilly put the proposal to Judge Gold, who was still meeting with the Cabinet crisis committee, stalling for time while the Mohawks tinkered with the wording of the latest draft. Finally, at 2:00 a.m., Gold called O'Reilly back. "We got a deal," he told him excitedly. O'Reilly called Kahnawake and Kanesatake to pass on the message. In Kanesatake, the small group of men waiting by the telephone was elated. At three o'clock in the morning, Maurice Gabriel drove around to all the barricades to tell the warriors the good news. The negotiations were about to get back on track.

There were still technical details to be worked out. Where would the deal be signed? Who would sign it? In times past, the war chiefs had signed treaties for the Mohawk nation, so there was some discussion about getting "diplomatic immunity" for Allan Delaronde, the Kahnawake war chief, to pass through the SQ barricades to get to Kanesatake to sign the deal. But others said the agreement was not a treaty, and that it would be more appropriate for the secretaries of the Longhouses in Kanesatake and Kahnawake to act as signatories.

Late the next afternoon, two warriors on a motorcycle held the Mohawk warrior flag aloft as they led a cavalcade of dignitaries through Kanesatake, to the entrance of the Pines. A dirt pile, criss-crossed by barbed wire, still blocked the road into the Pines. A warrior stepped gingerly onto the wire to hold it down, so the dignitaries would not catch their dress pants on it as they filed over the barricade and into the clearing. Tom Siddon smiled, winking at one of the Mohawk women as he took his seat at the table beneath the flags. If he was uncomfortable, he tried hard not to show it. He had often sworn that he would never cross the barricades to talk to armed warriors. Now, here he was getting ready to sign a document in the middle of the Pines. There were no arms in sight, but several warriors, their faces obscured by kerchiefs and dark sunglasses, stood among the other Mohawks. And then, after most copies of the agreement had already been signed, a masked warrior unexpectedly sat down at the far end of the table. He proceeded to sign his Mohawk name to the documents on behalf of the Mohawks of Akwesasne.

A last-minute decision had been made by some of the Mohawk negotiators to have the agreement signed by representatives of each Mohawk territory. Though a number of other Akwesasne Mohawks, including Loran Thompson, were in the Pines, someone told "4-20," a seventeen-year-old warrior from Akwesasne, to sign on behalf of his home reserve.

The move took the Longhouse secretaries completely by surprise. When 4-20 sat down, Walter David Sr. looked over at the Quebec and federal ministers to gauge their reaction. They said nothing, so he felt it would be inappropriate to intervene.

Later, most Mohawks acknowledged it was a serious mistake to allow a masked warrior to sign the agreement. Even those who believed it had been the right thing to do refused to reveal who had made the decision.

"If I had been there, I would have prohibited it," says Francis Boots, the Akwesasne war chief. "A few individuals thought they could slap Canada in the face."

Others agreed it was a move designed to embarrass Tom Siddon — which backfired on the Mohawks. It left Denise David-Tolley and Ellen Gabriel convinced, rightly or wrongly, that someone on the inside was conspiring to make sure the ensuing negotiations would fail. It shifted the focus of public attention to the question of the warriors' legitimacy. "It took everything off the issues of the land and what had happened to us on July 11," David-Tolley said later.

After the ceremony, 4-20 presented Alan Gold with a neatly folded Warrior Society flag as thanks for his work. "This must be a Mohawk nation flag," Gold remarked, smiling broadly, as he unfolded it and held it aloft for the television cameras.

"It's a warrior flag," an annoyed Walter David Sr. whispered to him loudly. He had expected that the Quebec judge would be given the blue and white "Hiawatha belt," the flag symbolizing the Haudenosaunee, or Iroquois Confederacy. Again, someone in the Pines had wanted to make a point — to show the world that the Quebec and federal governments had recognized the legitimacy of the warriors.

The public reacted to the signing ceremony with fury. Radio talk-show hotlines lit up with calls from indignant Quebeckers who labelled the event a farce and accused the governments of hypocrisy. "The governments said they would not negotiate under the gun, and lo and behold, on television we see the opposite," said one disgruntled Oka resident. "How do you explain that?" A short time later, a Liberal member of the Quebec National Assembly, René-Serge Larouche, quit his party, saying he was "sickened to see a sovereign nation negotiate on bended knee with terrorists."

The sensation created by the warrior's signature eclipsed the gestures of goodwill made by all sides that afternoon. Nevertheless, Tom Siddon, who had refused two weeks earlier to criticize his deputy minister when Harry Swain labelled the Mohawk warriors "criminals" and "an armed gang," now spoke sympathetically of the difficult times the Mohawks of Kahnawake and Kanesatake were living through, and of the great historical and spiritual significance of the Pines to the "people of the Mohawk nation." He vowed that "July 11 will never happen again."

Even while solemn words were being exchanged in the Pines, all hell was breaking loose on Montreal's south shore.

The nightly demonstrations on Highway 138 near the main Mohawk barricade were continuing to swell, and the crowds were growing angrier and uglier. On Sunday August 12, while the signing ceremony was taking place in the Pines, the Sûreté du Québec riot squad was battling demonstrators from Solidarité Châteauguay on the St. Louis de Gonzague Bridge, a revolving bridge that crosses the St. Lawrence Seaway near Valleyfield, west of Châteauguay. The demonstrators planned to block the shipping lane by parking their cars on the bridge.

By early afternoon, about 150 people had arrived at the scene. They broke into a fenced-in compound for construction materials, stole a pile of concrete bricks, and stacked them across the road, erecting their own barricade. Yvon Poitras, the former SQ officer who had become the leader of Solidarité Châteauguay, sported a badge that read "I am a hostage in Châteauguay" as he gave interviews to journalists.

"We'll stay here as long as the Mercier Bridge remains blocked," Poitras said. "We are at the point of no return. We have nothing left to lose."

Eighty officers in riot gear marched onto the bridge, trying unsuccessfully to push back the crowd. Someone tore the helmet off one officer's head and started to wrest his riot stick out of his hands. The officer was left beaten and pale, blood streaming from a gash on his forehead. More police reinforcements came running.

The police kept moving forward, banging their nightsticks rhythmically on the metal guardrails of the bridge and pulling people out of the cars where they had taken shelter. One CBC cameraman, who refused to follow the SQ's orders to stop filming the riot squad's advance, was knocked down by the police and forced to turn over his videotape.

Seven people were arrested, including Yvon Poitras. A crowd of enraged demonstrators followed police to the SQ detachment at nearby Ste. Martine, apparently intending to try to free those who had been arrested. They stormed the detachment, breaking windows and smashing police cars. Outnumbered by the mob, the police locked themselves into the building. Then the crowd moved on towards the barricade near the Mercier Bridge, the scene of nightly demonstrations since the Mohawk warriors had taken the bridge on July 11.

What followed was the worst night of rioting since the standoff had begun. This time, the Mohawks were all but forgotten by the mob. After the confrontation on the St. Louis de Gonzague Bridge, the police were now the enemy, and the crowd's fury was directed at them. By 9:30 p.m., the mob had swelled to several thousand. Once again, it was a family affair. More than one man arrived with a baseball bat in one hand and a child gripping the other. Someone climbed onto a police cruiser and smashed its dome light and its windshield. With that act of vandalism, a collective roar went up in the crowd. Young men advanced menacingly towards the line of officers, waving baseball bats and tire-irons, rattling the metal gate that separated the police from the mob. Still more people surged forward, knocking over the barricade and forcing the police to retreat several metres. Protesters peeled chunks of pavement off the roadside curbs, heaving them and anything else they could lay their hands on — eggs, bricks, rocks — at the police. RCMP officers, called in to reinforce the Sûreté du Québec, stood shoulder to shoulder on the front line, protecting the SQ officers behind them. Few of the officers carried protective shields. One middle-aged policeman was struck in the chest with a flying brick and collapsed on the ground.

The mob lit fires in the street, wrenched open a fire hydrant, and smashed more police vehicles. By then thousands of people were crowding the road and spilling out into the parking lots of the adjacent shopping centre and gas stations. The police launched round after round of tear gas to force the crowd back. With each volley, the crowd would move back, crying, choking, and coughing, some covering their mouths with their shirt-tails.

Then the police charged, chasing people down the street, tackling some of them and arresting them. Some hid behind parked cars; others took refuge in a hotel lobby.

Once again, journalists were a target for the mob's rage. About thirty angry men surrounded a radio reporter, wrestling with her, trying to tear away the purse where she had hidden her recording equipment.

"If you stay here one more second you won't have a face!" one man screamed at her. Two or three men pursued her down the street until she got to her car and drove away.

By 1:00 a.m., when the crowd had finally dispersed, thirty-five people had been taken to hospital, including ten RCMP officers. Many of the RCMP privately resented the fact that they had been directed to stand in front of the provincial police, where they suffered the brunt of the mob's fury towards the SQ.

For the following two nights, the riots continued. Demonstrators threw golfballs and Molotov cocktails at the RCMP officers who were again on the front lines. The police retaliated with tear gas. On the third night, rioters overpowered a semi-trailer whose driver found himself among the mobs while trying to deliver vegetables to the IGA store near the barricade. The truck was surrounded by the rioters, and before the driver had time to react, someone had unhitched the trailer from the cab. Within moments, the trailer's door was forced open and the truck was emptied of all its contents. The rioters lobbed cobs of corn and onions at the police, along with hockey pucks, golfballs, ·rocks, and bits of pavement. The clothing of one SQ officer was set ablaze by a Molotov cocktail. Another policeman was injured by a flying brick.

By the end of the third night of violence, the SQ officers on the front lines at Châteauguay had had enough. They complained that they had been prevented from doing their jobs, ordered not to further antagonize the crowd by making more arrests. Publicly criticized by their superiors for their assault on the St. Louis de Gonzague bridge, fed up with serving as cannon fodder for the angry mobs, their backs to the Mohawk warriors they were supposed to be watching, the police went to their union, which threatened to pull its members out of Châteauguay if they did not get more support from the government of Quebec.

Observers said the RCMP were clearly better trained than the SQ in crowd control. "When the RCMP busted someone, nobody got hurt," said one photographer. "There would be one guy at his head, two guys at his feet, one guy to search him and handcuff him. When the SQ moved in, it looked like a rugby scrum. And everybody they arrested went off bleeding, limping, or crying."

On the fourth night of the riots, August 15, the SQ tried the approach of the local Châteauguay police, who, from the start of the crisis, had mingled with the crowds at the barricade. Instead of lining up shoulder to shoulder and advancing on the crowds, the police officers wandered among the protesters, chatting with them and attempting to restore a level of trust. It worked like magic. That night there were no new acts of violence.

The pressure on Premier Robert Bourassa reached a new level of intensity after the signing ceremony and the fever-pitched riots in Châteauguay. It had now been a week since he had called for the help of the Canadian Armed Forces, but there was no sign that the army was ready to storm the barricades. The crowds in Châteauguay expected and wanted a military attack. "How much time does it take for the army to get here?" one Châteauguay man asked impatiently.

But the army commander, Lieutenant-General Foster, took a cautious approach. After a preliminary assessment of the Mohawk fortifications and firepower, the army concluded that the warriors were a highly organized paramilitary force, and Foster was anxious to end the standoff peacefully. In a briefing to reporters on August 9, he said the consequences of an armed assault on the Mohawk barricades would be "quite frankly, unthinkable."

One of Foster's main tasks was to convince provincial authorities that the use of armed force would not resolve the crisis, though the Cabinet crisis committee was deeply divided over the usefulness of continued negotiations with the Mohawks. Native Affairs Minister John Ciaccia was convinced that a military solution to the crisis would only plant the seeds for future armed conflicts with the Mohawks and other aboriginal people. "I don't think you have an army large enough to protect every pylon in the north," he told his Cabinet colleagues, referring to the possibility that an armed attack on the Mohawks could set the stage for violent confrontations with the James Bay Crees over future hydro development in northern Quebec. But Ciaccia was dismissed by the rest of the committee as a Mohawk sympathizer. The senior Cabinet member on the committee, Claude Ryan, took a cautious and analytical approach. He wanted "law and order" restored, but he was reticent about using force. Premier Robert Bourassa was also cautious, weighing all the options carefully. Virtually everyone else on the crisis committee wanted the army to move in.

"Most of these people had no idea of what the consequences of their desires were," Foster said later. The army had calculated that a military assault on the Mohawk barricades would require the evacuation of everyone within a ten-kilometre radius of the Mercier Bridge. Both the army and the warriors had .50-calibre machine guns, and stray bullets could travel as far as nine kilometres. An estimated 100,000 people would have to have been evacuated "just to be sure that no one dies accidentally," Foster said. "Even then, there would be a good chance of something going wrong. Those kind of potential consequences had to be explained."

The army later acknowledged that Foster "convinced provincial authorities that the use of arms in assault would not help resolve the Mohawk crisis." A senior federal official admitted privately in mid-August that there would likely have been several resignations among the top army commanders if Bourassa had ordered them to attack the Mohawk barricades. The senior official said Brian Mulroney was equally opposed to a military attack because he did not want to go down in history as "the butcher of Oka."

The army's reluctance to launch an assault left some provincial officials chafing. In the midst of the army operation, Public Security Minister Sam Elkas said Quebec was considering creating a paramilitary police force — a kind of provincial National Guard — to handle future racial conflicts and social unrest. One provincial official complained that Quebec's plans for a quick end to the standoff had been thwarted by the federal government. "We have found out that the Canadian army comes complete with strings attached," the official said.

In the strained constitutional climate that followed the demise of the Meech Lake accord in June, any public hint that the Quebec government's agenda was being influenced by Ottawa made many Quebeckers bristle. From the start of the crisis, the relationship between Ottawa and Quebec had been a complicated balancing act. The province's negotiator, Alexander Paterson, said later that the "easy relationship" between Bourassa and Mulroney prevented the crisis from escalating into a political tug-of-war between the two governments. "They would pick up the phone and talk to each other, and all the crap would fall away in thirty seconds," Paterson recalls.

On August 13, the day after the first night of heavy rioting and attacks on police on the Highway 138 barricade in Châteauguay, Premier

Robert Bourassa asked General John de Chastelain, the Chief of Defence Staff, to move troops closer to the scene to calm the situation. Early in the morning of August 15, six hundred soldiers of the Royal 22nd Regiment's 3rd Battalion rolled into St. Rémi, south of Châteauguay, and set up camp on the parking lot of a local sports complex. More troops were deployed in nearby St. Hubert, in St Benoit, fifteen kilometres northeast of Oka, and in Blainville, thirty kilometres farther east. In all, 2,650 soldiers, accompanied by more than a thousand vehicles, armoured personnel carriers, and other equipment, were in place by August 16, ready to move up to the barricaded territories.

By then, the team of international observers had arrived in Montreal. They were members of the International Federation of Human Rights, most of them lawyers or judges from western Europe. On August 14, they had signed a protocol agreement with the federal and provincial governments and the Mohawk nation, covering where observers would be stationed and what their duties would entail. Observers were to be posted at eight barricades in Kahnawake and Kanesatake, to verify that the August 12 agreement was being honoured, and two observers would monitor the negotiations between the Mohawks and the federal and provincial governments.

The chief federal negotiator was Bernard Roy, a prominent Montreal lawyer and former principal secretary to Brian Mulroney. For his effort, Roy was paid $225 an hour, plus expenses. Alexander Paterson, also a lawyer and the newly appointed chairman of McGill University, represented Quebec at the talks. Roy was a trusted friend of Mulroney and had direct and immediate access to the prime minister's office at all times. Paterson was a respected member of Quebec's anglophone community and the founding chairman of the English rights group, Alliance Quebec. In 1976, he had helped negotiate a solution to a long and bitter school strike. He was also a close personal friend of Quebec Native Affairs Minister John Ciaccia.

Paterson assumed that he would be reporting directly to Ciaccia but learned otherwise at a meeting of the Cabinet crisis committee, whose members were as deeply divided among themselves as the Mohawks whose factionalism the committee often complained about. "Nobody trusted anybody," Paterson recalls. He told the Cabinet crisis committee that he would not take advice from the entire committee, and that he would report directly to Ciaccia. At that moment, the Cabinet ministers around the table exchanged glances and asked him to leave the room. When he returned, Ciaccia said to him, "You won't be reporting to me, Alec." That was when Paterson realized that although he was still officially Native Affairs minister, Ciaccia had been effectively stripped of his authority. Paterson insisted then that he be allowed to deal directly with the premier. After that, he spoke to Bourassa or one of his top aides every night.

Both Paterson and Roy were experienced negotiators, who could be expected to handle the inevitable media scrutiny with dignity and aplomb. They assumed they could approach this crisis as they would any prolonged labour dispute, negotiating around the clock until they had an agreement on the dismantling of the barricades. But neither man had ever worked with the Mohawks before. The clash of cultures was obvious from the first day of negotiations.

The Mohawk approach to negotiations was to bring together everyone they felt they might need to explain their history, their treaties, and their land claims. The night before August 16, when the talks were scheduled to begin, Paterson and Roy received a list of fifty-four people who would serve as Mohawk negotiators, advisors, and spiritual leaders at the negotiations. Paterson seemed befuddled and irritated when he arrived at the hotel in the Montreal suburb of Dorval, where the talks were to take place. "I can't negotiate with fifty-four people," he told reporters. "It's unacceptable."

Most of the Mohawk negotiators were hard-line Mohawk nationalists, including Diane Lazore, Francis Boots, and Loran Thompson from Akwesasne, Joe Deom and others from the Kahnawake Longhouse, and Ellen Gabriel, Walter David Sr. and other members of his family from Kanesatake. The two Kanesatake community members who had been appointed to the talks in mid-July, Maurice Gabriel and Mavis Etienne, were also there to help present Kanesatake's land claims. Kahnawake's elected grand chief, Joe Norton, and elected chief Billy Two Rivers were among the few key negotiators on the list who were not from the Longhouse. The Mohawks insisted that most of their fifty-four people were simply observers who would be called to the negotiating table only if their expertise was required. But if they needed to arrive at a consensus on a government proposal, the Mohawks would draw on the advice of everyone present.

When the Mohawks arrived at the Dorval Hilton on the first day of talks, they were already feeling angry and harassed. Those who had travelled by bus from Kanesatake had seen an SQ officer videotaping their departure, and they had stopped the bus until the videotape was turned over to a provincial official. As they trooped into the meeting room, the Mohawks faced a barrage of questions from reporters. They had agreed to the government negotiators' request for a news blackout, but that agreement had not been conveyed to the media. Reporters chased them around the hotel, even into washrooms, pleading for a word or two on how negotiations were progressing. One journalist even sneaked into the kitchen adjacent to the meeting room and tried to eavesdrop on the talks. The event became a media circus. The Mohawks, taking their vow of silence seriously, would not throw as much as a "no comment" in the journalists' direction. Later the Mohawks were furious to learn that Roy and Paterson had stopped to talk to reporters, even though they did not divulge the substance of the talks.

The day ended in such frustration for everyone — the reporters, the Mohawks, and the government negotiators — that the next day's talks were moved to a secret location, a restaurant in an out-of-the-way industrial park in the city of Laval. Even there, however, negotiations did not go smoothly. The federal government had hired a consultant from Quebec's largest public relations firm, National Public Relations, to prepare government negotiators for media briefings. The same firm was handling the public relations strategy for the Oka town council. The consultant, Guy Côté, sat in on the talks for part of the day, until the Mohawks found out who he was and demanded his ejection from the room. Now the Mohawks were convinced that the federal government was going through the motions of negotiating merely as a public relations exercise to conceal the fact that a military attack was being prepared.

The army, however, had no intention of launching a surprise attack, despite the desires of some Cabinet ministers. In fact, Paterson considered the army commander to be his greatest ally. Lieutenant-General Foster was prepared to stall the army's approach as long as there was progress in negotiations.

"I was desperately trying to pull documents out of the Mohawks — to do anything to hold back the army," Paterson recalls. "I was absolutely convinced there was going to be shooting if the negotiations failed. The army agreed absolutely. General Foster pleaded with the governments to understand that."

However, Paterson had nothing to offer the Mohawks in negotiations. He had only one mandate: to get the barricades down. Bernard Roy was permitted to discuss the land issues in Kanesatake, but Ottawa required him to follow the principles of the so-called "framework agreement" that had been totally rejected by the Kanesatake Mohawks many months earlier. He was not permitted to make any undertakings on behalf of Ottawa until the barricades were dismantled and the Mohawk weapons were disposed of. His federal contract required him to obtain the dismantling of the barricades "prior to substantive negotiations" and prohibited him from recognizing Mohawk sovereignty "in the international sense." Neither negotiator had any margin of manoeuvre.

The Mohawks interpreted the narrow mandates of the negotiators as a clear indication that Ottawa and Quebec did not want a negotiated settlement. From their perspective, the "terms" of the dismantling of the barricades meant the minimum conditions that would have to be met first — that is, the recognition of Mohawk sovereignty and their right to defend their territory. Implicit in that recognition was freedom from prosecution for what they considered to be an act of self-defence. The two sides were entering negotiations with completely different sets of assumptions.

On August 18, talks had moved to La Trappe, the monastery a few kilometres east of Oka. That move eased tensions considerably, because the site was close to Kanesatake and the setting was peaceful and private. The monks had already shown their sympathy for the Mohawks by helping bring food to the settlement earlier in the summer, and that gesture had established a certain level of trust. That day, the Kanesatake Mohawks presented their list of demands: the transfer of title to the Pines and the existing Oka golf course to the Longhouse people of the Iroquois Confederacy, an independent inquiry into the July 11 raid, a return of sacred and historical articles held by Canada and Quebec, and a written commitment to negotiate Kanesatake's short-term land needs with the Longhouse people.

By the time talks broke off for a day of reflection on August 18, the Mohawks had spent the better part of three days lecturing the provincial and federal negotiators on Mohawk customs and treaties. They had given the negotiators a detailed overview of the Mohawk sovereignty position, of the Two Row Wampum treaty, of international indigenous rights agreements, and the Great Law of Peace. The federal government does not recognize the Two Row Wampum treaty, which was negotiated between the Mohawks and the Dutch, the first Europeans to settle among the Mohawks, and most of the officials at the talks were not interested in listening to the Mohawk arguments — but Paterson and Roy agreed it was important to hear the Mohawks out. Paterson found himself intrigued by their history, which was new to him.

His intrigue turned to surprise when Loran Thompson pulled out his Iroquois Confederacy passport, complete with Canadian customs stamps from occasions when Thompson had crossed the American-Canadian border. The customs stamps were proof that the Canadian government had accepted the passport, despite its refusal to recognize Mohawk sovereignty. Paterson borrowed the passport and showed it to Premier Bourassa when they met the next day. "What do you think of that?" Paterson asked the premier. Paterson recalls that Bourassa was just as surprised to see it as he was.

Apart from the passport, however, Paterson had nothing to show or tell Bourassa when they met that Sunday, nor did Roy have anything to report to Mulroney. When talks began, Paterson had told reporters optimistically that he hoped to see the bridge open by the weekend of August 18. By that weekend, however, the Mohawk negotiators had not even broached the subject of the barricades.

Early in the negotiations, the Mohawks had revealed that they had prepared a plan for the dismantling of the roadblocks. Paterson asked for the plan each morning, but after three days of negotiations, he had not yet seen it. "I read the Great Law of Peace," he said later. "I knew they would never give up the arms. But surely, I told them, you've got to realize that if you don't make a gesture, this thing is not going to end." He suggested they bury their arms in a sealed casket — although he did not know if the government would agree to his proposal — and told the Mohawks he could not stretch his mandate any further.

On Friday, August 17, Bourassa had called on the army to replace the exhausted members of the Sûreté du Québec on the barricades at Kahnawake and Kanesatake. The soldiers spent the weekend loading backpacks, checking communications equipment, tearing down their camps and preparing for their next move. At dawn on August 20, hundreds of trucks, jeeps, and armoured personnel carriers rumbled onto the streets of St. Rémi and the other towns where the army had set up its makeshift camps, and headed towards Châteauguay and Oka.

The standoff was entering a new and dangerous phase, but the Mohawks were happy to see the departure of the hated SQ. As the army arrived, the Kahnawake warriors put up signs to taunt the Quebec police for being unable to cope with the Mohawks. The police put up their own signs: "Thanks for the overtime." The Mohawks responded: "Don't thank us. You pay the taxes."

By the time the first army vehicles arrived in Châteauguay at 9 a.m., a crowd of bystanders had already been waiting at the Highway 138 barricade for hours to witness the event. The crowd watched approvingly as soldiers set to work removing the concrete blocks the Sûreté du Québec had set up at the roadblock, unravelling rolls of razor wire and staking it along the boulevards and across the highway. An armoured personnel carrier pulled onto the parking lot of a gas station near the old roadblock, and two more APCs stationed themselves under the nearby traffic lights on Highway 138.

Lieutenant-Colonel Robin Gagnon, the commanding officer of the troops at Châteauguay, walked into the no-man's-land on Highway 138 and shook hands with a small group of warrior leaders who had left their own barricade to meet him. The onlookers in Châteauguay were aghast, and an angry noise rumbled through the crowd as they hissed their displeasure. The crowd had come to the barricade expecting to see a show of military strength, not this sign of goodwill toward the warriors. "It's a comedy," one man complained. "The army, shaking hands with terrorists!"

Gagnon's gesture marked the beginning of a surprisingly cordial relationship between the army and the Kahnawake warriors. A few days earlier, three of the Kahnawake warrior leaders — Cookie Mc-Comber, Michael Thomas, and the warrior codenamed Windwalker — had agreed to meet a group of army officers to establish some ground rules about patrols and communications between the two sides. After the army arrived on August 20, Gagnon met daily with two or three warriors at a grove of maple trees near Highway 132. Each side brought food and beverages, and the Mohawks and Gagnon would sit in lawnchairs drinking Tang and coffee and munching on cookies and doughnuts while they discussed the army's proposals. On one occasion, the warriors took off their masks briefly so that Gagnon could see their faces, to show him he had their respect. Most of the warrior leaders were veterans of the U.S. Army and had served in Vietnam and other wars, so they spoke in the military jargon that Gagnon understood.

Gagnon and the Kahnawake warriors agreed to establish "land lines" — portable phones connected by wires — to provide communications between the army and the warriors at the barricades. This was intended to prevent accidents and to ensure that each side was aware of the other's movements. Gagnon promised that his soldiers would not aim their weapons at the warriors as long as the warriors did not aim at the soldiers.

Gagnon and his officers treated the warriors as professional soldiers. Although this may have been a deliberate strategy by the army to make the warriors feel important, the atmosphere of military respect gave the army officers a negotiating advantage that the politicians never had.

At the same time, Gagnon kept an iron fist in his velvet glove. He said he preferred a non-violent solution, but kept the warriors off balance by warning that he might be ordered to attack the barricades at any time. It was never clear whether he was bluffing or not. "He was a pussycat," one warrior said. "He wanted a peaceful solution. But he could have been conning us."

For his part, Gagnon was struck by the way the Mohawks reached decisions. "The chiefs have no decision-making power whatever," Gagnon said later. "They must constantly consult their people and reach a consensus." He regretted that he knew so little about Mohawk traditions when he was assigned to the operation at Kahnawake. "It would have helped beforehand to be familiar, not only with their demands, but also with their culture and traditions," Gagnon said. "Their outlook is altogether different from ours."

While the replacement of the police by the military went smoothly at the barricades in Kahnawake, the army was given a hostile reception at Kanesatake. The Kanesatake warriors had refused to meet the military officers before the army began its advance on August 20, so the delegates who agreed to go to the army's temporary headquarters at St. Benoit were not warriors but a team of community volunteers — three women and two men. At their two meetings with Lieutenant-Colonel Pierre Daigle, the officer in charge of the Kanesatake operation, Daigle showed them maps, explaining how the army was going to replace the police at the SQ checkpoints. "Why can't we move up to here?" Daigle repeatedly asked the Kanesatake liaison team, referring on the map to the unmanned Mohawk barricade at North Pole. The army wanted to position itself in a place where it could keep the Mohawks within eyesight, and the SQ checkpoint was over a kilometre away from North Pole. But the Mohawks refused to give Daigle permission to advance beyond the police perimeter.

Daigle would not be dissuaded from his plan, however. Shortly after dawn on August 20, he went to North Pole, where he put his proposal directly to Walter David Jr. and three Akwesasne warriors — Bill Sears, Harold Oakes, and Robert "Mad Jap" Skidders. The warriors balked. If the army moved forward, the soldiers would discover the Mohawks' bluff. "There were no Mohawks within two miles of North Pole at that point," Bill Sears explained later. "We didn't have the manpower to man those barricades."

Daigle abandoned any hope of reaching the same kind of "friendly arrangement" with the Kanesatake warriors that Gagnon had struck in Kahnawake, and he ordered his men to set up a post four hundred metres south of the SQ checkpoint. It was several hundred metres short of North Pole, where Daigle wanted to position his troops, but the advance was still enough to convince the Mohawks that the army was going to close in on them. When the rest of the Mohawk negotiators involved in talks at La Trappe found out about the army's manoeuvre, they cancelled the talks that were scheduled to resume on August 20. They returned to the Treatment Centre and fired off messages to Robert Bourassa and Brian Mulroney, informing them that the negotiations would not resume until they had a promise that the army would not advance any farther.

The army's negotiating strategy, which proved so successful in Kahnawake, was difficult to implement in Kanesatake. In Kahnawake, the warriors had a clear military command structure, and they had experienced military men who were prepared to deal with the army on a "soldier-to-soldier" basis. The Kahnawake leaders were also under growing pressure from their own community to get the barricades down. Mobs in the surrounding suburbs were blocking food and provisions from coming into the reserve, and people were going hungry. In early August, the federal government had bought the land that had been slated for the Oka golf course expansion, and many Kahnawake Mohawks were asking how long they could be expected to keep up the barricades that had been erected as a gesture of solidarity.

But in Kanesatake, the warriors had no clear military structure or chain of command. Dennis "Psycho" Nicholas, the Kanesatake warrior who had been "head of security" throughout the spring, was now devoting most of his time to a blossoming romance with a Mohawk woman named Cathy Sky. The gap in authority was being filled by others, including a warrior who had the respect and trust of most of the men, a Kahnawake Mohawk known as Muddy House. He was a powerfully built man who derived his combat experience from his years at Ganienkeh, the Mohawk territory in upstate New York. Since he stayed behind the scenes at Kanesatake, journalists rarely caught a glimpse of him, but he was a mentor to some of the inexperienced warriors, giving them advice and teaching them how to handle their weapons. A fervent Mohawk nationalist, he was fiercely opposed to the Kahnawake warriors' decision to negotiate with the army.

Several others at the Treatment Centre held varying degrees of influence over the warriors. One of them was Mad Jap, the fifty-three-year-old Akwesasne Mohawk who took charge of internal communications among the warriors and later controlled external communications with the police and army. Everyone assumed from his tough bearing that he was an army veteran, but in fact he had no military experience. "I was the senior person — by age and by voice of authority, voice of command," he explained later.

Francis Boots, the Akwesasne war chief, and Loran Thompson, the uncompromising Mohawk nationalist and faithkeeper from Akwesasne, were in charge of spiritual guidance for the warriors at Kanesatake. While Thompson was participating in the government negotiations, he would often wander from one warrior bunker to the next at night, updating the men on the day's events. He wanted to keep their spirits high, so he told them the negotiations were going well. But as talks dragged on and it became clearer there was no settlement in sight, many warriors became discouraged. Some felt Thompson was just stringing them along to keep them on the barricades.

Many of those who had been in Kanesatake during the first weeks of the siege had deserted the barricades by the time the army moved in. Some of them were bored or exhausted after the endless nights of patrols; others had simply lost faith in the negotiations. Even the Akwesasne war chief, Francis Boots, now believed that the warriors had done enough to guarantee that the land would be protected. He reminded them that they had come to Kanesatake to protect the land — not to fight the army. Boots never actually told the warriors to quit, but he laid out the facts, pointing out that the focus of the crisis had shifted away from the Pines and over to Kahnawake and the mobs in Châteauguay. But most of the warriors rejected the idea of quitting.

By the time the army arrived on August 20, the warriors and warrior supporters who remained at Kanesatake were the most fervent of the Mohawk idealists and militants. A motley collection of men and women from Kanesatake, from other Mohawk territories, and from aboriginal nations across Canada, they were nevertheless "the distillation of the ideal," according to one of the men. They were not prepared to make any compromises until their sovereignty was recognized and they were unwilling to play any friendly games with Lieutenant-Colonel Daigle.

The army's unilateral decision to advance beyond the SQ checkpoint on August 20 worried the Kahnawake warriors, who feared the move might spark a gunfight between the Kanesatake warriors and the soldiers. That same day, they asked Colonel Gagnon for a helicopter so they could fly to Oka and calm things down. Three warrior leaders from Kahnawake — Cookie McComber, Michael Thomas and Windwalker — got into an army helicopter and flew to Oka, accompanied by an army officer.

The warrior leaders knew they were taking a dangerous gamble. The army could simply have arrested them and carted them away. "I felt very uncomfortable getting into that helicopter," Thomas recalled. "But it was a risk we knew we had to take."

The helicopter landed on Highway 344, near the army's new position on the edge of Oka, at the bottom of the hill just east of Main

Gate. When the three warriors emerged from the aircraft, they were wearing black fatigues to remind everyone that they regarded themselves as professional soldiers. While the military officers waited at the helicopter, the Kahnawake warriors proceeded up the hill to the Treatment Centre, ignoring the shouts of reporters who demanded to know who they were.

Many of the Mohawks at the Treatment Centre were not impressed by the black fatigues, nor by the insistence of the Kahnawake warriors that the same kind of protocol should be established between the army and warriors in Kanesatake as had been set up in Kahnawake. The Kahnawake leaders said the warriors should make an agreement with the soldiers to sling their weapons if they happened to meet each other while out on reconnaissance patrols. The three men had brought with them their plan for dismantling the barricades on their reserve and suggested that a similar plan be drawn up in Kanesatake.

When the Kahnawake warriors suggested that one of the defenders of Kanesatake take charge of maintaining contact with the army, Joe "Stonecarver" David, the artist-turned-warrior, reluctantly agreed to meet Daigle. By then, Stonecarver had been off the barricades for several weeks, working with the faithkeepers who had come from other territories to conduct spiritual ceremonies for the people in the Pines, then joining the negotiating team at the Trappist monastery. He took on the new role of military liaison only because no one else wanted to do it, and he insisted, when he met the army officers, that he was not a warrior leader. His only role would be to pass on the army's requests to the rest of the people in the Pines. At the urging of the Kahnawake warriors, he agreed to accept a "land line" at the main barricade to communicate with the army, which they said would prevent misunderstandings if an incident occurred. But Stonecarver told Lieutenant-Colonel Daigle that the warriors were not interested in any other protocol arrangements — indeed, that they were not even prepared to make use of the land line.

Bill Sears accompanied the Kahnawake warriors back to the helicopter, where Brigadier-General Armand Roy was waiting with his officers. Sears listened as the Kahnawake warriors made Roy an offer: as a first step towards "military disengagement," they were prepared to open one lane of the Mercier Bridge to public buses and emergency traffic. "That will make Canada very happy," Roy said, smiling. "And it will make my mandate much easier."

Roy had been ignoring Sears, but now he looked at him and asked, "What do you think of that?"

Sears smirked. "I think I'm going to get ready to start ducking some bullets," he said coolly.

The military commander turned back to the Kahnawake warriors. "I will give you two or three days to open the bridge," he told them. "If not, I will complete my mandate and start pushing my men in."

By the following day, August 21, tensions had eased considerably. The Kanesatake negotiators agreed to return to the talks at the Trappist monastery. At Main Gate, which had been turned into a comfortable outdoor living room, complete with a tarpaulin shelter, a car seat for a couch, lights, and a TV set, the Micmac warrior called The General kept watch on the army. He joked about how pleased he was to have a new telephone — the communications link to the army. "Now we can order pizza," he said.

Back at the negotiating table, the Mohawks submitted reams of documents, all of which were variations of their proposal for the recognition of Mohawk sovereignty based on the concept of the Two Row Wampum treaty. They demanded that the federal government commit itself to comprehensive negotiations to define a new relationship between the Mohawk nation and the government of Canada following the dismantling of the barricades. They also wanted an undertaking from the government that there would be no arrests or other legal proceedings until those comprehensive talks were concluded.

Some reporters claimed that a demand for the legalization of bingo and gambling had been put on the table. In fact, those issues were never brought forward. For the Mohawks, legalized gambling was almost a frivolous question, as their intention was to negotiate a means of charting their own political and economic destiny within the historic territory they call Kanienkehakeh. The aim of the proposed long-term negotiations was to arrive at a "peace treaty" that would define and reunify Kanienkehaka (Mohawk) territory and would cover issues such as resource rights, economic development, reciprocal trade agreements, taxation and tariffs, and jurisdictional defence.

The Mohawks did not recognize the jurisdiction of the province of

Quebec over their territory. Accordingly, they made a point of virtually ignoring Alexander Paterson, directing their questions and statements almost exclusively to Bernard Roy. They referred to Paterson as "Little Brother" and to Roy as "Big Brother." Paterson and Roy did not mind. They started addressing each other the same way.

Throughout that week of talks, the chaos in the suburbs around Kahnawake was jeopardizing the negotiations. Mobs had succeeded in blocking off all access into and out of Kahnawake. Angry crowds in LaSalle had cut off the last remaining exit from the Mercier Bridge, the only emergency route out of Kahnawake. Others patrolled the water, trying to stop Kahnawake residents from crossing to Dorval by boat. The police stood by, making no apparent effort to prevent the roving gangs from venting their frustrations on any vehicle that tried to enter the reserve. Even the international observers were prevented from entering Kahnawake by bat-wielding gangs: they had to be airlifted to the reserve by helicopter.

On August 22, more people with baseball bats showed up at John Ciaccia's lakefront property in Dorval, where Ciaccia had allowed the Kahnawake peacekeepers to set up a landing dock. When the Kahnawake negotiators returned to the dock that evening for the trip back to their reserve, an angry mob tried to stop them from boarding the waiting boats.

Eba Beauvais, one of the Kahnawake clan mothers, was making her first trip back to Kahnawake since joining the Kanesatake Mohawks in the Pines in early July. The scene at the dock terrified her. The crowd pressed up close, a man jostled her, and she felt something sharp stab into her head. One of the international observers took her arm. "I'm going to walk you to the boat," he whispered to her. "Walk slowly. Don't look around." She could feel his arm trembling with fright. As they neared the boat, one of the Kahnawake peacekeepers standing on the dock yelled, "Jump!" She leapt into the boat. When she put her hands to her head to find out what had stabbed her, she felt a pen sticking out of her scalp, caught in her thick hair which had protected her from serious injury. As soon as the Mohawks had fled, the peacekeepers tore the dock apart and dragged it back to Kahnawake.

After the loss of the dock, the journey to the negotiating table at the monastery became a logistical nightmare for the Kahnawake Mohawks, as did the co-ordination of negotiating strategy between Kahnawake and Kanesatake. Until the dismantling of the dock, the Kahnawake Mohawks had travelled to Kanesatake each night to plan the next day's presentation. This was impossible now, and the apparent lack of unity became obvious to the government negotiators. Each morning, the Mohawks would have to take long recesses to discuss their negotiating strategy before the talks could get underway.

Joe Deom would begin each day's negotiating session by reading out a litany of the latest examples of human rights abuses against the Mohawks. On August 23, he told the negotiators what had happened to Annette Diabo, a Kahnawake Mohawk who had been forced to have her baby at home because she could not get to a maternity hospital. Haemorrhaging after the difficult birth, she had to be rushed to a hospital in Montreal, but an angry mob blocked the Kahnawake ambulance for over an hour. Diabo was finally transferred to a second ambulance that came from Montreal, but the crowd refused to let that ambulance leave. They insisted on sending someone into the vehicle to confirm that it did indeed contain a frightened, exhausted woman, weak from loss of blood, and a newborn squalling baby, still unwashed after her birth. "Maybe they figured I was hiding weapons under my blanket," Diabo said later. Her little daughter, Toksnwane:'s ("the people are protecting her") was fine, but her doctor told Diabo she could have died if she had been detained much longer.

Joe Deom broke down as he read the story of Annette Diabo's experience. Women around him at the negotiating table cried silently. Paterson and Roy were also shaken up. But Paterson was growing desperate as the talks were increasingly delayed by the complaints of human rights abuses. The daily recitation was taking up hours of precious negotiating time, and Paterson and Roy were beginning to despair of ever obtaining the only document their governments were willing to accept — the plan to dismantle the barricades.

On the morning of August 23, the negotiating bus left Kanesatake on schedule, heading down Ste. Germaine Road toward the Trappist monastery. Just past North Pole, in the no-man's-land between the Mohawk and military lines, they were met by two armoured personnel carriers. The soldiers told the negotiators that the APCs were to escort them to the monastery because the army had received threats directed at the negotiating team. The Mohawks did not believe the army's story, thinking that the army was looking for an excuse to make an advance towards North Pole. Joe Norton and Billy Two Rivers, who were already waiting for the rest of the negotiating team at the monastery after travelling from Kahnawake, raced to the spot where the bus had stopped on Ste. Germaine Road near North Pole, to find out what was going on. They found Ellen Gabriel standing on the road, seething with anger. She returned with them to the monastery, where she marched up to Paterson and Roy and gave them a tongue lashing, accusing them of authorizing a military advance. "You are going to be responsible for the death of our people," she told Paterson. The negotiators knew nothing about the army's move, but Gabriel did not believe them.

The Mohawks' suspicions of the army's motive were well founded. On the pretext of protecting the negotiators, the APCs began to roll forward towards a new military position which would be established just a few metres from the Mohawk line. Everyone in Kanesatake rushed to North Pole, and the negotiations were cancelled. Stonecarver confronted Lieutenant-Colonel Daigle about the move, but Daigle simply pointed to Wanda Gabriel, one of the members of the Kanesatake military liaison team, who was standing nearby. "Ms. Gabriel gave me permission to move forward," Daigle told Stonecarver.

Wanda Gabriel was furious. "You're lying," she told Daigle. She and other members of the liaison team had insisted that they could not approve any military advance without a consensus among the people who were still living in Kanesatake. According to Gabriel, Daigle then changed his story. Because no protocol had been set up between the army and the Kanesatake warriors, the army had no choice but to advance to a position where they could keep the warriors in sight, Daigle said. There was no changing his mind. Three days earlier, the Kahnawake warriors had promised to try to open one lane of the Mercier Bridge if the army guaranteed it would not advance on Kanesatake. But the bridge was still closed, and the army decided that the surprise advance in Kanesatake might pressure the Kahnawake Mohawks into dismantling the barricades more quickly.

Stonecarver stormed off, angry enough to change out of his civilian clothes, put on his camouflage gear and join the other warriors for the first time in weeks. The rest of the day was a bizarre and dangerous dance between the Mohawks and the advancing soldiers at North Pole. Warriors crouched in the ditches, their guns locked and loaded. John Cree and others walked in front of the APCs, trying to block their advance, but they were bumped aside. Native Mexican spiritual people, who had come to Kanesatake to show solidarity with the Mohawks, walked around the APCs, drumming and chanting. One of them held aloft an eagle feather attached to a stick and walked up to an advancing APC, placing the feather in the barrel of its .50-calibre machine gun.

Women and children stood in front of the soldiers, trying to stop them from rolling their razor wire across the road at their new position. "Is this what you call peaceful negotiations?" one of them demanded. The soldiers ordered the women to move back, accusing them of using their children as shields.

One soldier, seated atop his APC, was less than enthusiastic about his job. "These people are convinced that they're right," he said to a journalist, looking down from his perch high up on the APC. "They have a certain patriotism. Unfortunately, they are tossing aside the laws of our white governments. They're in a vicious circle. As long as we don't recognize them as a nation with their own protective force, we can't accept that they can bear military arms. But as long as they don't possess military arms, they will not be able to affirm their rights as a nation."

By evening, the army had established its new position. Soldiers drove stakes into the road to hold fast their razor wire and set up camp in a nearby field. Armoured personnel carriers pointed their powerful guns towards Kanesatake. The Mohawks dragged up a trailer from Main Gate to set up their own sentry post at North Pole. Two rows of razor wire a few metres apart were all that separated the army from the Mohawks.

Several more families left Kanesatake that night. They had held out for six weeks, determined not to be forced out of their homes. But now they began to believe that the army really would attack, and they feared for their lives.

Still, there were many people, especially the elderly, who refused to leave. "I've still got two hands left," seventy-eight-year-old Muriel Nicholas said emphatically to one of the people at the emergency food bank who tried to convince her to go. "I'll go down fighting with my two hands." Nicholas had sons and grandsons defending Kanesatake and she was proud of their willingness to fight. She treasured a photograph of Apache, the young warrior standing astride Main Gate above Oka on July 11, his rifle raised defiantly in the air. "If I had a gun, that would have been me," she said, raising her gnarled fist.

Talks continued at the Trappist monastery for two more days — an exercise in frustration for everyone at the table. There was growing disagreement among the Mohawk negotiators about how to proceed. Joe Norton and Peter Diome were ready to present Kahnawake's plan for disengagement, but the others wanted to wait until they had a commitment from the government to settle the other issues.

The government negotiators were asked to leave the room for long stretches while the Mohawks debated their next step. The level of paranoia was high. The Mohawks were so certain the room was bugged that they moved their deliberations outdoors. On Saturday, August 25, they borrowed a portable typewriter from one of the monks and banged out yet another version of their draft agreement on the lawn outside the monastery. This draft set out a plan to remove the barricades and replace them with checkpoints. Only commercial buses, ambulances, and people with authorization from the Mohawks would be entitled to use the Mercier Bridge and highways through the territories. The Mohawks demanded immunity from search, arrest, and prosecution until they had concluded their long-term negotiations on a new relationship between the Mohawks and the governments of Canada and Quebec.

At the end of the afternoon, after nearly every Mohawk in the room had taken a turn at making passionate speeches on the stakes in these negotiations, Bernard Roy stood up and announced he would have to go back to his government and conduct a "post-mortem" of the talks. The Mohawks stared at him, appalled by his choice of words. There were too many guns pointed at each other just a few kilometres away from the negotiating room to make any slips of the tongue about death.

Though Roy later told Alexander Paterson he was not yet at the point of calling it quits, it was at that moment that negotiations effectively ended. Prime Minister Brian Mulroney classified the Mohawk demands as "bizarre." Paterson told Premier Bourassa he was unwilling to return to the talks. "You have nothing left for me to tell those people," Paterson told Bourassa. "Unless you and Mulroney get together and decide you're going to give them an inquiry, for instance. If you want me to go back and say that, I will. But I'm not going back to stonewall anymore, because it doesn't make sense. My role is finished."

On August 27, Bourassa made a dramatic announcement. He asked the army to dismantle the barricades. "We cannot have in Canada or in Quebec this type of democracy or pseudo-democracy that permits citizens, no matter what the value of their ultimate cause, to choose which laws they are going to follow," Bourassa said.

The Chief of Defence Staff, General John de Chastelain, confirmed that the army intended to move in on the barricades and he urged the warriors to abandon their positions. "We cannot fail," he told reporters. "We are all that is left."

In Kanesatake, the warriors went on red alert. Despite that, a strange calm prevailed. Joe Deom said the Mohawks were not intimidated by the army's announcement, and they were awaiting a military assault with "peaceful hearts and tranquil minds."

"We are unified," said Deom. "Our spirits are strong." But he warned that if the army did attack, "we will turn our hearts and minds to war, and it too we will wage with all our might."

Loran Thompson sat under the shade of a pine tree near Main Gate, telling journalists the story of Deganawidah, the Peacemaker. His riveting green eyes lit up as more reporters gathered around him on the grass to hear him describe the Great Law of Peace. The ominous warnings from the politicians and military commanders seemed to have little effect on the surrealistic routine that had come to dominate the lives of the Mohawks behind the barricades. All night, the buzz of helicopters could be heard overhead.

On August 28, civil protection authorities went door to door through the town of Oka, advising citizens to leave their homes in case shooting broke out. At the community centre in Kanesatake, Red Cross officials carried in stretchers, body-bags, and other emergency medical equipment. Linda Simon and other members of the emergency measures committee had tried to persuade the army to declare the road leading north from Kanesatake a "neutral zone" so that the Red Cross would have easy access to the Mohawks if emergency medical help was needed, but the army had refused, saying its own medical personnel would look after anyone killed or wounded in the conflict.

Margaret Gabriel, a volunteer at the food bank, burst into tears when she saw the stretchers being carried to the back of the school gym. One of her daughters, Brenda Gabriel, was staying at the warrior headquarters at the Treatment Centre, which would surely be a prime target if the army moved in. Suddenly the helicopters, the APCs, and the military equipment that had become commonplace at Kanesatake took on a very real meaning. At the Treatment Centre, too, stretchers and medical supplies were brought in, and Cathy Sky, who was a nurse, began setting up a first aid station and morgue at the Centre.

In the afternoon, warriors and journalists gathered in front of the TV at Main Gate. Lieutenant-General Foster was holding a televised news conference to announce the army's plans. "We will not fire first," he said, "but we will take such action as is necessary for self-defence, which depends completely on Mohawk reaction."

Foster announced that the army would increase its marine, aerial, and ground surveillance at Kahnawake and Kanesatake as part of its preparation for dismantling the barricades, and warned the citizens of Oka and Châteauguay that they might be ordered to evacuate their homes. Others, outside the immediate danger zones, might be asked to remain indoors, away from their windows and in their basements.

Foster showed a videotape of the Mohawk defences, which consisted of TV clips and aerial photographs and gave the army's assessment of the warriors' firepower. As the warriors watched the video depiction of their fortified bunkers and their apparent vast array of weaponry, many of them burst out laughing. Their psychological tactics had succeeded. The military seemed to believe that they had rocket launchers and anti-tank missiles.

The warriors were calm and unruffled, but others in the community were distraught. Reverend Louis Marie Gallant, an Anglican priest who had been maintaining a vigil at the northern barricade, looked in disbelief at the large Red Cross signs that had been placed in front of the community centre. "If there is any bloodshed tonight, I hope God will forgive us," Gallant said, his voice breaking.

Early that evening, moments after Prime Minister Mulroney made a final appeal to the warriors to dismantle their barricades, two CF-5 fighter jets streaked through the air above Kahnawake and Kanesa-take, and the ground shook. It was an intimidation tactic, an ominous warning of the army's power. But it only made the warriors angrier and more defiant. "We're going to knock those out of the sky," said Joe Deom as the CF-5s screamed overhead.

CHAPTER 14
Disappearing Act

The Recapture of the Mercier Bridge

Joan Lacroix kept her eyes on the bumper of the car in front of her, driving as fast as she dared through the mobs that crowded both sides of the road at the north exit of the Mercier Bridge at LaSalle. Her car was part of a convoy of about seventy-five vehicles filled with women, children, and old people who were being evacuated from Kahnawake on the afternoon of August 28. There was no easy way out of Kahnawake — angry demonstrators gathered at every exit on the south shore, as well as at the north end of the bridge — but the convoy's organizers had decided to take the route over the bridge, informing the Sûreté du Québec of their plan and requesting police assistance. There had been only thirty demonstrators at the LaSalle exit when the cars drove onto the Mercier Bridge at 2:00 p.m. But by the time the Mohawks were allowed to drive off the bridge, after they had been detained for two hours in the sweltering heat while police searched their cars, the angry crowd in LaSalle had swelled to nearly four hundred people. They had been alerted to the evacuation of Kahnawake by broadcasters on the popular Montreal radio station, CJMS.

A contingent of about forty SQ officers, along with thirty members of the RCMP, pushed the crowd back to clear a space large enough for the cars to pass. As soon as the first car snaked its way through the crowd, the mob surged forward again. About twenty young men in shorts and tank tops who were standing on the west side of the road scrambled onto a nearby dirt mound and began picking up rocks, bricks, and other bits of debris and hurling them at the cars as they drove by.

The hooting of imitation Indian war cries rose from the crowd. "Fucking sissies!" someone yelled at the departing cars. "Let the army at you!"

A rock shattered the window of one passing car. "Good!" one woman shouted in approval. The RCMP officers standing near the mob gestured at the rock throwers to stop, but only a few did, and the police made no move to restrain or arrest any of them.

Lacroix could see that the cars ahead were being struck by flying rocks, but the police signalled her to keep going forward. They told the evacuees to close their windows, lock their doors, and drive as fast as they could. There were cars in front of Lacroix and cars on her tail and nowhere to go except straight through the menacing crowd. Five times, she heard the thud of rocks hitting her car. Her frightened sixty-seven-year-old mother was sitting next to her. Her father, an ailing seventy-six-year-old French Canadian, was lying down in the back seat. Then a huge rock, nearly the size of a football, came crashing through the back window. "I'm hit," her father moaned. The small boulder had landed squarely on his chest. There was glass in his hair, and he was covered in blood.

Lacroix kept driving, one hand on the wheel, one hand reaching back to comfort her father. She was crying and so was her mother. Lacroix struggled to keep the car under control as they crawled through the narrow passage littered with rocks and debris.

At least six Mohawks were injured by flying rocks and broken glass in the evacuation. Young children were traumatized. A week after the incident, Joe Armstrong, a seventy-one-year-old Kahnawake Mohawk who had been among the bridge evacuees, died of a heart attack in a Montreal hospital. Although he had not been physically injured by the stone-throwing mobs, other Mohawks attributed his death to the stress and tension of the ordeal.

"We would have been better off staying home," Lacroix said the day after the evacuation. "The army would have been more civilized."

With the army on Kahnawake's doorstep, she and hundreds of other Mohawks had finally decided to flee, fearing a military attack on the Mohawk barricades. They had endured weeks of food shortages, taunts from protesters who burned Mohawk effigies on the barricades, and the boredom of being trapped on the reserve all summer, but the threat of an army invasion was too much for them. The men — their sons, brothers and husbands who were staying behind — had told them to leave. The police had guaranteed them safe passage. But afterward, as they sat in Dorval hotel rooms and school gyms, keeping an eye on their restless children, many of the Mohawks regretted their decision to leave. They felt like fugitives in a foreign land, just a couple of kilometres across the river from home.

The hatred of the mobs in Châteauguay and LaSalle also took a heavy toll on the members of the International Federation of Human Rights who had been monitoring events in Kanesatake and Kahnawake since August 16. The international observers were not there to take sides in the conflict, but the mobs saw them as Mohawk sympathizers. For several days the observers had travelled to the two communities without serious difficulty, but by the weekend of August 25 they had become a prime target for mob attacks. By then, the mobs had cut off virtually all access to Kahnawake by road, bridge, and river. On August 24, a car carrying four human rights observers tried to enter Kahnawake by Highway 207. When the car was attacked by a group of men armed with baseball bats, the police and soldiers standing a few metres away did nothing to stop the attack, and the car was forced to retreat. The observers returned to Kahnawake at dawn, after the mobs had left, and walked into the reserve on foot. Later in the day, they had to be airlifted out of Kahnawake by helicopter, because there was no other safe route out.

"The only persons who have treated me in a civilized way in this matter here in Canada are the Mohawks," said Finn Lynghjem, a Norwegian judge. "The army and the police do nothing. It's very degrading ... degrading to us, and perhaps more degrading to the government who can't give us access."

On August 27, when Robert Bourassa announced that official negotiations with the Mohawks were over, the premier asked the international observers to leave. They pulled out reluctantly, warning Quebec and Canada of the "dangerous precedent" that had been set by breaking off the talks, and feeling rudely treated by the Quebec government, which had failed to consult them about the decision to end negotiations. From their observation of the talks, they refuted the governments' claim that the Mohawks had not shown good faith in the discussions. "Everyone made an effort," said Gerald McKenzie, head of the Quebec League for Rights and Liberties and a member of the international federation. It was obvious to the observers that the government negotiators had not been given a mandate to deal with the fundamental issues.

After the departure of the international federation, church observers and local human rights activists stepped in to fill the vacuum. Clergy from the United Church of Canada, who had been active in both communities since the beginning of the crisis, now believed they had a crucial role to play as independent witnesses. On August 27, two United Church ministers from Ontario, Susan Eagle and Peter Hoyle, travelled to Kanesatake. They had planned to bring in a shipment of food and stay for a day or two, and they encountered no problems getting into Kanesatake with their loaves of bread and other staples. But then the army informed them that no other clergy would be allowed in after them. They decided to stay for as long as they felt they were needed.

When another clergyman, Burn Purdon, tried to enter Kahnawake by Highway 132 with a carload of food, a mob surrounded his car, rocking it and letting the air out of its tires. The local Ste. Catherine police were standing a few metres away, but they refused to intervene, saying that Purdon's car was on a provincial highway and was therefore outside their jurisdiction. When the SQ arrived, Purdon appealed to them, arguing that he was performing a clergyman's duty, which he had a legal right to do. One of the officers laughed at him. "Everything is upside down today," he told the minister. "Because the Mohawks are not keeping the law on their side of the barricades, I am sorry, I can do nothing to uphold the law on this side." The officer insisted that the Mohawks did not need food.

Purdon was forced to drive the car on its flat tires to a sideroad until help arrived. As the mob followed him and started to harass him, the SQ just stood by and watched. Purdon was now on a local road, outside provincial jurisdiction, and by then the Ste. Catherine police were nowhere in sight. "It was a terrifying experience," Purdon recalls. "I never did get that food through."

On August 28, the day of the stone-throwing incident, John Ciaccia was participating in another round of urgent negotiations. This time the talks were secret, since Robert Bourassa had already cancelled all official negotiations.

Throughout the summer, Ciaccia had kept in touch with anti-warrior factions in the Mohawk territories and in other Iroquois communities. On August 7, he had held a meeting in Montreal with two anti-warrior Iroquois Confederacy chiefs, Leon Shenandoah of Onondaga and Tom Porter of Akwesasne, hoping that they could offer the government an alternative to negotiating with the militant Mohawks.

Shenandoah appointed Harvey Longboat of the Cayugas and John Mohawk of the Senecas to see if there was anything they could do to resolve the crisis. On August 10, the two men travelled to Kanesatake and met about twenty Mohawk negotiators, including Joe Deom, Loran Thompson, Ellen Gabriel, and Mavis Etienne. But the Confederacy chiefs were not welcomed by the Mohawks. Shenandoah and Porter had publicly condemned the warriors during the standoff, and many of the Kanesatake warriors saw the Confederacy delegates as traitors to the Mohawk cause. They also felt that the Confederacy chiefs had acted improperly by meeting Ciaccia on August 7 without first consulting the Mohawk negotiators.

John Mohawk and Harvey Longboat told the Mohawk negotiators that their demands — for example, the request that any disputes between Canada or Quebec and the Mohawk Nation be resolved at the World Court in the Hague — were unrealistic. But they did not succeed in persuading the Mohawk negotiators to dilute their proposals. Two days later they turned down Ciaccia's invitation to join the talks. They told the Cabinet minister that their intervention at that moment might just confuse negotiations, but they promised to return if the next round of talks broke down.

The elderly Longhouse chief in Kanesatake, Samson Gabriel, had stayed in the background most of the summer after two of his trusted advisors, Curtis Nelson and Allen Gabriel, had had a falling out with the people of the Pines at the end of June. But in late August, with negotiations between the militant Longhouse negotiators and the governments going nowhere and with the army closing in on Kanesatake, Samson Gabriel decided to act. Following the traditional protocol for seeking help from Iroquois nations, the chief gave strings of wampum to Curtis Nelson and Allen Gabriel, who took the wampum to Confederacy leaders in each of the Iroquois territories: to the Mohawks in Akwesasne; to the Onondagas at Onondaga, near Syracuse, New York; to the Cayugas at the Six Nations reserve in southwestern Ontario; to the Senecas at Tonawanda, near Buffalo, New York; and to the Oneidas at the Oneida reserve, near London, Ontario.

Only the Oneidas refused to accept the wampum. There was a longstanding political rift between the Oneida Longhouse chiefs and the Confederacy headquarters at Onondaga, which was anti-warrior. The Oneidas had a good relationship with the warriors and had already received a wampum directly from the Kahnawake Longhouse Mohawks earlier in the summer. They had sent two of their chiefs, Bob Antone and Terry Doxtator, to help the warriors.

On August 25, the day the negotiations at the Trappist monastery collapsed, the Confederacy leaders had held an emergency meeting at Onondaga. They appointed a peacemaking delegation, which met with John Ciaccia in Toronto on August 26. The Confederacy chiefs estimated they would need at least a week to consult the Mohawk communities on new proposals to bring back to the government, but the Cabinet minister said they did not have that much time. "How much time do we have?" Onondaga Chief Oren Lyons asked Ciaccia. The minister left the room, made a phone call, and came back with an answer. "You have forty-eight hours to come to a conclusion or there will be a military solution," he said.

The next day, the Confederacy representatives consulted the Longhouse people at Kanesatake, and even those who had just taken part in the failed round of talks grudgingly agreed to let them try to revive the stalled negotiations.

On the morning of August 28, Kahnawake's elected chief, Joe Norton, got a phone call from John Mohawk, asking him to meet for coffee at the Dorval Hilton to discuss the Confederacy's proposals. When he walked into the hotel room, Norton was astonished to find a roomful of negotiators. He had had no forewarning that another round of negotiations was underway, and he had come unprepared. Among the federal and provincial officials in the hotel room were John Ciaccia and Roger Gagnon, an assistant deputy minister in the federal Department of Indian Affairs. Aside from Norton, Ciaccia and Gagnon were now to be negotiating with an entirely new collection of Mohawks: the militant nationalists were gone, replaced by the Iroquois "peacemaking" team — including Kanesatake Longhouse Chief Samson Gabriel, Allen Gabriel, and Curtis Nelson — as well as Kanesatake's former band council chief, Clarence Simon, Chrystal Nicholas, and a coalition of other Kanesatake moderates who had been trying to persuade the government to negotiate with them ever since they had severed ties with the Mohawk nationalists in early August.

The Iroquois Confederacy and the Kanesatake coalition were strange allies. Many of the coalition leaders accepted the authority of the Indian Act and strongly opposed the Longhouse. The Confederacy leaders, by contrast, were traditional Longhouse believers who rejected the Indian Act. But the two groups were united in their desire to strike a quick deal to end the standoff peacefully. They considered the demands of the Mohawk warrior negotiators to be unrealistic.

Paul Williams, a lawyer for the Confederacy, had already drafted a fifteen-point proposal for ending the standoff, which was tabled as soon as Norton arrived. Norton wanted advice on the proposal and called in several people — the Kahnawake elected council's constitutional advisor, Arnold Goodleaf, and other members of the original fifty-four-person Mohawk negotiating team, including a militant Akwesasne Mohawk, Diane Lazore, and one of the Oneida advisors, Chief Bob Antone. Williams and the Confederacy delegates were not happy to see them. The clock was ticking down on the government's forty-eight-hour deadline, and Williams feared that the militants would throw up obstacles in order to block a quick agreement. He insisted that the fifteen-point proposal could not be substantially altered.

Unlike the proposals of the warrior negotiators, the Confederacy proposal did not explicitly demand the recognition of Mohawk sovereignty and the Two Row Wampum treaty, but it did call on the governments to recognize "long and friendly relations and alliances between the Confederacy and the Mohawks and the Crown." By implication, Williams told the Mohawks, that meant the government would be accepting the Two Row Wampum treaty, which would force it to recognize the Mohawks' right to defend their own land.

Under the Confederacy proposal, a "supervisory committee" of officials from Canada, Quebec, and the Confederacy would oversee the military disengagement and the dismantling of the barricades, and the Confederacy would be responsible for destroying the weapons of the warriors. The proposal was supported by the Kanesatake coalition and by several Mohawks from Kahnawake who were strongly opposed to the warriors, but neither of those groups had any influence over the Mohawk nationalists who had led the standoff all summer. And the nationalists had grave misgivings about the Confederacy proposal. By signing the draft agreement, the warriors would have accepted Quebec's right to lay charges against them. One clause in the fifteen-point proposal said the warriors could raise the legal question of whether a Quebec court had jurisdiction over their cases, but any criminal defendant can raise jurisdictional questions in court. The Confederacy proposal would give the Mohawks no special legal rights. Moreover, as Joe Norton later pointed out, the proposal might have jeopardized Kahnawake's hard-won autonomy on policing matters, since it conceded that peacekeeping on the reserve would be supervised by a committee which included both Quebec and Canadian officials. Norton feared the Confederacy would be issuing an invitation to the Quebec police to regain control of the reserve.

Another major concern of the Mohawk nationalists was that the words "Mohawk Nation" did not appear anywhere in the Confederacy document. They felt that the agreement undermined the principle of Mohawk sovereignty, which the warriors had fought for all summer and which had already been recognized to some extent when the Quebec and Canadian governments had signed the "nation-to-nation" agreement on human rights on August 12. The more cynical of the Mohawk nationalists suspected that the Confederacy had deliberately left out any mention of the Mohawk Nation in order to reassert control over the militant Mohawks and "put them in their place."

Despite their misgivings, some of the warrior negotiators felt the Confederacy proposal was better than the alternative — a possible attack on the barricades by the Canadian Armed Forces. The negotiations continued, and after eight hours of talks, the federal and provincial officials had agreed to most of the points in the Confederacy proposal. By the end of the first day of negotiations, the only outstanding point was the question of legal protection for the warriors. Williams suggested that there should be an independent review of each warrior's case. The Confederacy's position was that anyone who had picked up a gun to defend Mohawk territory was probably not a criminal, but someone who had uttered threats or destroyed property or shot another person was in breach of both Canadian and Confederacy law and should be prosecuted in an appropriate tribunal.

Ciaccia was willing to consider such a proposal, but it was rejected outright by Quebec Justice Minister Gil Rémillard, one of Ciaccia's strongest rivals on the Cabinet crisis committee. Rémillard refused to consider any option that might limit his discretionary powers as attorney-general. Rémillard's opinion carried more weight than Ciaccia's in Cabinet by now, since Ciaccia was operating on his own, without the sanction of the Quebec government, despite the presence of officials from the Quebec Justice Ministry and the Native Affairs Secretariat at Dorval. If the premier and the Cabinet crisis committee disliked any tentative agreement, they could effectively cut Ciaccia adrift without much political fallout.

While this round of secret talks got underway on August 28, a separate set of negotiations was taking place in another room of the same Dorval hotel. Sam Elkas, Quebec's Minister of Public Security, and Lieutenant-Colonel Robin Gagnon, the senior military officer in the Kahnawake area, were meeting with two Kahnawake Mohawk representatives to discuss the possible dismantling of the Mohawk barricades. They talked for about an hour. Then the two Mohawks returned to Kahnawake to consult the warriors at the barricades.

At about 3:30 p.m., the Mohawks returned to the hotel to talk to Gagnon and Elkas again, accompanied, this time, by several prominent warrior leaders with military experience. Gagnon proposed that the army and the Mohawks would jointly dismantle the barricades, and he promised that the army would conduct no raids or searches for guns at Kahnawake after the Mercier Bridge was open — as long as the guns were kept out of sight and the Mohawks stopped wearing masks and camouflage gear. It was a polite fiction: if the warriors put away their guns and masks, the army would pretend the warriors were gone. It would give the army an excuse to refrain from invading the reserve, which would inevitably lead to bloodshed. "If we don't see any guns, there aren't any guns," Gagnon told the warriors. "As far as I'm concerned, the weapons are gone."

The Mohawks realized they would be vulnerable to arrests by the police after the barricades came down, but according to Mohawks who attended the negotiations, Elkas promised that the Quebec police would not enter the reserve after the barricades were dismantled. For his part, Gagnon promised that the army would gradually withdraw from Kahnawake over a period of two or three weeks as the situation calmed down. He also proposed that the army and the Mohawks would jointly patrol the bridge and the highways leading out of the reserve. Unarmed Mohawks would travel with military officers in the joint patrols.

None of Gagnon's offer was put in writing. It was a "gentleman's agreement" on a "military-to-military" basis, according to Billy Two Rivers, who participated in the talks.

Gagnon's proposal was considered seriously by most of the warriors because he said he had orders to take down the barricades by force if they were not dismantled voluntarily. Some of the warriors thought he was bluffing, but the threat of an armed assault grew more real as the day progressed and the army began to mobilize its equipment. Lieutenant-General Kent Foster and Brigadier-General Armand Roy called a news conference at the Armed Forces base in St. Hubert to warn people who lived near the barricades to prepare for a "limited evacuation," recommending that residents who lived close to the evacuation zones stay away from their windows and hide in their basements, out of the path of stray bullets, once the army moved in on the warriors. Journalists reported how the army's Leopard tanks could be used to smash through the barricades. The army seemed to be gearing up for an attack.

The Mohawk leaders in Kahnawake knew they could not maintain the barricades much longer. Community support for the barricades — so solid throughout late July and early August — was dwindling fast. The number of men on the barricades had fallen sharply as many warriors believed they had done enough to support the Mohawks of

Kanesatake. Some simply returned to their jobs; others made it clear that they were not prepared to engage in warfare against the army's tanks. By the last days of August, only about ten warriors armed with AK-47s were still manning the barricades. The other warriors had only shotguns and .22-calibre hunting rifles. Some barricades were manned by no more than two or three warriors. "Eventually people were going to notice there was nobody at the barricades," one warrior said later.

After reaching the unwritten agreement with Gagnon and Elkas, the Mohawk leaders returned from Dorval at around 6:00 p.m. and went immediately to the Kahnawake Legion Hall, which was packed with about one hundred warriors. After listening to the report on Gagnon's offer, they bombarded Billy Two Rivers and the other nego-tiators with questions. "There was a lot of concern that there would be a double-cross," Two Rivers recalled. "They were concerned that nothing was in writing."

The atmosphere at the Legion Hall was emotional, and the debate was angry. Powerful speeches were made by supporters and opponents of the dismantling proposal. In the middle of the debate, the men at the Legion received word of the LaSalle mob's stoning of the fleeing Mohawks that had taken place that afternoon, and the tension mounted even higher.

As the veteran warrior leader Paul Delaronde spoke, the warriors listened respectfully. He was cynical about Gagnon's offer and said the warriors should be cautious. But others feared bloodshed and arrests if the barricades stayed up. They were convinced the tanks would come rolling in.

"We thought it over," Billy Two Rivers says. "We might last a day or two, but the machine would eventually roll over us. So we took the prudent way out."

One of the warrior squad leaders, codenamed Little Marine, asked the warriors if they were willing to pull the trigger if the army rolled in. "How many people here are willing to shoot?" he asked. "Who's willing to give the order to shoot? If you just keep backing up (without shooting), you're going to look like a bunch of fools." Most of the warriors admitted that they weren't willing to shoot.

There was also the danger of a military assault on the barricades at Kanesatake, where there were fewer warriors and fewer guns. By easing the tensions at Kahnawake, the warriors believed they could help the Mohawks in the Pines.

The final vote at the Legion Hall, in an informal show of hands, was about 80 per cent in favour of dismantling the barricades. The meeting ended at midnight.

While the warriors were meeting at the Legion Hall, a traditional Longhouse meeting had already begun at the Kahnawake Longhouse. The building was filled to capacity. The Confederacy's proposal was presented by Joe Norton, who had returned to Kahnawake earlier in the evening with Oren Lyons and John Mohawk from the Confederacy. Then Lyons and Mohawk were called upon to explain it. Many people attacked it as a sellout. They were not prepared to allow the Confederacy to destroy their guns. Nor were they willing to accept criminal charges against the men who had manned the barricades.

When the Legion meeting was over, the warrior leaders arrived at the Longhouse to seek the approval of the women, children, and elders about the agreement they had just reached to dismantle the barricades. Everyone went into their clans and debated the options. Some people wanted to maintain the barricades until the government yielded to their earlier demands, but by the end of the meeting, at 5:00 a.m., all had agreed to bring the barricades down.

Meanwhile, John Ciaccia had to consult his Cabinet colleagues on the Confederacy's proposal. Along with Sam Elkas and other senior officials, he flew back to Quebec City that evening for an emergency meeting of the Cabinet crisis committee. There was a violent thunderstorm that night, and the little F-27 pitched and yawed and shuddered so violently that many of the people on board were certain the plane was going to crash. At one point, the plane dropped fifty feet without warning, and everything that was not nailed down or belted in went flying.

But the hellish flight was nothing compared to the crisis meeting that followed. Convinced that he could still get a deal with the Mohawks, Ciaccia demanded more time to negotiate, but most of the crisis committee was opposed to any further negotiations. It appeared that the clock had run out and that nothing was going to stop Robert Bourassa from sending in the army. Alexander Paterson, who had accompanied Ciaccia to the meeting, was the only ally Ciaccia had left in the room. There was no doubt in Paterson's mind that some of the Mohawks were prepared to be martyred. Screaming at the premier — something no elected politician in the Cabinet would have dared to do — Paterson warned him of the strong likelihood that blood would be shed. And he made it clear to the premier that no amount of explaining would sway international public opinion in Quebec's favour if Mohawks died.

In spite of the crisis committee's hostility to the idea of continuing negotiations, Ciaccia flew back to Dorval the next morning, August 29, to resume talks with the Mohawks and the Confederacy negotiators. The pressure was intense. Ciaccia announced that they had until 4:00 p.m. to reach a deal or the army would start moving. Then he received a series of phone calls — the new deadline was changed to 2:00 p.m., then 1:00 p.m., then noon. When the noon deadline was set, it was already 11:45 a.m.

But the army had not moved. Joe Norton called back to Kahnawake. "Are the guys ready to fight?" he asked. Norton was told that only a few of the warriors were still prepared to hang tough.

Ciaccia took Norton aside and asked him to tell the warriors to delay the dismantling of the barricades as long as possible, to give the negotiators enough time to reach agreement on the last contentious points. The warriors had already been delaying as long as they could. The army had wanted the dismantling of the barricades to begin at eight o'clock that morning, and pressure was mounting. By 2:00 p.m., 675 soldiers and 200 army vehicles had left the Farnham military base, about fifty kilometres east of Kahnawake, heading in the direction of the reserve. There were reports that the much-vaunted Leopard tanks had been loaded onto flatbed trucks and were on their way.

The Mohawks are still not certain whether the army was bluffing to put extra pressure on them to accelerate the dismantling. But many — including Kahnawake gas station owner Jack LeClaire, who had become the official liaison between the Mohawks and the army — took the military threat very seriously. Some of the Mohawks believe Colonel Gagnon persuaded General Roy to delay the attack, since he knew the warriors were on the verge of dismantling the barricades.

At one point, Gagnon told the warriors he had to have the bridge by the afternoon. If not, he would be relieved by Lieutenant-Colonel

Greg Mitchell and presumably Gagnon's promises would disappear. "It was a scare tactic," Little Marine said later.

There was also a disagreement over who was going to take the barricades down. The army wanted to use its own equipment, but the warriors insisted on doing it themselves. Finally, they agreed to carry out the task together.

Late in the afternoon, Mohawks and soldiers gathered at the barricade on Highway 132, near Ste. Catherine. Some of the warriors still wore their masks and camouflage uniforms, but they carried no weapons. The soldiers and the warriors joked with each other, promising to play a round of golf together once the barricades were down. Then several Mohawk women burned tobacco and prayed that the eyes and ears of the men on both sides of the barricades would be opened so there might be peace and understanding among them. Jack LeClaire and Colonel Gagnon symbolically lifted the first rocks on the barricade. The dismantling had begun.

"We're taking down this first barricade with the Mohawks as a gesture of mutual goodwill," Gagnon told reporters. Behind him, two army bulldozers tore apart the barricade on one side of the highway, and a Mohawk driving a bulldozer smashed into the barricade on the other side.

A short time later, at the Châteauguay barricade on Highway 138, a single Mohawk walked toward the army line and signalled for a soldier to approach. They were joined by three Mohawk women and a couple of other soldiers. As the soldiers watched, the Mohawks began dismantling the barricades. A feeble cheer went up from the crowd of several hundred gathered on the Châteauguay side of the barricade. Some expressed disappointment. "As far as I'm concerned," one Châteauguay resident said, "the army should have gone in there and shot everything that moved."

Gagnon stayed true to his promise that the army would not detain any warriors unless they were armed. There were no guns in sight, so no arrests were made. Both Gagnon and LeClaire were evasive about the disappearance of the weapons. "I haven't seen anyone armed on the reserve this afternoon," LeClaire told reporters.

"They did the smart thing," said one moderate Mohawk in Kahnawake. "They couldn't stop the army from doing what they wanted to do. So they pulled a disappearing act. The weapons disappeared from the scene. You couldn't fight it out — there was no point to it."

During the violent thunderstorm on the night of August 28, the warriors were astonished by a strange sight in the skies above Kahnawake. Several military helicopters were flying in a bizarre pattern, dropping low over the reserve and then roaring upward. The warriors immediately called the army on the land lines. "What the hell is going on?" they asked the officers. "Those are your airplanes," the officers replied.

At first, the warriors did not grasp what was going on. But soon they understood. It was all an elaborate hoax, designed to create the impression that the warriors had fled Kahnawake in an organized airlift.

The army was under intense pressure from hawkish politicians who wanted a military invasion of Kahnawake to arrest all the warriors and seize every weapon. But the senior military commanders knew that an invasion would inevitably lead to a bloodbath. The warriors would never sit back and allow the army to roll into the village and conduct a house-to-house search for weapons. They would fight back, and there would certainly be violence. So the story of the airlift was invented.

Outside the reserve, some reporters had seen lights in the evening sky on August 28. They knew there was activity by aircraft, but it was too dark to see the military helicopters. When reporters asked about the mysterious flights over the reserve, the army said that fifteen flights had been made by "unknown" aircraft. Soon the media were reporting that the warrior leaders had escaped from Kahnawake with their weapons in an organized "air-bridge." Reporters claimed that the aircraft were Cessnas. Politicians denounced the army for allowing the warriors to escape. The tale of the Cessnas entered Quebec mythology as accepted fact.

After the fake airlift, the pressure on the army eased, as the military could claim that a house-to-house search was unnecessary now that the guns were gone. Equally anxious to avoid a military invasion, the warriors played along with the Cessna story. They also enjoyed the idea that outsiders thought they had their own "air force," capable of mysteriously slipping past the Canadian army.

Key warrior leaders now admit that the Cessnas never existed. "We all knew it was bullshit," says Little Marine, a squad leader for the Mohawks on Highway 138. "It was fabricated."

If the warriors had wanted to flee, there were far easier ways to do it than by taking an airplane in the middle of a thunderstorm. Throughout the summer, the warriors had come and gone by car, by boat, or on foot through the bush. At the end of the standoff, most of the warriors simply stayed in Kahnawake, took off their masks, hid their guns, and blended back into the community. The safest place for the weapons was right in the village, where the police were unlikely to enter. When the leaders ordered them to hide their arms, some of the warriors panicked and dumped them anywhere. Some were later found by children in ditches, creeks, and schoolyards, but most were hidden where they could be retrieved later — in basements or buried outside.

Earlier in the summer, the warriors had tried to convert Highway 138 into a temporary airstrip where food supplies could be landed. They painted white marks on the highway to help aircraft land. But the highway was never used as a landing strip. By late August, it was impossible for airplanes — even small Cessnas — to land on the highway. The warriors had torn up the pavement to make anti-tank trenches, and there was no safe stretch of road on which to land.

Some of the warrior leaders slipped out of Kahnawake during the first week of September. But the key players were still active in Kahnawake at the end of August, after the alleged airlift. Many of them were involved in an aborted attempt to recapture the Mercier Bridge on September 3.

The dismantling of the barricades at Kahnawake on August 29 was carried live on television, and it was this coverage that brought the news to the warriors at Kanesatake, who had no inkling of the deal their brothers at Kahnawake had struck with the army. Some of the key advisors at the Treatment Centre had been informed of the plans of the Kahnawake warriors, but the message had not been passed on to the warriors in the Pines. Journalists and warriors crowded around a TV at the main barricade near Oka when regular programming was interrupted to carry scenes of the Kahnawake barricades coming down. The warriors were shocked and disheartened at the images of Mohawks and soldiers working side by side to dismantle the barricades. One warrior anxiously flipped from channel to channel, as if he hoped to find some explanation on a different station.

The warriors and the Kanesatake Mohawks in the Pines huddled in small groups, trying to figure out what it all meant for them. Some were ashen-faced. Physically cut off now from Kahnawake — the boat trips had stopped after police began cracking down on the "Mohawk Navy," arresting three warriors that week — and still uneasy about the cordial relationship between the Kahnawake warrior leaders and Gagnon, they felt isolated from Kahnawake and did not understand the intense pressures that led to the dismantling. They felt betrayed and began to believe there was nobody they could trust anymore. Walter David Jr. sat on his all-terrain vehicle in the shade of the Pines, his head in his hands.

Some of the women emerged from the Treatment Centre, burning tobacco and sprinkling ashes along the highway, to protect the people behind the barricades from harm. Ellen Gabriel planted a frightening-looking mask — a gift from the Mexican spiritual people — at the top of a pole on one of the dirt barricades. It stared down menacingly at the soldiers posted on the road below.

The small band of warriors remaining at Kanesatake were the most militant and uncompromising of all the Mohawks. As they became more isolated, the tension grew worse. Feeling certain he was going to die in a battle with the army, Stonecarver went to the home of his invalid mother to say a final goodbye. He was crying as he left her house, but his mother was stoic, refusing to shed a tear. She wanted to give her son the strength to keep on fighting. But a few minutes later, when he returned to the house, he found her sobbing uncontrollably.

An avowed pacifist until July 11, Stonecarver had made a difficult and life-altering decision on the morning of the police raid to pick up a gun. He had done it for the love of the land, for the memory of his ancestors, and for his family, who were nearly all in the Pines. But one by one, the warrior's brothers and sisters had backed away from the fight. They rarely showed up in the Pines anymore, and they were trying to convince Stonecarver to lay down his gun.

At the community centre in Kanesatake, women organized cots and mats for the children who were sleeping overnight in the school gym. About fifty people were staying there around the clock, afraid to return to their homes in case the army advanced at night. Altogether, about three hundred people were left in Kanesatake. The soldiers at the army's roadblock at North Pole told them they would not be allowed to return to the community if they left.

Standing outside the community centre, his arms crossed, a flushed and angry Mohawk by the name of Willy Nelson was threatening to pick up a gun if the army tried to enter Kanesatake. Nelson was normally calm and jovial, but now he felt there was nothing left to joke about. The father of five was not a warrior. His wife Joyce was working full-time at the food bank, and he had helped to organize the security patrol that protected the vacated houses in Kanesatake. He had also served on the Kanesatake military liaison team until he quit in disgust after the army broke its word and advanced on North Pole on August 23. Now he was simmering with anger as reports filtered back into the community from Kanesatake Mohawks who said they had been beaten and tortured by the provincial police.

Angus Jacobs, a forty-seven-year-old Mohawk from Kanesatake, had been on his way to go shopping with his wife, Janet Nicholas, when he was picked up by police. He returned to Kanesatake bruised and almost voiceless. He alleged that he had been taken to a barn off a dirt road near Oka, where he was choked and kicked by police, who demanded to know who killed Marcel Lemay.

A second Mohawk, a nephew of Janet Nicholas named Daniel Nicholas, was picked up on a boat on the lake. He was taken to the police detachment at St. Eustache, where he was questioned about the events of July 11 and shown videotapes of the summer's events. He said he was tied to a chair and slapped and beaten. Then a police officer lit a cigarette and asked him if he wanted one. When he replied that he did, Nicholas said the officer crushed the burning cigarette on his stomach. Tears ran down his face. "The kicks hurt, but nothing hurt like that burn," he said later. The police asked him to sign a blank deposition, which they would fill in later with his statements. He refused. He claimed he was so badly bruised that police detained him for several days, waiting for the swelling to go down before he appeared in public at the St. Jérôme courthouse to be formally charged.

Everyone in Kanesatake was exhausted. They had desperately hoped for a breakthrough at the talks that were continuing between John Ciaccia and the Confederacy in Dorval. Now that the barricades were coming down in Kahnawake, they felt more isolated than ever. In the evening, Stonecarver's brother Dan David talked to reporters near the Pines. "This place holds the key to everything," he said. "This is where everything started, and this is where it must end."

At the Dorval Hilton — by now known in Kanesatake as the "Hilton Reserve" because so many Mohawks were staying there — negotiations continued throughout the afternoon of August 29. Confederacy officials took time off to burn tobacco in a garden behind the hotel, to pray for a peaceful resolution to the conflict. By mid-afternoon, John Mohawk and Oren Lyons felt so optimistic about the progress in the talks that they decided to leave the negotiations in the hands of the other Mohawks and Confederacy delegates. Soon after they left, word arrived from Kahnawake that the barricades were coming down. Talks recessed late in the afternoon. When the negotiators regrouped at 8:30 that evening, the room was packed with Mohawks from all factions. But the talks, which had given the Confederacy delegates so much optimism just a few hours earlier, now disintegrated quickly.

Roger Gagnon, the assistant deputy minister of Indian Affairs who had been participating in the negotiations for the past two days, suddenly announced that he was merely an observer at the talks. He said he had no mandate from the federal government to accept any deal reached at Dorval. Gagnon also insisted that a clause be inserted in the document to specifically state that the agreement was not a treaty. This infuriated Paul Williams. The Confederacy lawyer's strategy was to get the government's signature on the document and argue later that it was indeed a treaty. Williams suspected that Gagnon's proposed clause was designed to allow the government to break its commitments after the deal was signed.

Ciaccia, too, was furious with Gagnon and demanded that he make some phone calls to get a commitment from Ottawa if indeed he lacked an official mandate. Gagnon never received that mandate. Instead, Tom Siddon told reporters that no negotiations were taking place. The federal government's decision to desert the talks, after Gagnon's intense involvement, "was a devastating blow to all of our efforts," said Oren Lyons.

But before the Confederacy had time to recover from that blow, Arnold Goodleaf, the Kahnawake council's constitutional advisor, tabled a new proposal from his community, which called for the establishment of formal relations among Quebec, Canada, and the Mohawk Nation, consistent with the Two Row Wampum treaty, and for the disputed land at Kanesatake to be transferred from the federal government to the Mohawk Nation. It asked for an independent inquiry into the police raid of July 11, and it called for long-term negotiations to redefine the political relationship between Canada and the Mohawks. In short, Goodleaf put forward most of the demands that the governments had rejected in the previous round of talks.

Goodleaf's proposal led to a temporary suspension of negotiations. Government representatives left the room, and the Mohawks launched into a confrontational debate that lasted most of the night. Accusations flew thick and fast. Crawford Gabriel and other members of the Kanesatake coalition accused Joe Norton and the Kahnawake elected council of selling out to the warriors. Norton, in turn, accused the Kanesatake group and the anti-warriors from his own community of sabotaging the aims of the Mohawk nationalists. The Confederacy representatives left to discuss the situation among themselves. At 2:00 a.m., Paul Williams and Harvey Longboat returned to say they had decided to leave. They told the Mohawks they had done what they could. Now it was up to them to try to come to an agreement among themselves and with the governments.

Ciaccia was called back into the room. He said he had to attend a Cabinet meeting the next morning, August 30, and talks could not resume before early afternoon. He was still hoping for a slowdown in the dismantling of the barricades, to buy time with his government to reach an agreement.

The next afternoon, Allen Gabriel and Curtis Nelson returned to the Kanesatake Longhouse to seek support for the Confederacy's proposal, but most of the Mohawks at the Longhouse were hostile towards it. Stonecarver saw the Confederacy proposal as a betrayal of the warriors. He stormed out of the Longhouse, vowing to remain in the fight until the end. John Cree, the Mohawk faithkeeper who had always presented a serene face in public, was equally opposed to the Confederacy proposal. He lost his temper and left the meeting angrily.

Early that evening, Allen Gabriel and Curtis Nelson went to the Kanesatake community centre and talked to Joyce and Willy Nelson, Linda Simon, and some of the other Mohawks, most of whom backed the moderate coalition of Kanesatake Mohawks and supported the Confederacy plan. Then they planned to go to the Treatment Centre to talk to the warriors who had not attended the Longhouse meeting. But Dennis "Psycho" Nicholas, who was a good friend of the two Mohawk negotiators, warned them to stay away from the Treatment Centre because the warriors were enraged at the Confederacy's proposal. The men left and returned to Dorval.

Meanwhile, the Mohawk negotiators were milling around the Dorval Hilton, waiting for the talks to resume. Ciaccia was nowhere in sight. Finally, just before 8:00 p.m., Robert Bourassa's office released a terse press release, stating that Quebec was cancelling the negotiations because of the departure of the Confederacy delegates. The Mohawks were shocked. John Ciaccia was taken completely by surprise. No one had imagined that the talks would be called off.

Some of the Mohawks blamed Roger Gagnon for sabotaging the talks with his sudden pullout. Others blamed Joe Norton for rejecting the Confederacy proposal. But the Kahnawake grand chief had no regrets. He remained convinced that it was better to have no deal to agree to than one that jeopardized the Mohawks' autonomy.

Ultimately, the actions of the Mohawks and the Confederacy negotiators may have been irrelevant. John Ciaccia had little hope of persuading the Quebec Cabinet to approve the deal. "I don't think the Quebec government would ever have signed that document," Alexander Paterson said later. "Ciaccia would have recommended it, but the justice minister [Gil Rémillard] would have done everything in his power to stop it."

The dismantling of the Kahnawake barricades and the opening of the Mercier Bridge took eight days. For the first day or two, everything went smoothly and the army patrolled the bridge every two hours, escorted by Mohawks. But after Ciaccia's request to stall the dismantling on August 29, Norton asked the warriors to keep the bridge closed for another forty-eight or seventy-two hours. The Mohawks slowed down the pace at which they were filling in the anti-tank trenches on the highways.

By August 30, the army had become extremely impatient with the delays. Robin Gagnon was meeting the warriors two or three times a day to discuss the dismantling. Finally, during a meeting under the maple trees, Gagnon told the warriors: "I have bad news. My orders have changed." His implication was clear: the army was prepared to advance into the reserve.

Two of the warrior leaders, Michael Thomas and Windwalker, were furious. "Let's settle it, right here, one on one," they told Gagnon. "Why involve all these people? If you're the commander, come on." After a brief argument, the two warriors stormed off in disgust. "Fuck you," they told Gagnon as they left.

Thomas and Windwalker had always been skeptical about Gagnon's promises. They had warned the Mohawks that the army might come rolling into Kahnawake as soon as the barricades were dismantled. But the weary people of the community had accepted Gagnon's assurances that the army would stay outside the reserve.

"People wanted to believe it," Michael Thomas recalls. "A lot of people were shell-shocked. There were false hopes. People were grabbing for straws. When Gagnon dropped the bomb that his orders had changed, I knew exactly what would happen. I felt raped."

Four days later, on September 3, Paul Delaronde led a group of warriors in an aborted attempt to recapture the Mercier Bridge. The army rolled into the reserve and put razor wire checkpoints at all entrances to the village. By then, Gagnon had been replaced by Lieutenant-Colonel Greg Mitchell, and the Mohawks had no one to hold responsible for the army's broken promise.

Meanwhile, at Kanesatake, the relationship between the warriors and the army was becoming increasingly tense. Several incidents had nearly touched off a gunfight. At the army post at North Pole, military flares were accidentally tripped, sending the warriors into a panic. The army was constantly testing the warrior lines. One night, a soldier on reconnaissance stole a warrior flag from the barricade at Sector Five at the north entrance to the Pines.

On August 24, the day after the army had advanced on North Pole, Ronald "Lasagna" Cross decided to return to Kanesatake from Kahnawake, where he and Gordon "Noriega" Lazore and a couple of other Mohawks had been exiled for trashing a non-native's vacated house during a drunken party. It was difficult to keep out a warrior who was determined to return. Knowing there was a shortage of warriors in Kanesatake, Lasagna convinced his friend Gerald "Slim" Marquis, a former U.S. Marine, to take a boat with Lasagna and Noriega across the Lake of Two Mountains to Kanesatake. It was the last boatload of fresh recruits for the Kanesatake warriors. The Lake of Two Mountains was now so heavily patrolled that, after the arrival of Lasagna and Noriega, the warriors decided it was no longer a safe route to use.

For several days, Lasagna took over the face-to-face dealings with the army in Kanesatake, helping to establish land lines at a couple of the barricades and working out guidelines for where the soldiers could travel in their patrols. The army had established a camp on the mountain north of Kanesatake, and they sought and obtained permission to cross into Mohawk territory to bring food and latrines to their mountain camp. When an army truck crossed into the territory without seeking permission from the warriors, Lasagna accused the soldiers of breaking the agreement. He radioed for the warriors to bring up their front-end loader and threatened to dig a trench across the middle of the road to stop the army from any further incursions.

The rolls of razor wire across the roads leading in and out of Kanesatake gave the appearance that the army had tightly encircled the settlement, leaving no way for the warriors to escape. But that was another polite fiction. The army kept hoping that the warriors at Kanesatake would pull the same disappearing act as the Kahnawake warriors. They even informed the warriors that they had left open a safe corridor through the woods and mountains north of Kanesatake, which came to be known as the "back door."

The Mohawks at the Treatment Centre got several telephone calls from senior military officers reminding the warriors that the "back door" was still open and assuring them that the corridor would be entirely safe. "They asked why we weren't using the back door," recalls Paul "Sugar Bear" Smith, an Oneida warrior from Wisconsin who was stationed at Kanesatake. And during the negotiations between Lieutenant-Colonel Gagnon and the Kahnawake Mohawks on August 28 at the Dorval Hilton, Gagnon asked why the warriors at Kanesatake had not disappeared through the "back door."

Although the federal government publicly condemned the warriors and promised to use the full force of the law on them, federal officials clearly hoped that the warriors would disappear. In mid-August, a senior federal official privately admitted that the army was taking steps to ensure that the warriors could slip away at any time. "We could wake up one morning and find the warriors all gone," he said.

Although the existence of the back door was common knowledge among the warriors, they were worried that the Quebec police might be waiting in ambush at the other end of the corridor. And even if they were guaranteed safe passage, most of the warriors preferred to remain behind the barricades. They knew they would be abandoning any chance for political gain if they put down their guns and escaped. Throughout the summer, the Mohawks had been in touch with the European Parliament, trying to raise awareness of the Mohawk crisis at the international level, and by late August they were still hoping for action from that quarter. They also wanted to hold out at Kanesatake until the Canadian Parliament resumed sitting in September. That would put the spotlight on the federal government and force it to respond to the crisis.

Many of the Mohawks who remained in Kanesatake were unhappy about Lasagna's return. Most of the other hotheads, particularly a couple of the warriors from the community who were known drug users, had long since dropped out of sight. (At least two of them were staying in hotels in Dorval, taking advantage of the government's compensation package for Kanesatake residents who left the community.) Lasagna was the most dangerous of the loose cannons who remained in Kanesatake, and some people were afraid that he might get drunk again and do something stupid. They were worried that Lasagna, as the best-known symbol of the warriors, would become a target for the army, and they wanted him out of Kanesatake.

One of the few warriors who seemed to enjoy publicity, Lasagna boasted about the prowess of the warriors to an editor from the mercenary magazine *Soldier of Fortune* and nonchalantly posed for the cameras whenever he roared up to the main barricade on his motorcycle. (Even his best friends among the warriors called him a "media slut," and his own mother, Ann Cross, predicted that her son Ronnie would get into trouble because he was such a publicity hound. When yet another batch of pictures of Lasagna landed on one news editor's desk, he asked a reporter, "Are you sure Lasagna isn't the only warrior at Kanesatake?")

Late on the night of August 28, during the same thunderstorm that raged during the fake airlift at Kahnawake, Lasagna and four other warriors (Noriega, Gerald "Slim" Marquis, Eldred "War Horse" Jacobs, and 4-20) decided to test the army's perimeter. They walked quietly along a trail west of North Pole and slipped into the bush on the mountain. They had no flashlight, but the flashes of lightning helped them to see. After they had walked three or four kilometres, they decided to bunk down for a short rest in the woods until sunrise. Just after dawn, they resumed their trek. They rounded a corner and found two armoured personnel carriers parked on the trail in front of them, but there were no soldiers in sight.

Trip flares had been set up around the APCs. Lasagna and Slim dismantled them and stole a box of flares that was sitting nearby. Then the warriors climbed up onto the APC and opened the hatch. They could see the soldiers sleeping inside. They slammed down the hatch and tore off into the woods, whooping and hollering as they ran. The soldiers woke up in a hurry and moments later their commanding officer arrived. When he saw all the trip flares gone, he flew into a temper and chewed out his men. The warriors sat up on the mountainside, eating apples they had picked in a nearby orchard, laughing as they listened to the officer lecturing his troops.

Lasagna and Slim, who had become separated from the other three warriors, debated whether they should continue their escape through the woods. Slim started talking about the women and children still at the Treatment Centre. "We couldn't leave those kids," Slim explains. They met up with the other men and began the long hike back to the Pines.

By then there were only about thirty-five warriors still on active duty in Kanesatake. Of that number, fewer than a dozen were from the community. A number of the Kanesatake men had simply put away their weapons and stayed home.

Just outside Oka, hundreds of Mohawk supporters were keeping vigil at a peace camp in a field near Paul Sauvé Park. Among them were seventy Maliseet Indians from New Brunswick. The Maliseets had travelled to Oka in a convoy of cars and a school bus, hoping to act as a human shield between the army and the warriors. Their caravan had been stopped east of Quebec City by seventy armed SQ officers with dogs who spent two hours searching the Maliseets before finally letting them go.

Gilles Proulx, the CJMS talk show host who had supported the Châteauguay crowds at the Kahnawake barricade, brought his mobile studio to the main army barricade at Oka on August 31. Dozens of Proulx's fans followed him to the town. Although the police prevented them from entering Oka, they stayed nearby, parking their cars at Paul Sauvé Park, close to the peace camp. The scene turned ugly when one of Proulx's followers ripped an anti-Bourassa sign from a demonstrator. Inside Oka, the townspeople crowded around Proulx's mobile studio as he interviewed Mayor Jean Ouellette. They applauded his verbal attacks on the Mohawks on the other side of the barricade, a few hundred metres away.

Late that afternoon, Dr. Réjean Mongeon and his wife Andrea returned to their farm and veterinary clinic near the north entrance to the Pines. Throughout the summer, the Mongeons had supported the Mohawks, despite the fact that they had lost tens of thousands of dollars in business and had been forced to move many of their animals off their farm. They were intent on maintaining their friendship with the Mohawks, and when they left their home for several days in late August, had entrusted the property to one of the warriors, who had promised to take care of it. Instead, they found their house ransacked and vandalized. They exploded in anger, refusing even to accept help from Ronnie Bonspille, the head of the ambulance service, who knew that Dr. Mongeon had a history of heart trouble. Bonspille was worried that the veterinarian might have a heart attack on the spot.

The Mongeons rushed to Oka to report what had happened. Back at the community centre, the Mohawks agonized over what had happened to the Mongeons. "These are our neighbours, friends to the natives here," said an exhausted Joyce Nelson, who was still unpacking a long-awaited shipment of food at ten o'clock that night. "Once these warriors are gone, we have to stay and live with these people."

Some of the Mohawks wanted to take action against Lasagna and Noriega, who were believed to be responsible for the vandalism. Some people talked about turning the two warriors over to the police. The rumours soon reached Lasagna and Noriega and a couple of their Mohawk friends from the community. Late that night, they decided to go looking for Ronnie Bonspille, who they believed was planning to "rat" on them. They found Bonspille parked at the junction of Highway 344 and Ste. Germaine Road. Francis Jacobs, one of the Mohawk men on the security patrol, and his teenaged son Cory were parked beside Bonspille. Francis Jacobs and his son got out of their vehicle. So did Lasagna and his gang, armed with baseball bats and guns. Someone let off a shot. Ronnie Bonspille could see what was coming. He fled toward the military position at North Pole, crossing the army line, and was taken into custody.

Other warriors rushed to the scene to intervene, but Francis and Cory Jacobs had already been badly beaten, and Lasagna's gang had headed over to Ronnie Bonspille's house to look for him. Bonspille's son Bobby slipped out of the house and into the bush just as they arrived. They trashed the two ambulances parked in Bonspille's driveway, then smashed the windows of the house.

The Jacobs were taken to the community centre at the school gym. They were bruised and swollen, and both of them were in shock. Francis Jacobs did not want to see a doctor, but he was in rough shape. The Mohawks made arrangements for an ambulance to meet the Jacobs family at North Pole.

In the meantime, the other warriors had found Lasagna and his gang. They were disarmed and taken to a house, where one of the warriors was posted to guard them. A couple of the warriors went to the community centre and assured everyone that the maverick gang had been disarmed and would be punished. But somehow Lasagna slipped away.

By then it was nearly morning. About a dozen people were awake at the community centre, drinking coffee and discussing the night's events, trying to decide what to do with Lasagna and Noriega and the other men. No one was anxious to turn them over to the police, but neither did they want them in the community any longer. With the threat of an imminent invasion by the army and with this explosion of violence behind the barricades, everyone felt that the world was crumbling around them.

Dan David heard a noise and looked towards the door. "Oh-oh," he said. "Here comes Lasagna." Lasagna glared at Dan David as he walked into the school gym, banging the floor with an aluminum baseball bat. He began to yell.

"You fuckers," Lasagna shouted. "You've stabbed us in the back. Those guys were going to turn us in, turn us into the cops, and you guys were going to let them."

Dan David slipped upstairs and tried to call the Treatment Centre. The line was busy. When he walked back into the gym, the room was silent, except for the sound of Lasagna banging the baseball bat. The warrior had a pistol on his hip. One of the Mohawk men in the room had a gun. He was trying to signal the woman in front of him to get ready to drop. If Lasagna made a move for his pistol, the man with the gun was going to try to take him out first.

Lasagna shouted and yelled for what felt like hours. Everyone thought he was high on something. He unloaded all his anger. "I came here for the land," he told them. "I came here to fight for you people. I came here to defend you people, and you were going to stab me in the back. You guys have deserted us! You guys have betrayed us. It's not just those two fuckers that we beat up — it's all of you. You're not worth fighting for. You're nothing but dogs. And you know what we do with dogs — we shoot 'em."

For many long moments, everyone in the room was convinced he was prepared to do it. Lasagna kept waving his bat at one of the Mohawks, then banging it on the floor. Nobody moved. Finally, Lasagna had talked himself out. Then he began pleading.

"I didn't really mean it," he told them. "Look, we're here to protect you, you know what I mean? You have to support us."

But his pleas had come too late. Everyone had the image of Francis and Cory Jacobs' bloodied faces in front of them, and they felt no pity for Lasagna. They were exhausted, and suddenly everyone wanted the long, hot, dirty summer to be over.

CHAPTER 15
Bayonets and Helicopters

The Final Siege

As the sun rose over the deserted farms of Kanesatake on the first morning of September, the Mohawks awakened with a sense of foreboding. The story of the assaults on Francis Jacobs and Ronnie Bonspille had spread quickly through the community, and they knew that the incident could give the army an excuse to push through the barricades.

The warriors had already disarmed Lasagna and Noriega and posted a sentry to watch over them. Everyone was fed up with the two mavericks. Because of the shortage of experienced military men in Kanesatake, older warriors such as Lasagna and Noriega were supposed to be the leaders, but somehow they kept screwing up.

Early in the morning, the warriors and their supporters gathered at the Treatment Centre to discuss the assaults. Lasagna gave his side of the story, but he failed to sway his listeners, who agreed that disciplinary action was necessary. The residents of Kanesatake had scheduled another meeting for 2:00 p.m. at the community centre to discuss the matter with the warriors, but most already knew what the verdict would likely be: Lasagna and Noriega would be evicted and turned over to the police.

As they waited for the afternoon meeting, Ellen Gabriel and Denise David-Tolley felt drained and demoralized. They walked down to the beach and gazed at the water and talked about the craziness of the whole affair. They could see police boats all over the lake, and they could feel the gathering forces around them. "I guess it was at that moment that I kind of broke," David-Tolley remembers. She stared blankly around, wondering vaguely if they should return to the Treatment Centre to warn the warriors about the police boats.

Meanwhile, the army was mobilizing its equipment and moving its armoured personnel carriers into position near the barricades. The army commander, Lieutenant-General Kent Foster, had concluded that a negotiated solution to the Kanesatake barricades was extremely unlikely. With the recapture of the Mercier Bridge, the army had little reason to fear any retaliation in Kahnawake if the troops advanced. The assaults on Ronnie Bonspille and Francis Jacobs were the final pretext the army needed.

Lieutenant-General Foster, who stayed in regular contact with provincial and federal politicians, had authorized the commander of the 5th Mechanized Brigade, Brigadier-General Armand Roy, to make the strategic decisions about the deployment of troops at the Oka barricades. Brigadier-General Roy and Lieutenant-Colonel Pierre Daigle, the two highest-ranking officers at the scene, ordered their soldiers to prepare for a decisive advance on the warrior defences. Major Alain Tremblay, the leader of C company in Daigle's battalion, was assigned to lead the crucial phase of this "encirclement operation." Daigle instructed two other companies to support Tremblay's advance, boosting the number of soldiers in the operation to a total of about four hundred.

The day was sunny and the crickets were chirping as the armoured vehicles rolled forward at about 1:00 p.m. They pushed through the North Pole barricade with no opposition; it had been unguarded for several days. Soldiers walked through the fields beside the APCs and helicopters flew overhead. At the community centre, Mohawks frantically telephoned the Treatment Centre to make sure the warriors knew about the army's advance. "They're coming in," shouted a panic-stricken voice on the Kanesatake radio station.

About twenty soldiers were jogging toward the western barricade on Highway 344. This one, too, was unmanned. The warriors simply didn't have the manpower to protect all the barricades at once. The soldiers came to the pile of overturned cars, checked to make sure it was unguarded, then continued running down the highway toward the community centre. Behind them, a convoy of APCs rumbled up to the barricade. An army bulldozer brushed the cars aside, and the APCs rolled right through. After shielding the western flank of the community for nearly two months, the barricade of wrecked cars was swept aside like a pile of Dinky toys.

Weeks earlier, the army had promised to notify the warriors of its movements. And so, as the APCs roared down the highway, a fax message arrived at the warrior headquarters, giving official notification of what was already obvious — the army had begun the final stage of its operations.

Brigadier-General Roy issued a statement to the media to explain the army's advance. He alluded to the assaults on Ronnie Bonspille and Francis Jacobs. "I am growing increasingly concerned about the potential of violence in the area, given the existing tensions between Mohawk factions and the number and type of weapons they have at their disposal," Roy said in the statement. "I have therefore decided to adjust the deployment of my troops with the intent of ensuring the safety of the civilians and my soldiers in the area. This is neither an aggressive act nor an offensive action."

Despite the assaults, Francis Jacobs continued to defend the warriors. Only a small handful were responsible for the attacks, he told reporters. "It doesn't mean the rest of the warriors are doing the same thing. I know the others and they're good people, standing up for what they believe in."

The army's advance was relentless. The APCs rumbled past the community centre, rolling steadily towards the next warrior barricade on Highway 344. As soon as they saw the soldiers, the people of Kanesatake gathered their children and ran into the community centre. About 150 people, including Ellen Gabriel and Denise David-Tolley, were trapped inside the building as the army took control. All summer, this small group of Mohawk residents had stubbornly refused to leave the community. Now it was too late to flee.

Dennis "Psycho" Nicholas was caught unprepared when the army came rolling in. In a house at the western end of the community, he watched as the armoured vehicles lumbered past. Psycho had been a key warrior leader from the beginning, and he was determined to stay to the end. He loaded his guns into a truck, jumped in, and raced down the highway toward the Pines. Weaving in between the army vehicles and the soldiers, with his guns rattling in the back, he somehow reached the warrior headquarters without being stopped.

Another warrior was driving the wrong way from the Pines, heading straight toward the advancing army. He narrowly escaped the soldiers, but found himself on the wrong side of the military lines and had to go into hiding. For the rest of that week, the solitary warrior hid on the mountain north of Kanesatake, creeping down to an orchard below to steal apples to survive. He kept a close watch on the army and later said that if the soldiers had opened fire on the besieged Mohawks, he would have launched a one-man attack against them from behind.

A row of soldiers advanced through the fields, checking the empty farmhouses and looking for snipers. When they reached the community centre, the soldiers crouched around the building and pointed their guns at anyone who ventured outside. Dozens of Quebec police officers, dressed in riot gear, came in behind the army and soon occupied the western half of the community.

Six armoured vehicles rumbled down Highway 344 and stopped in front of a zigzag barricade of wrecked cars and piles of dirt, about a kilometre west of the Pines. They were confronted by a solitary warrior in a camouflaged golf cart — it was Richard "Boltpin" Two Axe, a middle-aged ironworker from Kahnawake who had commandeered the golf cart to patrol the roads inside the barricades. The unarmed warrior got out of his golf cart and stood in front of the first APC as it slowly rolled forward. The armoured vehicle bumped the warrior in the chest, but he refused to move. He was ready to go under the wheels. Finally the vehicle stopped and the driver waited for instructions.

Stanley Cohen and Mad Jap soon arrived at the zigzag barricade and began negotiating with an army officer, who made it clear that the troops intended to advance. After lengthy negotiations, the warriors abandoned their position. A military bulldozer ploughed through the piles of dirt, and the APCs rolled forward again.

North of the highway, Major Tremblay was leading another convoy of APCs along the backroads and into the Pines. They encountered no resistance from the warriors until they reached Sector Five, the Mohawk bunker on the edge of the golf course, where a single armed warrior, Leroy "Splinter" Gabriel, was nervously standing guard.

Splinter, one of the first warriors to notice the army's advance, had raced from his home in Kanesatake to Sector Five on his motorcycle to guard the back entrance to the Pines. But when the soldiers and armoured vehicles arrived at the bunker, he wasn't sure what he should do. He didn't have a two-way radio, and nobody had given him any instructions.

"Get off this land," Splinter shouted at the soldiers. "This is Mohawk land! You have no business here!"

For half an hour, the lone warrior blocked the armoured vehicles, dashing in and out of the woods to prevent the soldiers from advancing, until finally Jean Noel "Christmas" Cataford arrived at the scene to help him. Christmas had a radio, which the beleaguered warriors used to call their headquarters. "They're coming in," Splinter yelled into the radio, pleading for reinforcements. But he was instructed to retreat.

Christmas, a former Oka municipal worker who could not read or write and often depended on others to give him direction, loaded his gun when he saw the armoured vehicles rolling into the Pines. "Leroy, can I shoot?" he asked Splinter. "Give me permission to shoot." As the soldiers kept advancing, Christmas became more and more frustrated. Finally he raised his gun and fired it into the air.

Despite the obvious dangers, Tremblay decided to keep going. He ordered his troops to advance past the Mohawk bunker and down the dirt road into the Pines. "I took a calculated risk during that operation," Tremblay admitted later. "I was not supposed to push or advance so far, but the C.O. [commanding officer] had authorized me to exploit the terrain. We met resistance at the first barricades. I evaluated the situation and, despite the warriors' threats, I decided to continue the advance. The warriors seemed surprised and fell back."

As the soldiers advanced toward the Pines, more warriors arrived and they slipped into defensive positions behind the trees. They cursed and yelled at the soldiers, and there were brief shoving matches. Hunter Montour, carrying a warrior flag, blocked the advance of the armoured vehicles for several minutes. He glared at Tremblay and told him to keep out of the Pines, but the grim-faced officer was determined to push ahead. The young warrior walked away in disgust. "Somebody give me fucking permission to slug that guy," he said to the other warriors.

War whoops echoed through the woods when the Mohawks spotted a patrol of reconnaissance soldiers, their faces streaked with green camouflage paint. "Come on!" one warrior screamed as he lunged toward the reconnaissance soldiers. "Shoot!" He was restrained by a Mohawk woman, who grabbed him and dragged him away.

Mad Jap was pacing up and down the dirt road, barking orders into his radio, telling the warriors to hold their fire. At their meetings all summer, the warriors had agreed that they would not fire their guns unless the soldiers shot first. They realized that they would be slaughtered if there was a gunfight. Moreover, they had always insisted that their AK-47s were purely defensive weapons. But now, blinded by anger, the warriors found it difficult to restrain themselves. "Just be cool," Mad Jap shouted at the warriors. "You are not weak men. You are strong. So just listen. Relax."

Despite his orders, several of the warriors locked and loaded their AK-47s and were on the verge of firing at the soldiers. "I just felt like blasting every one of them," recalled Tom Paul, the Micmac warrior who was codenamed The General. "I was just waiting for that first shot. That's all it would have taken. I felt in danger of losing control. It didn't matter anymore."

The soldiers were carrying C-7 assault rifles, but they had been instructed to keep their fingers off the triggers. "*Restez calme*," Tremblay yelled at his men. "Don't move."

Unable to vent their frustrations, the warriors were close to the breaking point. With adrenalin pumping through their veins, they expected a gunfight at any moment. "Now that I look back, it was really stupid," one warrior said later. "We would have been wiped out in seconds."

A small group of reporters who were watching the confrontation on the dirt road asked Tremblay what was going on. "I'm just extending my perimeter," he replied with a steely smile. "I've taken three barricades now … As soon as I'm able to go forward, I'll go forward."

When the crisis was over, Tremblay described the confrontation in the Pines as "one of the most nerve-wracking actions" of the entire summer. The senior officers were praying that their troops would remain disciplined. "The soldiers had to have a lot of confidence in their superiors not to fire when a loaded weapon was aimed at them," Tremblay later told the Armed Forces magazine, *Sentinel*.

Back at the Treatment Centre, the Mohawk women were getting ready to hide in the basement with the seven children who still remained at the warrior headquarters. They had already rehearsed the emergency plan. Their medical supplies were ready, and the women had a supply of wet handkerchiefs and water with lemon juice in case of a tear gas attack.

Several kilometres to the west, the Mohawks trapped in the community centre were afraid that the military would allow the police to raid the building. Some of them rushed outside and screamed at the soldiers; others tried to calm them down. The soldiers ordered the Mohawks to stay in the building.

Throughout the Mohawk community, people were anxiously hiding in their houses. An armoured military vehicle was parked outside the house of Walter David Jr., and he was afraid to step out of his home in case he was arrested.

Late in the afternoon, an army vehicle pulled up to the community centre, followed by a bus with tinted windows. The bus seemed to be full of SQ officers. An army officer and an SQ officer ordered the Mohawks to leave the building, line up, and show their identification. But the Mohawks refused, convinced that they would be arrested and perhaps beaten by the provincial police.

Everyone was worried about the fate of the warriors who were still in the Pines. They stared down the highway toward the forest, trying to figure out what was happening. At six o'clock, when they saw the TV news, many of the Mohawk women began crying. Linda Simon couldn't take it anymore. She marched down the highway in her bare feet, ignoring the soldiers, refusing to acknowledge their commands to stop. She walked all the way to the Treatment Centre to find out if the warriors were safe.

Late that night, a parade of police vehicles cruised slowly down the highway and along the backroads, asserting their control of the territory where all the trouble had begun on July 11. The police taunted the Mohawks who were still trapped inside the community centre, pretending to point guns at them. After this display of force, the Mohawks became fearful of a police raid. They put their children in a safe room on the second floor of the school building and prepared wet rags in the case of a tear gas attack.

The Mohawks in the community centre were accompanied by church leaders who had volunteered to serve as human rights observers. Alarmed by the prospect of a police raid, they tried to figure out a way of protecting the Mohawks. They knew that the police were not allowed to raid a church, so finally they declared the community centre was a place of worship. The tactic seemed to work. The police stayed outside.

Meanwhile, at the Treatment Centre, some of the Mohawk women had been talking on the phone to traditional native healers, who promised to protect the warriors from the guns of the army. But they warned the women that the warriors must not fire a single gunshot at the soldiers. "If you shoot one round, that's it, the medicine won't be working with you anymore, and they can kill you all," a native healer told the Mohawk women.

Late in the afternoon of September 1, the soldiers placed a razor wire barrier in front of their new position on the dirt road in the Pines, south of Sector Five. Warriors confronted the soldiers in face-to-face staring matches, challenging them to drop their guns and fight with their fists. One of the warriors grabbed a soldier's gun, put the barrel into his mouth, and dared the soldier to pull the trigger.

The Mohawk women kept trying to calm the warriors. "We can't shoot," one of the women told the warriors. "The medicine people say we can't shoot or nothing is going to be on our side."

Among the troops at the front of the military advance was Private Patrick Cloutier, a twenty-year-old fresh-faced soldier from Quebec City. As he stood near the razor wire, a masked warrior strode up to him and glared into his eyes. Cloutier tried to ignore him by gazing straight ahead or turning away and pacing restlessly back and forth. In one of Cloutier's impassive moments, the tense staredown was captured in a photograph that became famous around the world as a symbol of the Oka crisis.

The warrior who confronted Cloutier was widely identified as Lasagna. In reality, it was Brad Larocque, the young Ojibway university student from Saskatchewan who had gone to Kahnawake to study the situation and had stayed to fight. As the confrontation continued, Larocque leaned close to the young soldier and whispered a long series of threats. He asked Cloutier if he understood the damage he would suffer if a bullet bit into him. In a soft voice, he gave a graphic description of the injuries a bullet could cause, boasting that his high-powered bullets would tumble upwards and eviscerate the soldier. "Getting nervous, perhaps? You should be," he said. "You're number one on my list. Did you join the army for this?"

All afternoon, Brad Larocque had wanted to fire his weapon at the soldiers. He was prepared to die, and he was frustrated when Mad Jap told the warriors to hold their fire. But now, as he faced Cloutier in the staredown, he wondered what would happen if he was killed in a shootout. "I've got no kids," he kept thinking to himself. "There's nobody to carry on for me."

Just then, two Mohawk women walked down to the front lines with pizza. It was a moment of absurdity — the warriors stopped their staredowns and took a break for dinner. Despite the army's relentless advance, the Mohawk women were trying to maintain the daily meal routine, if only to show the soldiers that the Mohawks could not be intimidated.

Early in the evening, tensions mounted again as the soldiers and the armoured vehicles continued their slow advance down the dirt road. By sunset, Tremblay and his soldiers had captured Hellhole, the last bunker in the Pines. Tremblay agreed to allow the Mohawks to take their possessions out of the bunker before the army advanced.

It was a humiliating job. As the soldiers watched, the Mohawks took apart their bunker and loaded everything into a wheelbarrow. When the soldiers told them to move faster, the Mohawks purposely slowed down. It was a tiny act of defiance, but it could not dispel their gloom at the loss of the Pines to the advancing army.

When night came, the warriors were left with a small piece of territory surrounding their headquarters in the Treatment Centre. Tremblay had promised he would not advance any farther during the night. Only two barricades were remaining — Main Gate on Highway 344 at the top of the hill above Oka and a makeshift barrier of toppled pine trees on the highway to the west. Depressed and demoralized, the warriors spent an uneasy night in the Treatment Centre, fearing that Tremblay might break his promise and try to storm their headquarters in the middle of the night.

At daybreak on the morning of September 2, army patrols were moving cautiously through the Pines, while military helicopters flew just above the trees. Inside the Treatment Centre, the warriors tried to ignore the tightening grip of the army. They chatted about baseball as they munched on a breakfast of sausages and pancakes. Faced with the overwhelming power of a modern army, the Mohawks knew it would be virtually impossible to defend their last remaining barricades on Highway 344. Instead they decided to concentrate on protecting their final stronghold on the clifftop, the rambling old building known as the Treatment Centre.

At 8:15 a.m., two dozen soldiers and three APCs advanced from the Pines, onto Highway 344, and moved quickly to Main Gate. As the warriors watched in silence, the soldiers sealed off the barricade with razor wire and started checking the overturned police vehicles and fallen trees for hidden explosives. A few hundred metres away, several warriors sat in lawnchairs at the entrance to the Treatment Centre. "They're facing a *fait accompli* each time we move," Tremblay told reporters. "They don't have any choice except to withdraw."

Despite their bitterness, the warriors were resigned to the loss of their main barricade. "It's just a pile of dirt," shrugged Mark "Blackjack" Montour. "It's theirs. It doesn't bother me. It's all a matter of time now."

An hour later, the warriors began digging bunkers and trenches in the woods on both sides of the laneway that led to their headquarters at the Treatment Centre. Some of them seemed calm, but others were ready to explode with frustration. Late in the morning, Lasagna marched out of the Treatment Centre and walked toward the soldiers at the razor wire. After the army had rolled into the Pines, the Mohawks had no time to worry about Lasagna's erratic behaviour, and he had been rescued from the threat of eviction. Now he was free to be a warrior again. Surrounded by dozens of reporters and cameramen, he glared silently at the soldiers. Then he uttered a war whoop, turned on his heel, and walked back. "I just wanted to look at their faces before I kill them," he said.

Another warrior, The General, walked up to an army officer at the razor wire. "We're getting tired of waiting," he told the officer. "You plan to kill us all in here? I want to know now. If you're going to kill us all, do it now."

"I have nothing to say about that, sir," the officer told the warrior.

Unlike the Kahnawake warriors, the Mohawks at the Treatment Centre were relatively young and inexperienced. Their bunkers were poorly constructed, and they had little expertise in defensive strategy. Of the thirty warriors at Kanesatake, only two — Slim Marquis and Bill Sears — had military experience.

The lack of training among the Kanesatake Mohawks was a source of worry to the veteran warriors of Kahnawake. The face-to-face staredowns, for example, were a poor military tactic. By marching right up to the soldiers, the warriors exposed themselves to their enemy. "They lost the mystique of the unknown," said Michael Thomas, the U.S. army veteran and assistant war chief at Kahnawake. "When you're in the shadows and you can't be assessed, it scares the enemy. The unknown is the most lethal weapon you can use." The staredowns were also a public-relations fiasco. They allowed the soldiers to appear courageous and unflinching in their defiance of the warriors — an image that soon embedded itself in the consciousness of millions of Canadian television viewers.

Shortly after 5:00 p.m. on September 2, an army bulldozer and a demolition squad started tearing down Main Gate on Highway 344. For the first time since July 11, the highway was free of Mohawk barricades, and the warriors had lost the symbol of their power. The soldiers took down a Mohawk Vietnam Veterans flag from the barricade, folded it carefully, and handed it to Mad Jap in a brief ceremony. "We want to be respectful to their nation," said Lieutenant-Colonel Daigle.

At nightfall, the warriors huddled in their bunkers, whooping and yelling to keep up their spirits. It was another tense night. Army searchlights pierced the dark forest, and helicopters roared above the trees. The soldiers could hear the eery sound of Mohawk chants from a stereo near the front trenches. The chants were a psychological ploy, designed to play on the nerves of the soldiers as they waited in the darkness.

At 7:30 the following morning, Major Tremblay made his next

move. He led about fifty troops and five armoured vehicles in a swift advance along Highway 344 to the entrance of the laneway to the Treatment Centre. The warriors scrambled into their bunkers in the woods, pointing their guns at the soldiers who crouched in the ditches beside the highway. A gunshot echoed from the army side. The Mohawks were afraid that the soldiers would keep advancing toward their bunkers. They realized this could be the final assault of the summer.

The warriors and the soldiers were now just a few dozen metres apart, pointing their guns at each other, and the suppressed violence of both sides seemed about to explode at any minute. "Hold your fire," Lasagna barked at the warriors. They ducked behind trees and cursed the soldiers, but did not shoot.

Farther back, near the Treatment Centre, more warriors crouched in bunkers and peered across the gully that ran alongside the western edge of the building. They could hear the sound of armoured vehicles advancing noisily through the woods on the other side of the gully. "Do not lock and load," Mad Jap shouted at the warriors. "They're trying to get to your nerves. Don't let them. You are honourable men. You have to be a lot smarter than they are."

The warriors were prepared for a final shootout if the army advanced down the laneway toward the Treatment Centre. But instead the troops dug into their new positions and strung a roll of razor along the edge of the highway, blocking the entrance of the laneway, while the warriors watched nervously from their bunkers in the woods.

By this point, the Mohawk territory had been reduced to a few hundred square metres, bounded by Highway 344 on the north, the Lake of Two Mountains on the south, and the wooded ravines on the east and west. They were surrounded by four hundred soldiers equipped with machine guns, assault rifles, dozens of armoured vehicles, and military helicopters. Soldiers patrolled every side of the warrior headquarters, including the rocky shore of the lake. Inside the razor wire barriers, there were just thirty warriors, seventeen women, seven children, and a handful of advisors. The army knew that the warriors were weakened and isolated. After the soldiers had completed their final advance on the morning of September 3, senior military officers phoned the Treatment Centre and demanded that the Mohawks surrender unconditionally.

"The situation is desperate," said Terry Doxtator, an Oneida chief who had entered the Treatment Centre the previous day to serve as a negotiator for the warriors. "The people here will not surrender unconditionally. They are prepared to make their last stand for their land now."

Doxtator was flanked by another Oneida chief, Bob Antone, and an Oneida faithkeeper, Bruce Elijah. The three Oneidas, who had travelled to Oka from their reserve near London in southwestern Ontario in mid-August, played a crucial role in the final siege at the Treatment Centre. For years, the Longhouse had been an influential force at the Oneida reserve in Ontario, and the Oneidas had become the closest allies of the Mohawk warriors in the Iroquois Confederacy. While the official Confederacy leadership had criticized the warriors, the Oneidas had endorsed the warrior movement in a formal Longhouse sanctioning ceremony. Most of the warriors trusted the three Oneida leaders, and in the final weeks of the siege the Oneidas were increasingly influential as the official spokesmen and negotiators for the warriors — especially after the army refused to allow Joe Deom and other Mohawk negotiators to return to the Treatment Centre.

Doxtator and Antone pleaded with the army to give the Oneidas a couple of days to "cleanse the minds and hearts" of the warriors so that they could get rid of their anger and hostility and negotiate an "honourable disengagement." Outside the warrior headquarters, the senior commander of the Canadian army gave a guarantee. "There will be no more military movements on the perimeter," Lieutenant-General Kent Foster told reporters. "There will be absolutely no attack on the Mohawks here."

By a curious stroke of fate, the Treatment Centre was the perfect location for a lengthy siege. It was a huge building with a big kitchen, dormitories, and freezers full of food. From a military standpoint, it was easily defensible. It stood at the top of a cliff overlooking the lake and it was protected on three sides by gullies or steep inclines. The warriors had a modern communications network to maintain their links with the outside world — a computer, a fax machine, a cellular phone, and a bank of phone lines. The intercom crackled with messages for the warriors. "Psycho, line 2, Psycho," the switchboard operator said.

The warriors were armed with dozens of hunting rifles and semi-automatic weapons, some of which were equipped with armour-piercing bullets and tracer bullets. One warrior had a compound bow with explosive-tipped arrows. Their bunkers were stocked with homemade grenades (plastic canisters filled with gunpowder and steel pellets) and miniature napalm bombs (manufactured from liquid detergent, styrofoam, gasoline, and the fuse from an ordinary bullet).

Behind the warrior headquarters, the Mohawks conducted tobacco-burning ceremonies at dawn and dusk at a sacred fire that burned all day and all night. Inside the building, Bruce Elijah conducted healing ceremonies for the warriors. Doxtator tried to explain to the army that the spiritual healing could provide a peaceful settlement to the conflict, but the military officers were skeptical. They warned the warriors that they were not prepared to let the situation drag on indefinitely.

In addition to the Oneida negotiators, the key warrior leaders at the Treatment Centre were Loran Thompson, Mad Jap, Bill Sears, and Harold Oakes. Sears, a forty-one-year-old businessman and veteran of the Vietnam War, kept the lowest profile. Born to a white mother and a Mohawk father from Akwesasne, he had fought in Vietnam from 1969 to 1973. After working as an ironworker for the rest of the 1970s, he had entered the fuel oil business in New York State and become a millionaire with investments in shopping malls, jewellery stores, real estate developments, a construction company, and clothing retailers. He also operated the oldest bingo hall in Akwesasne. Sears sometimes boasted that he was worth $35 million to $40 million, and he paid for his restaurant meals with cash from a wad of hundred-dollar bills.

Sears had heard about the Great Law of Peace in his childhood, but he forgot most of it during his ironworking days, when he lived in black and Hispanic neighbourhoods in the northeastern United States. As he puts it, "they didn't have much call for the Great Law in Jersey City."

In 1979 and 1980, Sears was the leader of the vigilantes who besieged Loran Thompson and his supporters (including Mad Jap) at Raquette Point in Akwesasne. He had opposed the traditionalists at that point because his brother was an Akwesasne police officer who had been disarmed by the Longhouse followers at the beginning of the crisis in 1979. Later, however, he patched up his differences with Thompson's supporters and became a close friend of Mad Jap. Then, at the funeral of a friend in the mid-1980s, he heard the Great Law recited at a Longhouse ceremony. "It got me thinking about it again," he said.

After July 11, Sears organized benefits and food drives for the warriors, sending truckloads of food to the Pines. In August, he travelled to Kanesatake with his sidekick, Harold Oakes, a Mohawk business associate who organized construction training and employment programs in New York State. Both men decided to stay. Francis Boots, the Akwesasne war chief, designated Sears as the "head of security" at the Treatment Centre because of his combat experience and his calm disposition, which made him a stabilizing influence on the warriors.

Meanwhile, on the outskirts of Montreal, repair crews were working on the Mercier Bridge to prepare it for commuter traffic. But on the morning of September 3, as the army tightened its noose around the Treatment Centre, the workers on the Mercier Bridge were suddenly forced to abandon their work. A group of fifteen warriors from Kahnawake had returned and seized control of the bridge.

The move was originally intended to be a peaceful protest by Mohawk women and children, but a handful of warriors had taken over the event. They were inspired by Paul Delaronde, the veteran leader of the Kahnawake Warrior Society, who was unhappy with the voluntary dismantling of the Kahnawake barricades. The warriors seized the bridge and pulled out dozens of weapons, including their most deadly weapon — the .50-calibre machine gun.

The army was forced to dispatch dozens of armoured vehicles and soldiers to recapture the bridge. Realizing they were outnumbered, the warriors grabbed their weapons and raced away in a van. They tried to hide the guns in the Longhouse, but an army helicopter had spotted their route. A few hours later, a convoy of armoured vehicles rolled into Kahnawake, and the soldiers raided the Longhouse. They said the presence of guns on the Mercier Bridge had violated their agreements with the warriors.

At the Longhouse, the soldiers were confronted by a group of enraged Mohawk women who fought to prevent the troops from entering the spiritual home of the Longhouse people. Eventually the troops pushed the women to the ground, injuring two of them, and entered the Longhouse. The soldiers found a number of weapons in the building, including the .50-calibre machine gun. When the raid was over, the troops kept their armoured vehicles on the reserve, near the entrances to the village. The army had now gained control of half the Kahnawake territory.

Over the next few days, Allan Delaronde ordered a dozen prominent warriors to disappear from Kahnawake. Some had become targets for the SQ because they were perceived as the ringleaders of the Warrior Society, while others were considered a danger to the community because they were heavily armed and willing to resist any soldier who tried to arrest them. Among those who vanished from sight were Paul Delaronde and Michael Thomas.

Accompanied by his wife and adopted children, Paul Delaronde travelled secretly to the southern United States, where he succeeded in evading the police. Michael Thomas used false identification to take a train to Toronto, then flew to Miami, rented a car, and drove to Key West. He did not realize that the police were following his every movement. When he walked out of a restaurant in Key West, he was ambushed by fifty police officers brandishing semi-automatic weapons. Police snipers hid in the bushes and on the roofs of nearby buildings as Thomas was taken into custody.

The warrior encampment near Oka was surrounded by the blinding searchlights of the army's APCs, and the muffled roar of military helicopters could be heard above the trees. Throughout the night of September 3, the soldiers shot flares into the dark sky above the Treatment Centre. It was psychological warfare, designed to deprive the warriors of sleep and wear down their resistance.

Concerned that secret army patrols or snipers might be creeping through the bush, the warriors salvaged some bright lights from Xerox machines and wrecked police cars and used this makeshift equipment to illuminate the gullies. They took mirrors from the bedrooms and bathrooms of the Treatment Centre and pointed them toward the army's searchlights, directing the glare back at the soldiers.

At midnight, without any warning, a malfunctioning army flare plunged into a group of Mohawks behind the Treatment Centre, narrowly missing a Mohawk woman. Although no one was injured or killed, the warriors knew that was only by chance, and they were infuriated. The previous day, they had been upset by the reports of the army raid on the Kahnawake Longhouse, and they were enraged by the sight of Quebec police vehicles cruising through Mohawk territory in Kanesatake. The flare incident was the final provocation.

The next morning, several Mohawks marched up to the razor wire on the highway. Among them was Lorraine Montour, the clan mother and veteran Longhouse activist, who had almost been struck by the falling flare the night before. When she arrived at the front line, she discovered that the army had reinforced its razor wire barricade, moving it slightly closer to the warrior encampment around the Treatment Centre. "Our whole existence was flashing before my eyes," Lorraine Montour recalls. "It was all being wiped out."

The clan mother began to scream at a soldier on duty behind the razor wire. "Get out of here," she shouted. "I ain't afraid of you. No one is afraid of you or your army. You're never coming in here."

She shoved the soldier and pushed him backwards. After several shoves, the soldier fell and suffered lacerations from the razor wire. Finally he retreated. A dozen troops rushed to the confrontation as the Mohawks pushed the razor wire back toward the highway. "If you think the men are bad, the women are worse," one Mohawk woman shouted at the troops.

When the incident was over, military officers resumed their efforts to negotiate with the Mohawks, but little progress was made. The warriors wanted free passage for their negotiators, who were trying to consult Mohawk leaders in Dorval and Kahnawake. The army said it would permit the request, but only if the warriors surrendered the front-end loader they were using to dig their bunkers and trenches. The warriors refused. When the Mohawks asked for firewood and large rocks to build a sweatlodge for healing ceremonies, the army rejected the request.

As the day wore on, there were more confrontations between the army and the warriors. Many of the warriors wanted to fire warning shots at the soldiers and the low-flying military helicopters that constantly harassed their encampment at night. They had retreated as far as they could go, and their backs were, almost literally, against the wall. There was nowhere left for them to retreat — except a cliff and a steep fall to the rocks below. If the army tried to advance into the warrior compound, the warriors had privately decided that they would open fire. Faced with the real prospect of death, more than half the warriors had prepared their wills and made their final burial arrangements. The details were quietly sent to their families by phone or radio.

Meanwhile, Terry Doxtator and Bob Antone were begging the army to ease the constant pressure on the warriors. The army's pressure was intended to break the resistance of the Mohawks, but Doxtator and Antone were afraid that it would trigger a violent reaction. They telephoned the senior army officers to ask them to stop the low-flying helicopter flights and the flares. The confrontations had frazzled the nerves of the Mohawks, and Bob Antone was not sure the warriors would ever survive this final siege.

Back at the Dorval hotel, negotiations between the Iroquois Confederacy leaders and government officials had resumed at the request of the Confederacy. But the negotiators from Quebec and Ottawa were becoming more and more inflexible. On September 5, they withdrew John Ciaccia's offer of a week earlier and submitted a much more restrictive one. The Confederacy negotiators, led by John Mohawk and Oren Lyons, immediately rejected the government proposal and announced that they were leaving Dorval because the talks were pointless.

On the same day, a delegation of Confederacy chiefs and other native leaders — including Georges Erasmus and Elijah Harper — travelled to Ottawa to ask Indian Affairs Minister Tom Siddon to persuade the army to withdraw a hundred metres from its existing positions. The chiefs knew they had to reduce the dangerous level of tension around the Treatment Centre. But Siddon said he was powerless to grant the request.

At Kanesatake, a dozen reporters and photographers were still inside the warrior encampment. Their presence was a constant irritant to the army, which had adopted a deliberate strategy of isolating the warriors from the outside world. In a bid to force out the journalists, the army prohibited them from receiving essential supplies such as film, videotapes and batteries, and refused to allow any film to be shipped out.

All day and night, Bruce Elijah was conducting his healing ceremonies for the warriors in a small room in the Treatment Centre. He massaged them, relaxed them, and told them he was taking the bad medicine out of them. Late at night, all the Mohawks gathered around their sacred fire for a traditional "hatui" (false face) ceremony to help protect the warriors from harm. The false faces were wooden masks, carved from the trunks of century-old living trees. Because they were considered to be still alive, the masks were oiled and food was placed on their lips. The ceremonies were conducted by Mohawks and Oneidas who belonged to the hatui society, one of the traditional secret medicine societies of the Iroquois people.

At the beginning of the ceremony, everyone was given a cup of cedar-leaf tea, a traditional Mohawk medicine. Then the warriors stretched out their hands and the women gave each of them a spoonful of corn meal — one of the ancient foods that sustained the Iroquois culture. According to the Iroquois creation myth, corn grew from the grave of the Earth Mother who died after giving birth to the creator of the world. While wooden masks were carefully draped on a wooden log beside the fire, Bruce Elijah prayed for the safety of the soldiers. He told the warriors that they should not regard the troops as their enemy. Instead they should see the soldiers as "people with no spirit" who simply cannot understand the cultural beliefs of the Mohawks.

Despite the spiritual ceremonies, the level of tension was still dangerously high, and the army kept escalating its pressure tactics. In the middle of the night on September 5, the soldiers noticed that the Mohawks had left one of their mirrors unguarded near the front line. An army sharpshooter raced through a gap in the razor wire, grabbed the mirror, and rushed back to safety.

By September 6, the Mercier Bridge was open to commuter traffic, and the warriors at the Treatment Centre realized they had no bargaining power left. The army continued to tighten its restrictions on journalists. All television crews and reporters on the military side of the barrier were forced to move to a military compound several hundred metres down the highway, where they could no longer witness any of the confrontations.

In the afternoon, an army officer phoned Terry Doxtator with a proposal to end the standoff. The army was still following its strategy of bypassing the politicians and dealing directly with the warriors, a strategy which had worked well in Kahnawake. Under the army's proposal, the warriors would put down their guns and enter military custody until their trial in court, in return for the army's guarantee that they would be treated "in a humanitarian manner" and "with dignity." The proposal was intended to protect the warriors from possible retaliation by the Quebec police, who, the Mohawks were convinced, would brutally beat them in revenge for the death of Corporal Lemay.

The deal offered physical security, but it would still amount to a total surrender by the warriors, and it would criminalize the warrior movement. Doxtator phoned the army to say that the warriors had rejected it.

On the night of September 6, with only a dwindling handful of reporters and photographers inside the warrior encampment to scrutinize their behaviour, some of the soldiers felt free to vent their anger at the barrage of taunts and shoves they had received from the Mohawks. Shortly after midnight, the soldiers spotted a Mohawk woman at the razor wire. "You fucking bitch," they screamed. The Mohawks shouted back, and the verbal confrontation soon became uglier.

At the entrance to the Treatment Centre, the warriors had erected a plastic sheet to shield themselves from the army's blinding searchlights. The plastic sheet was a constant source of frustration to the soldiers because it prevented them from seeing the warriors' movements. As the verbal abuse escalated, the soldiers and the warriors began hurling stones at each other over the plastic sheet. One warrior picked up a baseball bat and wildly swung it at the razor wire barrier. Troops dashed across the highway to join the battle. "If you want to fuck around, we'll fuck around," an army officer shouted at the warriors.

As the soldiers raced back and forth with their guns drawn, they were silhouetted by the searchlights behind them, and the warriors could see only their huge shadows, looming darkly against the plastic sheet. A few moments later, a warrior threw a bedroom mirror and a baseball bat in the direction of the soldiers. The officer ordered his men to fix their bayonets, and some of the soldiers jabbed at the plastic sheet. Harold Oakes thought he could hear the soldiers loading their assault rifles. "Lock and load!" he ordered the warriors. Then there was the ominous click of guns being prepared to fire. Noriega dropped to one knee and pointed his gun. "Get out of my line of fire," he screamed at several frightened journalists who were caught in the middle.

The warriors finally cooled down when Mad Jap arrived. It had been the most dangerous episode of the siege and the Mohawks realized they had been risking a bloodbath. They admitted they had been on the verge of shooting, but they blamed the soldiers for provoking them by maintaining such high levels of pressure. "It's hard to keep a clear mind when all these psychological games are going on," one warrior said.

The next day, September 7, the senior Mohawk leaders at the Treatment Centre discussed the situation. They knew that a gunfight could be sparked at any time. They also knew it was the younger warriors with hot tempers who seemed to be goaded into confrontations with the soldiers. So the Mohawks ordered the younger warriors to stay away from the front line. "They put us away so we wouldn't fuck around with the army all night," Hunter Montour explained later.

Down in the town of Oka, Elijah Harper had been waiting for several days for permission to visit the warriors, in an attempt to help ease the standoff. On September 7, he was finally allowed to walk through the army lines. The warriors were astonished to see him strolling calmly into the Treatment Centre. For more than two hours, Harper listened to the Mohawks tell their story. When he left the warrior encampment, he issued a warning to the military: the constant pressure from the army was making it almost impossible to negotiate a solution to the siege. "The people here are not prepared to surrender," he said.

As the sun went down that evening, an uneasy silence began to settle over the warriors. They had anticipated a military response to the confrontation of the previous night, but now everything seemed quiet — perhaps too quiet.

In a foxhole in the woods, Randy Horne was feeling drowsy. He hadn't slept all day, and he was exhausted. As the night dragged on, he could feel himself nodding off.

Horne, codenamed Spudwrench, was one of the older warriors who had replaced the younger Mohawks in the front line positions. He was a forty-year-old ironworker from Kahnawake, a quiet, softspoken man. Perhaps because of his age, he was less alert than the younger men, and in the early hours of the morning he dozed off.

Just after 4:00 a.m., Spudwrench woke up abruptly to see a soldier stepping over him. When he brought his arms out of his sleeping bag to defend himself, he was immediately grabbed by two other soldiers on either side of the foxhole. He tried to call for help, but the soldiers began beating him on the head with clubs. Spudwrench pulled out a small knife and slashed at the soldiers, injuring them slightly, but the soldiers kept clubbing him furiously. He put up his hands to protect himself, but they kept swinging away, inflicting deep gashes on his skull and face. He lost consciousness as the soldiers dragged him away.

Another warrior, Splinter, was at a nearby bunker when he heard the noise of branches breaking in the woods. He rushed over and shone his flashlight toward the struggling men. By that time, the soldiers were trying to drag the unconscious warrior out of the woods and into the army's territory on the highway. But when they were caught in the flashlight's beam, they dropped Spudwrench and ran away. Blood was pouring from wounds all over the warrior's face as he staggered to his knees. Splinter lifted him up and carried him back to the Treatment Centre.

The warriors placed him on a wooden table in the makeshift medical room that had been set up in the Treatment Centre. His face was lacerated in several places, and there was a deep cut over one of his eyes. He was suffering from shock, shivering uncontrollably as the Mohawk women tried to wash the blood from his face.

As his wounds were treated, Spudwrench explained in a weak voice how the soldiers had beaten him. The warriors were incensed. One of the angriest was a bearded twenty-two-year-old Mohawk from Kahnawake, codenamed Sledgehammer. His name was Dean Horne, and the bleeding warrior was his father.

Deane Horne had a girlfriend, Vicky Diabo, and an infant daughter in the Treatment Centre. Although the Mohawks tried to keep them away from the medical room, Vicky Diabo caught a glimpse of the bloody face of the grandfather of her child, and she fainted.

In the medical room, Terry Doxtator grabbed a phone and called a hospital emergency room for advice. He spoke to a doctor, but the physician was suspicious and refused to help. "Give me some goddamn hints," Doxtator yelled at him. The doctor hung up.

At the front line, there was an eery silence. Darkness still shrouded the highway, and no soldiers were visible. Two journalists walked out of the warrior encampment to look for medical help for the battered warrior. When they crossed the highway, an army officer materialized out of the darkness. The journalists described the warrior's injuries, but the officer said he knew nothing about the incident. The journalists insisted that he get help.

A few minutes later, a military ambulance drove up the highway, and the soldiers said the warrior should be brought to the ambulance. But the Mohawks were distrustful. They wanted their own physician, Dr. David Gorman, to be sent into their encampment. The army refused. "If he's injured, he should be brought out," an officer told Mad Jap.

After a brief negotiation, the army agreed to send a blindfolded paramedic into the warrior headquarters. As security for the army, Bill Sears walked out of the encampment and put himself temporarily into the custody of several soldiers.

The paramedic examined Spudwrench and recommended that he be sent to a trauma centre. "I guarantee he will be brought back as soon as he is well," Tremblay told the warriors.

But the warriors, convinced that Spudwrench would be arrested by the provincial police if he left the safety of the encampment, insisted on waiting for their own physician.

At 4:30 in the morning, at his home near Malone, New York, Dr. David Gorman was wakened by a call from the Treatment Centre. Gorman had lived with Lorraine Montour for many years, and he was the stepfather of Mark and Hunter Montour. He had treated Mohawk patients at Akwesasne during his entire career, and he was a strong supporter of the warrior movement. When he got the emergency call, he jumped into his car and raced all the way to Oka at breakneck speed. After a brief search of his car, Gorman was allowed to enter the warrior headquarters at about 8:30 a.m.

Despite a severe shortage of medical supplies at the warrior encampment, Gorman did his best to treat the injured Mohawk with bandages and an intravenous tube. He recommended that Spudwrench not be moved until his condition had stabilized. "His injuries are very serious," Gorman told reporters at 11:15 a.m. "He has multiple lacerations, a possible skull fracture, and severe head injuries. He's semi-conscious. He has lost quite a bit of blood. It's possible that he could die. The next twenty-four hours will be very important."

Meanwhile, army spokesmen were scrambling to explain the brutal beating of the warrior. One officer said the troops had secretly sent a reconnaissance patrol into warrior territory because they suspected there was a new "defensive construction" in the encampment. Another officer said the plastic sheet at the front line had prevented the army from seeing what was happening inside. "We just wanted to find out what was going on in there," he told reporters.

But the official explanations failed to answer the key questions. The army had promised to give clear warnings before making any movements. It had promised no further advances against the remaining warriors. And it had promised to take every precaution to avoid bloodshed. All of those promises had now been broken.

By mid-afternoon, Spudwrench's condition had stabilized, and Gorman was ready to transfer him to a hospital. But the injured warrior was reluctant to leave. He wanted to stay with the Mohawks at the Treatment Centre. The physician glanced over at Spudwrench's wife, Stephanie. "It's up to you, Stef," he said.

Stephanie Horne was convinced that her husband was close to death. "If he dies, I'll never forgive myself," she told Gorman. They decided to take him to a civilian hospital in Montreal.

The army offered to transport the warrior in a military ambulance or helicopter, but the Mohawks did not trust the military. They phoned for a private ambulance, and at 4:25 p.m. it arrived at the front line. A few minutes later, Spudwrench was carried out of the Treatment Centre on a stretcher, his head covered with bandages. Beneath the bandages were basswood leaves, a traditional Indian medicine.

As the injured Mohawk was lifted into the ambulance, the warriors lashed out in anger. One warrior shoved a soldier. Another tried to tear down the razor wire barrier. "You're going to pay," a Mohawk screamed. Bruce Elijah, the Oneida faithkeeper, tried to calm down the warriors by brushing their bodies with an eagle wing, the traditional Iroquois symbol of protection. He believed it would dispel their anger and give them clear minds.

The ambulance pulled away and headed towards Montreal. What followed was a journey of strange twists and turns.

Stephanie Horne and David Gorman, accompanied by a military physician, sat in the back of the ambulance with the injured warrior. Spudwrench's eight-year-old daughter, Amanda, rode in the front seat with the ambulance driver. They were followed by a long procession of vehicles — an army vehicle, a police car, and a convoy of reporters.

The army had agreed to escort the ambulance to Notre Dame hospital in Montreal, but as the convoy raced toward Montreal at 140 kilometres an hour, a radio message came through, saying that a bomb threat had closed the hospital's doors. The driver was told to go to a hospital in nearby St. Eustache.

The convoy sped off to its new destination, but Gorman was suspicious, concerned that the provincial police were waiting to arrest Spudwrench at St. Eustache. He also suspected that the hospital was inadequately equipped for head injuries. When the ambulance arrived at St. Eustache, he refused to let the warrior out of the ambulance. So they headed off for Montreal again. By this time, the reporters had lost the trail. Partway to Montreal, the ambulance driver suddenly stopped his vehicle and called his dispatcher. The military doctor began arguing with the driver. They drove off again, and Gorman was told that they were going to Montreal General Hospital.

Instead, they somehow then ended up at Hotel Dieu, a hospital in the north end of the city. Gorman was convinced that the police had changed the dispatcher's orders. Military officers got out of their vehicle and ordered the ambulance driver to go to Montreal General Hospital.

Finally, when they arrived at the Montreal General, provincial police were swarming all over the building. Doctors ordered the uniformed officers to leave, but some plainclothes officers stayed in the hospital. Two days later, Spudwrench was released from hospital and placed under military custody. Despite the promises of Major Tremblay, he was not permitted to return to the Treatment Centre. On the morning of September 12, he was arrested by the provincial police on five charges, including possession of a dangerous weapon and rioting.

Meanwhile, inside the razor wire barriers, the sense of fear was palpable. There had been confrontations almost every day for a week now, and the tension seemed to be worsening. Senior executives of the CBC, worried about the danger of a deadly gunbattle, decided to pull their reporters and technicians out of the Mohawk encampment. They were the last remaining television crew inside the warrior headquarters.

As night fell, only a handful of journalists remained in the warrior compound. The mood was sombre. Stanley Cohen said he expected a final attack at any moment. "They're setting the stage for a bloodbath," he said.

CHAPTER 16
Walking Home

The Dénouement

On the night of September 8, the warriors held a ceremony to pray for peace. They were filled with conflicting emotions. Most wanted vengeance for the beating of Spudwrench, but they tried to purge themselves of those feelings, realizing that the slightest incident could touch off a gunfight that would end in death and defeat. Against the overpowering technology of a modern army, the warriors knew they would be wiped out in a matter of seconds. Despite the provocations, they decided to be cool and disciplined. "Don't play the game they want you to play," Bill Sears told the warriors. "If you get mad, go out and punch a tree."

Soon the warriors were taking a perverse pride in their refusal to fight. "They thought we would retaliate, but we fooled them," Mad Jap boasted to reporters a day after the beating of Spudwrench.

Some of the warriors were beginning to think about a possible end to the conflict. After rejecting the army's proposal of September 6, the warriors were now prepared to make a counter-offer. Terry Doxtator was helping to draft a new peace proposal, and he went from bunker to bunker to consult the warriors. "We're concentrating on the disengagement now," Doxtator told the small band of reporters at the Treatment Centre. "As far as we're concerned, we've won the war. Native people across Canada have virtually declared that the war is won."

After several drafts and revisions, Doxtator and the warriors gave their proposal to the army on September 11. It called for the creation of a joint commission of Iroquois representatives, federal and provincial officials, and human rights leaders, which would decide the outcome of any criminal prosecutions of the warriors. It would also investigate any violations of human rights and international law that may have occurred at Kanesatake during the standoff. In exchange, the warriors would lay down their arms — but they would stay at the Treatment Centre under the custody of military police. The weapons would be sealed in a neutral place until the joint commission decided how to dispose of them.

Quebec Premier Robert Bourassa immediately rejected the peace proposal. The province had little interest in negotiations at this point. With the Mercier Bridge open to traffic and the warriors under military control, there was no pressure on the provincial government. It could afford a long waiting game.

The next day, September 12, the soldiers fortified their barricades, erecting new rows of razor wire at the entrance to the Treatment Centre. They also began to build a tall platform for a more powerful lighting system that would tower above the plastic sheet protecting the warriors from the APC searchlights.

An army colonel phoned Bob Antone twice during the day, urging the warriors to surrender and suggesting that the army might consider amendments to its previous proposal for a peaceful disengagement. He also warned, however, that the army's patience was wearing thin — and he added an ominous note to the conversation by inquiring about the water supply at the Treatment Centre.

In the afternoon, the Mohawks spotted an eagle in the sky, soaring high above the Treatment Centre. They rushed inside to alert the other warriors, who came tumbling out of the building to stare in amazement at the bird. According to Iroquois mythology, the eagle watches for signs of danger and screeches a warning if it sees any external threats. But the eagle above the Treatment Centre remained silent as it hovered in the sky. It was a good omen, the Mohawks believed.

Bruce Elijah, the Oneida faithkeeper, took it as a signal to perform the white mask ceremony at the sacred fire behind the Treatment Centre. It was one of the oldest and rarest of all the Iroquois spiritual practices. Members of the False Face Society wore wooden masks as they danced in the darkness. Next morning, the masks were hanging on nails at each corner of the Treatment Centre, and remnants of corn meal could be seen in their mouths. In the past, the hanging masks were intended to protect Mohawks from the four winds. But now they were guarding against something more dangerous.

By mid-September, the first signs of autumn could be felt in the chill evening air. The twelve remaining journalists, who had been sleeping outside in sleeping bags and blankets, moved into the cramped basement of the Treatment Centre as the temperatures dropped.

The army, which was still trying to force the media to leave the encampment, did everything possible to make life miserable for the journalists. A few days earlier, an assistant to Defence Minister Bill McKnight had promised that the journalists' equipment and film would be allowed to pass through the military lines, and that a food supply would be guaranteed. But the army immediately broke this promise. Journalists were prohibited from sending film back to their newsrooms, and they were not permitted to receive any personal supplies from their employers. As a result, they had to rely on the Mohawks for food. In cellular phone calls and face-to-face meetings at the razor wire, army officers issued a series of ominous warnings to the journalists, hinting that a violent attack on the warrior headquarters might be imminent. "For your own safety, we strongly advise you to leave by nightfall," one officer told the reporters on September 13. But the journalists stayed.

Human rights groups in the United States and Britain sent letters of protest when they learned of the worsening restrictions on the media. The Canadian Association of Journalists later described the military censorship as "one of the worst attacks ever on the Canadian public's right to know." Even during the North-West Rebellion of 1885, journalists had been allowed to cover both sides of the conflict.

The army, however, was following a masterful strategy to maintain its control of the news flow. Twenty public relations experts from military units across the country were mobilized to prepare briefing documents for army spokesmen. They distributed glossy photos and videotapes of the weapons the warriors allegedly possessed. They analyzed every available newspaper and newscast across Canada and from as far away as Australia. They conducted media briefings twice a day for the journalists who were corralled at the military compound at Oka. Over the course of the crisis, they organized ten press conferences and prepared forty-five press releases and twenty-five sequences of possible questions and suggested answers for the official spokesmen. The army later estimated that its public relations campaign cost about $1 million.

As the siege dragged on, the warriors became better organized too. Each warrior was assigned to either the day shift or the night shift. Their bunkers were camouflaged with tree branches and covered with plastic sheets to protect them from the rain. Their network of trenches became more extensive. Bill Sears showed the warriors how to drive wooden stakes into the ground behind the Treatment Centre to prevent the army from dropping its troops out of helicopters in an airborne attack.

To break the boredom, some of the warriors chatted casually with the soldiers at the front line. Richard Two Axe, the middle-aged grandfather who drove the camouflaged golf cart, was perhaps the friendliest of the warriors, often trading jokes with soldiers on the other side of the razor wire.

Some of the soldiers, however, were blatantly racist and hostile to the Mohawks. One group of soldiers put up a large wooden sign near the warrior encampment with a misspelled message: "Lazagne Your Dead Meat." Much of their hatred was directed toward Alanis Obomsawin, an Abenaki filmmaker who has received the Order of Canada for her acclaimed National Film Board documentaries. All summer, she had been directing a film crew at Kanesatake, and now she was one of the last remaining journalists in the warrior encampment. Whenever she appeared at the razor wire, soldiers shouted racist insults at her and called her a "squaw." When she complained to an army officer, she was ignored.

By day, the atmosphere inside the razor wire was cheerful and relaxed. The warriors didn't bother wearing their masks anymore, except when in direct contact with soldiers at the front line. They busied themselves by collecting firewood and digging new bunkers. Lasagna picked up a broom and swept the front steps of the warrior headquarters. Mark "Blackjack" Montour softly strummed an acoustic guitar at his bunker. Brenda Gabriel painted landscapes with oils on a canvas on the back lawn. Loran Thompson played for hours with the children, teaching them Mohawk words and phrases.

At night, however, the mood was completely different. The forest was pitch dark and every strange noise seemed a portent of danger. Helicopters hovered low in the sky while Indian songs and chants sounded from the Mohawk stereo. Armoured personnel carriers were parked along the highway and the gullies, their searchlights and .50-calibre guns pointed into the warrior encampment. The bright glare of those lights, which were turned on and off at unpredictable intervals, created bizarre silhouettes and nightmarish shadows in the woods.

With the departure of Spudwrench's daughter, six children remained at the Treatment Centre. The youngest was the eleven-month-old infant daughter of Dean Horne and Vicky Diabo; the oldest was Waneek Horn-Miller, the fourteen-year-old daughter of Kahn-Tineta Horn. Politicians often accused the warriors of using the children as a human shield, but the accusation rang false in the context of Mohawk culture. The Mohawks have always viewed their children as miniature adults who learn by observing and studying the behaviour of others, rather than by strict classroom teaching. They do not believe in protecting their children from reality, nor do they see childhood as a time of innocence and illusion.

"We don't hide anything from them," Kahn-Tineta Horn said. "We show them what life is all about. We always have our children with us. This is our school. This is how we teach them. They see life as it really is. In our society, they have as many rights as the adults."

The children themselves were determined to stay at the Treatment Centre, and they rejected the allegation that the warriors were using the children as hostages. "They're not hiding behind the kids," Waneek said. "The men are willing to give up their lives, and so are the women and me. Leaving here would be like saying I don't believe in the cause."

Waneek was a grade ten student at Glebe Collegiate Institute in Ottawa, and she had never lived on an Indian reserve until the summer of 1990. "I lived comfortably in the city," she said. "I lived like the white people. I was really a sheltered kid. I didn't identify with the Indian movement. I didn't know what was so darn important about it. But now I do. I think Canada isn't as great a place as people say it is."

At the beginning of the siege, Waneek and her four-year-old sister,

Ganyetahawi, were frightened by the noise of the military helicopters, but they soon became accustomed to it. By the second week, the helicopters were lulling them to sleep at night. "I know I could get killed here, but I don't really care," Waneek said. "My cousin was killed in a drunk-driving accident and it didn't mean anything. If I died here, it would mean something. It would be for a cause."

Waneek's mother, Kahn-Tineta Horn, was a fifty-year-old former fashion model and Mohawk activist from Kahnawake who was dubbed "the Indian princess" at the height of her fame in the 1960s. She was arrested several times for her role in Mohawk protests and demonstrations, including the takeover of the international bridge at Cornwall in 1968. But in the early 1970s she took a job at Indian Affairs and disappeared from the public stage.

Over the next two decades, she raised a family of five children. Then, in 1988, she went on a leave of absence from her government job to complete a master's degree in Canadian Studies at Carleton University. In the summer of 1990, she joined the Mohawks behind the barricades at Kahnawake and Kanesatake. She was supposed to return to work in the first week of September, but she telephoned the department and asked for an extension. Instead, the department fired her for failing to report to work.

On September 13, the Quebec government made another effort to persuade the warriors to surrender. Although the only formal negotiations were those conducted between the army and the warriors at the Treatment Centre, the governments of Quebec and Canada were maintaining contact with the warriors through intermediaries such as Joe Deom and Terry Doxtator, who were now operating from the Dorval Hilton. Through these unofficial channels, Quebec tested a possible deal. Public Security Minister Sam Elkas was still refusing to make any significant concessions, but he was willing to let the warriors retain a little dignity if they agreed to enter military custody. Elkas assumed the warriors were just protecting their public image by vowing never to surrender. He thought they wanted a way to save face. "Jesus, I wish we could get away from the word 'surrender,'" Elkas told Joe Norton at a lunch meeting.

Elkas suggested a simple deal: if the warriors agreed to put down their weapons, he would promise to prevent any media coverage of the

Mohawks entering military custody. "What we thought is we would throw the bloody media out completely, get rid of them," Elkas told Terry Doxtator in a telephone conversation on the afternoon of September 13. "Maybe in an evening or a night or early morning operation we could move in and ensure that they would get vans or something like that, no sign of surrender *per se*. Lay down the weapons, get into the vans and just take off to Farnham [military base]. This way ... nobody would be seen, nobody would be humiliated in any way ... The media would only find out the next morning that these people were gone."

At the end of the telephone conversation, Elkas admitted he didn't like the military involvement in the Mohawk crisis. "We don't want the army there, and I just feel this is a terrible thing to have around," Elkas told Doxtator. "We're in Canada, we're not in the Middle East here."

Doxtator promised to take the Quebec offer to the warriors at the Treatment Centre. Meanwhile, the warriors had prepared a slightly revised version of their previous peace proposal. But before the latest proposals could be exchanged, the negotiating atmosphere was poisoned by a new incident. The telephones at the Treatment Centre suddenly went completely dead, and the army announced it had terminated all phone connections to the building.

Only a fixed hotline between the army and the warriors was still intact. Every other telephone — except the cellular phones belonging to Bob Antone and the reporters — was now dead. An army spokesman described the measures as "another turn of the screw," designed to prevent the Mohawks from talking to anyone except the army. The military wanted to "encourage serious warrior negotiations" by eliminating all "distractions," the spokesman said.

If that was the intent, it had the opposite effect. The warriors immediately broke off negotiations and withdrew their latest proposal. They unplugged the hotline. If an army officer wanted to negotiate, he would have to approach the warriors at the razor wire and talk face-to-face, Bob Antone said. He suggested that the army was "trying to cut down our international support" by cutting their link to the rest of the world.

The next day, the Mohawks discovered that their water supply had been terminated. For almost a full day, there was no running water in the Mohawk encampment. The army denied responsibility, but the warriors were skeptical, remembering the colonel's veiled threat just two days earlier. Late in the afternoon, the water supply was restored, but in the evening, the electrical power at the Treatment Centre was interrupted twice with no official explanation.

Despite the tightening of the army's grip around the warriors, the news was still getting out. The European Parliament passed a series of resolutions to condemn Canada and Quebec for violating the agreement of August 12 on international observers and human rights. The vice-president of the Parliament, Wilfried Telkamper, wrote a letter to Brian Mulroney on September 14 to protest the human-rights violations. "The cut-off of the telephone lines is an unjustified attempt to turn away international attendance and to resolve this conflict without any witnesses," he wrote.

Meanwhile, the warriors had prepared a message for the army as a formal response to the Sam Elkas proposal. The message was written on a sheet of paper, wrapped around a rock, and thrown at the soldiers on the highway. It said, "No. No. No." And it was signed: "The People of the Pines."

By the evening of September 14, a number of the journalists' cellular phones were mysteriously failing to work. One by one, they began to shut down. Bob Antone's phone was also knocked out of service. Again there was no explanation, but everyone knew it was no accident.

During the day, Brigadier-General Armand Roy had sent another proposal across the razor wire to the warriors. It was identical to the army proposal of September 6, with one exception: native constables would be allowed to act as observers when the warriors laid down their weapons and entered military custody.

Bob Antone responded the following afternoon with a letter to Brigadier-General Roy. He said the Mohawks were pleased with the idea of allowing natives to observe the disengagement process, but he insisted that the "political concerns" of the Mohawks would also have to be addressed in any disengagement agreement. "You propose a resolution that belittles this crisis through its criminalization and yet ignores its reality," Antone wrote. He asked Roy to explain whether the army had a mandate to negotiate on behalf of the federal or provincial governments, and whether it had any authority to negotiate the political concerns of the warriors.

On the afternoon of September 15, the army's public relations specialists organized a tour for the journalists outside the Treatment Centre. They ordered the photographers and reporters to wear bullet-proof vests, as if there was some danger of random shooting by the Mohawks. The journalists were paraded through the army lines, across from the Mohawk encampment, but they were not permitted to speak to any of the reporters or warriors inside the razor wire. They stood mutely staring at the Mohawks as if they were animals in a zoo. Several of the journalists inside the razor wire, who were increasingly frustrated by the military restrictions, tossed canisters of camera film to the reporters across the highway. Soldiers scuffled with the journalists and seized some of the film.

By now, the journalists had discovered the reason for the mysterious failure of their cellular phones. The SQ had secretly gone to a justice of the peace to seek a court order authorizing them to terminate the phones. Without giving the media any opportunity to defend itself in court, the justice had granted the police request. After the police instructed the telephone companies to obey the court order, the phones began to go dead. Only a few remained active because the police had been unable to determine their telephone numbers. Those phones were the final remaining link between the journalists and the outside world.

To obtain the court order, the SQ had alleged that the cellular phones were "in the control of criminals." They failed to mention that almost all the phones were controlled by journalists, and they seemed to make no distinction between the warriors and the other people in the encampment.

The police alleged that the people inside the razor wire compound were "plotting daily and regularly with the aim of committing criminal acts ... which could put thousands of citizens in danger." They told the court that a woman at the Treatment Centre had phoned someone in British Columbia on August 28 and asked for bridges to be blown up. A bridge was set ablaze in Vancouver a few days after that telephone call, they said, and the Lions Gate Bridge was closed to traffic. The police allegation was false, however. No fire was reported on the Lions Gate Bridge, and the bridge had never been closed. A railway bridge in the interior of British Columbia was damaged in a fire on August 24, but that was four days before the alleged phone call from the Treatment Centre.

The court order was obtained in such secrecy that the media had great difficulty finding out which court had issued the warrant. Several days later, when a Quebec court finally released the warrant that authorized the termination of the cellular phones, three newspapers — the *Globe and Mail*, the *Montreal Gazette* and the *Ottawa Citizen* — went to court to challenge it. They called the warrant a violation of the Charter of Rights and Freedoms. University of Ottawa law professor and constitutional expert Joe Magnet said the police had no legal right to muzzle the media. The Canadian branch of the international writers group, PEN, criticized the government for failing to invoke any parliamentary debate or special legislation such as the Emergencies Act to authorize military censorship. The group produced a letter from a federal official on September 7 which had promised that the "right to information" of the press inside the razor wire would be guaranteed.

The Canadian Association of Journalists held a meeting with Brigadier-General Roy, demanding that the cellular phone service be restored, but he rejected the request. He did agree to permit a lawyer to visit the journalists to inform them of their rights — but the meeting was cancelled a day later. The army cited "security reasons" to justify the cancellation.

Late on the night of September 15, as the journalists were watching TV in the basement of the Treatment Centre, the room suddenly went pitch dark and the TV went dead. There was a frightening silence as everyone realized that all the electrical power had been knocked out. The warriors went on red alert, anticipating an army attack at any moment. The children were herded into a safe room in the basement, and the journalists were ordered to remain downstairs.

As the silence stretched on, there was nothing to do but wait for the expected attack. The journalists sat in the darkened basement, which was lit dimly by a flickering candle. Several days earlier, they had placed a large sign outside the basement to identify it as the press headquarters, but they had no idea whether they would really be safe there if a gunfight broke out.

Joe "Stonecarver" David wandered into the basement with a flashlight, sat on a couch, and thumbed through an anthology of English literature. After reading in silence for a while, he began to read aloud in a quiet voice. As the journalists listened in darkness, he read a poem by Wilfred Owen, the anti-war poet who had documented the horrors of World War I. It was a poem about a soldier who dies an agonizing death in a mustard-gas attack. The soldier was "guttering, choking, drowning" as his blood came "gargling from the froth-corrupted lungs." The poem ended with an ironic reminder of "the old lie" of the patriots. "*Dulce et decorum est pro patria mori*" — it is sweet and honourable to die for one's country.

The journalists listened silently. When the warrior had finished reading the poem, they said nothing.

The power was restored after about ninety minutes, and the tension eased. The army denied it was responsible for the blackout.

At about eleven o'clock the following night, an envelope was passed across the razor wire to the warriors. It was a letter from Lieutenant-General Kent Foster, the army commander, who was responding to Bob Antone's written questions. Foster said he had received assurances from the Quebec and Canadian governments that they would begin "without delay" to discuss the "longer-term issues" of the Mohawks as soon as the warriors laid down their weapons — but he added an ominous warning. The army would fulfill its orders to restore public security "with or without your consent," the letter said.

Meanwhile, on the outskirts of Montreal, the people of Kahnawake were becoming more frustrated. The army still controlled half the reserve, and it showed no signs of leaving. Finally the elected council of Kahnawake hired constitutional lawyer Morris Manning to launch a court challenge against the army's presence on the reserve. In his request for a court injunction on September 14, Manning argued that Ottawa had lost control of the military, despite its constitutional responsibility for the armed forces. "Canada's army has been commandeered by the Quebec government and they are acting as a police force for the Quebec government where there is no riot, no disturbance," Manning said.

During the previous two weeks, the army had been conducting a number of raids in Kahnawake to search for weapons, and on September 18 it decided to conduct another search. This time the target was Tekakwitha Island, a deserted island on the edge of the Mohawk territory, connected to the mainland by a short bridge. Dozens of soldiers and provincial police officers landed on the western end of the island by boat and helicopter. As they advanced slowly toward the bridge on the eastern end of the island, hundreds of Mohawks rushed to the bridge to confront them.

About thirty soldiers tried to protect the bridge, but they were facing an angry mob of three hundred men, women, and children from all over the Mohawk community. None of them carried guns, but they screamed and shouted at the soldiers to leave the Mohawk territory. When the soldiers put up razor wire to protect themselves, the Mohawks simply tore it down and threw rocks and attacked the troops with their fists. The soldiers fought back with rifle butts. They charged at the Mohawks and fired several volleys of tear gas grenades, forcing some of the Mohawks to jump into the river.

Grand Chief Joe Norton and the Mohawk Peacekeepers tried to calm the angry crowd, but emotions were running high. The Mohawks regrouped and attacked again. They grabbed one soldier, dragged him into the crowd, and punched and kicked him into semi-consciousness. When they started choking him with a binocular strap around his neck, some of the soldiers were afraid he would lose his life. Another soldier had his ear almost ripped off.

Military reinforcements were rushed to the island by helicopter until, in the end, 140 soldiers were fighting the Mohawks on the bridge. Many of them were administrative clerks and vehicle technicians who had been dispatched to the island to help with the search for weapons, never expecting to encounter a huge brawl. Others were young infantrymen, fresh from recruit school. "Our troops were not prepared for riot control," Lieutenant-Colonel Greg Mitchell said later. "They were getting hit, thinking they were not allowed to hit back. What they should have been doing was hitting back to avoid being hit again."

Clouds of tear gas were drifting over to the Kahnawake hospital, just a few hundred metres from the island, forcing the administration to move its patients into closed rooms. June Delisle, the sixty-two-year-old hospital administrator who had been confined to a wheelchair for ten years because of muscular dystrophy, was so infuriated by the army's behaviour that she insisted on confronting the troops herself. Some of the Mohawks tried to persuade her to stay in the hospital, but she refused to back down. She rolled down the road to the bridge in her wheelchair. The Mohawks opened a path for her, and she pushed herself up to an army officer standing on the island. She warned him that a hospital was only five hundred metres away.

In a desperate effort to disperse the crowd of angry Mohawks, a soldier raised his semi-automatic rifle and fired warning shots into the air. A fleet of eight military helicopters began to airlift the soldiers to safety. When the seven-hour confrontation finally ended, about twenty soldiers were injured, including two who suffered concussions. Among the Mohawks, about seventy-five needed medical treatment for cuts and bruises, broken bones, and exposure to tear gas. Children as young as five and elderly people as old as seventy-two were injured in the battle.

The soldiers seized forty-seven guns from the island, but most were hunting rifles and shotguns. Only three of the weapons were illegal in Canada.

On the evening of September 19, Bob Antone received a curt letter from Brigadier-General Roy. There was "nothing left to clarify" in the army's previous offers, the brigadier-general wrote. The mandate of the military "will not change," he said. "All discussions will now be limited to our military offer for disengagement ... There will be no discussion of Oka land claims by anyone until the warriors have disengaged and placed themselves in military custody."

Roy's blunt message was the final insult for the warriors. Already frustrated by the lack of progress in the negotiations with the army, they now gave up in disgust. Bob Antone called a late-night news conference for the handful of reporters inside the razor wire, where he released an open letter to the Canadian people. "We will not again speak with the military," the warriors said in the letter. They said they were willing to lay down their weapons and enter military trusteeship if their political issues were addressed, but they were unwilling to negotiate with soldiers "who are unaccountable to anyone." The political leaders of Canada and Quebec, the letter said, "have ignored their oaths of office by delegating political decision-making to the military."

While the warriors were locked in their stalemate with the military, John Ciaccia had secretly travelled to Toronto on September 16 to negotiate with a team of Iroquois Confederacy leaders, including Oren Lyons, Harvey Longboat, Curtis Nelson, and Allen Gabriel. Although the Quebec Cabinet was aware of this latest initiative, Ciaccia made it clear that he had no official mandate from the province — he was simply making a personal effort to find a solution. There was no guarantee that he could persuade Quebec to approve any agreement. The Confederacy negotiating team was equally uncertain of its status. Many of the Confederacy leaders were not Mohawks; they were Senecas, Cayugas, and Onondagas who had frequently denounced the warriors in the past and therefore had little credibility among the warriors.

At 5:30 in the afternoon of September 16, the Confederacy negotiators had reached a tentative agreement with Ciaccia. The deal included a number of concessions by the minister, including a promise that Quebec would appoint a special independent prosecutor to decide whether to lay criminal charges against the warriors. The prosecutor, who would be acceptable to both sides, would ensure that all criminal charges and trials were fair.

Over the next four days, Allen Gabriel tried to bring the tentative agreement to the Treatment Centre for the warriors to approve, but the army refused to allow him to enter the warrior encampment. At the same time, the hardliners in the Quebec Cabinet were unwilling to support Ciaccia's tentative agreement. As a last resort, the Confederacy decided to hold a news conference in Toronto on the night of September 20 to release the tentative deal. They were hoping to put pressure on Quebec to accept the agreement, but the move was unsuccessful — the Quebec government flatly rejected Ciaccia's proposal.

News of the secret negotiations sparked an angry reaction among the besieged warriors at the Treatment Centre, who had known nothing about the tentative agreement. At midnight on September 20, Bob Antone phoned Confederacy lawyer Paul Williams to complain that the agreement had been negotiated without the knowledge or consent of the warriors. Williams said the agreement was designed to satisfy the public demands of the warriors, and he told Antone that the army had prevented the Confederacy from sending the deal to the warriors. But the rift between the warriors and the Confederacy continued to grow.

Earlier in the evening, Lieutenant-General Foster held a news conference to announce that his troops would gradually withdraw and be replaced by the Quebec police. "The army's mandate is nearing completion," he said. Despite the violence on Tekakwitha Island earlier in the week, Foster vowed that the army would complete its searches for weapons in Kanesatake and Kahnawake. It was a promise the army never carried out. The senior army commanders were reluctant to keep brawling with the Mohawks, and they allowed hundreds of weapons to remain in Kahnawake.

Meanwhile, the warriors had set a new record for armed confrontations in North America. September 20 was the seventy-second day of the crisis, and it topped the seventy-one-day armed standoff between American Indians and FBI agents at Wounded Knee, South Dakota, in 1973. The warriors were certainly in no danger of running out of food. They had stockpiles in the large kitchen of the Treatment Centre, and the army was permitting shipments to enter the warrior encampment from the Mohawk food bank at the Kanesatake community centre. But the food was carefully checked and rationed by soldiers who cut open the tins of food and stabbed the oranges with knives and bayonets to ensure that nothing was smuggled into the Treatment Centre. The army refused to permit anything else to cross the razor wire — not even the school textbooks that Waneek Horn-Miller had requested. The warriors responded by stealing a supply of warm clothing and appliances from neighbouring houses.

The besieged Mohawks were becoming desperate for cigarettes, which were strictly banned by the army. There was some irony in this situation. Many of the Mohawks had been smuggling truckloads of cigarettes in Akwesasne and Kahnawake for years, but now they couldn't get a single pack. They became so anxious that they began to roll their own homemade cedar-bark smokes, which they admitted were a poor substitute.

When the army learned of the cigarette shortage, one colonel sent a pack of Camels across the razor wire in a sealed envelope to Bob Antone. But the Oneida negotiator would not be tempted; he sent the envelope back to the soldiers with a message scrawled on it: "Bribes are not accepted."

These brief moments of defiance could not conceal the deepening sense of gloom in the warrior encampment. "The psychological games have taken their toll," Bob Antone admitted to reporters. "The feeling of isolation is closing in all the time."

As the siege dragged on, nerves were beginning to frazzle again. To taunt the warriors, the soldiers put a grinning Hallowe'en pumpkin on top of the sandbags of one of their observation posts. The warriors were fed up. When a military helicopter hovered low over the Treatment Centre in the middle of the night, Lasagna fired a flare gun in the direction of the chopper.

On September 23, the mood brightened a little. It was the first Sunday of autumn, and the warriors put down their guns temporarily to attend the wedding of Dennis "Psycho" Nicholas and his fiancée, Cathy Sky. About twenty-five warriors and Mohawk women gathered in the afternoon sunshine behind the Treatment Centre for the traditional Mohawk ceremony. The two faithkeepers, Loran Thompson and Bruce Elijah, led the ceremony in Mohawk and English.

Psycho and Cathy Sky had known each other for several years, but their romance had blossomed behind the barricades earlier in the summer and they decided they could not postpone the ceremony any longer. "We don't really know how much longer we're going to live," Psycho said.

Two of the senior warriors, Bill Sears and Harold Oakes, sat beside two clan mothers as substitutes for the parents of the bride and groom. As a military helicopter roared overhead and soldiers tried to figure out the meaning of this puzzling ceremony, Bruce Elijah burned sweetgrass and passed around a pipe for everyone to share. The Mohawks used a deer skin and an eagle feather to gently clean the eyes and ears of the warrior and his fiancée. It was a symbolic gesture, borrowed from the Mohawk condolence ceremony, intended to clear the vision and hearing of the couple so they understood the importance of their decision. They sipped water to clear their throats and allow them to express their feelings. Then the warrior gave a basket of cornbread to his fiancée to symbolize the food he would provide for her. She gave him a basket of cloth and leather to show her willingness to care for him.

When the ceremony was over, Bob Antone borrowed a journalist's phone and walked to a spot near the front line to make a call. It was the last place in the encampment where the phones still worked sporadically. For several days, the army and the Quebec police had been jamming the airwaves to disrupt the cellular phones, and now the tiny "window" near the front line was the last fragile lifeline between the warrior encampment and the outside world. Bob Antone phoned his negotiating team, led by Terry Doxtator, Joe Deom, and Seneca activist Mike Myers, who had now found temporary quarters in a church in the Montreal suburb of Pointe Claire. The negotiators and Antone agreed that the warriors would have to make a final decision within the next forty-eight hours. They had exhausted almost every possible avenue, and they had no bargaining power left. The negotiators were willing to make one last attempt to persuade Quebec to reach an agreement. They would lower their demands to the absolute minimum — but they realized there was little possibility of swaying the hardliners in the Quebec Cabinet.

Another crucial factor was about to come into play as well — the scheduled opening of Parliament the following day in Ottawa, which would focus political attention on the Mohawks. The federal government would likely be forced to make promises to improve the aboriginal situation in Canada. If there was any positive signal from the government while the Mohawks were still in their encampment, they might be able to claim a political victory.

Antone calculated that the warriors would remain in the national spotlight for most of the first week. By the end of the week, however, he expected that the Mohawks would be overshadowed by other political issues such as the GST controversy and the Persian Gulf crisis. He reached an agreement with the Pointe Claire negotiators: if some of the warriors were willing to leave, Antone would take them out. And if there were any holdouts who refused to leave, they could remain behind in the encampment.

The warriors held a meeting on the night of September 23 and agreed with Antone's idea of a forty-eight-hour deadline for a final decision. But several of the most militant warriors — including Lasagna and Noriega — missed the meeting because they were on the night shift. When they discovered later that the Mohawks were considering ending the siege, they became immediately suspicious of Antone's role in the decision, and the first serious rift among the warriors was created.

True to Antone's prediction, Liberal and New Democrat MPs started the new session of Parliament on September 24 by blasting the federal government for its handling of the Oka crisis. They accused the government of abdicating its responsibility for aboriginal people by leaving it to the army to settle the conflict.

Inside the razor wire, the warriors held long meetings to discuss their plans. Some of the Mohawks privately confided that the siege might be over within the next two or three days. They realized there was little to be gained by prolonging the standoff. Their negotiating team in Pointe Claire was preparing a last-ditch offer to settle the crisis, but most of the warriors were ready to lay down their weapons even if the offer was rejected.

Lasagna and Noriega, however, were angered by the idea of laying down their arms. Feeling pressured by the forty-eight-hour deadline, they were beginning to distrust Bob Antone. After accusing him of selling out, the two militant warriors marched out of the Treatment Centre and demanded to use a reporter's cellular phone. They wanted to phone the Pointe Claire office to find out what was going on. But when they got the reporter's phone, they couldn't figure out how to use it.

Shortly before 9:00 p.m. on September 24, Stanley Cohen emerged from the Treatment Centre and walked quickly down the dirt path to the razor wire barrier at the front. His bags were packed and he was ready to leave. His usual air of supreme confidence had vanished; he seemed nervous and shaken. Just before he walked into the custody of the soldiers, Cohen claimed that he was leaving to help with negotiations on the outside. But that was not quite the truth. After two months as an influential figure at the centre of the armed standoff, the radical lawyer from New York City had finally been evicted by the Mohawks.

When he first realized that the warriors were thinking about putting down their weapons, Cohen had reacted cynically, questioning and challenging some of the warriors — especially the younger and more aggressive ones, who were susceptible to his pressure. Although he never stated it directly, he clearly implied that the warriors should stay to the bitter end.

At that point, Bob Antone had confronted Cohen, accusing him of planting doubts in the minds of the warriors and preventing them from reaching a consensus. He couldn't figure out Cohen's motives. "Either you don't want this to end, or you're crazy," Antone told Cohen in a brief shouting match.

When Cohen refused to listen to the Oneida chief, Antone asked for a decision from the Mohawk women, including the clan mothers, who were the final arbiters of many of the key decisions at the warrior encampment. They ordered Cohen to leave.

By this point, some of the Mohawk women were beginning to suspect that Cohen might be a government spy who was trying to sabotage any agreement. It was an improbable allegation and almost certainly untrue, but the women were convinced of it. His abrupt eviction from the warrior encampment, followed by the accusation of spying, made for an undignified ending to Stanley Cohen's summer.

Later that night, the tensions among the warriors became increasingly obvious. Harold Oakes confronted Lasagna and Noriega over the cellular phone incident, but they reacted furiously. A few minutes later, they warned the journalists that they would throw the cellular phones in the river if they found Antone using one again.

At about 10:00 p.m., Oakes and Antone approached the journalists at their campfire to plead for permission to use a phone. They were desperately trying to contact their Pointe Claire office. "Things are at a critical stage," Oakes said. But the journalists, recalling the threats from Lasagna and Noriega, refused to lend their phones.

The warriors continued their meetings long into the night, arguing and debating the issue until dawn. Most of the Mohawks were now in favour of ending the standoff. Their negotiating prospects were bleak, they were isolated and powerless, and their living conditions were increasingly stressful. The lack of cigarettes had left some of them irritable and frustrated. Tempers were flaring and arguments were breaking out. The psychological warfare and the constant noise of military helicopters had worn down their resistance. Now they just wanted to get the whole thing over.

The warriors also realized they were losing their spot on the national stage. Two of the twelve remaining journalists had left the Treatment Centre in the previous two days and several others were on the verge of leaving. Across the country, public sympathy was ebbing away. The Mohawks could imagine themselves alone at the Treatment Centre with no negotiators and no witnesses. "That would be signing our death warrants," said one of the Mohawks.

On the afternoon of September 25, the negotiators at Pointe Claire called a news conference to announce their final proposal. Terry Doxtator described the offer as a three-step process of disengagement, but it boiled down to a simple deal: the warriors would lay down their guns and enter military custody if Quebec agreed to appoint an independent prosecutor to review the criminal charges against them.

The warriors' demands had been greatly weakened. The simple request for an independent prosecutor was a modest measure that several provinces had approved in controversial political cases in the past. The Mohawks were willing to postpone all negotiations on long-term issues, including sovereignty and land rights, until after the warriors had surrendered their weapons. For months, the federal and provincial politicians had insisted that these deeper issues could not be discussed until the arms were laid down. Now the warriors had decided to call their bluff.

Quebec reacted coldly to the latest proposal. Despite the precedents, Justice Minister Gil Remillard rejected the idea of an independent prosecutor. "One of our fundamental principles of law is that the Attorney-General decides who will be charged," he declared. It was increasingly obvious that Quebec would never agree to a negotiated solution. The negotiating team at Pointe Claire said the Mohawks would make no further proposals.

Inside the razor wire, most of the warriors had already decided to leave. "We've done what we came here to do," said Tom Paul, the Micmac warrior. "There's nothing else we can do now. I'm sure my people are proud of what we did here."

Richard Two Axe, the grandfather from Kahnawake, echoed the same sentiment. "It's come as far as it can go," he said. "What good is it to stay? That's it. Case closed."

Only a handful of warriors were still defiant. Led by Lasagna and Noriega, they were vowing to fight to the death. "I'm staying," Lasagna told a reporter. "We're not going to walk out of here and surrender to the army or the police. We're not criminals. We've never surrendered before, and we ain't going to do that now. We're going to live free or we're going to die."

Other warriors kept trying to persuade Lasagna and Noriega to accept the majority's decision. Stonecarver was worried that the handful of militants would destroy the Mohawk tradition of decision making by consensus. "I know the danger of being branded a fanatic," he said. "If five people stay, they could easily be discredited. It would be pointless to stay. If anybody decided to stay, it would be suicidal."

For most of the warriors, the final decision was painful. There was still no guarantee that the golf course lands would be transferred to the Mohawks, even though the property was now in the federal government's hands. And there was no guarantee of personal safety for the warriors. "We could just disappear into the court system and the jails for the next couple of years," said Stonecarver. "That's my biggest fear. Things will be a lot worse in some ways. There will be a strong police presence in the area, and it will make things very tense for a long time." His predictions were later proven to be entirely accurate.

Despite the risks, however, most of the warriors were prepared to lay down their weapons. The worsening internal conflicts were the final straw. As tensions mounted, Lasagna and Noriega were clashing with other warriors. "We're beginning to eat ourselves," Stonecarver admitted. "It seems like we're turning against ourselves now. It's like an animal that's beginning to gnaw on its own stomach because it's so hungry."

At about 8:45 p.m. on September 25, Bob Antone held a news conference for the journalists at the warrior headquarters. "We are planning on disengagement this week," he announced. He predicted that the siege would end within two or three days and that most of the warriors would unconditionally lay down their weapons and enter military custody.

The Oneida chief insisted that the disengagement would not be a surrender. The warriors expected the federal and provincial governments to fulfill their promise to negotiate long-term Mohawk issues after the disengagement. "The Canadian government has said it would provide a forum and serious discussions if there was a laying down of arms," said Antone. "We will do that without any guarantees. We will take the governments of Canada and Quebec at their word."

The next day, September 26, was the day of decision. In the morning, the Mohawks met in their clans to discuss a list of options. Should they stay or go? If they agreed to put down their weapons, when should they do it? Should they wait another day or two? And should they voluntarily go into military custody, or should they fight to escape?

Almost all the warriors were now prepared to put down their weapons. Their situation was rapidly deteriorating. They believed they had accomplished as much as they could: they had helped unite aboriginal people across the country; they had gained a promise of support from the European Parliament; and the House of Commons had agreed to an emergency debate on the Mohawk situation. A day earlier, Prime Minister Brian Mulroney had made a major speech on aboriginal issues in the House of Commons, promising to introduce a new aboriginal agenda for the country, including a faster pace of settlement for Indian land claims. Even if his promises were largely rhetorical, he had finally been forced to make aboriginal issues a higher priority. The warriors felt they had pushed as far as they could.

A few of the warriors, led by Lasagna and Noriega, were still in favour of continuing the siege. The clan mothers tried to persuade them to accept the consensus. "You're not going to prove anything by lying here in a pool of blood," Lorraine Montour told Lasagna.

For most of the warriors, the only question was when to leave. Some wanted to leave at noon the next day. Others wanted to remain at the encampment until the following Monday to avoid the danger of being kept in police custody over the weekend, which would increase the risk of beatings.

The clan meetings continued for several hours. Meanwhile, the Mohawks had devised a system of secret communications to bypass the cellular phones. The day before, they had been told to listen for a disguised message on the Kanesatake radio station at one o'clock in the afternoon. The message, originating from the Pointe Claire negotiating team, was relayed to Kanesatake and broadcast in cryptic Mohawk phrases on the local radio station at the appointed hour. Several of the Mohawks listened intently, translated it into English, and took it back to the warriors in their meetings.

The message began by congratulating the warriors for holding out as long as they had, praising them for their discipline and strength, and asserting that the warriors had accomplished as much as they possibly could without the loss of any lives. Now it was time to move to a different phase of the battle. They were officially relieved of their military duties. "Come home," the message said.

By about 3:30 p.m., the clan meetings had ended and each of the clans appointed a spokesman who reported to a general meeting. The consensus was clear: they were ready to leave. The only question now was the timing.

By now, the journalists had agreed to let the Mohawks borrow their cellular phones again. Some of the warriors called the chiefs and clan mothers of their home communities to confirm the decision to leave. Mad Jap phoned Francis Boots, the war chief at Akwesasne, and Boots authorized the Akwesasne warriors to leave. "Our mission is accomplished," Mad Jap said.

"It's time to carry our fight into the political arena," said Harold Oakes. "We've realized we are not getting anywhere by staying here."

At the front line, the soldiers realized the siege was coming to an end. They huddled with senior army officers, finalizing their plans for taking the warriors into custody. Dozens of Quebec police officers had joined the troops, and police cruisers were visible near the army lines. The police were anxious to get their hands on key warriors like Lasagna. They weren't willing to let their quarry escape into military custody.

When the warriors saw the provincial police officers, they knew they could not afford to wait any longer. If they wanted the option of military protection, they had to leave immediately. At about 4:00 p.m., the Mohawks discarded the option of waiting until Monday. They decided that they should leave the encampment as soon as possible.

A few minutes later, the warriors ordered the reporters to leave the Treatment Centre and walk to the front line. Then they started a bonfire behind the Treatment Centre and began burning everything that might be incriminating, including most of their internal documents and papers. Boxes of ammunition and handguns were tossed into the septic tank. The warriors dismantled their AK-47s and threw them hastily into the bonfire. Some of the guns were still filled with bullets, which exploded in the fire as the warriors ducked for cover.

One final question remained: should the Mohawks obediently enter military custody or should they resist? The warriors decided they had a right to walk home freely. "We're not surrendering or giving up," said Brad Larocque. "We'll walk out that gate and they'll have to come and get us."

Back at Pointe Claire, the negotiators had phoned an army officer to co-ordinate the disengagement and the army had agreed to allow several people to enter the Treatment Centre to monitor the process. Among them would be a lawyer, a church official, a representative from the Pointe Claire negotiating team, and an Iroquois spiritual leader who would collect the masks and pipes and other spiritual objects.

By 5:00 p.m., dozens of Mohawks were converging on Oka. Loran Thompson had secretly called a Mohawk friend in Kanesatake and asked her to arrange for assistance in Oka in case the warriors got past the soldiers.

Thick clouds of black smoke were drifting up from the bonfire behind the Treatment Centre. Military helicopters hovered low overhead, trying to figure out what was going on. The warriors shook their fists and waved their flags defiantly at the choppers.

Some of the last remaining holdouts were now reluctantly agreeing to put down their weapons. "I don't feel too goddamn good about giving up," said Noriega. "I'll go with the majority. If the majority want to go, I'll go."

But one last warrior was still unwilling to leave. Lasagna walked through the woods, near his bunker, still carrying his rifle. He was the only warrior who had not yet destroyed his weapon. As he paced through the forest, he brooded silently. No one knew what he would do.

At 5:34 p.m., Harold Oakes and Hunter Montour took down the warrior flag from a makeshift flagpole at the front line. They returned to the bonfire, where the warriors were gathering to mark the end of the siege. Almost everyone, including the women and children, had put on camouflage clothing. For seventy-eight days, the camouflage gear had been the warrior uniform. Now they donned the uniform again to symbolize their belief that the warriors were an army of defence for the Mohawks and their land.

At 5:45, Bob Antone called a senior army officer and informed him that the warriors were in the process of disengaging. But when he gave a list of the people who had been approved as observers for the disengagement, the officer said he knew nothing about it. He said he would check into it and call back in fifteen minutes.

At 5:52, the warriors removed their hats and stood before the sacred fire as Loran Thompson led them in a final tobacco-burning ceremony. Ten minutes later, when the ceremony was over, the warriors looked up and realized that Lasagna had joined them. His gun was gone. The warriors burst into spontaneous applause and came over to hug him. Tears rolled down Lasagna's face.

Then the Mohawks began yelling as they steeled their nerves for the walkout. Tom Paul was carrying the medicine bundle and eagle feather that had hung by the sacred fire for several weeks. Mad Jap ordered the younger warriors to make a final check of the bunkers to ensure that any incriminating evidence was gone. By 6:20, the warriors were ready to go. A few started down the path to the front line, but they were called back. There was a last-minute hitch.

A few minutes earlier, the army officer had phoned Bob Antone, denying any knowledge of the agreement to allow observers to enter. No one would be allowed into the encampment. The officer said the warriors had to walk out the front entrance with their hands up, walk quietly across the highway, and enter the buses that the military had arranged for them.

Antone was shocked. He argued for a while, but the officer was adamant. The church leaders who had already arrived at the barricades were informed that the army had unilaterally cancelled the agreement.

Antone grabbed the cellular phone and called Terry Doxtator, Joe Deom, and Mike Myers, who were driving from Pointe Claire towards Oka. The agreement had been cancelled, Antone told them, but the warriors were going to come out and head home anyway. They told him to hang on for twenty minutes to give them enough time to reach Oka. Antone checked his watch. It was 6:20 p.m.

Earlier in the day, Loran Thompson had urged the warriors to try an alternative route out of the encampment. Instead of leaving obediently by the front entrance, he wanted them to exit through the woods in the northeastern corner of the encampment. This would put them closer to the town of Oka, closer to the outside television cameras, and closer to freedom. For a while, Thompson thought his idea had been rejected. But later in the afternoon, a few of the warriors studied the situation from the front gate and realized that Thompson's idea just might work.

The warriors felt they had committed no crimes, had done nothing wrong, and had a perfect right to return home. Their plan was simple: they would exit in the corner, keep moving in the direction of Oka, and resist the army as long as they could. It would signal to the world that they were not surrendering.

The warriors knew they were vastly outnumbered by the four hundred soldiers who surrounded them. No one thought they had any realistic chance of breaking through the military lines. But the symbolism of the gesture was important to them. "We are leaving here with heads held high, with pride and dignity in having defended the land," the warriors said in an official statement as they prepared to walk out. "Never again will the governments of Quebec and Canada be able to treat the Indian people as a mere thorn in the side."

At 6:50 p.m., the Mohawks began marching down the path toward the front line — thirty men, sixteen women, and six children. They were singing a traditional Mohawk song and carrying the flags of the Iroquois Confederacy and the Warrior Society. Several of them were cradling the false faces and the other spiritual objects.

Halfway down the path, the Mohawks suddenly veered off into the woods, heading for the northeastern corner. As they reached the razor wire, a series of trip-flares went off, casting the warriors in a cloud of smoke and burning sparks, but they kept going.

Some of the warriors were carrying stretcher boards from the Treatment Centre, and now they threw the boards onto the razor wire. In a matter of seconds, they had clambered over the boards and across the wire. Caught by surprise, the soldiers didn't know what to do. Only a few soldiers were anywhere near the warriors as they walked onto the highway. They ordered the Mohawks to stop, but the warriors pushed past and kept going. The scene erupted into chaos. Soldiers were kicked and pushed to the ground as the warriors forged ahead. Major Alain Tremblay, the nemesis of the warriors for the past six weeks, rushed forward to try to stop the Mohawks, but he was knocked to the ground.

Loran Thompson and Vicky Diabo, carrying her infant daughter, were among the first to cross the razor wire. They cut through the front yard of an adjacent house and ran down the hill toward Oka. Behind them was Noriega, who strode purposefully down the highway in the same direction. Cathy Sky walked quickly beside Noriega.

In the confusion, the four Mohawks escaped from the soldiers and

reached the town. Journalists rushing up the hill from Oka were astonished to meet Loran Thompson walking casually down the road.
"What are you doing?" they asked. "We're going home," he said,
smiling broadly.

Inside the town, the four Mohawks were mobbed by their supporters. Several SQ officers raced toward Noriega and tried to grab him,
but a group of Kanesatake Mohawks rescued him and spirited him
away. The police grabbed Cathy Sky too, but she wriggled out of their
grip, crawled past a police officer, and escaped.

Wearing camouflage clothing and a hat with a feather in it, Noriega was an obvious target for the TV cameras as he roamed around the
town. A few minutes later, a gang of police officers leaped on Noriega and hurled him into a cruiser. Mohawk women and children fought
viciously with the soldiers and SQ officers in Oka as the police hustled
Noriega away.

Loran Thompson, meanwhile, had melted into the crowd. As a
faithkeeper, he was one of the few Mohawks who never wore camouflage gear. Dressed in an ordinary blue shirt and jeans, he was ignored
by the police. He jumped into the car of a Mohawk friend and disappeared.

Back on the highway at the top of the hill, scores of soldiers were
struggling to control the rest of the Mohawks. "Put them on the
ground," an officer screamed at his troops. As many as four or five
soldiers jumped on a single warrior, pinning the Mohawks down. Other warriors rushed to their rescue, trying to peel the soldiers off.

By now, dusk was falling and helicopters with powerful searchlights
were hovering overhead. The soldiers fixed their bayonets and pointed
their guns at the Mohawks. Some wrestled with the warriors, their
helmets and guns clattering to the ground. Everyone was yelling and
screaming. Even the Mohawk women were scrapping with the soldiers. Lorraine Montour was enraged when she saw three soldiers
fighting with her youngest son, Hunter. "You leave my son alone," she
shouted. Moments later, she herself had been knocked down by a soldier.

"Get off my mother," Hunter Montour screamed. He jumped on
the soldier but was immediately tackled by four other soldiers with
such force that his head smashed against the pavement. He was hauled

to his feet and his hands were cuffed behind his back. He stood swaying, feeling disoriented and faint.

Several soldiers clubbed the Mohawks with their rifle butts. A dozen skirmishes had broken out. Kahentiiosta was pinned down by several soldiers, and one of her young sons was crying. Laura Norton's fingers were bleeding from scuffles with the soldiers. Loran Thompson's brother, a warrior known as Wizard, held grimly onto a false face as he was dragged away. Blackjack used a Tae Kwon Do back-kick to knock a soldier off a warrior. Dean Horne was desperately searching for his infant daughter. "Where the hell is my baby?" he shouted as the soldiers pushed him back.

Mad Jap was lying in the ditch with two soldiers on him. There were tears in his eyes. "Help me," he begged a reporter. Another group of soldiers grabbed Lasagna and hustled him away. They immediately turned him over to the Quebec police, who had identified Lasagna as their most wanted warrior.

Brad Larocque's glasses were knocked to the ground as he was handcuffed. Larocque turned to a black soldier nearby and asked him to pick up the glasses. The soldier made no move. "Come on," Larocque said. "You must have been fighting all your life too. Haven't you ever stood up for something you believed in before?" The black soldier said nothing, but he picked up the glasses and carefully put them on Larocque's face.

The soldiers grabbed another young warrior, Donald "Babe" Hemlock, and threw him to the ground, knocking out the hearing aid he had worn ever since an ironworking accident. Hemlock asked them to retrieve the hearing aid, but instead a soldier crushed it under his boot.

Waneek Horn-Miller was clutching her four-year-old sister, Ganyetahawi, as they rushed down the highway toward Oka. They were quickly intercepted by several soldiers. "I'm walking home," Waneek kept telling the soldiers. She tried to push past them, but one of the soldiers jabbed at her with his gun. She felt a stinging pain in her chest, and she began screaming as the soldiers dragged her backwards. Her little sister was crying as she held tightly onto Waneek's leg. Waneek fell to the ground, but the soldiers kept pulling her back.

Finally, a senior officer ordered the soldiers to form a line across the highway. They advanced slowly toward the Mohawks, surrounding them and forcing them back into a small enclosed space. One of the soldiers smiled at Waneek. Losing control of herself, she kicked and punched the soldiers until Richard Two Axe pulled her off and tried to calm her down.

A few minutes later, Waneek noticed that her shirt was covered in blood. Only then did she realize that she had been stabbed with a bayonet. Seventeen hours would pass before she was treated by a doctor.

As chaos reigned around him, Stonecarver stood silently with a bewildered expression on his face. He felt an impulse to help his fellow warriors, but he was carrying one of the spiritual masks, and he felt obliged to shield it from the violence. The mask, he believed, had helped to protect the Mohawks from death. Soldiers tried to take the mask away from him, but he refused to give it up.

By about 7:10 p.m., the soldiers had gained control of the situation. Corralled in a small section of the highway, the warriors were forced to their knees and shackled with plastic handcuffs. Some of the warriors were too strong for the handcuffs. With a powerful flick of their wrists, they broke the shackles, forcing the soldiers to put several sets of plastic handcuffs on each warrior.

Two military buses were backed into position, and the Mohawks were loaded on board. At 7:50, the buses drove slowly away. More than a dozen provincial police cruisers escorted the vehicles on the long drive to the Farnham military base.

As the convoy rolled through Kanesatake, Ann Cross stood on her front porch and cheered the warriors. She looked for her son, Lasagna, as the buses drove past. There was no sign of him. Lasagna had already disappeared into the custody of the police.

Just before the warriors were loaded onto the military buses, the soldiers had ripped away their flags. But the Mohawks refused to concede defeat. They whooped and yelled as they broke free from the plastic handcuffs. Reaching through the windows of the buses, they clenched their fists and punched the air. Somehow one of them had managed to smuggle a warrior flag onto the bus. In a final gesture of defiance, the flag was unfurled and the convoy headed for Farnham under the insignia of the Mohawk Warrior Society.

Epilogue

Barely two hours after the end of the siege, Lasagna was in handcuffs at the SQ headquarters on Parthenais Street in Montreal. The police forced him to kneel in a corner of a room. "We're going to have a party with you," they told him. Then the beating began.

"Who killed Lemay?" the police kept asking Lasagna as they kicked and punched him. They aimed at his head and ears to make sure the marks wouldn't be visible, but the warrior turned his head so the blows would hit him in the face, where the bruises would show.

For hours, the beating continued. Lasagna spat blood at the police. "You might as well kill me now," he told them. "I'm not going to tell you anything."

The police played tape recordings of telephone conversations involving Lasagna and other warriors at the Treatment Centre. Every time they heard the threats he had made against the SQ, they hit him harder. Early the next morning, he pretended he couldn't breathe, and the SQ brought in a paramedic to look at him. They took him to a hospital for a brief examination. Then they brought him back to Parthenais, and the interrogation continued. By daybreak, his face was badly bruised and swollen, his right cheek was black and blue, and his right eye was almost closed by a large bruise over the eye.

Three journalists who had witnessed the walkout by the warriors at the Treatment Centre were handcuffed and questioned for hours by the police that same night. One was punched and kicked.

Five of the warriors, including Lasagna and Noriega and the younger warriors who were legally regarded as minors, were kept in police custody. The other warriors, along with the Mohawk women and children, were taken to the Farnham military base, where they were kept in the bus for most of the night. At about 4:00 a.m., the police entered the military base and began questioning the warriors.

Mark "Blackjack" Montour was singled out for special treatment. Forcing him to kneel with his nose to the wall, the soldiers kicked his feet apart, grinding his knees into the cement and his head into the wall. Then they grabbed him by the hair and yanked his head back. Behind him, other soldiers clicked the triggers of their guns.

Over and over again, the police asked the warriors about the death of Corporal Lemay. They demanded to know the whereabouts of "the warrior general, Loran Thompson." But the warriors refused to say anything.

Outside the gates of the military base, lawyers for the Mohawks spent hours arguing for permission to see their clients. They were eventually allowed to enter, but the army refused to let them be present at the interrogations. At 4:00 a.m, the army finally released the Mohawk children into the custody of their relatives. Later in the day, Bob Antone and Bruce Elijah were set free.

The chaotic end to the military siege at the Treatment Centre sparked a violent reaction in Kahnawake. Shortly after the warriors were carted away on the military bus, about two hundred Kahnawake Mohawks approached an army barricade on Highway 207 and a similar number of Mohawks advanced toward the military position on Highway 138. They were enraged that the soldiers continued to control half of their reserve. "We just want the army out of here," one Mohawk said. "They have no business here any longer."

Many of the Mohawks were brandishing baseball bats, pickhandles, lead pipes, and rocks. They carried plastic shields and gas masks to protect themselves against tear gas. The Mohawks attacked the army barricades, and the soldiers responded with volleys of tear gas, but the Mohawks kept advancing, bombarding the soldiers with rocks. One soldier was knocked to the ground, and fistfights broke out as the other soldiers rescued him.

The confrontation finally ended after the soldiers fixed their bayonets and fired warning shots into the air. One soldier was taken to hospital with head injuries, and several Mohawks needed medical treatment for injuries inflicted by the ricochet of tear gas grenades.

Over the next few days, the Mohawks began to fade from the public eye. Back at Kanesatake, the army searched the Treatment Centre and opened up Highway 344 to normal traffic. Meanwhile, the SQ began to lay criminal charges against the Mohawks who had been at the Treatment Centre. All of the Mohawk women were released from military custody after they were charged with offences such as rioting and obstruction of justice. But the warriors remained at Farnham, where they described themselves as "political prisoners."

Loran Thompson, who had disappeared in the confusion at Oka when the siege ended, had quietly slipped back to his home in Akwesasne. As the authorities hunted for him, he spent a peaceful weekend with his family and his newborn grandchild. A few days later, Thompson reported to the RCMP to fulfill the terms of his release on a previous charge of cigarette smuggling. The police arrested him and charged him with assaulting a peace officer.

Most of the warriors were released from military custody on October 5 after a series of criminal charges were laid against them. That night, they were given a hero's welcome at Kahnawake. Hundreds of Mohawks crowded into a village hall to cheer the warriors in a welcoming party that continued until the early hours of the morning.

After seventy-eight days in the extreme isolation of an armed standoff, freedom was a strange experience for the warriors. They tried to adjust to the routine of the outside world, but many of the warriors felt empty and depressed. Some of them suppressed their emotional turmoil by throwing themselves into a new series of battles in the courtroom and the political arena. The warriors saw their criminal trials as an opportunity to argue their case for Mohawk sovereignty. They prepared a long list of legal arguments, including a reference to the Two Row Wampum treaties of the seventeenth century. Under the terms of those treaties, the Mohawks were sovereign people who had jurisdiction over criminal matters in their own territory. The warriors believe the principles of the early treaties are still valid today.

Dennis "Psycho" Nicholas was the first of the warriors to be convicted. He was anxious to put the past behind him and get on with his new life with Cathy Sky. Instead of letting his case drag on indefinitely, he pleaded guilty in early January 1991 to three charges of possessing a gun for dangerous purposes, one charge of participating in a riot, one charge of obstructing police and soldiers, and one charge of possession of stolen property (the trailer that had been hauled to the barricades in Kanesatake). He was given a jail sentence of two years less a day.

In total, about 150 Mohawks were charged in connection with the Oka crisis. The key targets were Lasagna and Noriega, who were hit with dozens of criminal charges. For most of the winter, judges refused to give them bail. Lasagna remained defiant. A five-year sentence was offered in a plea-bargaining arrangement, but he rejected the offer. He stayed in jail, where he was elected vice-president of the prisoners in his wing. After nearly six months behind bars, the two warriors were finally released on $50,000 bail each.

Among the non-Mohawks, fifteen people were charged with throwing stones at the convoy of children and elderly people that had fled from Kahnawake at the end of August. The first to plead guilty, a middle-aged LaSalle man, was given an absolute discharge by a judge who seemed to sympathize with the rock-throwers. "At that time, in their own way, they had the impression they were defending their democracy," Judge Gérard Girouard said. The sentence was appealed, and the Quebec Court of Appeal said the judge's reasons for granting the discharge were "disturbing, to say the least." The court ordered the LaSalle man to serve twenty days in jail. The next two stone-throwers to appear in court were placed on probation. After making a $500 donation to charity, they were told they could apply for an official pardon to erase the criminal convictions from their records. The two men were anxious to avoid a criminal record because one of them was seeking a job as a security guard and the second had enlisted in the Canadian army.

Most of the Mohawk spiritual objects, including the wooden masks, disappeared into the custody of the police or the army. The Mohawks pleaded with the authorities to give back the masks, but they were never returned.

The cost of the Oka crisis was enormous. In financial terms alone, it was a disaster. Federal taxpayers spent $22 million to pay for the 3,700 soldiers involved in the military intervention. The Quebec government, which had sent 1,500 police officers to the barricades, spent a further $91.6 million on overtime bills and other police expenses, $13.5 million on a highway extension to bypass the Kahnawake reserve, and $23.5 million on compensation to homeowners and businesspeople whose lives were disrupted by the crisis. The total bill for both governments came to more than $150 million.

Corporal Marcel Lemay was the first victim of the Oka crisis, but he was not the last. An elderly Mohawk died of heart failure in early September, just a few days after he suffered the terror of the stone-throwing mob on the outskirts of Kahnawake. Another elderly man in Oka was poisoned by the tear gas that wafted down from the Pines on July 11. He never fully recovered, and died several months later.

In addition to the three deaths, there were hundreds of injuries to Mohawks, police officers, soldiers, and local residents. The lives of thousands of commuters and homeowners were seriously disrupted. Nearly all of the eighty-seven homes of non-Mohawks behind the barricades at Kanesatake were vandalized — some by Mohawks, others by non-natives who took advantage of the barricades. The total damage to property was estimated at $1 million.

Until Oka, the Canadian army had never been used against domestic rebels since the FLQ crisis of 1970. The territories of Kanesatake and Kahnawake had become the first war zone in Canada since Riel's North-West Rebellion of 1885. One provincial Cabinet minister described Oka as "the greatest crisis we have ever witnessed in Quebec, Canada, or even North America." Despite the historic importance of the crisis, however, most politicians seemed anxious to pretend it never happened. The Quebec government, which had promised a public inquiry into the crisis, cancelled its plans for an inquiry as soon as the siege ended.

More than ten months after the July 11 police raid, the Quebec government announced that disciplinary hearings would be held to examine the conduct of eight senior SQ officers and thirty-one junior officers during the Oka crisis. At the same time, Quebec's chief coroner finally ordered an inquest into the death of Corporal Marcel Lemay. An investigating coroner, Paul Dionne, concluded that Marcel Lemay was probably killed by a Mohawk bullet. However, Dionne admitted he was relying on the results of a police investigation that concentrated on interviewing SQ officers. The police did not interview most of the dozens of Mohawk men and women who were present in the Pines on the morning of July 11.

When racist incidents were discovered in police departments in Manitoba and Nova Scotia in the 1980s, judicial inquiries were called and public hearings were held. Quebec, however, has shown no desire to conduct a thorough review of the behaviour of its police force in the crisis of 1990 — despite evidence that the SQ often ignored or encouraged the Châteauguay mobs in their attacks on Mohawk civilians, church leaders, human rights activists, and journalists. Nor has it investigated the evidence of organized racism in the riots at Châteauguay.

The federal government was equally reluctant to hold an inquiry into the events of 1990. It refused to conduct an independent review of the crisis and it stalled when Opposition MPs tried to persuade the House of Commons Standing Committee on Aboriginal Affairs to hold an inquiry. After weeks of delays and backroom battles, the Tories finally permitted the committee to have public hearings. But the hearings were virtually useless because the key witnesses — the Quebec police and the Quebec government — refused to testify. One Cabinet minister explained that the province didn't want to "focus specifically on these unfortunate specific incidents which are not truly representative of the over-all situation and which were caused by a very small number of people."

One of the committee members, Liberal MP Ethel Blondin, asked the House of Commons to authorize the committee to subpoena some senior members of the Quebec Cabinet and force them to testify at the hearings, but Conservative MPs voted down her proposal. When some MPs suggested that the committee should visit Kahnawake and Kanesatake to conduct research on the crisis, the Tories vetoed that idea too.

Despite their lack of action on other fronts, the federal Tories were extremely busy in the public relations field. One of the first initiatives they took after the end of the Oka crisis was to launch an intense PR campaign in Europe. In an effort to repair Canada's badly tarnished image, two federal officials flew to twelve European cities in early 1991. Their mission was to provide an information package to Canadian diplomats so that they could neutralize the damage Oka had done to the country's international reputation.

The lobbying campaign was ineffective. A number of well-respected international agencies launched their own inquiries into the Oka affair, and the European Parliament sent a delegation to Canada to study the Mohawk issue. An international human rights federation conducted its own inquiry. In the autumn of 1990, a lawyer from Amnesty International came to Quebec to interview Mohawks who said they had been tortured with burning cigarettes by the Quebec police after they were arrested.

Under the National Defence Act, provincial governments are required to conduct an inquiry and submit a report to Ottawa whenever they request the intervention of the Canadian Armed Forces. Yet this requirement was virtually ignored by the Quebec government during and after the Oka crisis. Two months after it ordered the army into the Mohawk territories, Quebec finally submitted its report to Ottawa. It consisted of a brief letter from Claude Ryan, barely two pages in length. The letter gave no indication that any significant internal inquiry had been conducted.

John Ciaccia, the only Quebec Cabinet minister who showed any real understanding of native issues, was effectively stripped of all authority during the final weeks of the Oka crisis. It was clear that his sympathetic approach to the Mohawks had caused him to fall from grace in the Quebec Cabinet. When he asked to be removed from the Native Affairs portfolio, his request was granted in a Cabinet shuffle on October 5, 1990.

After the crisis was over, Quebec showed no serious interest in improving its relationship with aboriginal people. While the new provincial Native Affairs minister, Christos Sirros, travelled to Indian reserves throughout Quebec to listen to the concerns of chiefs and community leaders, the government showed how little it valued the opinions of native people when it failed to include a single aboriginal representative among the thirty-five people appointed to the Belanger-Campeau commission to examine Quebec's future. And the commission did not even include aboriginal issues among the topics to be addressed by its special forums.

Jean Ouellette, the mayor of Oka, steadfastly defended the municipal actions that had led to the July 11 police raid. "We would make the same decision [if the same situation occurred again]," the mayor said in his testimony to the House of Commons Aboriginal Affairs committee. Ouellette acknowledged sending the letter to the SQ that provoked the fatal police raid, but he denied any responsibility for the SQ's decision to enter the Pines on July 11. "We did not even know," he said. "I woke up at 5:00 a.m. and the helicopter was there."

The SQ seemed to learn nothing from Oka. They failed to introduce any cross-cultural training programs to help them understand the traditions and beliefs of the Mohawks and other native people. Instead of trying to improve their strained relations with aboriginal people, the SQ concluded that they needed high-powered paramilitary technology and espionage tactics to suppress native militancy. Two police officers were dispatched to the United States to shop for armoured vehicles, including Leopard battle tanks with 105-millimetre cannons and 7.2-millimetre machine guns. The SQ also established a new detachment in the James Bay region of northern Quebec and tried to recruit white residents of the region to become secret police informers on the activities of Cree militants.

Although the province vetoed the purchase of Leopard tanks, the episode symbolized the SQ's stubborn insistence that high-tech weaponry and a massive show of police strength were the best response to the warrior movement. The police established a heavy presence on the highways of Kanesatake and Kahnawake after the Oka crisis had ended. Throughout the winter of 1990–91, violent confrontations and brawls erupted between the police and the Kahnawake Mohawks almost every week. The Mohawks suffered broken limbs and black eyes in pitched battles with the SQ, and police vehicles were smashed and damaged.

But the lessons of history should have been obvious. Violence has never crushed the Mohawk rebellion. The governments of Quebec and Canada failed to defeat the Mohawk sovereigntists with police intervention in 1877 at Oka, 1899 at Akwesasne, 1924 and 1959 at Six Nations, 1973 at Kahnawake, and 1990 at Oka and Kahnawake. It is simply not part of the Mohawk character to be intimidated by a display of force. It only makes them angrier and tougher and inevitably leads to an escalation of the warfare.

Whenever they arrested a Mohawk, the police always asked the same question — "Who are your leaders?" But the uprising of 1990 was not the product of a handful of criminal masterminds. It sprang from the convictions of thousands of Mohawks who believed they were sovereign in their own territory. The warrior movement could not be destroyed by arresting a few leaders.

The proof came on January 8, 1991. By then, the Quebec police had arrested about 150 of the most militant Mohawks from Kahnawake, Kanesatake, and Akwesasne — including most of those who were perceived to be the ringleaders. Yet the warrior movement was still as strong as ever. As long as the police remained on Kahnawake territory, the Mohawks were willing to fight them. On the afternoon of January 8, a huge brawl took place between 180 police officers and 120 Mohawks on the outskirts of Kahnawake, in which 13 police officers and 6 Mohawks were injured. Both sides fired a fusillade of gunshots into the air, and the authorities were forced to shut the Mercier Bridge for two hours at the peak of rush hour.

Despite the obvious failure of its hard-line law-and-order approach, the provincial government has continued to insist that the Mohawks accept Quebec's jurisdiction over their territory. Negotiations between the Mohawks and provincial officials began on several occasions in late 1990 and early 1991, but the talks always collapsed when Quebec insisted that its police must retain the right to patrol the territory of Kahnawake. Even though the provincial police had stayed off the reserve from 1973 to 1990, Quebec seemed unable to contemplate the idea of Mohawk independence.

Yet by international standards, the Mohawks can make a strong argument for sovereignty: they were never conquered by military force; they have never agreed to give up their sovereignty; they signed treaties with European countries on a nation-to-nation basis; and they served as equal partners with Britain in military alliances.

The International Commission of Jurists has proposed a list of seven criteria to define a "people" who possess the right to self-determination. The criteria include: a common history, racial or ethnic ties, cultural or linguistic ties, religious or ideological ties, a common territory or geographical location, a common economic base, and a sufficient number of people. By this definition, the Mohawks and the other Iroquois nations satisfy all the criteria for status as a "people" with the right to self-determination.

"In the case of the Six Nations, there can be no doubt that their distinctive race, culture, historical development and political structure satisfy the objective requirements of peoplehood," an article in the *University of Toronto Faculty of Law Review* concluded in 1986. "Their consistent assertions of sovereignty and their continuing resistance to Canadian interference are evidence of a subjective perception of themselves as a people and of a will to exist as such. The Six Nations Confederacy, therefore, should be regarded as a 'people' in the context of the right to self-determination."

Despite this evidence, the governments of Canada and Quebec have flatly rejected the concept of Mohawk sovereignty. In a speech to the House of Commons in the fall of 1990, Prime Minister Brian Mulroney insisted that Indian self-government "does not and cannot ever mean sovereign independence within Canadian territory."

While denying the Mohawks the right to self-determination, Mulroney has accepted the moral authority of other populations to chart their own destiny. For example, he has argued that the Baltic republics in the Soviet Union have the right to self-determination, and he has never questioned Quebec's right to choose its own future. Constitutional experts have called attention to the strong parallels between the sovereignty claims of Quebec and those of the Iroquois. It is ironic that Quebec should be free to determine its own destiny, while Quebec's aboriginal people — with a longer history of sovereignty — should be denied that same freedom.

The fight for sovereignty during the summer of 1990 had a devastating effect on the people of Kahnawake and Kanesatake. Surveys conducted across Quebec since the end of the Oka crisis have found widespread hostility toward the Mohawks. They have been attacked and beaten in the streets of Montreal by gangs who called them "savages." In the winter and spring of 1990 and 1991, mobs of "white warriors" from Châteauguay threatened to invade Kahnawake. A petition was circulated in Châteauguay, demanding the elimination of Indian reserves and the assimilation of native people. "Let's take up arms and raid the reserve," one Châteauguay man told a meeting of city councillors in February of 1991. "Are you, mayor, ready to come with us and march on Kahnawake to abolish the reserve?"

In Kanesatake, the divisions between the Mohawk factions have become increasingly bitter. Under the pressure of the armed standoff, families and neighbours turned against each other. Many people lost their jobs. Linda Simon, who had helped to hold the community together by co-ordinating food shipments and emergency services throughout the summer, was fired from her job as director of education at the local elementary school. She had insisted on opening the school in early September, before the standoff was over, to help the children get back to a normal routine. Grand Chief George Martin and his absentee council had opposed the move, and they dismissed her from her job.

In the fall of 1990, Linda Simon led a group of Kanesatake Mohawks in a request for federal funds to establish a healing program to help cure the psychological wounds of the summer. They suggested that the program could be based on native spiritual traditions, including the concept of a "healing circle." The federal government rejected the request. Other communities, including Oka and Châteauguay, have received federal money for psychological help. Yet the community where it all began, Kanesatake, has been left isolated.

By spending $5.28 million to purchase forty hectares of disputed land in Kanesatake, the federal government finally halted the Oka golf course expansion. However, the government failed to purchase the heartland of the Pines — the traditional gathering place of the Kanesatake Mohawks. As long as the municipality of Oka continues to exercise legal control over the Pines, the dispute is almost certain to continue.

The police presence in Kanesatake was dramatically increased at the end of the crisis. Police harassment has become a daily reality in the Mohawk community, and bitter confrontations between the Mohawks and the police are frequent occurrences. Several times a day, SQ vehicles cruise up and down the sideroads, keeping a close watch on the Pines. If any Mohawks are seen lingering in the Pines, the police question them and order them to move on.

Early in 1991, a delegation of European parliamentarians came to the Mohawk communities to study the situation. When they arrived in Kanesatake, the Longhouse people gave the Europeans a tour of the Pines. But just as Ellen Gabriel was showing them the bullet holes in the trees, the police ordered the group to leave the area. The Europeans were amazed. They called it an abuse of power. "Policemen can do whatever they want in this country," one of the parliamentarians observed.

Ellen Gabriel and the other Mohawk nationalists in the Kanesatake Longhouse have continued to fight for the Pines. They oppose Ottawa's plan to create a federal Indian reserve in their community and they continue to insist that the Longhouse is the rightful government of Kanesatake. But when the federal government launched negotiations to transfer the disputed forty hectares of land to the Mohawks, it deliberately excluded the Longhouse people from the negotiations. Instead the government chose to negotiate with a coalition of moderate Mohawks (led by non-Longhouse people such as Clarence Simon and Crawford Gabriel) who played minor roles in the crisis of 1990. And so the original defenders of the Pines, the Longhouse people who prevented the forest from being converted into a golf course, have watched the moderate coalition reap the benefits of their struggle.

Tom Siddon, the federal Indian Affairs minister, ordered a plebiscite to be held on May 31, 1991, to determine whether the Kanesatake Mohawks wanted their leaders to be chosen by elections, rather than by clan mothers. The Mohawks voted 526–21 in favour of a system of elections. But less than half of the eligible Mohawks participated in the plebiscite, and the Longhouse followers refused to have any involvement in the vote. As they pointed out, the traditions of the Longhouse precluded their participation in a western-style election.

In Kahnawake, the costs of the summer conflict were equally heavy. For the first time in almost two decades, half the Mohawk territory has fallen under Quebec police control. Hundreds of Mohawks were criminalized and forced into hiding. Many were unable to leave the safety of the village; others risked arrest whenever they slipped in and out of the reserve. They couldn't even travel to their Longhouse without putting themselves under the threat of arrest. Traditional ceremonies at the Longhouse were disrupted by the heavy police presence on the highways. Police patrols on Kahnawake's highways were six times more frequent than they were before the crisis, and the SQ officers wore flak jackets and carried riot gear as they patrolled the area.

The Mohawks of Kahnawake carry the scars of a generation of near-constant warfare. The community has come to accept the presence of guns and police scanners, and Mohawk children are absorbing the atmosphere of violent confrontation. But the militarization of Kahnawake is a response to the constant threat of outside intervention. The simplest way to defuse the violent atmosphere would be to allow the Mohawks to govern themselves.

For the past century, Quebec and Canada have used police intervention to force their laws upon the Mohawk people. Beginning with the Indian Act of 1876, governments have repeatedly tried to impose their political system upon the Mohawks. The Mohawks had a simple choice: they could surrender or they could resist. They have chosen to resist. Only the technology of their resistance has changed. Once it was fists and rocks; now it is AK-47s.

The Mohawks have accepted the high cost of their battle, for its benefits have been substantial. In Kanesatake, the Mohawks prevented their traditional territory from being converted into a golf course. In Kahnawake, the Mohawks defended their community against the combined power of the provincial police and the Canadian army. At the end of the crisis of 1990, the SQ controlled the outskirts of Kahnawake, but they still did not dare to enter the village itself.

Through sheer stubbornness and willingness to fight, the Mohawks have effectively created Canada's first independent Indian territory. By consistently repelling the RCMP and the Quebec police, Kahnawake has become the only aboriginal community in Canada to successfully resist the symbols of federal and provincial authority. Despite the lack of legal recognition for their autonomy, the people of Kahnawake have achieved a form of sovereignty in practical terms.

The crisis of 1990 brought other benefits too: a greater sense of Mohawk pride, a stronger feeling of aboriginal unity across Canada, and a higher profile for aboriginal issues on the national stage. For the first time, millions of ordinary Canadians began to realize that the Mohawks consider themselves a sovereign people. At the peak of the crisis, an opinion poll found that aboriginal issues were rated as the top priority in the country by 48 per cent of Canadians. "The Oka crisis was, I think, in many ways a moral victory for aboriginal people," said Keith Spicer, chairman of the Citizens' Forum on Canada's Future. "For the first time anybody can remember, your causes, interests and values were on the television screens for weeks at a time," he told a native audience in the fall of 1990.

Nor was this just a passing fad. Long after the crisis had ended, Canadians continued to put pressure on Ottawa to solve aboriginal problems. The Spicer Commission was flooded with thousands of letters and phone calls from Canadians demanding justice for native people and a fair resolution of Indian land claims. In the spring of 1991, the federal government finally bowed to the pressure and promised an infusion of new money to accelerate the settlement of Indian land claims.

Despite the intense coverage of the Oka crisis in newspapers and telecasts across the country, the central facts of the crisis were obscured by a torrent of absurd allegations from politicians, police officers, military commanders, and media commentators. Many of these inaccuracies were spread by the police themselves. The Canadian Police Association, representing 34,000 police officers, placed an advertisement in newspapers across Canada, claiming that the SQ had not fired a single shot in the July 11 raid and that the Mohawks had provoked the raid by barricading major highways at Oka. It also alleged that Corporal Marcel Lemay was "murdered." The SQ, of course, has now admitted to having fired shots in the raid; the Mohawks barricaded a dirt sideroad, not a highway; and the courts have never established that Corporal Lemay was murdered.

The Sûreté du Québec, meanwhile, blamed the English press for giving the Quebec police a bad image. In an official statement, they accused the anglophone media of "settling accounts with Quebec" because of "political motives" somehow connected with the Meech Lake accord. The same kind of wild allegations were tossed around by many Quebec nationalists. One popular tract, which became a bestseller in Quebec, alleged that Oka was English Canada's "last excuse" — part of an anglophone conspiracy to blacken Quebec's reputation.

No such conspiracy existed, of course, and anglophones were not the only ones to criticize the conduct of the Quebec government and the SQ in the Oka crisis. The Quebec Human Rights Commission, for example, concluded that the police should have negotiated with the Mohawks instead of attacking their barricade in the Pines on July 11. It criticized the SQ for their arbitrary and unpredictable actions throughout the summer of 1990. Even some of the early leaders of the Quebec nationalist movement, such as Pierre Vallières, condemned the police and the Quebec government for their treatment of the

Mohawks. "The state is once again criminalizing a valid social protest, it is trying to dismiss social demands, demands for sovereignty, as criminal activities," Vallières said.

As for the anglophone media, a study by a researcher at the University of Western Ontario found "no purposeful journalistic bias" in the coverage of the Oka crisis by ten daily newspapers in central Canada. The media have exposed racism and police wrongdoing in every region of the country, not just in Quebec. Indeed, the same kind of media attention was focused on Manitoba and Nova Scotia when racism was uncovered in the justice systems of those provinces in the 1980s. It would be illogical to expect Quebec to be immune from criticism for its treatment of aboriginal people.

The Canadian Armed Forces contributed to the Oka confusion by trying to discredit the reporters who remained inside the warrior encampment in the final weeks of the military siege. One senior army officer accused the journalists of suffering from the "Stockholm Syndrome" — a psychological condition in which hostages sympathize with their captors. The accusation was totally groundless. None of the journalists were held against their will. The reporters were the only independent witnesses to the confrontations at the barricades in the final weeks. The accusations of psychological damage were a desperate attempt to discredit the only source of accurate information on the conflict.

Politicians were among the most significant sources of misleading information on the Oka crisis. In his testimony to the Aboriginal Affairs committee, Tom Siddon described the Mohawks as "immigrants" to Canada — ignoring the evidence of a blood connection between the Mohawks and the original inhabitants of the St. Lawrence Valley. He also claimed that internal divisions among the Mohawks had frustrated the government's efforts to solve the Oka land problem before the standoff began. Yet the Mohawks were united in their opposition to the golf course expansion. The government understood this unanimous opposition, but it allowed Oka to proceed with the golf project until violence finally erupted on July 11.

In a speech to the House of Commons, Brian Mulroney claimed that the Mohawks had "repudiated" a 1989 agreement on the Oka land question. In reality, no such agreement had ever existed. There was only a federal proposal that had been unanimously rejected by the

Mohawks. By consistently describing its land proposal as a "framework agreement" despite the absence of any agreement, the government diverted attention away from its own failure to settle the land issue.

Federal Justice Minister Kim Campbell claimed that the Mohawks had violated the "rule of law." Yet the Mohawks have never been a lawless people. They have consistently maintained their own system of justice, based on the Great Law of Peace. Under traditional Mohawk law, for example, it is illegal for anyone to commit assaults or acts of vandalism. When some of the warriors vandalized houses and assaulted people, Mohawk leaders made efforts to punish them, despite the chaotic conditions behind the barricades.

The rhetoric about the "rule of law" sidestepped the central question of whether or not Mohawk territory was actually subject to Canadian jurisdiction. Because of their belief in their own sovereignty, most of the Mohawks have never accepted the authority of Canadian law in their territories. The issue of Mohawk sovereignty has to be settled before there can be any agreement about the "rule of law" in Mohawk territory.

Historically, the "rule of law" was often wielded by Canadian governments to suppress aboriginal people. Until 1951, for example, a federal law made it illegal for Indians to follow their traditional spiritual practices, and another law prohibited Indians from raising money for land claims. Other laws made it illegal for Indians to vote in federal and provincial elections, and there were laws prohibiting Indians from leaving their reserves without government permission. After this long history of using the law as a weapon against aboriginal people, it was hypocritical for politicians to expect the Mohawks to respect the rule of Canadian law.

Some of Canada's top legal experts have questioned the federal interpretation of the "rule of law." For example, a group of twenty lawyers from the Queen's University Faculty of Law concluded that the routine laws of criminal procedure might not apply to the Oka situation. "The laws we apply must recognize international law, treaty law and the law of aboriginal rights as well as the ordinary law of criminal procedure," the lawyers said in a letter to Kim Campbell.

Bruce Clark, a lawyer from London, Ontario, who specializes in constitutional issues, has argued that the Mohawk warriors were in fact defending the rule of law. In some circumstances, Clark has said, it is legal to use force to defend existing rights — in this case, the rights conferred on the Mohawks by treaty and in the Royal Proclamation of 1763. "Self-defence and self-help are basic remedies, available even against the state; an inherent and ultimate safeguard against the arbitrary abuse of state power," Clark said.

Perhaps the most pervasive myth about the Oka crisis is the allegation that the warriors were a gang of criminals motivated by money. Brian Mulroney, for example, claimed that the Oka land dispute was "hijacked by a group of heavily armed people ... seeking to protect illegal commerce." He described the warriors as "terrorists" who were "acting against all of the peaceful and noble traditions of Canada's Mohawks." Although this claim has become conventional wisdom in Quebec, it is contradicted by all the available evidence about the warriors and their motivations.

There is no doubt that the warriors were and are strongly supported by a large number of the Mohawks. In Kahnawake, they are endorsed by the largest of the Longhouse factions, which itself is supported by a growing percentage of the Kahnawake population. The number of Longhouse followers in the community is now roughly equal to the number of people who follow the elected council. Because of the growing popularity of the traditional political system, the elected chiefs are now working closely with the Longhouse chiefs (including the warrior leaders) on many issues, and a merger of the two systems is planned. Despite differences of opinion on controversies such as the cigarette trade and high-stakes bingo, the elected council unanimously supported the barricades at Kahnawake in the summer of 1990. At the peak of the crisis, an estimated 80 to 90 per cent of the Kahnawake Mohawks supported the standoff.

There has never been any reign of terror in Kahnawake. If the Mohawks were living in fear of the warriors, they would be clamouring for the Quebec police to enter the community to rescue them. But instead of expressing any desire to be "protected" from the warriors, virtually all the Mohawks have agreed that the Quebec police must be kept out of their community.

In Kanesatake, there had been serious disagreements about the warriors' involvement in the spring of 1990. But after the police raid on July 11, most Mohawks rallied around the warriors, and there was strong support for the warriors at the peak of the crisis. Not until the end of August did that support begin to diminish.

The strength of the warrior movement will always be underestimated if it is perceived as a criminal or terrorist organization. No group of criminals could maintain the kind of community support that the warriors have achieved. Their popularity comes from their willingness to fight for the nationalist beliefs of the Mohawk people. It does not come from a simple desire to protect gambling and smuggling operations.

In recent years, the contraband cigarette trade has helped to finance the warrior movement in Kahnawake and Akwesasne, and hundreds of Mohawks, including some of the warriors, have become involved in cigarette smuggling. Several of those who led the armed confrontations in 1990, including Loran Thompson and Gordon "Noriega" Lazore, have faced charges of cigarette smuggling. Others have been involved in gambling casinos in Akwesasne. However, the basic demands of the warriors had nothing to do with tobacco or gambling. The fundamental ideology that united the warriors was their passionate belief in Mohawk sovereignty.

For many decades before the birth of the casinos and the cigarette trade, the Mohawks were doing exactly what they are doing today: fighting the police to defend their sovereignty in their own territories. The warrior movement itself was born in the late 1960s, almost twenty years before the advent of the casinos and the cigarette trade. Despite the prime minister's rhetoric about the "peaceful" traditions of the Mohawks, the reality is that the Mohawks have regularly used violence or the threat of violence to defend their territory against federal and provincial authorities, beginning with the battle of 1877 in Oka. If the cigarettes and casinos disappeared, the warrior movement would continue as strongly ever.

There is no question that a few of the warriors have unsavoury pasts. Some are former alcoholics and drug addicts. Others are quick-tempered youths with a penchant for violence. But there are hundreds of rank-and-file warriors in Kahnawake and Kanesatake today, and the vast majority of these are middle-class ironworkers and construction workers with families for whom they feel responsible. Few would fit the conventional definition of a criminal, yet all of them are willing to pick up guns to defend the Mohawk people.

"No one ever has gotten anywhere by being a nice guy," says John Mohawk, a Seneca Indian and professor of American studies at the University of Buffalo who has followed the warriors closely. "There's nothing inconsistent with people being rough and having criminal histories that contradicts [their] general goal ... The only way they can get power is with money and weapons, and they've taken steps to get as much money and as much firepower as they could and I don't believe for a moment they've abandoned their goal of Mohawk sovereignty."

At the end of the Oka crisis, most of the warriors quietly returned to their home communities. As they waited for their trials to begin, they slipped back into their old lives. Brad Larocque went back to his economics classes in Regina. Randy "Spudwrench" Horne was hired as an ironworker in Brooklyn. Mark "Blackjack" Montour got a job at a ski shop in upper New York State. Robert "Mad Jap" Skidders returned to his wife and children in a split-level house in Akwesasne. "Blondie", the fifteen-year-old warrior, was sent to a group home in the Laurentians. Tom "The General" Paul travelled to South Dakota for the hundredth anniversary of the Wounded Knee massacre. Bill Sears went back to his bingo hall in Akwesasne. Gerald "Slim" Marquis returned to his construction job — and, ironically, found himself working on repairs to the Mercier Bridge.

The warrior leaders of Kahnawake found peacetime activities to keep themselves busy. Donnie Martin began writing a book on the Iroquois philosophy of war. Michael Thomas and Cookie McComber helped construct a new headquarters for the Tae Kwon Do society. Paul Delaronde spent most of his time with his adopted children. But just before Christmas of 1990, the warrior leaders joined hundreds of other Mohawks in a convoy of vehicles that cruised slowly along the highways of Kahnawake, temporarily forcing the SQ and the RCMP to withdraw from the reserve. It was another signal that the warriors were prepared to keep resisting the presence of outside police agencies on their territory.

Waneek Horn-Miller, the oldest of the Mohawk children inside the razor wire in the final siege, returned to school at Glebe Collegiate in Ottawa. Her physician advised her to get plastic surgery to conceal the bayonet scar on her chest, but she refused. She wanted a visible reminder of the events of the summer. "I'm one of the only women who can say they were stabbed by the Canadian army," she explained.

On a clear day in the autumn of 1990, Joe David walked back up the mountain on the northwestern edge of Kanesatake. Near a dry stream bed, not far from a rocky bluff, he spotted an eagle feather on a branch of a tall birch tree. It was one of four feathers he had tied to the trees as a gift to the four directions on July 1, 1990 — just ten days before the police raid. It seemed that a lifetime had passed since he had said his prayer on the mountaintop. He took a crystal from his medicine pouch and placed it beneath the rocks to give thanks for protecting the warriors throughout the summer.

For months after the crisis had ended, Joe David brooded about the events of the summer. Long after the army had departed from Kanesatake, he thought he could still hear its helicopters hovering over the roof of his cabin. But he had no regrets about his decision to become a warrior. If the Mohawks hadn't taken a stand, he said, they would have been just "wooden cigar-store Indians."

When the Oka crisis was over, a fresh round of internal debates took place among the warriors. They discussed the contraband cigarette industry and the question of whether it should be based on free enterprise or whether it should be nationalized to benefit the entire Mohawk nation. They held meetings with the leaders of the Iroquois Confederacy to make tentative moves toward a reconciliation. And they even debated the question of guns.

"We need a review of our gun policy," said Mike Myers, the Seneca activist who had become a senior negotiator for the warriors in the final weeks of the Oka crisis. "I think they're a waste of time. We should get rid of them. We'll never out-gun the army and the police."

Myers noted that, in every confrontation with the army and the police after July 11, the warriors had been reluctant to fire their weapons. If the warriors are unwilling to pull the trigger, the guns are just "very expensive clubs," Myers said. He believes the warriors could be more creative in their tactics if the guns were gone. "It's better to fight with cheap clubs, as was demonstrated at Tekakwitha Island in the summer," he said. "This is like an intifada. We're up against a heavily armed enemy with sophisticated tools. We can be more successful with rocks and fists than with AK-47s."

Most warriors, however, decided that the guns should remain in the Mohawk arsenal. Despite the army raids in Kahnawake at the end of the crisis, hundreds of guns are still in the hands of the warriors. Of the estimated 500 to 600 guns held by the warriors at the peak of the summer, fewer than 150 were seized by the army. Several hundred guns are easily available to the Kahnawake warriors. "I still got my stash," confides one of the warriors who was arrested at the end of the military siege.

If anyone doubted the existence of the warrior arsenal, all doubts were erased on New Year's Eve in Kahnawake. To celebrate the arrival of 1991, the Mohawks took out their guns and fired them into the air, creating a twenty-minute fusillade of gunshots from hunting rifles, shotguns, and semi-automatic weapons. "It sounded like Vietnam," one Mohawk said.

On a cold night in early December, a warrior crept through the darkness of the forest surrounding the Treatment Centre. Carefully avoiding a security guard at the entrance, he slipped through the woods and approached the former warrior headquarters. He searched for a spot he remembered. Then he began digging.

Within a few minutes, the warrior had found what he was looking for. He lifted up a package from the earth. Inside the package was a handgun, a holster, and a knife. They were coated in oil, wrapped in plastic, and covered with dirt. The weapons were exactly where he had buried them at the end of the siege.

The warrior looked up into the trees. High up in the branches, glinting in the moonlight, several rifles were visible. Their hiding place was still undiscovered.

A few minutes later, the warrior crept back out of the woods. He had what he wanted. He was carrying the handgun and the knife.

Postscript

On a hot Friday afternoon in June 1992, a strange procession made its way through the Pines, stopping at the Mohawk graveyard at the edge of the parking lot for the Oka Golf Club, then winding its way along Highway 344 and up the gravel driveway towards the Onen'to:kon Treatment Centre. At its head was Ellen Gabriel, accompanied by Mr. Justice Louis Tannenbaum of the Quebec Superior Court. Behind them were the twelve members of the jury, followed by most of the thirty-nine defendants — the Mohawks and others who had been arrested as they walked out of the treatment centre on September 26, 1990.

The jury had asked to visit the Pines, to help them make sense of the plethora of maps and videotapes with which they had been presented over the weeks of testimony from army officers and members of the Sûreté du Quebec. Ellen Gabriel, the Kanesatake Mohawk who had acted as a spokesperson for the people behind the barricades throughout much of the crisis, was a witness for the defence. Every few metres, the judge asked her to stop and explain to the jurors where they stood in relation to landmarks on the map they had been given.

As they made their way towards the treatment centre, the centre's director hurried to meet them, alarmed by their unexpected appearance and worried that they might disturb the centre's clients. Tannenbaum agreed to stay clear of the residence, and he and the jury members began to return to the highway. But the defendants hung back, reluctant to leave.

It had been nineteen months since they had left this place — their final refuge in the seventy-eight day stand-off. Memories of the twenty-six days and nights they had spent together there, surrounded by the Canadian army and ringed in by razor wire, came flooding back. Hunter Montour and a few of the other men walked over to the edge of the forest, looking out across a steep ravine as if they expected soldiers to be on guard there still, staring back at them. Kahentiiosta drew in her breath at the view of the Lake of Two Mountains. "And look how much the trees have grown!" she exclaimed.

Walking around a volleyball net behind the treatment centre, they quietly formed a circle on the manicured lawn. No one spoke. But each of them remembered the last time they had stood in this spot, their sacred fire burning in the centre of that same circle, as they had prayed together and prepared to go home.

The trial of the thirty-nine Mohawks and their supporters had received scant coverage in the media, who had tired of the Oka story by now — nearly two years after the police raid that had sparked the crisis of 1990. The case was viewed as a curious footnote to an old story. The selection of a jury set a Canadian record: It took forty days to go through a panel of 643 potential jurors to select twelve impartial people — nine men and three women.

From the outset, it was clear this was no ordinary trial. On the morning it began, the smell of burning sweetgrass wafted into the large courtroom, as supporters of the Mohawks conducted a traditional rite of purification. Three of the defendants — Sandra Deer, Arlette Van Den Hende and Georgina Michell — had young babies, and they slipped in and out of the courtroom to nurse or play with their infants. Another defendant, Jenny Jack, had permission to remain in Ottawa, where she was involved in constitutional negotiations for the Assembly of First Nations. Paul Smith, the Oneida warrior from Wisconsin, refused to appear in court because he did not recognize the Canadian judicial system. His girlfriend, Beverly Scow, who was also charged, remained with him and their infant child in Wisconsin.

Throughout the trial, there was an unusual lack of decorum. The defendants did not rise to their feet when the judge and jury entered and left the courtroom. Tannenbaum instructed the jury not to interpret that as a sign of disrespect or defiance. He accepted the Mohawks' argument that it was not their custom to show deference in that fashion.

More than a year earlier, the same judge had ruled that Mohawk witnesses were free to take their oaths on a string of wampum — the traditional way that promises and commitments are made. So when Ellen Gabriel and other Mohawks took the stand as witnesses in the trial, clan mother Eba Beauvais stood before each of them with her wampum and, speaking Mohawk, had them pledge an oath to the Creator.

The trial lasted seven weeks. The indictments against the Mohawks related only to the final twenty-six days of the crisis. They were charged with participating in a riot and obstructing peace officers. The men also faced charges of possessing a weapon dangerous to the public peace.

Midway through the trial, one of the defence lawyers argued that the Crown prosecutor had no criminal evidence against five of his clients. The judge agreed and directed the jury to acquit all five. The remaining defendants could have made the same lack-of-evidence argument, but they refused to resort to the technicalities of Canadian criminal law. They chose to defend the legitimacy of their actions. Deprived of a public inquiry or other official forum to tell their version of the events of 1990, they wanted to turn the courtroom into a political arena, where they could finally put a spotlight on the history of their land fight.

The defendants did not deny they were participants in the stand-off, nor that many of the men carried weapons. However, Bob Antone, the Oneida chief, testified that the weapons were only intended to be negotiating tools, after all other avenues for resolving the conflict had been exhausted. He said the guns would only have been used if women and children behind the barricades had been attacked by the police or the army.

The Crown prosecutor in the case, Jean Pierre Boyer, argued that an acquittal of the Mohawks and their supporters would send a message to the world that Canada condoned the settling of disputes between neighbours at gunpoint. Tannenbaum accused him of trying to intimidate the jury. The judge said that if there was any message to be drawn from the evidence, it was contained in the letter sent by Quebec's native affairs minister, John Ciaccia, to Oka Mayor Jean Ouellette two days before the crisis. In that letter, Ciaccia warned Ouellette that a failure to resolve the dispute could lead to a confrontation with serious consequences for the Mohawks and for Quebec society.

Despite his obvious understanding of the historical issues that led to the crisis, Tannenbaum had little choice but to apply the strict rules of criminal law to the case. He instructed the jury to ignore all evidence that did not specifically pertain to the criminal charges. That ruled out most of the Mohawk evidence on the history of the dispute, and it illustrated a key point that the International Federation for Human Rights had made in its 1991 report on the Oka crisis: the Canadian judicial system is fundamentally unsuited to deal with the underlying issues of aboriginal conflicts. The courts can only respond to the violent symptoms of an Oka crisis. They cannot resolve the deeper questions of land and sovereignty.

The verdicts came after four-and-a-half days of deliberations, during which there were hints of discord and anxiety in the jury room. On day three, the jurors asked what would happen if they could not agree on all verdicts. On day five — July 3, 1992 — one juror was discharged after he suffered an apparent heart attack.

Four hours after the twelfth juror was taken to hospital, the jury came forward with its verdict. The thirty-four remaining defendants were acquitted on all counts.

None of the Mohawks showed any emotion as they listened to the jury foreman repeat "not guilty" eighty-six times — once for every charge. Then Joe David stood up from his seat among the defendants and held an eagle feather high in the air. The others rose to their feet, raised their clenched fists and began to smile and laugh, their eyes brimming with tears.

Lorraine Montour hugged her sons, Hunter and Mark, unable to believe the verdict had been in their favour. "Faith in humanity," she said. "That's what I feel again, right now."

In the eighteen months following the Oka crisis, thirty other Mohawks were convicted in separate trials in the courthouse in St. Jérôme. Their crimes ranged from mischief to obstruction of justice, assault and weapons' possession. Some received fines, while others went to prison.

Hervey Nicholas received one of the stiffest sentences — a year in jail for weapons' possession, obstruction, rioting and blocking the highway. Nicholas was perceived as a warrior leader because he was carrying a walkie-talkie on July 11, 1990. In fact, he was just one of many Kanesatake Mohawks who flocked to the Pines that morning.

For several months during the fall of 1991 and winter of 1992, the public's attention had focussed on Ronald "Lasagna" Cross, the most notorious of the Oka warriors. Cross, along with Gordon "Noriega" Lazore and Roger "20-20" Lazore, had faced a total of fifty-nine charges ranging from mischief to aggravated assault.

In contrast to the relaxed atmosphere of the trial of the thirty-nine defendants, security at the trial of Cross and the two Lazores was extremely tight. Every person entering the St. Jérôme courthouse was checked for weapons by security guards armed with metal detectors. Towards the end of the trial, after Cross had failed to appear for a second time — both times due to an alcohol and cocaine binge — he was detained and brought into the courthouse bound in handcuffs and leg shackles each day.

On January 22, 1992, after three months of testimony and forty-one hours of jury deliberations, Ronald Cross was acquitted of twenty charges. But he was found guilty on another twenty, including all the charges related to the beating of his fellow Mohawks, Francis Jacobs and his son Cory, and for vandalizing the ambulances operated by Kanesatake's emergency service. He was also convicted on weapons charges, and for uttering threats and the assault of a soldier. He was sentenced to four years and four months in prison.

Gordon Lazore was acquitted of nine charges, but he was convicted of assault, use of a firearm, and vandalizing the ambulances. He was sentenced to twenty-three months imprisonment.

Roger Lazore was acquitted on all charges. And the jury acquitted the three Mohawks on all charges related to the vandalism of two houses owned by non-natives in Kanesatake, including the Mongeon farmhouse.

"*Où est la justice?*" roared a headline in *La Presse* the next day. "Where is the justice?" was the reaction of Bernard and Solange Lemay, whose home was trashed during the stand-off.

In his sentencing report, Mr. Justice Benjamin Greenberg made it clear he did not intend to belittle the tragedies that befell the Lemays and other victims of the crisis. The Mohawks had been cleared on those charges for want of sufficient evidence against them. But his lengthy discourse during sentencing also made it clear that Greenberg had a complex and sophisticated view of the motivations of the Mohawks. The Crown prosecutor, Francois Briére, had portrayed Ronald Cross as a common criminal. Greenberg had a different assessment of Cross.

"I am satisfied that he was not motivated by greed or reasons of personal gain," Greenberg said. "He acted out of a deep anger, rage, desperation and a sense of hopelessness, all the result of the systematic discrimination and racism against his people over several centuries."

Greenberg said Cross's image as a warrior ringleader was purely a creation of the media. "Although he was prominent, was aggressive, and, yes, was often violent, there was absolutely no evidence adduced before me to suggest that he was *the leader* or even *a leader* of the militant Warrior Society at Kanesatake during the crisis. In fact, the evidence was to the effect that, prior to the Oka crisis, he was not even active or involved in the Warrior Society. It appears that he was galvanized into action by the fear of the Mohawks regarding the proposed expansion of the golf course."

Greenberg followed this with a stirring indictment of Canada's treatment of its first peoples:

"For years, decades, even centuries, the aboriginal people of this country have endured, at best, indifference, neglect and unfairness and, at worst, open hostility, contempt, discrimination and racism.... The aboriginal peoples occupy a special place in the firmament of Canadian society. They were the original inhabitants of this country; this continent. The white man, the European settlers, came here and, by dint of their superior numbers (and) state of technological development and, hence, by force of arms, took the land from the natives."

Greenberg talked at length about the historical relationship between aboriginal nations and Canada's colonizers. "Even before the Confederation of Canada as a Nation in 1867, the British Sovereigns, and the Sovereigns of France before them, dealt with the Indians here as though they were quasi-sovereign nations themselves," he noted. He also reviewed the history of the land dispute at Oka, examining the 1912 decision of the predecessor of Canada's Supreme Court, the Privy Council in London. It ruled that the Mohawks did not have legal title to the Two Mountains seigneury, but it left the door open to a negotiated settlement that never took place.

"It is against that background that one must try to understand the attitude of the Mohawks to the proposal approved by the municipal council of the village of Oka in March 1990 to enlarge the Oka golf course, which they feared would disturb 'the Pines' and the ancient Mohawk cemetery located there," he said. "It must be recalled that the Mohawks had opposed, unsuccessfully, the building of the original golf course some thirty years earlier."

Greenberg delved further back into court records and looked at the appeal court ruling that had been sent to the Privy Council in 1911. He was struck by the fact that the term "*les sauvages*" (the savages) was used forty-one times in the judgment to describe the Mohawks of Kanesatake. Greenberg suggested that even in 1911, "savage" was probably a pejorative term.

"That is but one example of the contempt, discrimination and racism which the native peoples of Canada have endured over the centuries, and it came there not from an uneducated man on the street, but from a Judge of the highest Court of Quebec," he said.

While the long and cumbersome trials played themselves out in courtrooms in Montreal and St. Jérôme, the Quebec police and the Mohawks continued to wage their guerrilla warfare at Kahnawake. The checkpoints surrounding the village of Kahnawake have become the frontline battleground for the struggle over Mohawk sovereignty. Throughout 1991 and 1992, there were frequent clashes between the police and Mohawks at the checkpoints. The violence was perhaps inevitable, because Quebec still rejected the fundamental concept of Mohawk self-government.

Claude Ryan, the Quebec public security minister, continued to insist that the Mohawk checkpoints were illegal. He demanded the dismantling of the checkpoints around Kahnawake, even though the small wooden huts at the entrances to the village were the only protection the Mohawks had to shield themselves from a police invasion. Ryan insisted that Quebec must be the predominant authority in the policing of Kahnawake. He said the Mohawk Peacekeepers which patrolled the village were an illegal organization (even though the Peacekeepers were federally funded), and he criticized Ottawa for giving official recognition to the Peacekeepers. Ryan said the Peacekeepers must be trained by the Quebec police and ultimately must be responsible to the provincial government.

This, of course, was a recipe for permanent conflict. While the Mohawks stubbornly fought for their right to govern themselves, the Quebec police maintained a heavy presence on the highways around Kahnawake, harassing the Mohawks as much as possible. Any motorist with a dark skin was stopped and searched. At least a dozen Quebec police officers were assigned to the borders of Kahnawake each day. Every officer was required to work four hours of overtime on each shift, at a total cost to taxpayers of $50,000 per day.

There were sporadic negotiations between the Mohawk leaders and the Quebec authorities in 1991 and 1992. But the negotiations always foundered when Quebec insisted on the right to send the provincial police into Kahnawake. When the Mohawks proposed that the Peace-keepers be officially recognized as the legitimate police force at Kahnawake, the Quebec negotiators said the idea was unacceptable unless the Peacekeepers were under Quebec's control. And as long as the Mohawk checkpoints were still in operation, Quebec refused to discuss any other aspects of self-government at Kahnawake.

The Kahnawake Mohawks were determined to keep the Quebec police at bay. At a series of community meetings, the people of Kahnawake confirmed that the checkpoints would remain. Grand Chief Joe Norton said the Mohawks would be willing to dismantle the checkpoints only if there was a guarantee that the Quebec police would not invade the village. Even if the checkpoints might eventually be removed, Norton said the Mohawks would retain an "early warning mechanism" to alert the village if the Sûreté du Québec tried to enter.

In the meantime, Kahnawake was holding a separate series of negotiations with Ottawa, and these talks were slightly more fruitful than the Quebec negotiations. On December 13, 1991, Joe Norton signed an agreement with the federal government to begin negotiations on "a new relationship between Canada and Kahnawake." The agreement, however, was interpreted in two different ways. To the federal government, it was just another discussion about a form of native self-government within Canada. But to the Kahnawake chiefs, it was an implicit recognition of Mohawk sovereignty.

The conflicting views were symbolized by the dual role of the federal cabinet minister who signed the agreement. The minister, Monique Landry, believed she was signing the accord in her capacity as the junior minister of Indian Affairs. But the Mohawks knew that

Monique Landry had another title: she was also the Minister of External Relations. In their view, Kahnawake was signing an international treaty with Canada's Minister of External Relations.

Under the terms of the agreement, Canada and Kahnawake would discuss the details of Mohawk jurisdiction in a long list of areas: health, education, justice, trade and commerce, social services, environment, land management, and financial matters. Claude Ryan was outraged by the agreement. Ryan and the Quebec government wanted the policing question to be settled before anything else was discussed.

At the same time, there were Mohawk traditionalists who felt that Joe Norton had made too many concessions. They were afraid that the agreement would allow Canada to set limits on Kahnawake's autonomy. And they were worried that the negotiations with Quebec on the policing question might lead to a dismantling of the checkpoints.

Three days after Norton and Landry signed their agreement, a small group of traditionalists seized the offices of Kahnawake's elected council. (Most of them were members of a small Longhouse faction that had always opposed the larger pro-warrior Longhouse.) After a day of confusion, the traditionalists walked out of the council building. But the brief takeover was the spark for a big community meeting the next day. Close to a thousand Mohawks flocked to the meeting, and there was much discussion of the community's 1979 agreement to move to a form of traditional government. Many people were frustrated that Kahnawake had still not taken concrete action to scrap the elected council and establish a new government that would follow the ancient Great Law of Peace. Under pressure from the community, Joe Norton promised that he would accelerate the move to traditional government.

Throughout the first half of 1992, there were more meetings and debates about the concept of traditional government at Kahnawake. The elected council and the Nation Office both launched their own studies of the issue, and two draft proposals were widely circulated in the community. There were still plenty of disagreements about the details, but Kahnawake seemed closer than ever before to its dream of traditional government. In the first week of July 1992, Joe Norton was re-elected as the grand chief of the Kahnawake Mohawks. It now seemed possible that this might be the final election under the Indian

Act system of government in Kahnawake.

In Kanesatake, by contrast, an elected system was once again entrenched, after more than two decades of a modified form of traditional government. The federal government had refused to negotiate the land issue until the thorny issue of leadership in the community had been cleared up. In the spring of 1991, a team of federal consultants conducted a plebiscite in Kanesatake to determine whether the majority of band members wished to hold elections or to continue allowing clan mothers to select the chiefs. For Mohawk traditionalists, neither option was acceptable: they would never agree to electing a chief and council under the Indian Act system, but they viewed the so-called "Six Nations Traditional Hereditary Chiefs" who were then in power as a weak, homogenized version of governance whose only link to Mohawk traditional government was the name they had chosen for themselves when the clan-based council had been adopted in 1969.

Despite the refusal of traditional Mohawks to participate in the process, the plebiscite went ahead. Of those who voted, most favoured a return to an elected system. In June 1991, Jerry Peltier — an Ojibway adopted through marriage into Kanesatake, who had led the push for band elections — was elected the interim Grand Chief. His mandate was renewed in a second election in June 1992. But the community remains splintered and unable to agree on how to deal with outside forces. An attempt to resolve the policing issue failed because the community could not reach agreement on various proposals to set up its own police force. The Sûreté du Quebec continued to patrol the territory, and there were sporadic clashes between the SQ and Mohawks who are unhappy with their presence.

In Akwesasne, meanwhile, there was another significant election in 1991. For the first time in many years, a group of warrior supporters was elected to the Mohawk council on the Canadian side of the reserve. Instead of being a powerful enemy of the warriors, the elected council was now a more accurate reflection of the community, and the new councillors helped to bridge the gap between the warriors and the anti-warriors.

There were other signs of progress in Akwesasne. A peace centre was established to conduct mediation and conflict resolution work in the community. One of its staff members was Francis Boots, the war chief who had been a prominent leader in the Oka crisis. Meanwhile, a lacrosse league was revived at Akwesasne, and the traditional Iroquois sport attracted players from all of the main political factions. The unifying force of the league was another reason for the reduced tensions at Akwesasne.

While there was plenty of activity in the Mohawk communities in the two years after the Oka crisis, the governments of Quebec and Canada continued to show little interest in resolving the underlying issues of the crisis. A parliamentary committee urged the federal government to hold a judicial inquiry into the events at Oka, but the recommendations were ignored. Neither the federal nor the Quebec governments were willing to appoint a public inquiry into the crisis of 1990. By the middle of 1992, there still had not been an inquest into the death of Corporal Marcel Lemay. And there still had been no disciplinary proceedings against 39 police officers who were cited for misconduct during the Oka crisis. Both the inquest and the disciplinary proceedings had been postponed until after the trials of the Oka warriors.

Despite the official stonewalling in Ottawa and Quebec, independent groups submitted their own reports on the human rights abuses at Oka, and the conclusions were highly critical of the federal and provincial governments. The International Human Rights Federation, in a 1991 report, described a litany of human rights abuses by the Quebec police and the Canadian army. It said the police had systematically discriminated against native people at Oka by arresting Mohawks under improper conditions and harassing anyone with a native face. The federation, based in Paris and accredited by the United Nations, said the Quebec and Canadian governments should have pursued negotiations instead of sending the army into Oka. It criticized the police and the army for blocking shipments of food and medicine, and it condemned the police for refusing to protect Mohawks from well-organized gangs of whites. Claude Ryan rejected the entire report. "That we should feel guilty? Not me," he said.

Amnesty International, meanwhile, put Canada on its list of human rights violators. Amnesty said it had identified six cases of alleged police mistreatment of Mohawks which "merit rigorous official investigation." In a report in early 1992, Amnesty published photographs of

Ronald Cross, showing the bruises and wounds he received after his arrest at the end of the crisis.

Another report, by a Quebec law professor and a Montreal criminologist, said the Sûreté du Québec had failed to control its officers during the Oka crisis. The report, released in early 1992, concluded that the Quebec police were virtually unaccountable to anyone. It said the police force had refused to reform itself, the disciplinary proceedings against individual officers were only a result of external pressure, and the question of who ordered the police to attack the Mohawk barricades on July 11, 1990, was still a mystery.

In February 1992, the Sûreté du Québec finally instituted a two-day cross-cultural training course for its members — a move long demanded by the union representing the police force's officers. However, the fourteen-hour course on intercultural and interracial relations did not specifically deal with aboriginal issues. The failure of the police to confront their ignorance of Mohawk values and customs is a virtual guarantee that the same kinds of prejudice and misunderstanding will be a factor in future conflicts.

The stonewalling by Ottawa and Quebec contributed to another trend: an increasing militancy among the Mohawks and a growing polarization between natives and non-natives in Quebec. According to a report by Canada's secret intelligence agency, the Warrior Society continued to gain influence in Mohawk communities in Ontario and Quebec in the aftermath of the Oka crisis. The report, prepared by the Canadian Security Intelligence Service in the fall of 1991, said the warriors were especially popular among younger Mohawks.

At the same time, hostility against aboriginal people in Quebec was growing worse. Radio talk-show programs were jammed with callers who complained bitterly about the Mohawks and the Crees. One radio station persuaded 240,000 people to write letters to Hydro-Québec, alleging that the utility was showing favouritism to natives by giving some Akwesasne Mohawks a $300 credit to compensate them for inaccurate electricity bills. Natives were perceived as the enemies of Quebec's interests, from James Bay to the Meech Lake accord. When national chief Ovide Mercredi went to the Quebec National Assembly to appear before a constitutional committee, the provincial politicians were openly hostile. They refused to allow him to perform a traditional native ceremony at the start of the meeting. Eventually they permitted the ceremony to proceed, but some of them labelled it a "joke" and a "circus."

For the warriors, the road from Oka was filled with twists and turns. Many of the Mohawks were still embroiled in the justice system. Bill Sears was jailed in the United States after he was convicted of perjury. Paul Delaronde was arrested in New York State for his role in the Ganienkeh barricades of 1990. Michael Thomas, the assistant war chief at Kahnawake, was acquitted of charges in connection with the same stand-off.

Other Mohawks were moving into new areas of politics and culture. Billy Two Rivers became a movie star for his prominent role in *Black Robe*, one of the most popular films of 1991. Donnie Martin, the Kahnawake assistant war chief and military philosopher, moved to Europe to work at the Mohawk embassy in the Netherlands. With the help of European friends, he produced his first album — a collection of his own songs, including several songs with warrior themes. Joe David, the Kanesatake artist-turned-warrior, returned to his artistic roots. One of his installation pieces was displayed at the Canadian Museum of Civilization in Ottawa as part of *Indigena*, an exhibition of aboriginal artists in 1992.

Brad Larocque, the Saskatchewan Ojibway who was the "unknown warrior" in the famous photograph of the face-to-face staredown with the Canadian soldier Patrick Cloutier, spent months working on environmental issues with the Peigan Lonefighters in Alberta. In the summer of 1992, he began working as a writer and lay-out artist on the Saskatchewan aboriginal art journal *Iron Bow*. (Cloutier, meanwhile, served 45 days in military detention in the spring of 1992, after he admitted using cocaine.) Jenny Jack, the Tlingit woman who had travelled from British Columbia to help the warriors during the Oka crisis, completed her law studies successfully and worked as an advisor on traditional government to the Assembly of First Nations during the 1992 constitutional talks.

Richard Two-Axe was finally able to spend time with his young daughter to whom he had sung songs over the cellular telephone during the final weeks of the crisis. He worked at home in Kahnawake, repairing golf clubs. Ronald "Lasagna" Cross, too, was able to spend time with his new wife and infant son, after he and Gordon Lazore were granted bail while they awaited their appeals. They sought a retrial on the grounds that the Crown had withheld evidence.

The legal battle was not yet over, either, for Shaney Komulainen. She was the widely-respected photojournalist who was charged with threatening a soldier with a machete during the stand-off between warriors and the army in the Pines on September 1, 1990 — the same day she took the prize-winning photograph of Larocque and Cloutier. From the start it was clear that the charges were a case of mistaken identity, at best. At her trial, Komulainen's own photographs showed the woman she had apparently been confused with — a small Mohawk woman with long, brown hair. Komulainen is blonde and nearly six feet tall. Eleven reporters and photographers, including an army photographer, testified that Komulainen had done nothing but take pictures.

On November 27, 1991, Komulainen was acquitted on all counts. Her legal bills, which were paid by the Canadian Press wire service agency, amounted to more than $100,000. She wrote letters to all levels of government, demanding an inquiry into the decision to file charges against her. In April 1992, the Quebec Police Ethics Commission agreed to investigate the conduct of the SQ officers who were involved in her case. The officers could be brought before a disciplinary hearing if the probe concludes they failed to do their job properly.

When the Oka jury announced the acquittals in July 1992, one warrior was conspicuous by his absence. Tom Paul, the Micmac poet and spiritual leader known as "The General" during the Oka stand-off, died suddenly of a heart attack in February 1992. The veteran of Wounded Knee and many other confrontations was just forty-eight when he died in the home of a friend near Kanesatake.

The Micmacs in Tom Paul's home reserve of Eskasoni asked for Mohawk "runners" to accompany the body home, so Joe David and Mike Mayo made the final trip with the veteran warrior. His body was dressed in the black, red and gold of the Warrior Society, and four feathers from his namesake — Mestaghuptaasit Kitpu, or Spotted Eagle — were laid across his chest. Tom Paul was respected by the Micmacs as one of the first to revive the traditions of the pipe, the drum and the sweatlodge among his people. He had asked to be buried in a traditional Micmac ceremony, and his wife and close friends insisted that his spirit should be honoured through the customs he had fought so hard to preserve. There was resistance from the local priest and Catholic family members, but eventually a compromise was struck. For the first time in Eskasoni's history, the priest allowed the traditional drum into the Catholic church.

Outside the church, it was bitterly cold, and snowdrifts were piled two metres high. As Joe David and Mike Mayo and the other pallbearers carried the casket inside, Micmac singers sang their ceremonial songs to the beat of Tom Paul's beloved drum. High above them, in the winter sky, an eagle slowly circled.

In November 1991, Jean Ouellette was re-elected as mayor of Oka. He received more than twice as many votes as his sole opponent, Jules Sauvé — the first candidate to challenge Ouellette in sixteen years. Sauvé, a school board administrator, had promised an open government and regular consultation with Oka's Mohawk neighbours. But most of Oka's citizens preferred Ouellette's hardline approach.

In the summer of 1991, the town of Oka received $435,000 in federal grants to set up an economic development corporation and to try to bring back the tourists who had been barred from the town during the crisis of 1990. Ouellette, who admitted he had not invited ideas from the Mohawks or even visited neighbouring Kanesatake in the year since the crisis had ended, seemed to believe that the Mohawks might be a useful attraction for tourists. "They could set up an Indian village, like you see when you drive through the United States," he said. "They could do their rain dances or whatever." He also suggested that Oka could organize bus tours of the former barricade locations, dropping off visitors at the golf club for a drink, followed by dinner in a restaurant in town.

By 1992, the luxury homes that faced the entrance to the Pines still stood empty, deserted by their owners. The "forgotten" families of Oka had been made into celebrities by Gilles Proulx, the virulently anti-Mohawk radio announcer, who launched an appeal for financial support for the homeowners as they awaited compensation from the federal government.

Negotiations on the unsettled land question moved slowly. The Mohawks and government negotiators were once again on a collision course, with completely different views of the land dispute. With the crisis over and the sense of urgency gone, the government returned to the language and content of the so-called "framework agreement" which the Kanesatake Mohawks had rejected in 1989. The federal plan was to create a "contiguous land base" for the Mohawks by negotiating to buy houses from non-natives living near the Pines, and eventually from people living in the parish of Oka. Twenty-five million dollars was budgeted by the federal treasury to pay the bills.

The Mohawks maintained that they had an historic right to the entire seigneury of Two Mountains. They questioned how the government could purchase land which the Mohawks had never given up. The federal government proposed that the Mohawks swap their claim on the contentious luxury homes in exchange for title to the Pines, but the proposal nearly caused what federal negotiator Bernard Roy called "the fragile atmosphere of peace" to disintegrate. The government was forced to withdraw its offer. Two years after the crisis, the majestic pine forest where it all started — the land at the heart of the centuries-old dispute — still legally belonged to the town of Oka.

A Note on Sources

This book is the product of research that began in March 1990, when the Mohawks of Kanesatake first occupied the Pines. Beginning with that event, the authors attended almost all the key events that marked the crisis of 1990. Our notebooks cover hundreds of news conferences, confrontations, protests, scrums, announcements, and personal interviews. We conducted interviews with more than two hundred people, including Mohawks from all factions, federal and provincial politicians, police and military officers, bureaucrats, lawyers, academic specialists, and other key players in the drama of 1990. We gathered information in Oka, Kanesatake, Kahnawake, Akwesasne, Ganienkeh, Ottawa, and Montreal. Although the personal interviews were the primary source of information, we also obtained material from academic research papers, government studies, court documents, transcripts of hearings, media reports, and many other sources. Following is a summary of the major published sources of information for each chapter.

CHAPTER 1   **Get Ready to Rock and Roll**

The physical details of Corporal Marcel Lemay's death and the Sûreté du Québec's version of its actions on July 11, 1990, are contained in the report of Coroner Paul G. Dionne, *Rapport d'investigation du Coroner*, Quebec, May 27, 1991.

CHAPTER 2   Golfballs among the Headstones

Historian Michel Girard's unpublished "Historical Study of the Forest of the Village of Oka" tells the complete story of the reforestation of the Pines in Oka in the late 1800s.

For more information on the conflict over Mohawk government at Kanesatake, the land issues and the events leading up to the 1990 crisis, see *The Summer of 1990*, the report of the House of Commons Standing Committee on Aboriginal Affairs (Ottawa, 1991).

CHAPTER 3   Camouflage and Ugly Sticks

For details on the role played by the Quebec Human Rights Commission and for its analysis of the conflict, see *Le Choc collectif: Rapport de la Commission des droits de la personne du Québec* (Montreal: Commission des droits de la personne du Québec, 1991).

CHAPTER 4   The Two Dog Wampum

Claude Pariseau's thesis entitled *Les Troubles de 1860–1880 à Oka: Choc de Deux Cultures*, presented to McGill University for his master's degree in history in 1974, is an invaluable study of the historical dispute over the land title of the Lake of Two Mountains seigneury and the relationship between the Oka Indians and the Seminary of St. Sulpice. For shorter synopses of the dispute, see Richard C. Daniel, "The Oka Indians vs. the Seminary of St. Sulpice," in *A History of Native Claims Processes in Canada, 1867-1979* (Ottawa: Department of Indian Affairs Research Branch, 1980); Larry Villeneuve and Daniel Francis, "The Oka Indians," in *The Historical Background of Indian Reserves and Settlements in the Province of Quebec* (Ottawa: Department of Indian Affairs Research Branch, 1984).

Controversy over "The Oka Question" generated a wealth of published works on the issue in the late 1800s. The best sources include *The Seminary of Montreal: Their Rights and Titles* (St. Hyacinthe: Courier de St. Hyacinthe, 1880); Beta (pseudonym), *A Contribution to the Proper Understanding of the Oka Question* (Montreal: Witness, 1879); Jean Lacan, *Mémoire sur les difficultés survenues entre Messieurs les Ecclésiastiques du Séminaire de St-Sulpice de Montréal et certains Indiens de la mission d'Oka, Lac des Deux-Montagnes* (Montreal: Séminaire de St- Sulpice, 1876). For a narrative of late nineteenth-century life among the Oka Mohawks, including a description of the events leading to the burning of the church in 1877, see the autobiography *The Life of Rev. Amand Parent: Eight Years among the Oka Indians* (Toronto: William Briggs, 1894). For a synopsis of the church-burning trials, see J.V. McAree, "Iroquois Indians Triumph at Oka," *Toronto Globe and Mail*, November 28, 1944.

A brief history of the Sulpician mission at Lake of Two Mountains can be found in John Porter and Jean Trudel, *Le Calvaire d'Oka* (Ottawa: The National Gallery of Canada, 1974). For an account of the history of the Mohawks under the Sulpicians at the mission at Mount Royal, see William Fenton and Elisabeth Tooker, "Mohawk," in William C. Sturtevant, ed., *Handbook of North American Indians,* vol. 15 (Washington: Smithsonian Institute, 1978), pp.15:466-80. The historical arguments on the links between the Mohawks and the Saint Lawrence Iroquoians can be found in J.B. Jamieson, "Trade and Warfare: The Disappearance of the Saint Lawrence Iroquoians," *Man in the Northeast* (Spring 1990) 39:79-87; Bruce Trigger and James Pendergast, "Saint Lawrence Iroquoians," in William C. Sturtevant, ed., *Handbook of North American Indians,* vol. 15 (Washington: Smithsonian Institute, 1978), pp. 15:357-61.

For a synopsis of French and British policies towards the Indians, see *The First Peoples in Quebec* (La Macaza, Quebec: Native North American Studies Institute, 1973). A detailed analysis of those policies and the legal history of the Mohawk claim at Oka is contained in *The Oka Indian Land Claim*, prepared by lawyer Peter Hutchins and submitted to the Government of Canada in June 1977.

CHAPTER 5   **Bulldozers in the Pines**

The fascination of the *Montreal Daily Star* with the saga of Chief Joseph "Kennatosse" Gabriel provided a goldmine of information on life in Kanesatake in the early twentieth century. See "Chief of Iroquois Seeks King Edward," *Montreal Daily Star*, April 28, 1902; "Chief of Tribe Threatens War," *Montreal Daily Star*, May 26, 1902; "Guarded against Arrest 'Kinnatosse' Talks to Star," *Montreal Daily Star*, May 28, 1902; "Detectives Hot on Trail of Chief Kennatosse: Indians Purchase Arms," *Montreal Daily Star*, June 19, 1902; "Chief Kennatosse Is Still Defiant," *Montreal Daily Star*, June 5, 1902; "Will Only Obey King's Commands," *Montreal Daily Star*, June 13, 1902; "Oka Indians Are Divided in Opinion," *Montreal Daily Star*, May 11, 1909; "Famous Lawsuit between Indians and Sulpicians," *Montreal Daily Star*, June 23, 1909.

For an account of the twentieth-century history of the Oka land dispute, including excerpts from the testimony of Émile Colas before the Joint Committee of the Senate and the House of Commons on Indian Affairs, see the *Oka Indian Land Claim*, prepared by Peter Hutchins and submitted to the Government of Canada in June 1977.

A thorough examination of the recent history of factionalism in Kanesatake is available in court documents submitted to the Federal Court of Canada in *Six Nations Traditional Hereditary Chiefs* vs. *Her Majesty the Queen and Richard Gabriel*, February 1991. A descriptive account of the Kanesatake Longhouse can be found in W.G. Spittal, "A Mohawk Condolence at Oka, P.Q. April 1964," in an appendix to the Iroqrafts reprinting of Arthur C. Parker, *The Constitution of the Five Nations or The Iroquois Book of the Great Law* (New York: New York State Museum, 1916).

CHAPTER 6   Cowboys of the Sky

For historical information on Kahnawake, see David Blanchard, *Seven Generations* (Kahnawake: Kahnawake Survival School, 1980); David Blanchard, *Kahnawake: A Historical Sketch* (Kahnawake: Kanien'kehaka Raotitiohkwa Press, 1980); Johnny Beauvais, *Kahnawake: A Mohawk Look at Canada and Adventures of Big John Canadian* (Kahnawake, 1985); and Mary A. Duke, "Iroquois and Iroquoian in Canada, " in R. Bruce Morrison and C. Roderick Wilson, eds., *Native Peoples: The Canadian Experience* (Toronto: McClelland and Stewart, 1986).

Sources on Mohawk ironworkers include Joseph Mitchell, "The Mohawks in High Steel," in Edmund Wilson, *Apologies to the Iroquois* (New York: Farrar, Straus and Cudahy, 1959); David Blanchard, "High

Steel: The Kahnawake Mohawk and the High Construction Trade," University of Chicago Department of Anthropology, 1981; and "Sky-walkers: A History of the Indian Ironworker" (Brantford: Woodland Cultural Centre).

For descriptions of contemporary government in Kahnawake, see J. Rick Ponting, "Institution-Building in an Indian Community: A Case Study of Kahnawake," in Ponting, ed., *Arduous Journey: Canadian Indians and Decolonization* (Toronto: McClelland and Stewart, 1986); and Mohawk Council of Kahnawake, *Institutions of Mohawk Government in Kahnawake* (Kahnawake: Mohawk Council of Kahnawake, 1990).

CHAPTER 7   Romans of the New World

There is a wealth of historical information on the Mohawks and the other Iroquois nations. Among the best sources are Bruce Trigger, *Natives and Newcomers: Canada's "Heroic Age" Reconsidered* (Kingston: McGill-Queen's University Press, 1985); Barbara Graymont, *The Iroquois in the American Revolution* (Syracuse: Syracuse University Press, 1972); John A. Price, "Huron and Iroquois: Warfare among Tribal Farmers," in Price, *Indians of Canada: Cultural Dynamics* (Scarborough: Prentice-Hall, 1979); Francis Jennings, *The Ambiguous Iroquois Empire* (New York: W.W. Norton, 1984); Anthony F.C. Wallace, *The Death and Rebirth of the Seneca* (New York: Random House, 1969); *Traditional Teachings* (Akwesasne: North American Indian Travelling College, 1984); William N. Fenton, ed., *Parker on the Iroquois* (Syracuse: Syracuse University Press, 1968); Lewis H. Morgan, *League of the Iroquois* (New York: Dodd, Mead and Company, 1901); Elisabeth Tooker, "The League of the Iroquois: Its History, Politics and Ritual," in William C. Sturtevant, ed., *The Handbook of North American Indians* (Washington: Smithsonian Institute, 1978); A. Roy Petrie, *Joseph Brant* (Don Mills: Fitzhenry and Whiteside, 1978); and David Blanchard, *Seven Generations* (Kahnawake: Kahnawake Survival School, 1980).

For twentieth-century Iroquois history, see Six Nations Indian Museum, *Deskaheh: Iroquois Statesman and Patriot* (Akwesasne: Akwesasne Notes); E. Brian Titley, *A Narrow Vision: Duncan Campbell Scott and the Administration of Indian Affairs in Canada* (Vancouver: University of British Columbia Press, 1986); Darlene M. Johnston, "The Quest of the Six Nations Confederacy for Self-Determination," *University of Toronto Faculty of Law Review* (1986) 44: 1–32; Andrew T. Thompson, *Report of the Commissioner to Investigate and Enquire into the Affairs of the Six Nations Indians* (Ottawa: Department of Indian Affairs, 1923); and Edmund Wilson, *Apologies to the Iroquois* (New York: Farrar, Straus and Cudahy, 1959).

CHAPTER 8 The Psychology of Fear

For a description of the revival of Mohawk activism, see Laurence M. Hauptman, *The Iroquois Struggle for Survival: World War II to Red Power* (Syracuse: Syracuse University Press, 1986); Peter Matthiessen, "Akwesasne," in Matthiessen, *Indian Country* (New York: Viking Press, 1984); Ward Churchill and Jim Vander Wall, *Agents of Repression: The FBI's Secret Wars against the Black Panther Party and the American Indian Movement* (Boston: South End Press, 1988); and various issues of *Akwesasne Notes*, 1969–1973.

For information on Moss Lake and Ganienkeh, see Gail H. Landsman, *Sovereignty and Symbol: Indian-White Conflict at Ganienkeh* (Albuquerque: University of New Mexico Press, 1988); and Richard Dean Campbell, *The People of the Land of Flint* (Lanham, Md.: University Press of America, 1985).

CHAPTER 11 War Songs and Black Wampum

Among the key sources for Mohawk theology are Paul A.W. Wallace, *The White Roots of Peace* (Philadelphia: University of Pennsylvania Press, 1946); William N. Fenton, ed., *Parker on the Iroquois* (Syracuse: University of Syracuse Press, 1968); Louis Hall, *Warrior's Handbook* (Kahnawake: 1979); Louis Hall, *Rebuilding the Iroquois Confederacy* (Kahnawake: 1989); and Tom Porter, "Traditions of the Constitution of the Six Nations," in Leroy Little Bear, Menno Boldt, and J. Anthony Long, eds., *Pathways to Self-Determination: Canadian Indians and the Canadian State* (Toronto: University of Toronto Press, 1984).

CHAPTER 12 **Shock Waves**

Land claims are documented in numerous reports by governments and native organizations. Among the sources for this chapter are *Living Treaties: Lasting Agreements* (Report of the Task Force to Review Comprehensive Claims, 1985); Assembly of First Nations, "Backgrounder on the Current Crisis in First Nation–Canada Relations" (Ottawa: 1990); Canadian Human Rights Commission, "A New Commitment: Statement of the Canadian Human Rights Commission on Federal Aboriginal Policy" (Ottawa: November 21, 1990); and *Globe and Mail*, July 17, 1990, p. A4.

CHAPTER 14 **Disappearing Act**

For the RCMP account of the events of August 28, 1990, see RCMP Commissioner Norman Inkster's report, "Incidents between Demonstrators and Mohawks, North Exit of Mercier Bridge, LaSalle, Quebec."

CHAPTER 15 **Bayonets and Helicopters**

The army's version of events in September 1990 is documented in Gerald Baril, "Mission Accomplished," *Sentinel: Magazine of the Canadian Forces* (1990) 6; 1–8; and in testimony to the House of Commons Standing Committee on Aboriginal Affairs, March 19, 1991.

Index